THE CRAFT OF SOFTWARE TESTING

SUBSYSTEM TESTING

INCLUDING OBJECT-BASED AND OBJECT-ORIENTED TESTING

Prentice Hall Series in Innovative Technology

Dennis R. Allison, David J. Farber, and Bruce D. Shriver *Series Advisors*

Bhasker	*A VHDL Primer*
Blachman	*Mathematica: A Practical Approach*
Chan and Mourad	*Digital Design Using Field Programmable Gate Arrays*
El-Rewini, Lewis, and Ali	*Task Scheduling in Parallel and Distributed Systems*
Jenkins	*Designing with FPGAs and CPLDs*
Johnson	*Superscalar Microprocessor Design*
Kane and Heinrich	*MIPS RISC Architecture, Second Edition*
Kehoe	*Zen and the Art of the Internet: A Beginner's Guide. Third Edition*
Lawson	*Parallel Processing in Industrial Real-Time Applications*
Nelson, ed.	*Systems Programming with Modula-e*
Nutt	*Open Systems*
Rose	*The Internet Message: Closing the Book with Electronic Mail*
Rose	*The Little Black Book: Mail Bonding with OSI Directory Services*
Rose	*The Open Book: A Practical Perspective on OSI*
Rose	*The Simple Book: An Introduction to Internet Management, Second Edition*
Schröder-Preikschet	*The Logical Design of Parallel Operating Systems*
Shapiro	*A C++ Toolkit*
Slater	*Microprocessor-Based Design*
SPARC International, Inc.	*The SPARC Architecture Manual, Version 8*
SPARC International, Inc.	*The SPARC Architecture Manual, Version 9*
Strom, et al.	*Hermes: A Language for Distributed Computing*
Treseler	*Designing State Machine Controllers Using Programmable Logic*
Wirfs-Brock, Wilkerson, and Wiener	*Designing Object-Oriented Software*

THE CRAFT OF SOFTWARE TESTING

SUBSYSTEM TESTING

INCLUDING OBJECT-BASED AND OBJECT-ORIENTED TESTING

Brian Marick

Testing Foundations, Champaign, Illinois

PTR PRENTICE HALL, ENGLEWOOD CLIFFS, NEW JERSEY 07632

Library of Congress Cataloging-in-Publication Data

Marick, Brian.
        The craft of software testing: subsystem testing including object-based and object-oriented testing/Brian Marick.
        p.   cm. -- (Prentice Hall series in innovative technology)
        Includes bibliographical references and index.
        ISBN 0-13-177411-5
        1. Computer software--Testing.   I. Title.   II. Series.
QA76.76.T48M36   196f4
005.1'4--dc20

94-11423

CIP

Acquisitions editor: Paul Becker
Editorial assistant: Maureen Diana
Cover design: Wanda Lubelska
Cover design director: Jerry Votta
Copyeditor: Diana Leith
Indexer: Robert J. Richardson
Interior design: Gail Cocker-Bogusz and John Morgan
Illustrations by Gail Cocker-Bogusz
Manufacturing Manager: Alexis R. Heydt
This book was composed in FrameMaker on a UNIX platform from nroff source files.

Published by Prentice Hall PTR
A Simon & Schuster Company
Englewood Cliffs, New Jersey 07632

PostScript is a registered trademark of Adobe Systems Incorporated.

ViSTA® is a registered trademark of Veritas Software.

The publisher offers discounts on this book when ordered in bulk quantities. For more information, contact Corporate Sales Department, PTR Prentice Hall, 113 Sylvan Avenue, Englewood Cliffs, NJ 07632. Internet: dan_rush@prenhall.com; Phone: 201-592-2863; FAX: 201- 592-2249.

Printed in the United States of America
10 9 8 7 6 5 4 3 2

ISBN   0-13-177411-5

Prentice-Hall International (UK) Limited, *London*
Prentice-Hall of Australia Pty. Limited, *Sydney*
Prentice-Hall Canada Inc., *Toronto*
Prentice-Hall Hispanoamericana, S.A., *Mexico*
Prentice-Hall of India Private Limited, *New Delhi*
Prentice-Hall of Japan, Inc., *Tokyo*
Simon & Schuster Asia Pte. Ltd., *Singapore*
Editora Prentice-Hall do Brasil, Ltda., *Rio de Janeiro*

To my parents

Contents

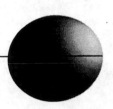

PART *1* The Basic Technique

CHAPTER **4**

**Test
Specifications**   *93*

PART *2* Adopting Subsystem Testing

PART *3* Subsystem Testing in Practice

PART 4 Examples and Extensions

An Example of Testing Derived Classes   *378*

Object-Oriented Software 2: Dynamic Binding   *400*

PART 5   Multiplying Test Requirements

PART 6 Appendices

APPENDIX *A*

Test Requirement Catalog (Student Version) *449*

**Test
Requirement
Catalog** *462*

APPENDIX *C*

POSIX-Specific Test Requirement Catalog (Sample) *486*

APPENDIX *D*

Question Catalog for Code Inspections *490*

APPENDIX *E*

Requirements for Complex Booleans Catalog *497*

**Checklists
for Test
Writing** *504*

Preface

This book is about "testing in the medium." It concentrates on thorough testing of moderate-sized components of large systems. I call these components subsystems. Good testing of subsystems is a prerequisite for effective and efficient testing of the integrated system.

The book aims to present a sensible, flexible, affordable, and coherent testing process so that subsystem testers needn't waste time wondering what to do next. It also provides detailed techniques and tricks of the trade so that testers know how to do that next task well. In short, the book answers these common questions:

▲ How do I design tests?
▲ What are typical tester errors, and how do I avoid them?
▲ How do I implement tests?
▲ How do I know whether my tests are any good?
▲ How do I know when I'm done?

The Intended Audiences

The book is addressed to three audiences. The first is the individual programmer responsible for a subsystem like a device driver, a lexical analyzer, a class library, or the communications substrate of a client-server system. In many organizations, these programmers test their own code. That's very efficient, but it often leads to problems. Most programmers don't know enough about testing and haven't integrated their knowledge into an efficient, effective strategy. Even those who know more than most have trouble finding their own mistakes—it's hard for a person who didn't think of a special case in design to notice it during testing. That problem is not necessarily overwhelming, provided the programmer is aware of it and makes conscious efforts to counter it. This book can help because one of its fundamental premises is that everyone—programmers and independent testers alike—makes mistakes of this kind. Subsystem testing is designed to reduce their number and also reduce the harm done by those that remain.

I don't pretend that all programmers will want to become expert testers, though most do a good job when given the right support. Part of that support is the advice of an expert. Such experts make up the second audience. They consult with tester/developers, help them with tricky problems of test design, review solutions, point out oversights, ease the implementation, and review quality estimates to ensure they're used effectively. A single testing consultant can greatly help many developers. Of course, these experts are also doing testing of their own, be it subsystem or system testing.

As the above implies, subsystem testing is best done alongside subsystem development. Testing's end product is a set of tests, but the intermediate results can be used during the design process or in design reviews. They help you find the all-important design and specification mistakes early, before they're (expensively) turned into code that has to be (expensively) rewritten.

The final audience is programmers or testers responsible for testing changes, especially bug fixes. Changes present special problems. They have a way of breaking "unrelated" parts of the subsystem, so they must be carefully tested, but within tight limits on the amount of testing that can be done.

All of these audiences will use the code in their test design. The code is not the only source of testing information, but it is an essential one. The examples in the book are written in C, except for the chapters on object-based and object-oriented testing, which use C++. You need to be able to read the examples to use the book, but the techniques are applicable to other languages. My background is in UNIX, so some of the examples are drawn from that world. I've avoided or explained system dependent details, so people from other environments should have little trouble.

Other Audiences

System testers will have two problems with this book. Most system testers work exclusively from the system's external interface. They will find certain parts of the book useful: Abbreviated cause-effect testing, catalog testing, the test design framework, the emphasis on test variety, the checklists of common testing errors, and the discussion of coverage. The first problem for system testers is that they want to see those topics presented without reference to code, whereas subsystem testers need them in the context of code. It wasn't possible to satisfy both desires in one book, so system testers will have to skim some parts and do a certain amount of extrapolation and translation in others.

The second problem is that this book isn't enough. System testing is the hardest kind of testing. It builds on risk analysis: Where are high-visibility or high-severity problems likely? What specific testing techniques can efficiently target those problems? How can the quality of those particular tests be estimated? Good system testing requires innovation of a sort not described here.

In contrast, risk analysis is less central to subsystem testing. You use risk analysis to decide how much effort to spend on a particular subsystem. Once that's done, the testing process is uniform—one subsystem is approached much like another, something that would be a grave mistake in system testing.

I've used this book in a one-semester course at the University of Illinois. Most of the students are master's degree candidates expecting to go into industry. As such, they are primarily interested in how to test and how testing fits with the rest of software development, but they also need theory and exposure to techniques not yet practical. In that class, this book is supplemented with journal articles and lectures on system testing. For self-study, I recommend [Beizer84] for system testing. [Morell89] is a useful survey of the literature. The IEEE Transactions on Software Engineering, ACM Transactions on Software Engineering and Methodology, IEEE Software, and the proceedings of the ACM Symposia on Testing, Analysis, and Verification (now called the International Symposium on Software Testing and Analysis) are readily available sources—browse them.

The Book's Organization

Part 1 is a tutorial for subsystem testing illustrated with a running example. The example is simplified in several ways: It assumes that you have a thorough specification of what the program is to do, that the subsystem will present no problems in test implementation, and that you have the time to test completely.

Part 1 contains a lot of material. Trying to adopt all of it immediately is risky, especially when you have a product shipping soon (and who doesn't?). Gradual adoption is better. Part 2 discusses what can be inexpensively and nondisruptively done right away and what parts should be added. It also discusses how to get better at subsystem testing.

Part 3 removes the simplifications of Part 1. One chapter discusses how large subsystems are chosen and tested. Others cover how less complete, less rigorous, or missing specifications are handled and what to do when you don't have enough time. The important topic of testing bug fixes and other changes is also covered here.

Part 4 contains a further example. I recommend that you work through it in detail, comparing what you do to what I did. You don't learn much about a craft by reading about it. You learn by apprenticeship: first by watching an expert tackle a problem, then by tackling problems yourself with the expert looking on. This second example simulates that as closely as possible within the confines of a book.

The other chapters in Part 4 extend the basic ideas of subsystem testing to new situations such as testing based on input syntax, testing consistency relationships, and testing object-based and object-oriented subsystems. Not only are these useful topics in themselves, they also show you how to extrapolate subsystem testing to your own circumstances.

Subsystem testing makes some simplifying assumptions that are not always true. Part 5 shows how to determine when they're not true and what to do about it. However, the assumptions are true enough often enough that you don't need this material for effective testing.

The appendices contain the catalogs used in subsystem testing. Appendix F contains checklists to use during testing. The experienced tester will use this part of the book as a continual reference.

The book ends with a glossary. Terms in the glossary are written in italics the first time they appear.

After You've Read the Book

You will have questions and objections. Send them to me. I prefer to get mail over the Internet. Your can reach me at marick@testing.com. My surface mail address is:

Brian Marick
Testing Foundations
913 West White Street
Champaign, IL 61821
USA

I cannot promise to answer all mail. However, I will answer the best or most common questions, and I plan to make the answers available over the Internet and also possibly in hardcopy form.

Acknowledgments

I must above all thank Dawn for being the perfect wife: for comfort and support; for the integrity and thoroughness of her own work, a constant inspiration; and for talks about medicine that somehow magically turned into ideas about testing.

Professors C.W. Gear and Ralph Johnson at the University of Illinois made the decision that led to this book—they exposed students to some stranger from industry who wanted to teach about testing. Those students who suffered through the first semester of "Software Testing: Practice and Theory" asked too many questions. When I found that I didn't have good answers—and that no one else had answers that satisfied those stern critics—I decided to write a book. Five years later, here it is, and I hope the answers are finally good enough.

Many students since then have contributed to my collection of answers. Chris Bachman, Mark Brodie, John Conneely, Heather Ferguson, Eddie Gornish, Robert Greanias, Thomas Hoch, Steve March, Rocco Martin, Mike Murphy, Kaiyu Pan, Georgios Papagiannakopoulos, Jim Pirzyk, K. Wolfram Schafer, Jun Sun, Evan C. Thomas, Jane Wang, Johnny Zweig, and others whom my sieve-like memory has forgotten can all find their contributions in this book.

Most of what I've learned I've learned on the job. Dave Carr, Randy Clayton, Dan Defend, Peter DeWolf, Glenn Kowack, and Dan

Putnam taught me much. Special thanks to Mark Holderbaugh and Fran Wagner for their detailed comments on an earlier draft in addition to everything else. And I must give blanket acknowledgment to all the people who created the bugs I've found or looked at. One learns through mistakes; thankfully, they didn't all have to be my own. Special thanks to L. Peter Deutsch for permission to use a bug of his in this text and for the fine software he writes. Tandem Computers, through Mark Tompkins, paid me to (among other things) adapt parts of subsystem testing to a new environment, an experience that deepened my understanding of what to teach and how to teach it. Claude Fenner, Glen Michtom, Paul Trompeter, Keith Stobie, and Joan Zimmerman never failed to give me more work to do, but always usefully. Further thanks to Tandem for their specific support of this book. James Bach and Robert Hodges helped with comments on earlier drafts. John Baldwin helped with the inspection catalog.

What I know might have remained a chaotic bag of tricks had not the testing research community built a framework to support it. Like any skeleton, it's largely invisible, but no less important for that. The research community, especially Dick Hamlet, also deserves credit for encouraging a sometimes difficult and obtuse outsider.

Dennis Allison asked me if I had ever thought of writing a book—just about the time the first draft was done. Except it wasn't really the first draft. Paul Becker was extremely patient until the real first draft arrived. Diana Leith removed more commas than I thought the whole manuscript contained. John Morgan had the job of dealing with an extremely touchy manuscript after it was "converted" from troff to FrameMaker. He has my thanks, my apologies, and my promise never to inflict that on anyone again.

Glen Myers provided the title, a takeoff on his fine book, *The Art of Software Testing*.

Finally, I thank Dave Fields, who helped Dawn paint while I frantically worked on the final draft. I'll do the same when you write a book.

An Overview
of Subsystem Testing

First, a joke:

A mathematician, a physicist, and an engineer are told, "All odd numbers are prime."

The mathematician says, "That's silly. Nine is a non-prime odd number."

The physicist says, "Let's see. Three is a prime, five is a prime, seven is a prime—looks like it's true."

The engineer says, "Let's see. Three is a prime, five is a prime, seven is a prime, nine is a prime, eleven is a prime..."

Testing is like the joke. A tester is given a false statement ("the system works") and has the job of selecting, from an infinite number of possibilities, an input that contradicts the statement ("Then why does it crash when you type in a line longer than 72 characters?"). You have to avoid both the physicist's error (not trying the right value) and the engineer's (trying the right value, but not noticing the contradiction). You want to be like the mathematician, finding the right counterexample with a minimum of wasted effort. That's the topic of this book.[1]

Some Unavoidable Terminology

The term "bug" is not very precise. Sometimes the imprecision doesn't matter, but it's often useful to distinguish three different senses of the word.

---

1. The metaphor of software testing as searching for a counterexample to a conjecture is due to [Podgurski92].

❒ **error**

An *error* is a mistake made by a developer. It might be a typographical error, a misreading of a specification, a misunderstanding of what a subroutine does, and so on. Errors are mostly located in people's heads.

❒ **fault**

An error may lead to one or more *faults*. Faults are located in the text of the program. More precisely, a fault is the difference between the incorrect program and a correct version. For example, we may describe a fault as "the program used < when it should have used <=" or "the program is missing the code that checks for an error return from the `write` subroutine".

❒ **failure**

The execution of the faulty code may lead to zero or more *failures*, where a failure is the difference between the results of the incorrect and correct program. If the `write` routine never returns an error indication, the faulty program will never fail. A particular fault may cause different failures, depending on how it's been exercised.

These terms are from [IEEE83]. In this book, I'll still use "bug" when that more general term is appropriate.

Failures are detected by comparing the actual output of the program to the expected output. In almost all cases, the expected output is gotten from the *specification*. For purposes of this book, the specification is any external, independent description of the program, including especially user documentation. Specifications are often incomplete, incorrect, ambiguous, or contradictory, so it may be the specification that's wrong, not the program. Finding specification faults is another part of the testing task.

Fundamental Assumptions of Subsystem Testing

Subsystem testing depends on these assumptions, which are described in more detail in this chapter.

1. Most errors are not very creative. Since errors are clichéd, methodical checklist-based approaches will have a high payoff.
2. Faults of omission, those caused by a failure to anticipate special cases, are the most important and most difficult type.
3. Specification faults, especially omissions, are more dangerous than code faults. They're also harder to find.
4. At every stage of testing, mistakes are inevitable. Later stages should compensate for them.
5. How thoroughly the tests exercise the code (code coverage) is a good *approximate* measure of their quality. Because it's an approximation, coverage must be used with extreme care.

Motivating the Technique

Tests can be derived from both the specification and the program. The derivation is done, in principle, by predicting likely programmer errors or likely program faults, then writing tests to detect them. In the practice of test design, testers don't make these explicit predictions. Instead, they use general rules abstracted from common errors. One simple general rule is "always test boundary conditions". If the specification requires that argument A must be greater than zero, the tester would try the value zero. (We'll ignore the other side of the boundary for this example.)

What likely error justifies that choice? Programmers can't get their relational operators right, so they're forever writing

```
if (A < 0) exit_with_error_message();          /* buggy */
```

when they should be writing

```
if (A <= 0) exit_with_error_message();          /* correct */
```

Zero is the only value that makes the buggy program take the false branch when the correct program would take the true branch.

You can do a lot of good testing armed with a few simple rules, the three most basic being:

1. If the specification identifies a case to handle, there's a reasonable chance the programmer either forgot to handle it or handled it incorrectly. So you should try that case.
2. Not all cases will be identified in the specification. If the code attempts to handle a particular case, there's a reasonable chance it will fail. So you should try that case.
3. For each case identified above, preferentially test the boundary values.

(In the testing literature, these rules are called "equivalence class partitioning with boundary values." This type of case analysis can be applied to the logical structure of the specification, as in cause-effect testing [Myers78], or to the input syntax as in syntax testing [Beizer90]. Case analysis is used in subsystem testing as well, but this introduction focuses on what's unusual about the technique.)

These rules work well, but require either the program or the specification to identify all the relevant cases. They don't, not always. The specification writer may have missed a special case; if so, the programmer almost certainly did as well. Or the special case may be an implementation detail of the sort that isn't relevant to the specification. If the programmer missed it, the specification also won't identify it.

Missed special cases are called *faults of omission*. This is an example of a low-level fault of omission:

```
write(file_descriptor, buffer, amount);
```

This code does not check whether the `write` fails. It should read

```
if (write(file_descriptor, buffer, amount) == -1)
    handle_the_problem();
```

> ## A Summary of Subsystem Testing
>
> Build the test requirement checklist
>   Find clues
>   Expand clues into test requirements
> Design the tests
>   Combine test requirements into test specifications
>   Check the test specifications for common testing mistakes
> Supplement testing with focused code inspections
> Implement test support code
> Implement the tests
> Evaluate and improve the tests
>   Measure code coverage
>   Use results to find undertested or missing clues
>   Find more test requirements for those clues
>   Write more test specifications

As an example of a higher level fault of omission, a specification for the client side of a client-server application might describe the recovery procedure when the server crashes, but fail to anticipate the case that the server might resume transmissions before recovery is complete.

Faults of omission are critically important. For example, [Glass81] found them to be the most common type of fault in delivered avionics systems. And most maintainers will recognize the sinking feeling that comes when a customer calls with some completely unanticipated—but reasonable—special case, one that will require a major design change. Far better to find those bugs before the product is released.

How to do this? Let's first consider coding and low-level design omissions.

Every system is a mixture of the unique and the mundane. A compiler may have new and novel register allocation techniques. An operating system may have clever and complex virtual memory algorithms. But the cleverness is surrounded by ordinary routines doing ordinary things, and it's largely implemented using the same sort of code programmers write again and again in their careers. Test design builds on the ordinary, because ordinary code contains ordinary mistakes. Boundary-handling code and the associated off-by-one faults are the simplest example, one that every tester knows.

Much of the difference between the skilled tester and the novice tester lies in knowing how to test for other ordinary faults. The skilled tester can look at a program and rattle off sentences like these:

"This routine takes a pointer argument. Such routines often fail to handle null pointers."

"This option makes the program search for a matching file. Code that searches sometimes breaks when the match isn't found. If there is a match, it's best to put it in the last position, or the first."

"This command line option takes an argument. Programs often fail drastically when no argument is given and the option is the last word on the command line."

Experienced testers have a catalog of programming clichés and associated errors in their head. The Test Requirement Catalog, included with this book, lists many of these for the benefit of inexperienced testers and experienced testers without perfect memories. The catalog is effective at finding low-level omissions because it was developed with those in mind.

Higher level specification omissions are much more difficult. To find them, you must understand the unique aspects of the system and match those against your understanding of the system's unique environment. It's a creative (or creatively destructive) task, and a general purpose testing technique can't provide that creativity. What it can provide is room for creativity:

▲ by providing an orderly framework for test design, so that you don't get bogged down by inessentials;
▲ by getting the mundane tests out of the way efficiently, leaving you with time and brainpower to design the unique tests;
▲ by helping you avoid common test design mistakes.

The first requirement of test design is that it be methodical. Many programming errors are due to lapses of attention; some special case slips the programmer's mind. The cases that are easy for a programmer to overlook are just as easy for the tester to overlook, and a tester who does not proceed by careful, thorough steps will miss bugs in a flood of detail.

Subsystem testing divides test design into three stages: finding clues, expanding them into test requirements, and combining test requirements into test specifications.

Three Elements in Test Design

❏ **test specifications**
Test specifications describe exact inputs to a program together with exact expected outputs.

Example: LIST has the null string as its single element; expect return value 5.

❏ **test requirements**
Test requirements describe useful sets of input that should be tested.

Example: LIST must have a single element (value unspecified).

Example: Use the null string as some LIST element.

❏ **clues**
Clues are the sources for test requirements.

Example: LIST, a list of strings

Example: a list element, a string

Clues

The first stage in test design is searching for clues about what needs testing. These clues can be found in the program itself, in the specification, in bug reports filed against earlier versions of the system, from experience with similar systems, and so on. This book will concentrate on the first two sources.

These clues are written down in a checklist. By listing the clues, you focus your attention and reduce the chance that you'll omit a needed test. Here are some representative clues:

> searching for an element equal to ELT in the input LIST
> ELT < 0 is an error
> D_ELT is a count

That the program searches is a clue to write tests for likely searching faults. That the program classifies ELT is a clue to write tests checking for incorrect classification and incorrect error handling. That D_ELT is a count is a clue to write tests targeted to common faults involving counts.

Test Requirements

The clues describe what needs to be tested. The next step is to decide how to test them in order to discover likely faults. Off-by-one faults are always likely. In code that searches, such a fault might cause the search to stop one element early. To detect the problem, a matching element should be placed in the last position. Another likely error is to assume that a match will always be found. This leads to omitted code, and to catastrophic results when the search returns a "no match" indication. To detect the error, there should be no matching element in the LIST. Both of these descriptions of how to test searching—called *test requirements*—are useful enough often enough to be written down in the Test Requirement Catalog.

Here are those test requirements for searching, together with some for the other clues:

> searching for an element equal to ELT in the input LIST
> > found in the last position
> > not found
> ELT < 0 is an error
> > ELT = -1
> D_ELT is a count
> > D_ELT = 0
> > D_ELT = 1

Although test requirements are derived from likely errors or faults, the justification is not part of the test requirement. A test requirement is just a description of some input that's good at finding bugs.

The structure shown above is an example of a *test requirement checklist*.

Test Specifications

Test requirements are general descriptions of how to test a program. The first searching test requirement does not give precise values for ELT or LIST; it just says that the only match for ELT must be the last element of LIST. Further, it says nothing at all about the value of D_ELT. Before the program can be executed, these variables must be given exact values in a *test specification*. Here's an example:

TEST 1:
    ELT is 1
    LIST is [45, 5, 1]
    D_ELT = 1
EXPECT
    return value 2

Notice that the test specification describes exact expected output as well as exact inputs. That's very important for effective testing.

A test specification is created by picking inputs that satisfy one or more test requirements. The above test specification satisfies two, one for searching and one for D_ELT:

found in last position
D_ELT = 1

In subsystem testing, test specifications usually satisfy many test requirements. This leads to complex tests and test suites with more variety. Complexity and variety increase the chance of finding faults you didn't think of looking for. Because we're all imperfect testers, we have to enlist chance on our side.

Although this test specification satisfies test requirements, it does so poorly. Suppose the program uses D_ELT when it should use ELT, a not-unusual fault. Because this test gives D_ELT the same value as ELT, the program will produce the correct results the wrong way—and the fault will be missed. You should satisfy the searching requirement with some other value for ELT. Test specification creation requires both a procedure for combining test requirements and rules to reduce the chance that a test will miss a failure.

There are some types of faults that testing is poor at detecting. For example, suppose a program very occasionally fails to close an open file. A test that exercises that fault once would not cause a visible failure. Finding the fault by testing would require exercising it many times (until the program runs out of resources) at a much greater expense in time or hardware. It is better to augment test design with a focused kind of code reading. This reading is organized around a checklist of likely faults, the Question Catalog for Code Inspections. The catalog can be used to supplement the style of code reading or inspecting you already use.

SUPPLEMENTARY CODE INSPECTIONS

TEST IMPLEMENTATION AND THE SCALE OF TESTING

The implemented tests must cost as little as possible over the life of the system. Reducing lifetime cost requires automation. Manual or semi-automated tests are cheaper to develop, but they're too time-consuming and hence expensive to run often. For this reason, it's not unusual to run a manual suite only once, just before a new release, with the desperate hope that no bugs are found. Manual testing is also error-prone; people easily miss obvious failures, especially late Friday afternoon after a solid week of running tests.

Automated tests usually require special-purpose test support code and tools. This book discusses their general requirements. Since the particular requirements are determined by the test design and application type, it cannot go into great detail.

Reducing the cost of testing means reducing the amount of that support code. This raises an issue: what size subsystem should you test?

You could derive clues and test requirements from a single routine, combine them into test specifications for that routine, then write test support code that allows you to test the routine in isolation. This approach, called *unit testing*, is too expensive. Not only is the initial development of the support code costly, maintenance becomes a nightmare. The problem is that relatively small changes to the system can require changes to the support code for many units. The result is that unit tests are often abandoned—in which case, they're barely worth writing.

It is more efficient to test larger subsystems because less support code needs to be written. In the most thorough application of this technique, you select a subsystem, derive clues and test requirements from all the internal routines, from the interfaces between the routines, and from the entire external interface, then combine them all into test specifications. Based on those test specifications, you design support code to allow you to test the entire subsystem at once. This subsystem-scale support code is substantially cheaper than support code for each routine. Alternately, you can adapt the system to provide the testing support for its subsystems.

Fig. 1 shows an example of this approach. The large oval is a subsystem. The ovals inside it represent individual routines. Small black dots are test requirements. The ones outside the subsystem come from its specification, ones outside routines come from their specifications or code headers, and ones inside routines come from the code. The arrow represents a single test specification that satisfies many test requirements. The test is run by providing inputs to the subsystem and evaluated by examining its outputs.

Testing larger subsystems also has advantages in effectiveness. Because each routine participates in tests targeted to other routines, every routine is exercised more. Because test design emphasizes variety, all routines are exercised in many ways, including many unplanned ways. More bugs will be found by chance.

As subsystems increase in size, problems surface. It becomes harder to satisfy some test requirements, the amount of information to be managed increases the difficulty of test design, and the chance that a failure may escape detection grows. The approach of this technique is to test large subsystems and solve those problems, rather than to keep subsystems small enough that they do not arise.

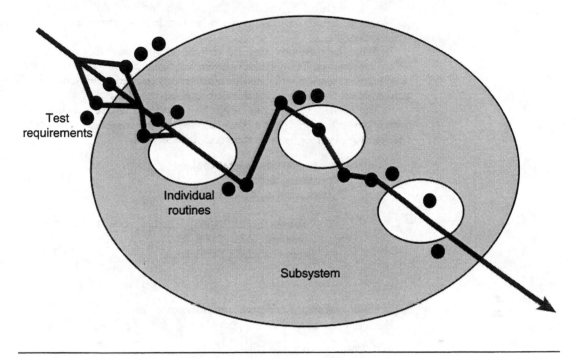

Test requirements

Individual routines

Subsystem

Fig. 1 One test specification satisfies requirements from many sources

Well-designed tests will cause failures. The underlying fault is most often in the code, but sometimes it's in the specification. A change in either will require updates to the test suite. The process of finding what updates are needed is largely the same as testing new code, but there are special constraints. The task must be narrowly focussed so that the cost of testing the change is in line with the cost of making it. Nevertheless, a change can have effects far removed from the modified lines of code, and testing's focus must not be so narrow that it misses those. Finally, there are certain characteristic errors people make when changing code, and a testing strategy should take them into account.

Changes are made for reasons other than to fix bugs. They are often made to add new features to the subsystem. These changes are tested in the same way as bug fixes.

A good set of tests will thoroughly exercise a subsystem. The tests will force all branches in both directions, force all subparts of branch tests to be both true and false, force all loops to execute zero, one, and more than one times, and force certain boundary conditions.

During test design, you should pay no attention to these criteria. For example, you should not write test requirements to force particular branches in particular directions. The test requirements gotten from other sources will usually do that anyway, so considering branches would be wasted thought.

After the tests are run, the criteria should be measured. This is called *test coverage*. Complete subsystem testing (not scaled down because of schedule pressure) will usually result in high coverage; for example, 95 percent of the branches might be taken in both directions.

The remaining branches might be considered test requirements to satisfy, but it is better to treat them as clues about weaknesses in the test design. For example, suppose this code is under test:

```
1       operation_failed = operation();
2       if (operation_failed)
3          switch (type_of_failure)
4             {
5                case FAILURE_TYPE_1: ...
6                case FAILURE_TYPE_2: ...
7                case FAILURE_TYPE_3: ...
8             }
```

A coverage tool might complain that the cases for failure types 1 and 3 had never been taken with a report like

line 5: case was taken 0 times.
line 7: case was taken 0 times.

The strong temptation is to write tests to cause those two failures and be done with it. However, what this coverage really indicates is that the tests only weakly probe operation's failure cases. More careful thought might reveal that operation can actually return a fourth failure type, one the caller makes no effort to handle—a probable fault of omission.

Careful thought is harder than finding simple ways to satisfy coverage. However, after thorough initial test design, handling coverage this way takes only a few percent of the total effort.

Coverage reveals test implementation mistakes as well as test design mistakes. For example, you may have thought you designed a test that passed a particular value to some internal routine, but in fact a higher-level routine intercepted that special case and handled it. The internal routine has not been correctly tested. Coverage is important in all testing, but it is crucial for effective subsystem testing.

When coverage shows nothing more to do, stop testing. (When subsystem testing has been scaled down because of schedule pressure, perfect coverage is not a realistic goal, but coverage can still be used to guide test suite improvement.)

In its examples, this book uses the Generic Coverage Tool, a freeware coverage tool provided by the author. Subsystem testing will work fine with other coverage tools.

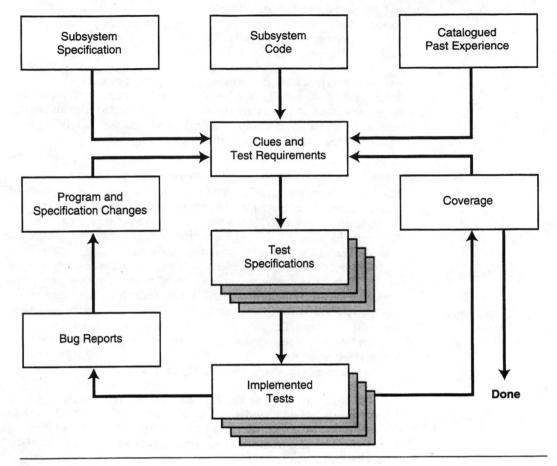

Fig. 2

Fig. 2 shows a picture of the entire subsystem testing process.

MORE CATALOGS

The preceding discussion has given the impression that there's a single catalog, the Test Requirement Catalog. In fact, that catalog is only one of many. It's the catalog that contains clichés used so widely that they'll be relevant to all readers. People working in special environments might also use special catalogs. For example, if a company builds its product line around a set of certain complicated data structures, a catalog containing test requirements specifically for those structures will be valuable. That catalog will be built by examining bug reports from existing subsystems.

The most common source of these special-purpose catalogs is reusable software. Just as programmers make errors using a cliché like searching for strings, they make characteristic errors when calling library routines. Ways of discovering the resulting faults can be placed in a catalog that accompanies the library. This book contains a small example of such a catalog for the standard C library.

Object-oriented software is a particular kind of reusable software. It has more structure than software written in purely procedural languages. That structure—the class, class inheritance, and dynamic binding—leads to power but also to characteristic faults. By associating a small catalog with each class and structuring catalogs in parallel with the inheritance structure, those faults can be specifically targeted.

EARLY TESTING

Many documents may be written on the way from an idea to a system or upgraded system. Some are specifications, which describe what the system is to do. Others describe how it is to do it. All can be wrong. Running tests often finds those bugs, but it's cheaper to find them before the code is written. The intermediate steps in subsystem testing can help.

Design documents of all types inevitably project their writer's point of view. They have a preferred reading that often obscures their own problems, especially their faults of omission. The reader has a hard time breaking free of that preferred reading. That's where the test requirement checklist is useful. Thinking about whether the design handles a test requirement is precise, focused, and different from other types of thinking about the design. Going through the checklist requirement by requirement can make design bugs leap out at you in a surprising way. This can be done during design or at a review.

But test requirements are abstract, and it's unfortunately easy to believe the design will handle one simply because it should. Our brains work with concrete objects differently than with abstractions, so thinking about the effect of a test specification can find faults missed by thinking about its component test requirements.

When I am a subsystem designer, I build the test requirement checklist alongside the design, and I constantly check the design against those requirements. When the design is finished, I build at least some of the test specifications. I expect that combining the test requirements and choosing specific inputs will jog my imagination into noticing problems with the subsystem's design. After they are fixed, and the test requirements and specifications are updated, I think in some detail about how the design would handle each test. That sometimes finds bugs; at the least, it's good preparation for writing the code. Then I implement the subsystem and the tests, trying always to write tests as soon as possible.

Most of the book will ignore this interplay of subsystem design and test design. For clarity, the explanation of subsystem testing will assume that everything, specification and code, is finished before testing starts. In practice, that's an inefficient use of testing.

This section introduces some of the theory of testing. You can use subsystem testing without reading this section, or any of the sections that use this terminology. But the theory is not complicated, and understanding it will make you a better tester.

A goal of testing is to execute the program with inputs that cause all faults to reveal themselves as failures. What does this require? Consider this program:

```
void
check_square(int do_square, double x)
{
    double y = x;
    if (do_square)
        y = x + x;      /* Should be x * x */
    printf("squared version larger? %d\n", y > x);
}
```

The fault is that + was used when * should have been.

❐ **reachability**

To provoke a failure, the program's inputs must cause the faulty statement to be executed. Those inputs satisfy a *reachability condition*. In this case, the reachability condition is that do_square is true.

❐ **necessity**

Next, the faulty statement must produce a different result than the correct statement. This is called the *necessity condition*. It describes the inputs that cause an incorrect internal state. In this example, X=1 will cause Y to have the incorrect value 2 (1+1) instead of the correct value 1 (1*1). However, X=2 will cause Y to have the correct value 4. The program calculated the right result the wrong way, so it won't fail on that input. The necessity condition for this fault is X!=2 && X!=0.

❐ **propagation**

Finally, the incorrect internal state must propagate so that it becomes visible in the program's results. For example, if X is 4, Y will be 8, where it should have been 16. However, both of these are greater than 4, so the faulty program will print

    squared version larger? 1

which is exactly what the correct program would have printed. The incorrect internal state has been "damped out" before it became visible. The *propagation condition* for the fault requires that x+x>x have a different truth value from x*x>x. That's true whenever x<=1.

These three conditions are called the *ideal fault conditions*. Their names are derived from [Offutt88] and [Morell83]. All three of them must be simultaneously satisfied for the fault to cause a failure. That is, you must test this program with inputs satisfying

    do_square true AND (X != 0 and X != 2) AND (X <= 1)

or, equivalently,

do_square true AND X <= 1 (except 0)

Only then will the incorrect program show a different result from the correct program.

The ideal fault conditions are derived from the faults in the program. You don't know what or where those faults are, of course, so the best you can do is approximate the ideal. This book is about practical approximations.

Subsystem testing's test requirements are most closely related to necessity conditions. For a given program, there are three sets of necessity conditions: those for the faults actually present in the program, a much larger set for the faults plausibly present in the program, and an infinite set for the faults possibly present in the program. (*Note*: An actual fault may not have been plausible. That is, you wouldn't have ever guessed the program could be wrong *that* way. Let's leave that topic aside for the moment.)

Test requirements should approximate the necessity conditions for the plausible faults in the sense that tests satisfying the test requirements should also satisfy the plausible necessity conditions. The test requirements are not identical to those necessity conditions because they're derived from different sources. They may be derived from plausible errors—by asking what inputs would find most faults caused by an error regardless of the precise manifestation. Or test requirements may be purely empirical, found by observing which inputs are good at provoking failures regardless of the underlying fault or error. If testing with the empty string catches bugs often enough cheaply enough, is it essential that we know why?

A second hope for the set of test requirements is that it be smaller than the set of plausible necessity conditions. On average, each test requirement should satisfy several necessity conditions, reducing the cost of test design. This is accomplished by deriving them from "higher-level" entities, such as specification and programming clichés. For example, the test requirements for a searching loop may detect several types of off-by-one faults without having to consider each of them separately. Or the empty string may exercise plausible faults in many locations without having to consider each location individually.

But even if test requirements are perfect (have the effectiveness of plausible necessity conditions, while being few enough to allow affordable test design), necessity conditions are only one of the three ideal fault conditions. The other two are reachability, causing the fault to be exercised; and propagation, causing the incorrect internal state to affect the program's result. In subsystem testing, these two conditions are handled in three ways:

❑ **design**

Some of the test specification design rules alert you to tests where reachability or propagation are doubtful. Approximating reachability is a topic in Part 5, though it is not part of the basic technique.

❑ **implementation**

In some cases, you should modify the subsystem to permit reachability and propagation. For example, if the results of an internal function return a complicated list structure but the entire system returns only TRUE or FALSE, there's a potential propagation problem. An incorrect list structure may yield the same eventual boolean value as the correct list structure. In this case, you should add test support code that prints out the list structure. Essentially, you've selectively made part of the intermediate state a part of the subsystem's results. The propagation condition is much more likely to be satisfied.

❑ **coverage**

Coverage is good—though not infallible—at detecting failures to satisfy reachability conditions. If reachability isn't satisfied, some code may not be exercised. Examining coverage often leads to realizing that the test and program are such that a necessity condition doesn't reach a body of code where it would be useful.

Given these, reachability and propagation are not usually major problems in practice. But the set of test requirements may be inadequate in one of two ways:

❑ **overly general**

A test requirement might not force a necessity condition. For example, a fault's necessity condition might be X!=0 && X!=2, while a test requirement might be X>0. If the test specification, by sheer bad luck, selected X=2, the fault would not be detected. Another possibility is that you have the following test requirements:

A true
A false
B true
B false

The fault's necessity condition is that A is true and B is true. Subsystem testing contains rules for discovering when test requirements interact and should be combined into compound test requirements like A is true and B is true. But when those rules fail, test specification design does not require that all combinations of values for A and B be used. (It would be too expensive.) There is no guarantee that any test specification exercises the necessity condition.

❑ **too small**

Because test requirements are not derived from actual faults, some test requirements might simply be missing.

These problems would be solved by enhancing the existing test requirements or discovering missing ones. Coverage often helps you do that, but only when the inadequate test requirements correspond to unexercised code. Often, though, they correspond to omitted code, and coverage says nothing about omitted code.

Test design that emphasizes variety and complexity helps counteract weak test requirements.

▲ Each test requirement is used often, and used in different ways. Because of this, the test suite is more likely to satisfy
`X!=0 && X!=2`.

▲ The chance of accidentally making a needed combination of two test requirements is increased. Because the test requirements for A and B will be satisfied together in a variety of tests, one of those tests is more likely to satisfy the compound necessity condition
`A true and B true`.

▲ Because the tests are complicated, the chance of accidentally satisfying completely unanticipated necessity conditions increases. Those test requirements may be plausible ones missed during test design, or implausible ones that no cost-effective testing technique could reliably discover.

Subsystem testing attempts to strike a balance between too many tests and the likelihood of omitted necessity conditions. In all of testing, we must compare the unknown probability that a new test requirement will find a fault to the better-known but still uncertain cost of that new test requirement. There is too much uncertainty to give a deterministic rule. However, a basic premise of this book is that explicitly thinking about sources of both cost and effectiveness will lead to better decisions.

Part 1

THE BASIC TECHNIQUE

This part of the book teaches you how to test subsystems. It assumes you've been given enough time and information. Part 3 discusses what to do in more realistic situations. Part 5 discusses some advanced topics. Subsystem testing relies on inspection checklists and catalogs of test requirements; they can be found in the appendices.

Subsystem testing is step-by-step procedure, in which each step builds on the previous steps (and also helps catch mistakes made there). The discussion follows the same sequence. This has the advantage of emphasizing an orderly, methodical process, and it makes the book a good reference for the practicing tester. It has the disadvantage that the reasons for a step may not be entirely clear until you see how the step is used.

The `sreadhex` example used here is a good one in most ways. It's small enough to fit in a book, but has enough content that each of the steps can be usefully applied. It's real code from a widely-used program, and it contains a real fault (since fixed). It has two disadvantages, though:

1. It's tightly coded, so it will take some effort to understand. It uses two C idioms that you might not have encountered before. (They're explained in the text.)

2. It's small. Larger subsystems allow fixed costs to be spread over lots of code. When testing `sreadhex`, all those costs are apparent, but the economies of scale aren't. That will make subsystem testing seem more expensive than it really is.

The Specification

The *specification* describes what the subsystem is to do. All subsystems have some sort of a specification. It may be a formal document, it may be the user's manual, it may be comments in the code, or it may not be written down at all. Even in the latter case, there is invariably some clear intent that allows some testing ("this sqrt routine probably returns the square root"). The less information in the specification, the less testing you can do, because the specification is the major source of testing clues. For example, sqrt may return some random garbage when given a negative number. But that's not necessarily a bug in sqrt: perhaps it's the caller's responsibility not to pass it illegal values. There's no way to tell without some sort of specification (perhaps a general coding standard that all routines should check all their inputs). Without a way to tell what it should do, there's no point in testing sqrt with negative numbers.

This part of the book uses a specification style, adapted from [Perry89], that makes clues about what to test easy to find. It distinguishes error cases from normal cases, separates normal cases from each other, and highlights logical connections among inputs. Real specifications are rarely this helpful, and Chapter 12 discusses what to do then.

1.1 THE ELEMENTS OF A SPECIFICATION

An interface to a subsystem can be described in terms of *preconditions* and *postconditions*. The preconditions describe the caller's responsibilities before calling a subsystem. The postconditions describe the subsystem's responsibilities.

1.1.1 Preconditions

Preconditions describe error cases. Preconditions are written as

> <Type>: <test>
>   On failure: <failure effect>

There are two different types of preconditions:

❑ **Validated**

The truth of a validated precondition's test is checked by the subsystem. It should cause the failure effect if the test is false (the precondition is *violated*). If the test is true (the precondition is *satisfied*), the failure effect does not happen. It is important that the failure effect be a complete description—nothing should be changed other than what it describes. If, for example, a failure effect should leave a temporary file lying around, that must be explicitly stated, otherwise it will be considered a bug.

❑ **Assumed**

The caller is responsible for ensuring the truth of an assumed precondition. The subsystem does not check it, so there is no failure effect. (Alternately, you can think of the failure effect as "anything at all could happen.")

The precondition test is written as natural language phrases, perhaps connected with the *combining operators* OR and AND. It's useful to highlight the combining operators because they play an important role in test generation.

Examples:

1. Suppose a subsystem requires that A, B, and C be strictly positive. If any of them are not, it returns the string "error". This precondition would be written

> Validated: $(A > 0)$ AND $(B > 0)$ AND $(C > 0)$
>   On failure: return string "error"

2. A subsystem requires either that the pointer argument P be non-null or that the NULL_OK argument be true. Ensuring this is solely the caller's responsibility; the subsystem doesn't check, and makes no promises about what happens if the precondition is violated. This precondition would be written

> Assumed: P is non-null OR NULL_OK is true.

3. Another subsystem might accept either null or non-null pointers but checks that whenever a non-null pointer is given, its count field is zero. This could be written as

Validated: PTR is NULL OR PTR->COUNT is 0.
On failure: Print "caller failure" to standard error.
Return -1.

The precondition is violated only when `ptr` is non-null and the `count` field is non-zero.

1.1.2 Postconditions

If all the preconditions are satisfied, one or more of the postconditions will apply. The postconditions describe the results of the subsystem. They are written in this form:

IF <trigger> THEN <effect>

or

IF <trigger> THEN <effect> ELSE <effect>

Example:

IF (A equals B) AND (B equals C)
    THEN return "equilateral"
IF ((A equals B) AND (B does not equal C)
   OR (A equals C) AND (B does not equal C)
   OR (B equals C) AND (B does not equal A))
    THEN return "isosceles"
IF ((A does not equal B) AND (B does not equal C) AND
    (A does not equal C)
    THEN return "scalene"

`IF-THEN-ELSE` statements aren't nested. That is, what comes after the `THEN` or `ELSE` is some effect of the subsystem. It is not another `IF` statement. This is sometimes inconvenient for writing specifications, but it's more convenient for systematically producing test requirements.

If a postcondition always applies, the trigger is omitted. This means that the action takes place whenever the preconditions are satisfied.

Postconditions are not necessarily exclusive. For example, if the subsystem always prints the date, it may be more convenient to write the postconditions as

Postcondition 1
    Display the date in date(1) format.

Postcondition 2
    IF (A < 0)
    THEN
        Prints "I've been called"

than as

Postcondition 1
    IF (A >= 0)
    THEN
        Display the date in date(1) format.
    ELSE
        Display the date in date(1) format.
        Print "I've been called"

1.1.3 Definitions

Definitions are used as shorthand. For example, if a subsystem processes a set of strings, a definition for an intermediate value may be useful:

UPPER_SET(SET)
    UPPER_SET(SET) contains the same strings as SET,
    except all mapped to upper-case.

Such a definition might be used in a postcondition:

IF UPPER_SET(FIRST-INPUT-SET) contains the string "TEST"
THEN
    <do whatever the postcondition does>

Definitions are convenient for writing specifications. They're also useful for testing because they focus attention on clues that need exploring.

Definitions can have more precise descriptions that will serve to generate test requirements. Here's an example:

STRIPPED_NAME(NAME)

STRIPPED_NAME is NAME with all leading "./" prefixes stripped. If nothing follows the final "./", it is not stripped.
Examples:
    STRIPPED_NAME("./") is "./"
    STRIPPED_NAME("./././") is "./"
    STRIPPED_NAME("././foo") is "foo"
    STRIPPED_NAME("foo") is "foo"

Precisely:
IF NAME is "./"
    STRIPPED_NAME(NAME) is NAME
ELSE IF NAME is composed of "./" concatenated to the front
of some SUFFIX
    STRIPPED_NAME(NAME) is STRIPPED_NAME(SUFFIX)
ELSE
    STRIPPED_NAME(NAME) is NAME

That might be used in this precondition:

> Validated: STRIPPED_NAME(INPUT) is shorter than INPUT
> On failure: ...

The fact that there are three cases to the definition of STRIPPED_NAME suggests that the precondition can fail in more than one way. The different possibilities should be tested.

Specifications are often incorrect. When you're looking at a specification, you should check it for common errors. (These checks apply to other styles of specification as well.)

1.2.1 Incompleteness

Are there any possible inputs that are not handled by any of the preconditions or postconditions?

1.2.2 Ambiguity

Look for pairs of postcondition triggers that apply at the same time and have contradictory effects:

> IF I is even THEN result is I-1.
> IF I < 0 THEN result is -I.

What is the result of I=-2?

The case where preconditions overlap is more common:

> Validated: I < 0
> On failure: return ENEG
> Validated: I even
> On failure: return EODD

I=1 violates both of these, and the specification doesn't say which value is returned. This is usually harmless, since the caller should be prepared for either result. Still, it may be a sign of an oversight.

2

Introduction to the SREADHEX Example

sreadhex is a routine from the GhostScript program, which processes the PostScript™ page-description language. This routine is used by permission of its author, L. Peter Deutsch. Although this version of the routine contains a fault, it has long since been fixed in later versions.

2.1 Motivation

sreadhex is a function that takes a string of characters that represent hexadecimal digits. Each character in the string represents a number. For example, the string "34AB" is interpreted as follows:

'3' represents 3.
'4' represents 4.
'A' represents 10.
'B' represents 11.

All such numbers can be represented in 4 bits:

3 decimal is 0011 binary.
4 decimal is 0100 binary.
10 decimal is 1010 binary.
11 decimal is 1011 binary.

Thus, the values of two characters can be packed into a single 8-bit byte, and a whole string can be packed into about half its length. That's what SREADHEX does. The original string "34AB" is packed into these two bytes:

Byte 1: 00110100
Byte 2: 10101011

Question: What should be done if there are an *odd* number of characters? Since two digits fit per byte, what would be done with the unused half of the last byte in the result string? That is, given "34ABF", what values should the ?'s below have?

Byte 1: 00110100
Byte 2: 10101011
Byte 3: 1111????

Answer: The solution is not to put the last digit in the result array, but to return it as a separate return value. Thus, the result string always has an even number of digits. In the above case, the result string would be

Byte 1: 00110100
Byte 2: 10101011

and the integer 15 (hexadecimal 0xF) would be returned. This "extra" return value is typically used in the next call to sreadhex. That is, if one call returns 15, 15 would be passed to the next call where it's used for the first four bits of the next result byte-array.

Question: What should be done if there are characters in the source string that do not represent hexadecimal digits?

Answer: sreadhex completely ignores them. Thus, all of these strings will yield the same result:

"34AB"
"3 4 A B"
"3G4GAMB-"

2.2 The Specification

Here is the specification for sreadhex. It's complex. Other styles of specification read more naturally but are harder to test. To make the specification easier to read, names of variables and definitions are uppercase when used in text (even though the variables are lowercase in the program).

sreadhex(str, rlen, nread, odd_digit, s)
STR is a byte array to fill. It's the destination.
RLEN is the maximum number of bytes to be filled in STR.
NREAD is a pointer to an integer. When the routine finishes, it leaves the number of bytes it used in that integer.
ODD_DIGIT is a pointer to an integer. The caller uses it to pass in the first digit (if the last call used an odd number of digits); the routine leaves either -1 or the extra digit in it after return. (The "odd" in ODD_DIGIT refers to its being set when there are an odd number of hexadecimal characters to be placed in STR.)
S is a null-terminated string. It is the source of hexadecimal characters.
sreadhex returns 0 or 1. 1 means SREADHEX ran out of characters before filling STR.

DEFINITIONS:
There are 22 hexadecimal characters. They are listed here,
along with their corresponding integer values.

'0'	0	'6'	6	'C'	12	'c'	12
'1'	1	'7'	7	'D'	13	'd'	13
'2'	2	'8'	8	'E'	14	'e'	14
'3'	3	'9'	9	'F'	15	'f'	15
'4'	4	'A'	10	'a'	10		
'5'	5	'B'	11	'b'	11		

➥*Notice that both uppercase and lowercase characters are used.*

HEX_CHAR[INDEX]
>This is the INDEXth hexadecimal character in S,
>ignoring nonhexadecimal characters. Suppose S is
>"Aa-0". Then,

>HEX_CHAR[0] is 'A'
>HEX_CHAR[1] is 'a'
>HEX_CHAR[2] is '0'

➥ *Notice that the dash is not counted. Numbering begins with 0.*

NUM_HEX_CHARS is the number of hexadecimal characters
in S. If S is "Aa-0", NUM_HEX_CHARS is 3.

START
>This is the location where the value of the first hexadecimal
>character in S is to be placed in STR.

>IF (*ODD_DIGIT == -1)
>THEN
>   START is 0
>ELSE
>   START is 1

DIGIT[INDEX]
>This is the INDEXth digit (4-bit chunk) of STR. Digits 0
>and 1 are in byte 0 of STR, Digits 2 and 3 are
>in byte 1, and so on. Remember that *ODD_DIGIT, if not -1,
>is placed in digit 0.

PRECONDITIONS:

1. Assumed: STR is a non-null pointer to an array that can
    hold RLEN bytes (hence 2*RLEN digits).
2. Assumed: RLEN >= 0.
3. Assumed: NREAD is a non-null pointer to an integer.
4. Assumed: ODD_DIGIT is a non-null pointer to an integer.

5. Assumed: *ODD_DIGIT is in the range [-1, 15].
6. Assumed: S is a non-null pointer to a null-terminated string.

7. Validated: RLEN is not 0.
    On failure:
        *NREAD is 0
        The return value is 0.

POSTCONDITIONS:

1. (An even number of digits that don't fill STR: use them all)
    IF START+NUM_HEX_CHARS < RLEN*2
      AND START+NUM_HEX_CHARS is even
    THEN
        A. The return value is 1.
        B. *NREAD is (START + NUM_HEX_CHARS)/2
        C. For any hexadecimal character in S at index INDEX,
           DIGIT[START+INDEX] = HEX_CHAR[INDEX]
           (For example, if character 0 is '9' and START is 0, 9
           is placed as the 0th digit of STR.)
        D. *ODD_DIGIT is -1.

2. (An odd number of digits that don't fill STR: use them all)
    IF START+NUM_HEX_CHARS < RLEN*2
      AND START+NUM_HEX_CHARS is odd
    THEN
        A. The return value is 1.
        B. *NREAD is (START + NUM_HEX_CHARS - 1)/2
        C. For any hexadecimal character in S at index INDEX
           except the final hexadecimal character,
           DIGIT[START+INDEX] = HEX_CHAR[INDEX]
        D. *ODD_DIGIT is set to the value of the last
           hexadecimal character in S.
3. (Enough digits to fill STR; ignore any excess)
    IF START + NUM_HEX_CHARS >= RLEN*2
    THEN
        A. The return value is 0.
        B. *NREAD is RLEN.
        C. For any hexadecimal character in S at index INDEX
           such that START + INDEX < RLEN*2
           DIGIT[START+INDEX] = HEX_CHAR[INDEX]
        D. *ODD_DIGIT is unchanged.

4. IF *ODD_DIGIT is initially >= 0
    THEN
        DIGIT[0] = the initial value of *ODD_DIGIT.

2.3
The Code

For future reference, here is the program. Because some of the code is fairly tricky, I've added some notes at the end.

```
26    typedef unsigned char byte;
27    typedef unsigned int uint;
28
29    /* Read a hex string from a stream. */
30    /* Answer 1 if we reached end-of-file before filling the string, */
31    /* 0 if we filled the string first, or <0 on error. */
32    /* *odd_digit should be -1 initially: */
33    /* if an odd number of hex digits was read, *odd_digit is set to */
34    /* the odd digit value, otherwise *odd_digit is set to -1. */
35    static byte decode_hex[257] = { 0 };        /* not initialized yet */
36    #define hex_none 0x10
37    #define hex_eofc 0x20
38    #define sgetc(s)   (*((s)++))
39
40    int
41    sreadhex(str, rlen, nread, odd_digit, s)
42        byte *str;
43        uint rlen;
44        uint *nread;
45        int *odd_digit;
46        register byte *s;
47    {    byte *ptr = str;
48         byte *limit = ptr + rlen;
49         byte val1 = (byte)*odd_digit;
50         byte val2;
51         register char *decoder = (char *)(decode_hex + 1);   /* EOFC = -1! */
52
53         if ( decoder[-1] == 0 )                 /* not initialized yet */
54           {  static char hex_chars[] = "0123456789ABCDEFabcdef";
55              int i;
56              memset(decoder - 1, hex_none, 257);
57              for ( i = 0; i < 16+6; i++ )
58                decoder[hex_chars[i]] = (i >= 16 ? i - 6 : i);
59              decoder[0] = hex_eofc;
60           }
61         if ( val1 <= 0xf ) goto d2;
62    d1:  while ( (val1 = decoder[sgetc(s)]) > 0xf )
63           {  if ( val1 == hex_eofc ) { *odd_digit = -1; goto ended; }
64           }
65    d2:  while ( (val2 = decoder[sgetc(s)]) > 0xf )
66           {  if ( val2 == hex_eofc ) { *odd_digit = val1; goto ended; }
67           }
68         *ptr++ = (val1 << 4) + val2;
69         if ( ptr < limit ) goto d1;
70         *nread = rlen;
71         return 0;
72    ended:*nread = ptr - str;
73         return 1;
74    }
```

☐ **line 38**

The program gets characters via `sgetc`. In the original program, `sgetc` got characters from a stream datatype; in this simpler version, it picks characters from a string.

☐ **lines 35,51**

The program uses a lookup table, `decoder`, to convert characters into values. The character is used as an index in the table. `decoder[character]` is the corresponding value.

The table is initalized the first time `sreadhex` is called. On line 51 `decoder` is set to point to the last 256 characters of the `decode_hex` array. The first character (`decode_hex[0]` or `decoder[-1]`) indicates whether the table has already been initialized.

☐ **lines 53-60**

`decoder` is initialized with `memset`, which sets every entry to `hex_none` indicating that the corresponding character is not hexadecimal. Then the entries for hexadecimal characters are set by iterating through a string of all such characters, calculating the value, and placing that in `decoder`. Note that the characters "abcdef" are given the same values as "ABCDEF". Character `'\0'` (which is found at the end of a C string) has value `hex_eof` (value 0x20), which causes `sreadhex` to return.

☐ **lines 61-67**

The first `while` loop finds the first digit in a byte; the second one finds the second. The loops skip nonhexadecimal characters. If the starting digit was passed in via `*odd_digit`, the first loop is skipped; thus, the first string character is used as the second digit. The test of whether to skip (line 61) is tricky. If the first digit is passed in, it should be in the range [0 .. 15]. -1 means no digit was passed in. The cast on line 49 converts the -1 to a large positive number, so that `val1 <= 0xf` evaluates to false.

Building the Test Requirement Checklist

The test requirement checklist is the heart of subsystem testing. A thorough checklist is essential for thorough testing. The checklist is built in two distinct steps. First, clues about what needs testing are extracted from the specification and perhaps the code. Here's a partial list of clues for sreadhex:

> Precondition 7
> STR, an array of bytes to be filled
> searching for the next hexadecimal character

The first clue says that Precondition 7 should be tested, but doesn't say how. That's the job of the test requirements. Test requirements describe inputs to be tried by at least one test. Here are some of the test requirements from the above clues:

> Precondition 7
>   RLEN is 0
> STR, an array of bytes to be filled
>   more than one byte is filled
> searching for the next hexadecimal character
>   found as first element
>   not found before end of string

The actual design of tests is deferred until the checklist is completed. This allows more efficient and effective test design.

Specification or Code?

The specification is the major source of clues since it describes what the subsystem is supposed to do. It isn't a complete source of clues since most subsystems contain implementation detail irrelevant to the specification. For example, the subsystem may sort small arrays using one algorithm and long arrays using another. That detail won't be mentioned in the specification, but the tests had better exercise both algorithms.

Looking at the code too early can be dangerous. The programmer may have made incorrect assumptions, embodying them in the code as faults. When reading the code, you may absorb those assumptions and be less likely to write tests that reveal the faults. However, as you'll see, ignoring the code when it's available can add time to test design (and may also reduce the effectiveness). The question of when to look at the code is one of those efficiency versus effectiveness tradeoffs that abound in testing. The answer depends on the particular situation and its risks. Here are some examples.

1. Suppose you're given a new, large subsystem to test. It is part of the external interface of the whole system. In this case, the greatest risk is that bad assumptions will lead to design and specification omissions. ("The user would never want to do *that*!") The cost of becoming "infected" by the developer's mistaken assumptions is high enough that you should avoid the code at first, even if it's available. Write test requirements from the specification, then augment them with test requirements from the code. Finally, combine them all into a set of test specifications.

2. When testing a small utility function or group of functions, assumption errors are less of a problem. Such routines are more likely to do something wrong than fail to do something. What errors of omission there are tend to be more clichéd, the type that can be found through methodical application of the Test Requirement Catalog. Even the original developer can find them. In such a case, there's little risk in looking at the code and specification together, and it saves time.

3. If—ideal world!—you as tester are involved before the code is written, you should draw up a test requirement checklist as soon as possible. You can use it as a specification review checklist. Many times you'll be able to ask the developers questions like "what if the user isn't in the permissions file?" and watch them realize they hadn't thought of that. Other times, simply mentioning a special case isn't enough. Many mishandled cases look perfectly reasonable in isolation, but are obviously wrong when you walk through a scenario that includes them. Test specifications are such scenarios, so write some of them as soon as possible and step through them as part of specification review.[1]

This chapter will first assume that you're looking at specification and code simultaneously, because that's easiest to explain. Later, we'll consider the modifications for looking at the code after the specification.

---

1. It's uncanny how some bugs just leap out of scenarios. Perhaps there's a part of the brain that answers "Error!" when asked "What would happen if X?" while another part answers "Sure!" when asked "Do I believe X?" See [Dennett91] for interesting speculations on how this might be.

Clues tell you what's test worthy about this program.

3.1.1 Preconditions and Postconditions

Preconditions and postconditions are clues because each one identifies at least two cases the program should handle (one where the condition is satisfied and one where it is not). You will surely want to try each case.

If you're using a different style of specification, you will need to do some thinking to discover the different cases. See Part 3.

Start the checklist by listing all the preconditions and postconditions:

> Precondition 1:
> Precondition 2:
> Precondition 3:

> Postcondition 1:
> Postcondition 2:
> Postcondition 3:

3.1.2 Variables

There will be test requirements based on the data the subsystem uses. These requirements will check for certain typical misuses of data. For example, if a program handles string variables, one useful test requirement is "the empty string". Programs sometimes mishandle that case.

Add *variables* as clues. "Variables" means arguments, global variables, data read from files, intermediate values mentioned in the specification, and so on—anything the program computes with. They can be found by looking at any part of the specification: the triggers, the effects of violated preconditions, and so on.

For example, if the subsystem works on the lengths of sides of triangles,

> triangle(a, b, c)
> int a, b, c;

the checklist should contain

> A, a length
> B, a length
> C, a length

Include a *type* for each variable. This type will help determine what test requirements are generated. Notice that the type is "length" instead of "integer". This is because that's what the integer arguments represent, and there may be special test requirements for lengths. For example, -1 is a pretty peculiar length but it's an unremarkable integer.

You don't need to be restricted to the types that can be used in a programming language. Much of what the type captures is the intent of the variable: What kind of thing is this, and what is it for? You may be puzzled by what type to write down. If so, just write down the first thing that comes to mind. Subsystem testing is not so rigid that it will fall apart unless the type is exactly right.

3.1.3 Operations

Add clues for each distinct major operation you can identify in the specification. Again, these clues can be found anywhere: the precondition effects, the text of definitions, etc. The examples will clarify what "major" means. As a first approximation, major operations are those that can be found in a Test Requirement Catalog such as Appendix B. "Searching" is a typical example. Most major operations would require at least several lines of code to implement. The only exceptions are the relational operators like <.

The specification may state explicitly what operations the subsystem performs ("this function searches the list..."). Or the operation may be implicit. If the specification refers to the "largest element in a list", that implies a searching operation. All these operations, explicit or implicit, should be listed as clues.

3.1.4 Definitions

Definitions usually represent intermediate data, that is, new variables. As such, clues should be listed for them. For example, this might be a definition in a specification:

UP-SET(SET)
    SET is a set of uppercase and lowercase characters.
    UP-SET is the corresponding set of uppercase characters.
      Example: UP-SET({'a', 'Z'}) == {'A', 'Z'}

and the specification might use that definition in a postcondition

Postcondition 2:
    IF UP-SET(input-set) contains 'R'
    THEN ...

You would have added `input-set` as a clue since it's a variable. You should also add another clue:

input-set, a set of characters
UP-SET(input-set), a set of characters

This new clue might correspond to an internal variable. Or it might not. Most programs convert between cases one character at a time without forming an explicit set. No matter: You'll get useful test requirements in either case.

3.2
Finding Clues
in the Code

After finding clues that describe what the specification says the sub-system must do and contain, look at what the subsystem actually does. To save time, scan the code quickly picking out variables, clichés, and function calls. You don't need to look at the detail because most of it will be accounted for automatically. The part that isn't will be handled by coverage.

3.2.1 Variables

The implementation may have more variables than the specification. For example, there may be intermediate counters, pointers, and so on. Add them to the checklist. Where before you might have had

> input_list, a list of counts

you might now have

> input_list, a list of counts
> median, the median value of input_list, a count

Note that the new clue describes median's relationship to input variables. Suppose you only wrote down

> median, a count

Later, you'll have to write a test to give median a particular value. You can't do that directly, since median isn't an input. You'll be annoyed that you have to go back and look at the code to discover how to set input_list to force median's value.

Structure members should be listed separately if they're used independently:

> file_table, a list of opened file names
> file_table->length, a length
> file_table->threshhold, a length

You should only write down variables likely to yield new test requirements. Since you haven't yet seen how *any* variables yield test requirements, you shouldn't expect to have a feel for which variables are worthwhile. After finishing this chapter, you'll have a better feel. But you probably won't be really comfortable until after you've used these techniques in your own testing.

Here is a typical example. Many local variables add no new information. Suppose a subsystem takes an argument, length, which describes the length of an array. You might see this definition in the code:

> int last_index = length+1;

Both length and last_index would lead to test requirements like

> zero-length array
> array of length one
> array with more than one element

so listing both would be a waste of time.

More Global Variables

In the previous step, you wrote down global variables used directly in the subsystem. But there may be hidden globals. Your subsystem may call a function F1 that sets a global, then a function F2 that uses it. Although that global isn't mentioned in the text of the subsystem, it's important that you list it as a clue. If you don't, you won't get test requirements for it. Without test requirements, all your tests will tend to give it the same value. If there are interaction faults between the assignment in F1 and the use in F2, your tests are unlikely to find them. Variety is required to find faults.

The best way to find hidden globals is to use a symbol-table or cross-reference listing tool. Apply it to the code used by your subsystem, find the globals, and write down any suspicious ones.[1] As with any variable clues, you'll need to use some judgement to decide which are not worthwhile.

Without such a tool, the best you can do is to examine the specifications (or, more likely, the source) of subroutines called by the subsystem. You'll have to decide whether to examine the subroutines called by *those* subroutines (and so on).

3.2.2 Clichéd Operations

Recognize clichés by looking for blocks of code that perform operations you've seen before. Examples are "searching a list", "sorting a list", and "decomposing a pathname to create a pathname for a temporary file". Often such clichés are set off by comments or blank lines. Loops often implement clichés.

At this point, don't worry about code details like individual branches or built-in operations like <. You'll consider those, if necessary, when you measure coverage. The goal is to become such a good tester that it's never necessary, because the test requirements you would have gotten from the details are automatically satisfied by test requirements from other sources (the specification and code clichés). If so, any time spent thinking about the details would have been wasted.

Quite often, the clichés you find in the code correspond exactly to operation clues you found in the specification. There's no need to list them again. Sometimes, the code clichés are new. Here are two examples:

1. You might have gotten a "sorting a list" clue from the specification. When you look at the code, you see that the program sorts small vectors (<= 15 elements) with an insertion sort and large vectors with quicksort. That would cause you to split the clue into two clues:

   sorting an array <= 15 elements (insertion sort)
   sorting an array > 15 elements (quicksort)

---

1. As an example, on UNIX you'd find the globals with `nm executable | grep '[BD]'`.

2. The specification talks of inserting elements into a table. When you look at the code, you see it uses a hash table for speed. That means there will be operations specific to hash tables, such as handling collisions. Those operations are not included in the specification—the user doesn't care how elements are inserted, just that they are. But you need to test collision handling, so you'd add "hash table collisions" as a clue.

(In both cases, the complicated operations—quicksort and hash table collision handling—would certainly yield more than just these clues.)

The most interesting case is when a specification clue doesn't correspond to anything in the code. Why not? Perhaps it's a bug, a fault of omission. Even if you discover a reason for the missing operation, it's usually a good idea to retain the existing clue. For one thing, the reason may be invalid. For another, the test requirements from the clue are probably still relevant—they're often inherently special cases that the code must handle correctly.

Each separate cliché is a separate clue, even if the same cliché is repeated twice. For example, if there are two searching loops in the code, both are written down as clues:

> searching for the maximum element in the input list
> searching for the minimum element in the input list

3.2.3 Function Calls

List all function calls as clues. If one corresponds to an operation you already wrote down, just modify the existing clue. For example, you might have found

> Sorting the INPUT list

in the specification. You now see that it's done by calling quicksort. In this case, change the clue to

> Sorting the INPUT list (via quicksort())

If there are several identical function calls, be sure to distinguish them. For example, if you were testing a function that called sreadhex twice, your checklist would contain these clues:

> sreadhex(), applied to the saved_stream
> sreadhex(), applied to the input_stream

> ➡ *You will need test requirements from each operation to ensure that each call is fully tested.*

The preconditions and postconditions are listed by number. Even assumed preconditions are listed. Later we'll see under which circumstances you wouldn't bother listing some of those.

Precondition 1
Precondition 2
Precondition 3
Precondition 4
Precondition 5
Precondition 6
Precondition 7

Postcondition 1
Postcondition 2
Postcondition 3
Postcondition 4
Postcondition 5

Deriving clues from variables and operations is more work than listing preconditions and postconditions. For easy reference, Fig. 3–1 shows the parts of the specification that will contain such clues. Refer to Chapter 2 for the full specification.

(1) sreadhex(str, rlen, nread, odd_digit, s)...
(2) returns 0 or 1...

(3) There are 22 hexadecimal characters. They are listed here...

(4) HEX_CHAR[INDEX]
This is the INDEXth hexadecimal character in S,
ignoring nonhexadecimal characters...

(5) NUM_HEX_CHARS is the number of hexadecimal characters in S.

(6) START
This is the location where the value of the first hexadecimal character in S is to be placed in STR.

IF (*ODD_DIGIT == -1)
THEN
    START is 0
ELSE
    START is 1

(7) DIGIT[INDEX]
This is the INDEXth digit (4-bit chunk) of STR. Digits 0 and 1 are in byte 0 of STR, Digits 2 and 3 are in byte 1, and so on. Remember that *ODD_DIGIT, if not -1, is placed in digit 0.

Fig. 3–1 The SREADHEX specification used for clues

1. The first set of clues comes from variables passed into the function:

   STR, an array of bytes to be filled
   RLEN, a count
   NREAD, a pointer to a count
   ODD_DIGIT, a pointer to an integer either -1 or [0..15]
   S, a string

2. Another clue comes from considering the return value:

   return value, a Boolean (0 or 1)

3. The definitions are a useful source of operations and variables. The first one defines which characters sreadhex moves into STR:

   a hexadecimal character, in range ['0' .. '9', 'A'.. 'F', 'a' .. 'f']

4. HEX_CHAR must skip over nonhexadecimal characters, which suggests a search for hexadecimal characters:

   searching for next hexadecimal character

5. NUM_HEX_CHARS is a count of hexadecimal characters in S:

   NUM_HEX_CHARS, a count of hexadecimal characters in S

6. START is just another way of talking about odd_digit, so nothing is written down (yet).

7. The definition of DIGIT suggests a digit as a range of values. The definition also describes digits as being packed two per byte. It seems that which half the digit is in might be important—that's a clue. As you'll see in a couple of pages, the same clue is gotten more straightforwardly in another way. That's OK: It's better to get the same information in two ways than not at all, because sometimes you'll miss it the first time.

   DIGIT, a location to be filled with an integer in range [0 .. 15]
   DIGIT, either the first or last half of a byte

Most of the work done by the specification is captured in the definitions. The precondition and postcondition actions are all simple. The most complicated operation is filling DIGIT from the HEX_CHARS. For example, Postcondition 1 says:

   C. For any hexadecimal character in S at index INDEX,
      DIGIT[START+INDEX] = HEX_CHAR[INDEX]
      (For example, if character 0 is '9' and START is 0, 9
      is placed as the 0th digit of STR.)

There are two steps to that operation: searching for the next hexadecimal character and putting its value in the appropriate half of a byte. Both of those already have clues from the definitions.

RLEN is a count of characters used, but not all characters are used. (Postcondition 3 describes the situation in which they're not.) Given how common off-by-one faults are, it might be reasonable to worry about the number of unused characters with a clue like this:

number of unused hexadecimal characters in S, a count

Had I missed this clue, its effect should have been rediscovered when creating test requirements. Were it missed there, one of the test design rules should rediscover it. Subsystem testing is designed so that each of its stages is a partial safety net for the stages before it.

3.3.1 The Code

Fig. 3–2 shows an abbreviated version of the code once more for easy reference.

```
41  sreadhex(str, rlen, nread, odd_digit, s)
42      byte *str;
43      uint rlen;
44      uint *nread;
45      int *odd_digit;
46      register byte *s;
47  {   byte *ptr = str;
48      byte *limit = ptr + rlen;
49      byte val1 = (byte)*odd_digit;
50      byte val2;
51      register char *decoder = (char *)(decode_hex + 1);   /* EOFC = -1! */
52
53      if ( decoder[-1] == 0 ) /* not initialized yet */
54          {   static char hex_chars[] = "0123456789ABCDEFabcdef";
55              int i;
56              memset(decoder - 1, hex_none, 257);
57              for ( i = 0; i < 16+6; i++ )
58                  decoder[hex_chars[i]] = (i >= 16 ? i - 6 : i);
59              decoder[0] = hex_eofc;
60          }
61      if ( val1 <= 0xf ) goto d2;
62  d1: while ( (val1 = decoder[sgetc(s)]) > 0xf )
63          {   if ( val1 == hex_eofc ) { *odd_digit = -1; goto ended; }
64          }
65  d2: while ( (val2 = decoder[sgetc(s)]) > 0xf )
66          {   if ( val2 == hex_eofc ) { *odd_digit = val1; goto ended; }
67          }
68      *ptr++ = (val1 << 4) + val2;
69      if ( ptr < limit ) goto d1;
70      *nread = rlen;
71      return 0;
72  ended: *nread = ptr - str;
73      return 1;
74  }
```

Fig. 3–2
The SREADHEX code

The temporary variables are just shorthand for essentials already listed. There's no point in writing them down again. ptr (line 47) is just the mechanism by which str is filled. Since str is already listed, listing ptr as a clue would be redundant. limit just makes checking rlen easier. val1 and val2 are covered by "oddness or evenness of DIGIT".

The initialization of the decoder array (line 54 and following) doesn't look promising: It will always be done the first time sreadhex is called, and it will always execute the same way. (The initialization is not dependent on any of the input variables.) Because of that, any test requirements gotten from "filling decoder array" or "memset call" would either be satisfied by every test, or by none. Listing them would be a waste of effort. There should be tests that call sreadhex after it's already been called to check whether it works when initialization isn't done. As you'll see, that happens naturally, so there's no need to write anything down. (If it doesn't happen, coverage—the last of the safety nets—will discover the missing tests.)

There are two while loops corresponding to searching for an odd digit or even digit. It seems that the "searching for next hex character" clue should be replaced by these two clues:

Searching for a value for an odd DIGIT
Searching for a value for an even DIGIT

These describe the consequences of "DIGIT, either the first or last half of a byte", so that old clue is also superseded by the two new clues.

The two while loops are wrapped in a larger loop, which fills str. That adds no information to the existing clue, "STR, an array of bytes to be filled."

The complete set of clues is shown on the facing page.

3.3.2 Where Do We Stand?

The list of clues distills the specification and code down to the essential elements (as far as test design is concerned). This focuses attention and helps ensure that nothing is missed. The next step is to decide how each of those elements is to be tested. Those are the test requirements. The step after that is to create test specifications that satisfy all of the test requirements.

The process of creating clues is not mechanical. Two different people will arrive at different sets of clues. The same person might find different clues at different times. The goal of subsystem testing is not to make all people uniform. While that would be desirable, it seems the result would be that everyone would be uniformly bad. Instead, the goal is to improve everyone, but perhaps unevenly. The discovery of clues is where individual differences have the most impact on effectiveness. The later steps in the process are either more mechanical or less sensitive to individual differences.

Precondition 1
Precondition 2
Precondition 3
Precondition 4
Precondition 5
Precondition 6
Precondition 7

Postcondition 1
Postcondition 2
Postcondition 3
Postcondition 4
Postcondition 5

STR, an array of bytes to be filled
RLEN, a count
NREAD, a pointer to a count
ODD_DIGIT, a pointer to an integer either -1 or [0..15]
S, a string
return value, a boolean (0 or 1)

hexadecimal character, in range ['0' .. '9', 'A'.. 'F', 'a' .. 'f']
searching for the next hexadecimal character (superceded)
NUM_HEX_CHARS, a count of hexadecimal characters in S

DIGIT, a location to be filled with an integer in range [0 .. 15]
DIGIT, either the first or last half of a byte (superceded)

number of unused hexadecimal characters in S, a count

Searching for a value for an odd DIGIT

Searching for a value for an even DIGIT

3.4 Test Requirements from Preconditions, Postconditions, and Definitions

Each precondition divides the subsystem's input into two groups: those inputs that satisfy the precondition, and those inputs that don't. Each postcondition does the same. Definitions are often little functions with (in effect) preconditions and postconditions of their own. Test requirements for these types of clues can usually be generated mechanically. The rules are explained in this section and summarized in Appendix F. They quickly become second nature.

3.4.1 Simple Validated Preconditions

If the precondition is simple (without AND or OR), there are two test requirements. One violates the precondition; the other satisfies it.

Here's an example:
From

> Precondition 1:
>   Validated: A must be even
>   On failure: Print "A must be even" and exit with status 1

you get this clue and requirements

> Precondition 1
>   A odd   ERROR
>   A even

The ERROR marker reminds you that "A odd" violates a precondition. The marker is important because "A odd" will be used to test whether the subsystem catches that violation. Such error tests are different than tests of normal use.

What does "A even" tell you? It requires that you write at least one test where A is even. But any test that violates no preconditions must have A even. Provided you're going to write any normal (non-error) test, the requirement adds no information. So there's no point in writing it down. The result of a simple precondition usually looks like:

> Precondition 1
>   A odd   ERROR

(This detail will be clearer after you've seen more about how test specifications are built. Leaving the non-ERROR requirement in does no harm—you'll simply discover later that it's redundant.)

3.4.2 Validated Preconditions Using OR

Preconditions that use the OR combining operator contain more information and yield extra test requirements.

> Precondition 1:
>   Validated: A OR B

yields

> Precondition 1:
>   A true, B false
>   A false, B true
>   A false, B false   ERROR

This is called the *OR rule*. Notice that one possibility is missing, A and B both true. Its omission is based on two general principles:

1. You can't test every conceivable requirement; some pruning is needed.
2. You should prune out requirements that have a poor record at finding faults.

The fourth possibility has such a poor record. That can be explained by thinking about the correct implementation and plausible faults. The correct implementation would look like

```
if (!(A || B))
    exit_with_error("Error:  A is %d, B is %d", A, B);
else ...
```

However, the programmer might forget to test one of the two cases, giving code like this:

```
if (!A)
    exit_with_error("Error:  A is %d, B is %d", A, B);
else ...
```

or

```
if (!B)
    exit_with_error("Error:  A is %d, B is %d", A, B);
else ...
```

Or the code might use the wrong logical operator:

```
if (!(A && B))
    exit_with_error("Error:  A is %d, B is %d", A, B);
else ...
```

The three-requirement set given by the OR rule is enough to find such plausible faults (and others besides). To see why, compare how the different alternatives handle each of the four possible test requirements:

Inputs		Correct Implementation	Incorrect Implementations			
A	B	!(A||B)	!(A&&B)	!A	!B	Plausible Faults
true	FALSE	FALSE	true	FALSE	true	!(A&&B), !(B)
FALSE	true	FALSE	true	true	FALSE	!(A&&B), !(A)
FALSE	FALSE	true	true	true	true	in then branch
true	true	FALSE	FALSE	FALSE	FALSE	in else branch

With the (A true, B false) requirement, the correct implementation evaluates to false. The plausible faults ! (A&&B) and !B evaluate to true. If the program is incorrect and if it contains one of those faults, this input will cause it to take the if in the wrong direction. The error message will be printed. That's a program failure, so the fault is discovered.

If, however, the program contains the !A fault, it will take the same branch as the correct program. The wrong code gets the right result, which means that this test cannot find the fault. The (A false, B true) requirement will, though.

That argument justifies two of the three OR rule requirements. It illustrates some of the ideas of fault-based testing [Morell90], mutation testing [DeMillo78], or Error-Sensitive Test Case Analysis [Foster80]. See also [Ostrand79]. Note that simply triggering the fault does not guarantee that it will lead to a failure. In this program, it did, because the wrong path immediately printed an obviously wrong message. In other cases, though, the wrong path might yield the right result by accident. That doesn't seem to be much of a problem for small subsystems [Offutt91], [Marick91]. It's more of a concern for large subsystems, but the solution lies in test implementation rather than test design. See Chapter 13.

The two remaining requirements, where A and B have the same value, do not seem to be needed. However, suppose there's no fault in the if test, but rather one in the error handling. For example, the program might be written

```
if (!(A | | B))
    exit_with_error("Error: A is %d, B is %d\n", A);
else ...
```

The programmer forgot the third argument to `exit_with_error`. That happens all the time, and compilers can't catch it for functions with a variable number of arguments. The two requirements (A true, B false), (A false, B true) that catch faults in the if test will both cause this program to take the else branch. They won't exercise `exit_with_error`, so they certainly can't find the fault. Only (A false, B false) can do that, so that requirement is valuable.

(A true, B true) doesn't seem to be. That's not to say that it will never find a fault. For a given specification and set of requirements, you can always think of a fault that won't be found by those requirements. Perhaps the complete program looks like this:

```
if (!(A | | B))
    exit_with_error("Error: A is %d, B is %d", A, B);
else
    printf("%d", 5 / (A - B));
```

This program will have a divide-by-zero failure only when A and B are both true[1]. But such a fault is rare enough that it's not worth always writing a special test for the fourth requirement. Although the (A true, B true) requirement may be added back in a later stage, in this stage it's pruned out.

The pruning is particularly valuable when the OR has more than two terms. In abstract terms, the rule is that given this precondition:

Precondition 1:
    (A1 OR A2 OR ... OR An)

there are N+1 test requirements:

    A1 is true, all others are false
    A2 is true, all others are false
    ...
    An is true, all others are false
    All the A's are false.   ERROR

---

1. Assuming that in this program "true" means the value 1.

Each of the first N cases checks for one of the A's being left out of the implementation (as well as for other plausible faults). The fault-based approach thus leads to the same rule as cause-effect testing [Myers79]. Without the OR rule, you would have 2^N test requirements. As a concrete example, for this precondition:

Precondition 1:
>   (File1 empty OR File2 empty OR ... OR FileN empty)

there are N+1 test requirements:

File1 is empty, all others are non-empty

File2 is empty, all others are non-empty

...
FileN is empty, all others are non-empty
all the files non-empty.   ERROR

The OR operator is sometimes used in cases where the second clause is meaningless if the first is true. For example, given

>   P is NULL OR P->field has value 5.

A mechanical application of the OR rule yields these requirements:

P is NULL, P->field has value other than 5.	(true, false)
P is not NULL, P->field has value 5.	(false, true)
P is not NULL, P->field has value other than 5.	(false, false)

But P->field's value is meaningless when P is NULL, so the first requirement can be simplified to

>   P is NULL

Such combinations will sometimes be written as "EITHER...OR":

>   EITHER P is NULL OR P->field has value 5.

That has no effect on testing; it's entirely to make specifications a little easier to read.

3.4.3 Validated Preconditions Using AND

The other combining operator is AND:

Precondition 1
>   Validated: A AND B
>   On failure: ...

yields

Precondition 1
>   A true, B true
>   A true, B false   ERROR
>   A false, B true   ERROR

In a multi-way AND, one requirement has all terms true. Then there are N requirements where exactly one of the terms is false.

Since any non-error test must satisfy (A true, B true), that requirement can be left out of the checklist. That wasn't the case for the OR precondition because there were two distinct ways to satisfy it. You can't be sure that test specifications will satisfy each way unless they're listed explicitly.

3.4.4 Validated Preconditions with Combinations of ANDs and ORs

Suppose you have a complex precondition like

Precondition 1
    Validated: A AND (B OR C)
    On failure: ...

When testing an expression that mixes ANDs and ORs, use the Requirements for Complex Booleans Catalog (Appendix E). That catalog contains this entry for such an expression:

A && (B || C)

A	B	C	Whole Expression
1	1	0	true
0	0	1	false
1	0	0	false
1	0	1	true
0	1	0	false

(The C operators && and || are used because they're easier to spot when scanning the catalog. 1 and 0 are used instead of "true" and "false" because they're more visually distinct.)

An alternate approach is to apply the AND/OR rules to the two operators separately. From the outermost AND operator, you'd get three cases for AND:

Precondition 1
    A true, (B OR C) true
    A true, (B OR C) false   ERROR
    A false, (B OR C) true   ERROR

The OR operator would add its three cases:

Precondition 1
    A true, (B OR C) true
    A true, (B OR C) false   ERROR
    A false, (B OR C) true   ERROR
    B true, C false
    B false, C true
    B false, C false

Which approach should you use? The catalog requirements are slightly more effective, so use them. If, however, the boolean expression is not in the catalog, handle the operators independently. When you learn to work with real specifications (Chapter 12), you'll see that considering operators to be independent simplifies your life. Optional Chapter 25 goes into the relationship between the two approaches in more detail. As a practical matter, either works well. Time spent worrying about which one is best in a particular situation would be better spent elsewhere.

3.4.5 Assumed Preconditions

Assumed preconditions differ from validated preconditions in that the subsystem is not required to handle violations. There is no "on failure" action. Therefore, there's no point in writing down ERROR requirements. The rule for converting an assumed precondition to requirements is:

1. Start with the same requirements as for validated preconditions.
2. Throw out the ERROR requirements.
3. If there's only one requirement left, throw it out, since it must be satisfied by every test. (No test should violate the assumed precondition).

For simple preconditions and preconditions using AND, that means assumed preconditions yield no test requirements. An OR yields two. Given

> Precondition 1:
> Assumed: LENGTH is even OR LENGTH is 1

the OR rule gives you two requirements that satisfy the precondition:

> Precondition 1:
> LENGTH is even, LENGTH is not 1
> LENGTH is odd, LENGTH is 1

These two requirements are internally redundant. If LENGTH is even, it surely isn't 1. If LENGTH is 1, it is surely odd. They can be shortened to:

> Precondition 1:
> LENGTH is even
> LENGTH is 1

It's important to write them down, since this precondition might be your only clue that there's something special about even lengths.

Combinations of ANDs and ORs also yield more than one non-ERROR requirement. For example,

> Precondition 1
>   Assumed: A AND (B OR C)

gives the two cases where B OR C is true:

> Precondition 1
>   B true, C false
>   B false, C true

A must always be true, so it doesn't need to be written down. All that needs to be listed are the different ways in which the precondition can be true, which means listing the requirements from the OR subexpressions.

Since assumed preconditions that don't involve OR never lead to test requirements, don't write them down as clues. But beware of a common mistake: not writing down any assumed preconditions, even if they do involve OR.

3.4.6 Postconditions

Postconditions, like preconditions, divide input into groups. The difference is that failing to satisfy a postcondition is not an error. It just means the postcondition doesn't apply to that input. So postconditions are handled like preconditions, with these exceptions:

1. None of the requirements are marked as ERROR requirements.
2. If the postcondition has no trigger (no IF), it must be satisfied by every non-error test, so there's no requirement to write down.
3. If the postcondition has a trigger, it always yields at least two requirements. None of them can be dropped (as were the non-ERROR requirements for simple preconditions and preconditions using AND).

Here's a set of simple postconditions:

> Postcondition 1:
>   Print "Hello, world"

> Postcondition 2:
>   IF A < 0
>   THEN print "Less than zero"
>   ELSE print "More than zero"

> Postcondition 3:
>   IF B AND C
>   THEN print "B and C"

Postcondition 4:
    IF D OR E
    THEN print "D or E"

and here's the resulting checklist:

Postcondition 1
Postcondition 2
    A < 0
    A >= 0
Postcondition 3
    B true, C true
    B true, C false
    B false, C true
Postcondition 4
    D true, E false
    D false, E true
    D false, E false

Notice that some of the requirements under a postcondition satisfy the trigger and some do not. Writing a requirement under a postcondition doesn't mean it causes that postcondition to happen. It just means it was derived from that postcondition.

Postconditions often neatly partition the possible inputs of the subsystem. Here's an example. It will be worked out in laborious detail. With practice, you go immediately from the postconditions to the final requirements.

Postconditions:
1. IF the optional argument was not given
    THEN ...

2. IF the optional argument was given AND it's <= 0
    THEN ...

3. IF the optional argument was given AND it's > 0
    THEN ...

Those postconditions would lead to these clues:

Postcondition 1:
Postcondition 2:
Postcondition 3:

The test requirements for Postcondition 1 are the trigger and its negation:

Postcondition 1:
    1.1. The optional argument was not given.
    1.2. The optional argument was given.

(The test requirements are numbered for later discussion.) The AND rule applies to Postcondition 2:

> Postcondition 2:
> 2.1. Optional argument was given, it's <= 0   (true, true)
> 2.2. Optional argument was given, it's > 0   (true, false)
> 2.3. Optional argument not given, it's <= 0   (false, true)

The first thing to notice is that 2.3 is nonsensical. If the optional argument is not given, its nonexistent value can't be less than 0. The test requirement should say only "optional argument not given". But that's already been written down (1.1). It's *redundant*, so it shouldn't be listed again.

You might not notice that a test requirement is redundant. At worst, this leads to an excess test specification, and that doesn't happen often.

The next thing to notice is that test requirement 1.2 is automatically true if either 2.1 or 2.2 is true. Those two test requirements are *refinements* of 1.2. Rather than write them down under the Postcondition 2 clue, they can be indented under 1.2:

> Postcondition 1:
> 1.1. The optional argument was not given.
> 1.2. The optional argument was given.
>   2.1. Optional argument was given, it's <= 0
>   2.2. Optional argument was given, it's >= 0

It is common to generate a test requirement from one clue, then write it down under another. By doing that, you lose track of where the requirement came from. This slight disadvantage is outweighed by having a more compact, logically structured checklist without redundancy.

Such an indentation structure means that two tests for the indented test requirements would be better than one test for the "parent" test requirement. There's reason to believe the subsystem may handle the two cases differently.

To be precise, by refining a test requirement, you're making these statements:

1. Fewer inputs satisfy a refining requirement than satisfy the original requirement. This is certainly true in the previous example where the two refinements divide 1.2 in two. But refinements don't have to neatly partition the original requirement. As another example, consider

Precondition 1 (A >= 0)
    A < 0   ERROR
      A = -1   ERROR

A=-1 is certainly a subset of "all A values less than 0."

2. You predict that a test for the original might not find a bug that a refinement would catch. This is because a bug might happen only for inputs that satisfy the refinement. Since the original allows other inputs, you could satisfy it without trying the bug-revealing inputs. In the last example, A=-1 will detect an off-by-one fault that no other negative A would find.

3. You predict that the inputs excluded by the refinement wouldn't find any bugs that the refinement won't also find. The prediction in the example is that any bug found by A=-2, A=-3, . . . will also be found by A=-1.

The checklist is a set of predictions about which refinements are cost-effective. Testing is the process of narrowing down an infinite number of inputs into a small set you can afford to try, so some refinement is inevitable. You have to make the best predictions you can, without generating an unmanageably large number of tests.

It's not unusual to miss a refinement. If you do, you end up with both the original and refined requirements in different parts of the checklist. This may result in testing input values that you otherwise wouldn't have bothered with, but the worst that can happen is that you have an extra test specification.

3.4.7 Definitions

Earlier, you saw this example of a definition:

UP-SET(SET)
    SET is a set of uppercase and lowercase characters.
    UP-SET is the corresponding set of uppercase characters.
    Example: UP-SET({'a', 'Z'}) == {'A', 'Z'}

and these clues associated with its use:

    input-set, a set of characters
    UP-SET(input-set), a set of characters

But UP-SET is defined in terms of something. In fact, a more rigorous definition of UP-SET has to be something like this:

> For each element of SET,
>   IF it's uppercase
>   THEN it is in the UP-SET
>   ELSE its uppercase equivalent is in the UP-SET

This looks a lot like a postcondition. It splits SET into two cases—in fact, it creates two test requirements: whether the characters are uppercase or lowercase. The clues could be refined as follows:

> input-set, a set of characters
>   a character is uppercase
>   a character is not uppercase
> UP-SET(input-set), a set of characters

Notice that, unlike the earlier examples, the test requirements are not mutually exclusive. If input-set were { 'A', 'b' }, it would satisfy both test requirements. That would be fine. You usually want to satisfy as many test requirements as possible with the fewest test specifications.

"A character is uppercase" is something to test, but it will certainly be refined with better test requirements, ones that describe more precisely *which* uppercase characters to test. Those refinements might come from preconditions, postconditions, other definitions, or the Test Requirement Catalog. Use of the Test Requirement Catalog will be described after this section is applied to the sreadhex example.

3.5 Finding Test Requirements for SREADHEX

The preconditions are reproduced in Fig. 3–1.

None of the assumed preconditions use OR, so they produce no useful test requirements. To illustrate this lack of useful effect, Precondition 1's true requirement will be listed and used throughout the sreadhex example.

Validated Precondition 7 is a simple precondition, so only its ERROR requirement should be written down. The non-ERROR

Fig. 3-1 SREADHEX preconditions.

1. Assumed: STR is a non-null pointer to an array that can hold RLEN bytes (and 2*RLEN digits).
2. Assumed: RLEN >= 0.
3. Assumed: NREAD is a non-null pointer to an integer.
4. Assumed: ODD_DIGIT is a non-null pointer to an integer.
5. Assumed: *ODD_DIGIT is in the range [-1, 15]
6. Assumed: S is a non-null pointer to a null-terminated string.

7. Validated: RLEN is not 0
    On failure:
        *NREAD is 0
        The return value is 0.

requirement will also be retained to show how it adds nothing to test design (but does no harm, either).

Here are the requirements from the preconditions:

Precondition 1:
    STR is a non-null pointer to an array that can hold RLEN bytes.

Precondition 7:
    RLEN is not 0
    RLEN = 0   ERROR

After the preconditions come the postconditions. They are summarized in Fig. 3–2.

<table>
<tr><td>

1. (An even number of digits that don't fill STR: use them all)
    IF START+NUM_HEX_CHARS < RLEN*2
      AND START+NUM_HEX_CHARS is even
    THEN ...

2. (An odd number of digits that don't fill STR: use them all)
    IF START+NUM_HEX_CHARS < RLEN*2
      AND START+NUM_HEX_CHARS is odd
    THEN ...

3. (Enough digits to fill STR; ignore any excess)
    IF START + NUM_HEX_CHARS >= RLEN*2
    THEN ...

4. IF *ODD_DIGIT is initially >= 0
    THEN ...

</td><td>

Fig. 3–2 SREADHEX postconditions.

</td></tr>
</table>

The first postcondition uses AND, so it generates these test requirements:

START+NUM_HEX_CHARS < RLEN*2, START+NUM_HEX_CHARS is even	(true, true)
START+NUM_HEX_CHARS >= RLEN*2, START+NUM_HEX_CHARS is even	(false, true)
START+NUM_HEX_CHARS < RLEN*2, START+NUM_HEX_CHARS is odd	(true, false)

Postcondition 2 uses the AND rule to give:

START+NUM_HEX_CHARS < RLEN*2, START+NUM_HEX_CHARS is odd	(true, true)
START+NUM_HEX_CHARS >= RLEN*2, START+NUM_HEX_CHARS is odd	(false, true)
START+NUM_HEX_CHARS < RLEN*2, START+NUM_HEX_CHARS is even	(true, false)

The first and third of these are redundant with Postcondition 1's, so they should not be listed again.

Postcondition 3 doesn't use AND or OR, so only the trigger and its negation are possible test requirements:

START+NUM_HEX_CHARS >= RLEN*2
START+NUM_HEX_CHARS < RLEN*2

These are less refined than ones already listed, so they are ignored.

Postcondition 4 gives
*ODD_DIGIT is initially >= 0
*ODD_DIGIT is initially < 0

Fig. 3-3 Checklist after preconditions and postconditions.

Fig. 3-3 shows the test requirements so far.

Precondition 1
    STR is a non-null pointer to an array that can hold RLEN bytes.
Precondition 7
    RLEN is not 0
    RLEN = 0   ERROR
Postcondition 1
    START+NUM_HEX_CHARS < RLEN*2, START+NUM_HEX_CHARS is even
    START+NUM_HEX_CHARS >= RLEN*2, START+NUM_HEX_CHARS is even
    START+NUM_HEX_CHARS < RLEN*2, START+NUM_HEX_CHARS is odd
Postcondition 2
    START+NUM_HEX_CHARS >= RLEN*2, START+NUM_HEX_CHARS is odd
Postcondition 3
Postcondition 4
    *ODD_DIGIT is initially >= 0
    *ODD_DIGIT is initially < 0

➡ *The variable and operation clues have had nothing added yet—omitted to save space.*

The definitions come next. Fig. 3-4 shows the definitions that have either explicit or implicit IF statements. START uses an IF..THEN construct. Its test yields:

*ODD_DIGIT == -1
*ODD_DIGIT != -1

These two requirements can be merged with those already found for Postcondition 4:

Postcondition 4
    *ODD_DIGIT is initially >= 0
    *ODD_DIGIT is initially < 0

*ODD_DIGIT==-1 refines the second requirement, so it's added there. *ODD_DIGIT!=-1 is automatically satisfied whenever *ODD_DIGIT>=0, so it's not worth listing. Postcondition 4 now looks like this:

CHAP. 3 BUILDING THE TEST REQUIREMENT CHECKLIST

Postcondition 4
     *ODD_DIGIT is initially >= 0
     *ODD_DIGIT is initially < 0
          *ODD_DIGIT==-1

START
          This is the location where the value of the first hexadecimal
          character in S is to be placed in STR.
          IF (*ODD_DIGIT == -1)
          THEN
               START is 0
          ELSE
               START is 1
HEX_CHAR[INDEX]
          This is the INDEXth hexadecimal character in S,
          ignoring nonhexadecimal characters.
          HEX_CHAR("Aa-0")[0] is 'A'
          HEX_CHAR("Aa-0")[1] is 'a'
          HEX_CHAR("Aa-0")[2] is '0'

     ➡Notice that the dash is not counted. Numbering begins with 0.

DIGIT[INDEX]
          This is the INDEXth digit (4-bit chunk) of STR. Digits 0
          and 1 are in byte 0 of STR, Digits 2 and 3 are
          in byte 1, and so on. Remember that *ODD_DIGIT, if not -1,
          is placed in digit 0.

Fig. 3-4 SREADHEX definitions.

These START requirements raise a question. Many of the test requirements from the postconditions involve START:

     Postcondition 1
          START+NUM_HEX_CHARS < RLEN*2, START+NUM_HEX_CHARS is even
          START+NUM_HEX_CHARS >= RLEN*2, START+NUM_HEX_CHARS is even
          START+NUM_HEX_CHARS < RLEN*2, START+NUM_HEX_CHARS is odd
     Postcondition 2
          START+NUM_HEX_CHARS >= RLEN*2, START+NUM_HEX_CHARS is odd

Each of those has to be satisfied in at least one test. But perhaps they should be satisfied with both values of *ODD_DIGIT? That would lead to this checklist:

Postcondition 1
    START+NUM_HEX_CHARS < RLEN*2, START+NUM_HEX_CHARS is even
        *ODD_DIGIT ! = -1 (START is 1)
        *ODD_DIGIT = = -1   (START is 0)
    START+NUM_HEX_CHARS >= RLEN*2, START+NUM_HEX_CHARS is even
        *ODD_DIGIT ! = -1 (START is 1)
        *ODD_DIGIT = = -1   (START is 0)
    START+NUM_HEX_CHARS < RLEN*2, START+NUM_HEX_CHARS is odd
        *ODD_DIGIT ! = -1 (START is 1)
        *ODD_DIGIT = = -1   (START is 0)
Postcondition 2
    START+NUM_HEX_CHARS >= RLEN*2, START+NUM_HEX_CHARS is odd
        *ODD_DIGIT ! = -1 (START is 1)
        *ODD_DIGIT = = -1   (START is 0)

This is not the same as the way the definition was used with the refinement of Postcondition 4. There, new test requirements were put in the best place in the checklist. Here, *copies* of the new requirements are put in four different places. It's a multiplication rather than a refinement. Should it be done?

The rule is not to multiply requirements unless there's clear evidence it's needed. Anything else can quickly lead to a combinatorial explosion of tests. In the basic technique, that evidence is given by the AND and OR combining operators, and the multiplication happens as part of the AND and OR rules. Other sources of evidence are given in Part 5. They're not so important that they should be included in basic subsystem testing.

Like the earlier example of a string with uppercase and lowercase characters, a rigorous definition of HEX_CHAR would have to say something about "IF a character in S is a hexadecimal character...". No more needs to be written to get two requirements for S:

    S, a string
        a character in S is hexadecimal
        a character in S is not hexadecimal

(You'll see later that the Test Requirement Catalog does a better job with test requirements for hexadecimal and nonhexadecimal characters.)

In the same way, `DIGIT` suggests there's a difference between filling even and odd digits. However, there are already clues for this distinction:

Searching for a value for an odd DIGIT
Searching for a value for an even DIGIT

and I know that the catalog will give me good requirements for those clues, better than simply adding some like:

an element is added as an odd digit
an element is added as an even digit

So I won't do anything more with `DIGIT`.

The updated checklist can be found in Section 3.8.

3.5.1 Where Do We Stand?

This part of subsystem testing is a simple case analysis. The preconditions and postconditions explicitly group the inputs the subsystem should treat differently. Many definitions also group inputs, though not always as obviously as preconditions and postconditions do. Listing a test requirement for each group ensures that it will be tried.

Most test specifications will be built by satisfying several requirements at once. For example, we could specify this input to `sreadhex`:

STR is a 100-byte buffer, initialized to all '2'
RLEN has the value 2
ODD_DIGIT points to an integer containing 0.
S is the string "9"

That input satisfies these test requirements:

STR is a non-null pointer to an array that can hold RLEN bytes.
RLEN is not 0
START+NUM_HEX_CHARS < RLEN*2, START+NUM_HEX_CHARS is even
*ODD_DIGIT is initially >= 0

`sreadhex` should put 0 and 9 in the first two digits of `STR`, set `*NREAD` to 1, set `*ODD_DIGIT` to -1, and return 1. If it doesn't, there's a fault.

These requirements are not enough. There are more groups of inputs, ones only implicit in the specification. As in this section, each group of inputs will be described by a test requirement, but the clues will be different. They will be the subsystem's operations and variables.

3.6
Test Requirements from Catalogs

Operation and variable clues also lead to test requirements but in a different way. They're found by using catalogs. Three catalogs are included in the reference material. Appendix A, "Test Requirement Catalog (Student Version)," is easiest to use when learning. Appendix B, "Test Requirement Catalog (Standard Version)," is the complete catalog, applicable to a wide range of programs. Appendix C, "POSIX®-Specific Test Requirement Catalog", contains some extra test requirements tailored to POSIX-compatible programs.

The easiest way to learn a catalog is to watch someone use it. This section briefly explains the organization of a catalog, applies one in detail to `sreadhex`, then summarizes the rules for catalog use.

3.6.1 Catalog Organization

A catalog is a collection of test requirements, indexed by variables and operations. It is scanned sequentially. The format allows you to skip obviously irrelevant parts easily. For example, if your application doesn't process text, you can skip the PRINTING TEXT and READING TEXT sections, and perhaps all of STRINGS AND TEXT. Take a moment to look over the student catalog (Appendix A) now.

Catalog entries use two types of annotations.

IN, OUT, IN/OUT

A variable can be an input, output, or intermediate variable. Input variables are given to the subsystem to control its processing. Output variables are set by the subsystem. Intermediate variables are set during processing and affect later processing.

Variable requirements are labelled as IN, OUT, or IN/OUT. An IN requirement is good for input or intermediate variables. An OUT requirement is good for output or intermediate variables.

For example, when two input values are pointers of the same type, an IN requirement says to create a test specification where they point to the same object. Programs often contain faults because programmers assume that can't happen. But suppose a subsystem has two result variables that are pointers. It's much less likely that forcing them to point to the same object will discover a fault.

OUT requirements, like all test requirements, are requirements on the inputs, just expressed in terms of the outputs. For example, if there's a test requirement that says the result should be an empty string, it's really requiring that there be a test specification with inputs that cause an empty string result. This is an important distinction in one case. Sometimes people write down OUT test requirements that are impossible; perhaps the subsystem, according to the specification, can never produce an empty string. If you can't make a test satisfy such a requirement, it's not worth writing down.

INLINE

Operation test requirements are of two kinds: requirements that check for an incorrectly implemented operation, and requirements that check for an incorrect use of an operation. Suppose you've got a clue

Searching for TARGET in LIST

Looking at the code, you may see one of two things:

```
match = search(target, list);
```

or

```
for(rover = list; rover != NULL_NODE; rover=rover->next)
{
  if (rover->tag == target->tag)
      break;
}
```

In both cases, you'd want to try a test specification in which `target` was not present in `list`. Subsystems that search sometimes assume they will always find what they're looking for. The catalog contains that test requirement for searching. It also contains a test requirement that the match be the first element in the list. This checks for an off-by-one error in the implementation. If `search` is a tested library routine, writing a test for that requirement will not be cost-effective.

Some operation test requirements apply only to *inline operations* and should be omitted when library routines are used. These are marked INLINE in the catalog to remind you to use them only when testing new implementations, not reused code.

If you don't have access to the code, you may not know how searching is implemented. See the end of this chapter.

3.7
Using the
Catalog
with
SREADHEX

Explaining the use of the catalog is hard to do on paper, because you, the reader, need to look at three things at once: the catalog, the growing test requirement checklist, and the explanation of how new entries are added to the checklist. Things get even more cumbersome when the checklist grows to more than a page. In this section, a catalog entry and the explanation of its use will be given on the left-hand page. The right-hand page will show the test requirement checklist (perhaps abbreviated) with new entries and changes in bold font. This presentation will give you a good understanding of using matching entries, but a lesser one for the process of searching the catalog and deciding which entries match. The MAX example in Part 4 will give you more of an opportunity to do that.

Some of the test requirements in the catalog will be immediately recognizable as good things to test. Some will be perplexing—why is *that* worth testing? The ultimate answer is an appeal to history: it's worth testing because it's been able to find faults. The odder test requirements may not reveal faults often, but they raise the cost of testing very little, and they incidentally serve to force variety in the test specifications (a topic of the next chapter).

Notation: Catalog entry names will be capitalized. Thus, the first catalog match is "Boolean." It matches sreadhex's return value. Boolean's entry reads as follows:

⟶ BOOLEAN

• 1 (true)	IN, OUT
• 0 (false)	IN, OUT
• Some true value not 1	IN

Since the return value is an output variable, the OUT requirements are appropriate. However, they are redundant. Suppose they were added:

return value, a boolean (0 or 1)
    0
    1

When Postcondition 1 is triggered, sreadhex returns 1. There's already a requirement that triggers Postcondition 1. Therefore, the checklist already forces a test that satisfies "return value 1", so there's no point in listing it explicitly. The same is true of "return value 0", but due to Postcondition 3.

Redundancies can be easy to miss. However, the consequence of missing them is small. When you build a test specification, you always finish by checking which test requirements got satisfied by accident. If some did, you don't have to write special tests for them. If a test requirement is redundant with another, they always "accidentally" get satisfied together. Only if you miss noticing that the redundant requirement was also satisfied (and you often get several opportunities) will you end up writing an unnecessary test.

In my normal use of the catalog, my search for redundancies is far less thorough than in this example. Finding a few extra redundancies isn't worth the extra effort. (Also, the more subtle the possible redundancy, the greater the chance I'll miss a way in which it's not really redundant.)

The next page is the unchanged checklist from the preconditions, postconditions, and definitions. On later pages, the "return value" clue will be omitted to save space.

Precondition 1
    STR is a non-null pointer to an array that can hold RLEN bytes.
Precondition 7
    RLEN is not 0
    RLEN = 0   ERROR

Postcondition 1
    START+NUM_HEX_CHARS < RLEN*2, START+NUM_HEX_CHARS is even
    START+NUM_HEX_CHARS >= RLEN*2, START+NUM_HEX_CHARS is even
    START+NUM_HEX_CHARS < RLEN*2, START+NUM_HEX_CHARS is odd

Postcondition 2
    START+NUM_HEX_CHARS >= RLEN*2, START+NUM_HEX_CHARS is odd

Postcondition 3
Postcondition 4
    *ODD_DIGIT is initially >= 0
    *ODD_DIGIT is initially < 0
        *ODD_DIGIT==-1

STR, an array of bytes to be filled

RLEN, a count

NREAD, a pointer to a count

ODD_DIGIT, a pointer to an integer either -1 or [0..15]

S, a string
    a character in S is hexadecimal
    a character in S is not hexadecimal

return value, a Boolean (0 or 1)

hexadecimal character, in range ['0' .. '9', 'A'.. 'F', 'a' .. 'f']

NUM_HEX_CHARS, a count of hexadecimal characters in S

DIGIT, a location to be filled with an integer in range [0 .. 15]

number of unused hexadecimal characters in S, a count

Searching for a value for an odd DIGIT
Searching for a value for an even DIGIT

The next match is Comparison Operators (such as < or <=), and there are a lot of those in the postcondition requirements. The catalog entries will lead to refinements. I'll step through the first in laborious detail; with even a little experience, they're immediately obvious. (These early sections of the catalog contain the test requirements most testers know by heart. I still find them useful, because having a checklist helps me avoid oversights.)

The two test requirements under Postcondition 4 say:

Postcondition 4
    *ODD_DIGIT is initially >= 0
    *ODD_DIGIT is initially < 0
        *ODD_DIGIT==-1

The catalog gives these boundary conditions:

Specification only

➥*epsilon is 1 for integers.*

<, >=
  • V1 = V2 - epsilon
  • V1 = V2

"Specification only" indicates that these test requirements apply only to specification clues. Processing every < in the code is not worthwhile. Almost every test requirement you got would be redundant with test requirements from other sources, so the effort would be wasted. A few will probably be missed, but the Generic Coverage Tool (described later) will catch them. Some other coverage tools do not check relational operators; if you use these tools, you may need to design redundant test requirements based on operators found in the code to decrease the chance of missing some requirements.

You'll note that >= and < produce the same test requirements (they describe the same boundary). Here, V1 is *ODD_DIGIT, V2 is 0, and epsilon is 1, so the test requirements are:

    *ODD_DIGIT = -1
    *ODD_DIGIT = 0

The first of these is already in the checklist. It's not unusual for the catalog to duplicate specification test requirements, which is a slight waste of effort. But it's better to have to think about and discard redundant requirements than to miss some.

The second requirement can be added as shown on the next page.

Precondition 1
> STR is a non-null pointer to an array that can hold RLEN bytes.

Precondition 7
> RLEN is not 0
> RLEN = 0   ERROR

Postcondition 1
> START+NUM_HEX_CHARS < RLEN*2, START+NUM_HEX_CHARS is even
> START+NUM_HEX_CHARS >= RLEN*2, START+NUM_HEX_CHARS is even
> START+NUM_HEX_CHARS < RLEN*2, START+NUM_HEX_CHARS is odd

Postcondition 2
> START+NUM_HEX_CHARS >= RLEN*2, START+NUM_HEX_CHARS is odd

Postcondition 3
Postcondition 4
> *ODD_DIGIT is initially >= 0
> •   ***ODD_DIGIT==0**
> *ODD_DIGIT is initially < 0
> *ODD_DIGIT==-1

STR, an array of bytes to be filled

RLEN, a count

NREAD, a pointer to a count

ODD_DIGIT, a pointer to an integer either -1 or [0..15]

S, a string
> a character in S is hexadecimal
> a character in S is not hexadecimal

hexadecimal character, in range ['0' .. '9', 'A'.. 'F', 'a' .. 'f']

NUM_HEX_CHARS, a count of hexadecimal characters in S

DIGIT, a location to be filled with an integer in range [0 .. 15]

number of unused hexadecimal characters in S, a count

Searching for a value for an odd DIGIT
Searching for a value for an even DIGIT

The previous page described a methodical way to replace inequalities with equalities. Each pair of inequalities produced two equalities, which were then used as refinements. The result? Each inequality was refined with one specific equality that satisfied it, but just barely. That's the common testing trick of trying boundaries. The same can be done for the remaining requirements that use inequalities. For example,

START+NUM_HEX_CHARS < RLEN*2, START+NUM_HEX_CHARS is even

yields

START+NUM_HEX_CHARS < RLEN*2, START+NUM_HEX_CHARS is even
START+NUM_HEX_CHARS = RLEN*2-2, START+NUM_HEX_CHARS is even

Note that 2 had to be subtracted, not 1, because `RLEN*2-1` isn't even. The refinement uses the largest value of `START+NUM_HEX_CHARS` which is still less than `RLEN*2`.

The facing page shows the result for all four remaining inequalities.

Precondition 1
> STR is a non-null pointer to an array that can hold RLEN bytes.

Precondition 7
> RLEN is not 0
> RLEN = 0   ERROR

Postcondition 1
> START+NUM_HEX_CHARS < RLEN*2, START+NUM_HEX_CHARS is even
> - **START+NUM_HEX_CHARS = RLEN*2-2, START+NUM_HEX_CHARS is even**
> START+NUM_HEX_CHARS >= RLEN*2, START+NUM_HEX_CHARS is even
> - **START+NUM_HEX_CHARS = RLEN*2, START+NUM_HEX_CHARS is even**
> START+NUM_HEX_CHARS < RLEN*2, START+NUM_HEX_CHARS is odd
> - **START+NUM_HEX_CHARS = RLEN*2-1, START+NUM_HEX_CHARS is odd**

Postcondition 2
> START+NUM_HEX_CHARS >= RLEN*2, START+NUM_HEX_CHARS is odd
> - **START+NUM_HEX_CHARS = RLEN*2+1, START+NUM_HEX_CHARS is odd**

Postcondition 3

Postcondition 4
> *ODD_DIGIT is initially >= 0
> *ODD_DIGIT==0
> *ODD_DIGIT is initially < 0
> *ODD_DIGIT==-1

STR, an array of bytes to be filled

RLEN, a count

NREAD, a pointer to a count

ODD_DIGIT, a pointer to an integer either -1 or [0..15]

S, a string
> a character in S is hexadecimal
> a character in S is not hexadecimal

hexadecimal character, in range ['0' .. '9', 'A'.. 'F', 'a' .. 'f']

NUM_HEX_CHARS, a count of hexadecimal characters in S

DIGIT, a location to be filled with an integer in range [0 .. 15]

number of unused hexadecimal characters in S, a count

Searching for a value for an odd DIGIT
Searching for a value for an even DIGIT

The next appropriate catalog entry is for Counts, which applies to RLEN (the amount of STR to fill):

➠
- -1   IN
- 0   IN/OUT
- 1   IN
- >1   IN/OUT
- maximum possible value   IN/OUT
- one larger than maximum possible value   IN

The value -1 would violate assumed Precondition 2, which requires RLEN >= 0.

The value 0 is certainly a possible value for RLEN, but it's already in the checklist (under the Precondition 7 clue).

The value 1 is possible and unused, so I add it under the RLEN clue.

The value >1 is always redundant with "maximum possible value". It's only used when that requirement doesn't apply or would be too expensive to test. In this case, the maximum possible value does apply: it's the size of STR. (This may seem odd—isn't RLEN by definition the size of STR? In C, sreadhex can't know the size of STR except via RLEN. As you'll see when test specifications are built, it is odd, though for a slightly different reason. I'll list it for now.)

"One larger than maximum possible value" would mean "larger than the size of STR", which would violate precondition 1:

> Assumed: STR is a non-null pointer to an array that can hold RLEN bytes (and 2*RLEN DIGITS).

NREAD, the number of bytes used, is another count. Since it's an OUT variable, only two catalog entries apply: 0 and the maximum possible value. In this case, the maximum possible value is RLEN. However, *NREAD is always assigned RLEN whenever Postcondition 3 is satisfied, so that's redundant. That leaves only

> NREAD, a pointer to a count
>   0

Why are three of the Count requirements not marked with OUT? There are two reasons: impossibility and low utility.

1. The values -1 and "one larger than the maximum" can't be used in test design. You *hope* that one of the tests will make RLEN be -1, because that would be a failure. But you can't design a test around hope. Without knowing what the fault is in advance, you couldn't write a test that satisfies the requirement. So there's no point in writing it down.

2. The value 1 isn't marked OUT because forcing output counts to 1 has no track record at finding faults.

NUM_HEX_CHARS is a property of S, an input variable, so all the entries apply. The value -1 is impossible. The value 0 is an interesting case: passing in a string without *any* hexadecimal characters. The value 1 applies. The value "maximum possible value" can be interpreted to mean "all characters hexadecimal (more than one)".

Precondition 1
>STR is a non-null pointer to an array that can hold RLEN bytes.

Precondition 7
>RLEN is not 0
>RLEN = 0   ERROR

Postcondition 1
>START+NUM_HEX_CHARS < RLEN*2, START+NUM_HEX_CHARS is even
>>START+NUM_HEX_CHARS = RLEN*2-2, START+NUM_HEX_CHARS is even
>START+NUM_HEX_CHARS >= RLEN*2, START+NUM_HEX_CHARS is even
>>START+NUM_HEX_CHARS = RLEN*2, START+NUM_HEX_CHARS is even
>START+NUM_HEX_CHARS < RLEN*2, START+NUM_HEX_CHARS is odd
>>START+NUM_HEX_CHARS = RLEN*2-1, START+NUM_HEX_CHARS is odd

Postcondition 2
>START+NUM_HEX_CHARS >= RLEN*2, START+NUM_HEX_CHARS is odd
>>START+NUM_HEX_CHARS = RLEN*2+1, START+NUM_HEX_CHARS is odd

Postcondition 3

Postcondition 4
>*ODD_DIGIT is initially >= 0
>>*ODD_DIGIT==0
>*ODD_DIGIT is initially < 0
>>*ODD_DIGIT==-1

STR, an array of bytes to be filled

RLEN, a count
- **RLEN=1**
- **RLEN=size of STR**

NREAD, a pointer to a count
- 0

ODD_DIGIT, a pointer to an integer either -1 or [0..15]

S, a string
>a character in S is hexadecimal
>a character in S is not hexadecimal

hexadecimal character, in range ['0' .. '9', 'A'.. 'F', 'a' .. 'f']

NUM_HEX_CHARS, a count of hexadecimal characters in S
- 0
- 1
- **all characters hexadecimal (more than one)**

DIGIT, a location to be filled with an integer in range [0 .. 15]

number of unused hexadecimal characters in S, a count

Searching for a value for an odd DIGIT
Searching for a value for an even DIGIT

There's one last Count in the checklist, the number of unused hexadecimal characters. Here, again, is the catalog entry.

- -1   IN
- 0   IN/OUT
- 1   IN
- >1   IN/OUT
- maximum possible value   IN/OUT
- one larger than maximum possible value   IN

The value -1 doesn't make sense. 0 does. However, any test that satisfies Postcondition 1 or 2 must use up all the hexadecimal characters in S, leaving 0 unused characters. So 0 is redundant with, for example, the existing requirement

START+NUM_HEX_CHARS = RLEN*2, START+NUM_HEX_CHARS is even

The value 1 is also redundant. The requirement under Postcondition 2 requires START+NUM_HEX_CHARS = RLEN*2+1, which means that there will be one unused character.

The value >1 is not redundant. It's also probably not useful. If there is a failure associated with this clue, it's almost certainly because sreadhex processes too many characters. A single extra hexadecimal character would cause the failure. It's unlikely that more than one would catch anything new. However, I'll include it. If I can use it easily in a test I'm writing anyway, I will. Otherwise, I'll skip it.

"Maximum possible value" could mean that all characters were unused, but that would be redundant with NREAD=0. "One larger than maximum possible value" doesn't make sense. Even if it did, it would be unlikely to find a fault that 1 and >1 don't.

Precondition 1
    STR is a non-null pointer to an array that can hold RLEN bytes.
Precondition 7
    RLEN is not 0
    RLEN = 0   ERROR

Postcondition 1
    START+NUM_HEX_CHARS < RLEN*2, START+NUM_HEX_CHARS is even
        START+NUM_HEX_CHARS = RLEN*2-2, START+NUM_HEX_CHARS is even
    START+NUM_HEX_CHARS >= RLEN*2, START+NUM_HEX_CHARS is even
        START+NUM_HEX_CHARS = RLEN*2, START+NUM_HEX_CHARS is even
    START+NUM_HEX_CHARS < RLEN*2, START+NUM_HEX_CHARS is odd
        START+NUM_HEX_CHARS = RLEN*2-1, START+NUM_HEX_CHARS is odd

Postcondition 2
    START+NUM_HEX_CHARS >= RLEN*2, START+NUM_HEX_CHARS is odd
        START+NUM_HEX_CHARS = RLEN*2+1, START+NUM_HEX_CHARS is odd

Postcondition 3
Postcondition 4
    *ODD_DIGIT is initially >= 0
        *ODD_DIGIT==0
    *ODD_DIGIT is initially < 0
        *ODD_DIGIT==-1

STR, an array of bytes to be filled

RLEN, a count
    RLEN=1
    RLEN=size of STR

NREAD, a pointer to a count
    0

ODD_DIGIT, a pointer to an integer either -1 or [0..15]

S, a string
    a character in S is hexadecimal
    a character in S is not hexadecimal

hexadecimal character, in range ['0' .. '9', 'A'.. 'F', 'a' .. 'f']

NUM_HEX_CHARS, a count of hexadecimal characters in S
    0
    1
    all characters hexadecimal (more than one)

DIGIT, a location to be filled with an integer in range [0 .. 15]

number of unused hexadecimal characters in S, a count
• 	>1

Searching for a value for an odd DIGIT
Searching for a value for an even DIGIT

There are several Intervals:

➡ *Values selected from a range including its endpoints [A,B] or from a range that doesn't (A,B).*
Epsilon is 1 for intervals of integers.

⫸ [A, B] (Both A and B are in the interval)
  - V1 = A - epsilon   IN
  - V1 = A   IN, OUT
  - V1 = B   IN, OUT
  - V1 = B + epsilon   IN

The first Interval is ODD_DIGIT, which is either -1 or in [0 .. 15]. The -1 case must be tested, but it's already in the checklist, under the Postcondition 4 clue.

The interval must also be tested. Having ODD_DIGIT outside the range would violate assumed Precondition 5 (*ODD_DIGIT is in the range [-1, 15]), so only the internal values of the interval apply:

ODD_DIGIT, a pointer to an integer either -1 or [0..15].
  0
  15

However, the first of these is also under the Postcondition 4 clue.

At this point in test design, I should have caught a mistake (but I didn't). There should be two Interval clues for ODD_DIGIT—one for its original value and one for its result value. As it is, all the test requirements are for the original value. There should be more:

ODD_DIGIT **result**, a pointer to an integer either -1 or [0..15].
  -1 (this is redundant with Postcondition 1)
  0
  15

As you'll see, no test requirements from other clues will force a test with either the 0 or 15 result value. That means that an off-by-one error in setting the result might be missed. The procedure for building test specifications assumes some test requirements were missed and tries to compensate. In this case, it will be only partially successful: There will be a test that sets the result value to 15, but none that sets it to 0.

I'm leaving this mistake in the text because it's a common one. Clues from output (and global) variables are easy to miss. Remembering my mistake will make you less likely to make one of your own.

The next interval clue has three intervals:

hexadecimal character, in range ['0' .. '9', 'A'.. 'F', 'a' .. 'f']

Values outside the intervals are possible—they are nonhexadecimal values, which are allowed in S. So, following the rules gives the results on the facing page.

Precondition 1...
Precondition 7...
Postcondition 1...
Postcondition 2...
Postcondition 3
Postcondition 4
    *ODD_DIGIT is initially >= 0
       *ODD_DIGIT==0
    *ODD_DIGIT is initially < 0
       *ODD_DIGIT==-1

STR, an array of bytes to be filled

RLEN, a count
    RLEN=1
    RLEN=size of STR

NREAD, a pointer to a count
    0

ODD_DIGIT, a pointer to an integer either -1 or [0..15]
- **15**

S, a string
    a character in S is hexadecimal
    a character in S is not hexadecimal

hexadecimal character, in range ['0' .. '9', 'A'.. 'F', 'a' .. 'f']
- **/**   **(ASCII character before '0')**
- **0**
- **9**
- **:**   **(ASCII character after '9')**
- **@**   **(ASCII character before 'A')**
- **A**
- **F**
- **G**
- **`**   **(ASCII character before 'a')**
- **a**
- **f**
- **g**

NUM_HEX_CHARS, a count of hexadecimal characters in S
    0
    1
    all characters hexadecimal (more than one)

DIGIT, a location to be filled with an integer in range [0 .. 15]

number of unused hexadecimal characters in S, a count
    >1
Searching for a value for an odd DIGIT
Searching for a value for an even DIGIT

Since I was thinking about characters, the string used to initialize the `decoder` array came to my mind.

```
53      if ( decoder[-1] == 0 )          /* not initialized yet */
54        {   static char hex_chars[] = "0123456789ABCDEFabcdef";
55            int i;
56            memset(decoder - 1, hex_none, 257);
57            for ( i = 0; i < 16+6; i++ )
58              decoder[hex_chars[i]] = (i >= 16 ? i - 6 : i);
59            decoder[0] = hex_eofc;
60        }
```

What if it was missing a character? I checked quickly, and it wasn't. But a simple editor mistake while changing something else in `sreadhex` could delete one, perhaps the '3'. That might not be caught by a code review (most people wouldn't check the string, since it was correct in the past). It would be embarrassing to write a thorough test suite that checked all kinds of boundaries and missed noticing that no string S containing '3' was processed correctly. A simple way to avoid this problem is to add a test requirement to use all of the nonboundary hexadecimal characters at least once.

This actually points up an earlier error in my test design. The first definition of the specification enumerates all the characters:

There are 22 hexadecimal characters. They are listed here...

That should have told me to use the Cases catalog entry instead of the Interval catalog entry. If I had, I would have seen:

⟹ V1 might be any of (C1, C2, ... Cn).
Specification only.

- V1 = each possible case.   IN, OUT
- V1 = some impossible case.   IN
  (If possible, choose boundaries, like C1-1 when the cases are integers.)

That would have given a requirement for each of the hexadecimal characters, instead of just the boundaries. For this example, I'll save space by lumping all the interior characters into a single requirement.

DIGIT is an Interval containing all numbers that can fit into four bits. Since values outside the interval are impossible, the requirements are:

DIGIT, a location to be filled with an integer in range [0 .. 15]
    0
    15

Precondition 1...
Precondition 7...
Postcondition 1...
Postcondition 2...
Postcondition 3
Postcondition 4...

STR, an array of bytes to be filled

RLEN, a count
    RLEN=1
    RLEN=size of STR

NREAD, a pointer to a count
    0

ODD_DIGIT, a pointer to an integer either -1 or [0..15]
    15

S, a string
    a character in S is hexadecimal
    a character in S is not hexadecimal

hexadecimal character, in range ['0' .. '9', 'A'.. 'F', 'a' .. 'f']
    /   (ASCII character before '0')
    0
    9
    :   (ASCII character after '9')
    @   (ASCII character before 'A')
    A
    F
    G
    `   (ASCII character before 'a')
    a
    f
    g
- **All of 1-8, B-E, b-e**

NUM_HEX_CHARS, a count of hexadecimal characters in S
    0
    1
    all characters hexadecimal (more than one)

DIGIT, a location to be filled with an integer in range [0 .. 15]
- **0**
- **15**

number of unused hexadecimal characters in S, a count
    >1

Searching for a value for an odd DIGIT
Searching for a value for an even DIGIT

S, the input, and STR, the output, are both collections of objects (characters and bytes, respectively). The General Collections section of the catalog applies.

➡️
• empty	IN/OUT
• a single element	IN/OUT
• more than one element	IN/OUT
• full	IN/OUT
• duplicate elements	IN/OUT

(may be an error case, or impossible)

❏ **• empty**

This applies to S. For STR, it's already satisfied by NREAD=0.

❏ **• a single element**

This applies to S and STR.

❏ **• more than one element**

This applies to both.

❏ **• full**

This is already satisfied for STR (via requirements that trigger Postcondition 3), and it's meaningless for S.

❏ **• duplicate elements**

This seems unlikely to be worthwhile since the hexadecimal characters do not interact, so I'll not include it. (It would be easy to satisfy, though.)

Precondition 1...
Precondition 7...
Postcondition 1...
Postcondition 2...
Postcondition 3
Postcondition 4...

STR, an array of bytes to be filled
- **a single element**
- **more than one element**

RLEN, a count
    RLEN=1
    RLEN=size of STR

NREAD, a pointer to a count
    0

ODD_DIGIT, a pointer to an integer either -1 or [0..15]
    15

S, a string
    a character in S is hexadecimal
    a character in S is not hexadecimal
- **empty**
- **a single element**
- **more than one element**

hexadecimal character, in range ['0' .. '9', 'A'.. 'F', 'a' .. 'f']...

NUM_HEX_CHARS, a count of hexadecimal characters in S
    0
    1
    all characters hexadecimal (more than one)

DIGIT, a location to be filled with an integer in range [0 .. 15]
    0
    15

number of unused hexadecimal characters in S, a count
    >1

Searching for a value for an odd DIGIT
Searching for a value for an even DIGIT

The arrays are Ordered Collections because they have a first and last element.

> ➡ *Whenever you're doing something to particular elements of an ordered collection (one with a first and last element), use the following requirements:*

⮕ • Doing it to the first element   INLINE
(There should be more than one)
• Doing it to the last element   INLINE
(There should be more than one)

That "doing" could be finding hexadecimal character to put in STR. This is done by the two `while` loops, so INLINE requirements apply. They are two distinct operations, and the requirements apply to each:

Searching for a value for an odd DIGIT.
    found as first element (more than one char)
    found as last element (more than one char)
Searching for a value for an even DIGIT.
    found as first element (more than one char)
    found as last element (more than one char)

Filling STR is also "doing something to an ordered collection". But any test that puts anything in STR will start with the first element. There are even separate requirements that ensure what's put in the first element is sometimes the value of *ODD_DIGIT and sometimes the first character in S. Any requirement that triggers Postcondition 3 ensures the last element will also be filled, so that's redundant as well.

Precondition 1...
Precondition 7...
Postcondition 1...
Postcondition 2...
Postcondition 3
Postcondition 4...

STR, an array of bytes to be filled
      a single element
      more than one element

RLEN, a count
      RLEN=1
      RLEN=size of STR

NREAD, a pointer to a count
      0

ODD_DIGIT, a pointer to an integer either -1 or [0..15]
      15

S, a string
      a character in S is hexadecimal
      a character in S is not hexadecimal
      empty
      a single element
      more than one element

hexadecimal character, in range ['0' .. '9', 'A'.. 'F', 'a' .. 'f']...

NUM_HEX_CHARS, a count of hexadecimal characters in S
      0
      1
      all characters hexadecimal (more than one)

DIGIT, a location to be filled with an integer in range [0 .. 15]
      0
      15

number of unused hexadecimal characters in S, a count
      >1

Searching for a value for an odd DIGIT.
- **found as first element (more than one char)**
- **found as last element (more than one char)**

Searching for a value for an even DIGIT.
- **found as first element (more than one char)**
- **found as last element (more than one char)**

Filtering out S's nonhexadecimal characters means using a subset of S to form STR. Subsetting is a common operation, though sometimes not obvious, and it often leads to useful test requirements. Here is the catalog entry:

▶ In all cases the starting collection should have more than one element.

- Filtering out no elements (subset is same as original)
- Filtering out one element
- Filtering out all but one element
- Filtering out all elements (subset is empty)

Since each while loop filters independently, these requirements apply to two separate operations. They can be added to the "searching for a value" clues.

These new requirements supercede some of the older ones for S. They are more precise than "a character in S is hexadecimal", "a character in S is not hexadecimal", and "S has more than one element".

If you think about the implementation, you'll realize that some of these requirements don't make much sense. Because of the way specifications and code are abstracted into clues, subsystem testing often results in such "unneeded" requirements. There are several reasons they turn out to be valuable. First, thinking about the implementation takes time. It can be more efficient to write a few extra requirements. Second, the code may be wrong and miss special cases these requirements will discover. Finally, even if the requirements are handled correctly, they're an easy way to force useful variety into the tests. (Test variety is a topic of the next chapter.)

Streams are a generalization that appears again and again in programs. A stream is processed by taking each element, doing something with it, then proceeding to the next element. Most loops can be interpreted as streaming operations, and what they "stream over" can be useful abstract data structures in their own right.

In sreadhex, elements from S are examined one by one and perhaps placed in STR. There are two elements of interest: hexadecimal characters and nonhexadecimal characters. Thus, this catalog entry seems useful. The value 1 would represent hexadecimal characters, 0 nonhexadecimal.

▶ **Streams with two kinds of values**
- Two or more elements, each with the first value   IN/OUT
  Examples: (0 0) (0 0 0)
- Two or more elements, each with the second value   IN/OUT
  Examples: (1 1) (1 1 1)
- Two or more elements, each appears   IN/OUT
  Examples: (1 0) (0 1) (1 0 1) (0 1 0 1)

However, each of these requirements is already satisfied by the subsetting requirements. That's as it should be: subsetting is a more specific operation.

Preconditions...
Postconditions...

STR, an array of bytes to be filled
    a single element
    more than one element

RLEN, a count
    RLEN=1
    RLEN=size of STR

NREAD, a pointer to a count
    0

ODD_DIGIT, a pointer to an integer either -1 or [0..15]
    15

S, a string
    a character in S is hexadecimal **(superceded)**
    a character in S is not hexadecimal **(superceded)**
    empty
    a single element
    more than one element **(superceded)**

hexadecimal character, in range ['0' .. '9', 'A'.. 'F', 'a' .. 'f']...

NUM_HEX_CHARS, a count of hexadecimal characters in S
    0
    1
    all characters hexadecimal (more than one)

DIGIT, a location to be filled with an integer in range [0 .. 15]
    0
    15

number of unused hexadecimal characters in S, a count
    >1

Searching for a value for an odd DIGIT.
    found as first element (more than one char)
    found as last element (more than one char)
- **all of several elements are hexadecimal (none filtered)**
- **exactly one of several elements is not hexadecimal (one filtered)**
- **exactly one of several elements is hexadecimal (all but one filtered)**
- **none of several elements are hexadecimal (all filtered)**

Searching for a value for an even DIGIT.
    found as first element (more than one char)
    found as last element (more than one char)
- **all of several elements are hexadecimal (none filtered)**
- **exactly one of several elements is not hexadecimal (one filtered)**
- **exactly one of several elements is hexadecimal (all but one filtered)**
- **none of several elements are hexadecimal (all filtered)**

The catalog contains these requirements for Pointers:

⮚	• null pointer	IN/OUT
	• pointer to a true object	IN/OUT
	• if several arguments are pointers of the same type, have them all point to the same object. (This catches faults where the routine uses the argument when it should have made a copy.)	IN

There are several pointers. The assumed preconditions rule out the use of null pointers. All pointers are therefore "pointers to a true object", so that's not worth writing down. Although it's not explicitly ruled out, having NREAD and ODD_DIGIT point to the same integer would certainly be a caller error since sreadhex fills them with different information.

The next applicable section is Strings, which suggests "the empty string". That's already written down under S's header.

There are no changes to the checklist.

Preconditions...
Postconditions...

STR, an array of bytes to be filled
    a single element
    more than one element

RLEN, a count
    RLEN=1
    RLEN=size of STR

NREAD, a pointer to a count
    0

ODD_DIGIT, a pointer to an integer either -1 or [0..15]
    15

S, a string
    empty
    a single element

hexadecimal character, in range ['0' .. '9', 'A'.. 'F', 'a' .. 'f']...

NUM_HEX_CHARS, a count of hexadecimal characters in S
    0
    1
    all characters hexadecimal (more than one)

DIGIT, a location to be filled with an integer in range [0 .. 15]
    0
    15

number of unused hexadecimal characters in S, a count
    >1

Searching for a value for an odd DIGIT.
    found as first element (more than one char)
    found as last element (more than one char)
    all of several elements are hexadecimal (none filtered)
    exactly one of several elements is not hexadecimal (one filtered)
    exactly one of several elements is hexadecimal (all but one filtered)
    none of several elements are hexadecimal (all filtered)

Searching for a value for an even DIGIT.
    found as first element (more than one char)
    found as last element (more than one char)
    all of several elements are hexadecimal (none filtered)
    exactly one of several elements is not hexadecimal (one filtered)
    exactly one of several elements is hexadecimal (all but one filtered)
    none of several elements are hexadecimal (all filtered)

The catalog contains General Searching Requirements, which apply to the two searching clues.

- • Match not found
- • Match found (more than one element, exactly one match)
- • More than one match in the collection
- • Single match found in first position   INLINE
  (it's not the only element)
- • Single match found in last position   INLINE
  (it's not the only element)

"Match not found" is already satisfied by "none of several elements are hexadecimal". "Match found" is satisfied by "exactly one of several elements is hexadecimal". "More than one match" is satisfied by "all of several elements are hexadecimal". Again, this is expected, since taking a subset is a special kind of searching.

The two INLINE requirements also apply, since the search is by while loops. "Single match found in last position" is already satisfied by "found as last element". "Single match found in first position" isn't quite satisfied by "found as first element". The requirement already in the checklist allows more than one hexadecimal character, whereas the Searching requirement doesn't. The searching requirement is more specific because you don't want a match later in the list to disguise the fact that the first match was missed. Whether such a disguise is successful depends on what's done with the matching element. In sreadhex, it's unlikely to be, but it won't do any harm to be more specific:

Searching for a value for an odd DIGIT.
    found as first element (more than one char)
-     **after the first, all are nonhexadecimal**
    found as last element (more than one char)

This is now more specific than "exactly one of several elements is hexadecimal", since it says which one is hexadecimal. The new requirement can be placed indented under the old one (after being rewritten for clarity).

I now noticed something I'd missed earlier: I didn't notice that "found as last element" also refines "exactly one of several elements is hexadecimal". It can be indented too.

sreadhex contains Continued Searching:

Here, searching can be resumed from the last element found.

- • Further match immediately adjacent to last match

This requirement is satisfied by "all of several elements hexadecimal."
This is the last match in the catalog.

Preconditions...
Postconditions...

STR, an array of bytes to be filled
      a single element
      more than one element

RLEN, a count
      RLEN=1
      RLEN=size of STR

NREAD, a pointer to a count
      0

ODD_DIGIT, a pointer to an integer either -1 or [0..15]
      15

S, a string
      empty
      a single element

hexadecimal character, in range ['0' .. '9', 'A'.. 'F', 'a' .. 'f']...

NUM_HEX_CHARS, a count of hexadecimal characters in S
      0
      1
      all characters hexadecimal (more than one)

DIGIT, a location to be filled with an integer in range [0 .. 15]
      0
      15

number of unused hexadecimal characters in S, a count
      >1

Searching for a value for an odd DIGIT.
      found as first element (more than one char) **(superceded)**
      found as last element (more than one char) **(moved)**
      all of several elements are hexadecimal (none filtered)
      exactly one of several elements is not hexadecimal (one filtered)
      exactly one of several elements is hexadecimal (all but one filtered)
-     **only hexadecimal character is first of several**
-     **only hexadecimal character is last of several**
      none of several elements are hexadecimal (all filtered)

Searching for a value for an even DIGIT.
      found as first element (more than one char) **(superceded)**
      found as last element (more than one char) **(moved)**
      all of several elements are hexadecimal (none filtered)
      exactly one of several elements is not hexadecimal (one filtered)
      exactly one of several elements is hexadecimal (all but one filtered)
-     **only hexadecimal character is first of several**
-     **only hexadecimal character is last of several**
      none of several elements are hexadecimal (all filtered)

3.8
Where Do We Stand?

The complete checklist is shown when it's used in the next chapter. The next page summarizes how the catalog is used.

This on-paper presentation inevitably makes the process seem too long. Decisions that take seconds to make take paragraphs to explain. What's difficult to follow while reading would be obvious were I there to point with my finger and sketch a quick example.

You may be particularly worried about refinements and redundancy since the discussion seemed to spend an inordinate amount of time on them. In practice, it's faster. Before adding a new group of requirements, I make a quick scan to look for refinements. I don't care if I miss a few, since they're easily caught during test specification design. The discussion here was more thorough for two reasons: to save space in the checklist, and so that your reading wouldn't be disrupted by discovering unnoticed refinements or redundancies and wondering about them.

Subsystem testing is designed to be robust in the face of inevitable mistakes, such as not noticing refinements. Any process that can't tolerate and recover from human error won't work. That's why subsystem testing has a series of stages, each of which is, in part, a safety net for the previous work.

This stage relied mostly on the list of clues. The specification and code were largely ignored because they'd been boiled down to their essentials.

Earlier, much was made of not multiplying requirements unless there's clear evidence it's needed. Two separate `while` loops are such evidence, which is why each has its own duplicate set of requirements. Had the code not been available, the need for two separate searching clues would have been hidden and there probably would have been one set of requirements under the S clue. Even with the code, an oversight is certainly possible. What safety nets would have caught this problem?

1. Test specifications are constructed in ways that increase their variety. This might have the effect of exercising each loop with each of the requirements.

2. Part 5 discusses specific ways of catching such oversights, as well as more complicated interactions. For example, `sreadhex` uses two loops together in a slightly complicated way. Other than separating them out as two operations, their interaction was ignored. The assumption is that requirements for one will exercise the interaction with the other. Chapter 26 discusses whether that assumption is really true.

3. If one of the loops were underexercised, coverage might reveal it.

Note that the code has to be available at some point for the last two of these safety nets to work. Although the code is less important than the specification, it's essential for thorough testing.

At this point, the checklist contains requirements from what the program is supposed to do and from the variables and operations it uses. There are two remaining sources: function calls (integration requirements) and raw inspiration (error guessing).

1. Scan the catalog sequentially. For each possibly relevant operation or variable type, ask if it's a clue in the checklist. If so, add the test requirements.

2. If the operation or variable entry isn't a clue, ask if it should be. Be sure to do this, since much of the virtue of the catalog is that it can jog you into realizing there's something more to test.

3. If you're working strictly from the specification, especially consider operations and variables that you think might be used in the implementation. A good test requirement for a likely implementation is probably also good for any actual implementation. This is especially true when the actual implementation is a clever, efficient one that cleverly and efficiently fails to handle some special case.

3.9
A Summary
of Rules
for Using
Test Requirement
Catalogs

3.9.1 Where and Whether a Requirement Should be Added

Not every matching test requirement should be added, and not every one will be added in quite the same way. Here are the cases to look for:

1. Use IN catalog entries for input or intermediate variables. Use OUT entries for output or intermediate variables.

2. Use INLINE catalog entries for operations implemented as inline code. Don't use them if the operation is a function call. If you don't know the implementation, use the entries, but mark them with DEFER. (See the end of the chapter.)

3. Specification-only catalog entries don't apply to clues found only in the code.

4. If a test requirement violates an assumed precondition, don't use it. Testing it means nothing since any result is allowable.

5. If no possible input can satisfy the test requirement, don't use it. (Since the catalog is general, not all test requirements will make sense in every case.)

6. If a test requirement violates a validated precondition, add it as an ERROR requirement. It will be most convenient to add it under the precondition's clue, so you always know immediately what precondition it's violating.

   Sometimes you find a case that you can't believe the subsystem handles, yet it's not ruled out by any precondition. (Null pointers, for example.) This is often because the specification is incomplete—you've found a bug in it.

7. If a test requirement refines an existing test requirement, add it indented under that test requirement. You've now narrowed the previous test requirement down to a more exact and, you hope, more fault-revealing case.

8. If the test requirement adds nothing to an already-existing test requirement, don't use it. For example, suppose you find the test requirement A < 0 in the catalog when you already have A=-1 in the checklist. Since the existing text requirement is already more refined, don't add the new one. (If they'd been added in the other order, the A=-1 test requirement would have refined A<0.) It is easy to make a mistake and add duplicate test requirements. At worst, adding a less-refined test requirement will increase your workload later, but probably only slightly.

9. Remember that the catalog gives test requirements useful for a broad range of programs, meaning that they may not be useful for *this* program. You can use your own judgement and leave doubtful requirements out. But remember that many of the test requirements in the catalog are targeted to faults of omission, the hardest faults to find. Be wary of discarding a test requirement because "it's not relevant to the code". It may seem irrelevant only because you share mistaken assumptions with the programmer. (Especially if you *are* the programmer.) It's better to try the requirement and see whether it's really irrelevant, especially since additional requirements do not usually cost much.

3.10 Integration Test Requirements

When you've finished scanning the catalog, consider again all the clues that came from subroutine calls. Those clues that correspond to catalog entries (e.g., search) have been given requirements. But clues that didn't match need them. Also, some calls may partially match (e.g., find_match_and_update, which searches and then does something else). Those need more requirements. How are they found?

People make two kinds of mistakes when calling subroutines:

1. They do something wrong. For example, an argument might be given in degrees when it should be in radians, or a function might be declared as

int F(int length, int dollars);

but the arguments are passed in the wrong order, as F(dollars, length).

2. They forget to do something. The most usual error is forgetting a possible return value (for example, by assuming that an open always succeeds).

The latter is more important because it's harder to test. (It's easy to forget the same condition the programmer did.) Test requirements for the omissions will also often catch incorrectness, so concentrate on them.

Requirements from the called routine's postconditions

The first source of test requirements is the subroutine's specification. Write down test requirements that cause that routine to execute each of its postconditions. For example, if the routine is a triangle classification routine that has three postconditions, one to return `equilateral`, one to return `isosceles`, and one to return `scalene`, the calling subsystem isn't well tested unless each of those has been returned and handled by the caller. Do this even if the calling subroutine handles all three return values identically. The point is to discover whether it should be handling one of them differently.

In particular cases, exercising each postcondition may be too thorough: Perhaps two postconditions differ only in ways that cannot be relevant to the caller. For example, suppose they differ only in what they print to the output. This difference cannot affect the caller, so it need not be considered. Of course, judging what "cannot affect the caller" can be difficult—suppose the two postconditions set some global variable that doesn't appear in the caller's text. There might be an integration fault because some other called routine uses the global:

Caller
    Calls routine1().
        Routine1() sets Global to either 0 or 1.
    ...
    Calls routine2().
        Routine2() does something horribly wrong when
        Global is 1.
    ...

It's best to be cautious.

Requirements from the called routine's preconditions

You should also think about whether it is possible for the caller to violate one of a called function's preconditions. If it can violate an assumed precondition, that's a bug. If it can violate a validated precondition, a test is needed to check whether it handles the failure result correctly. Write down a test requirement that causes the caller to violate the called routine's precondition. That test requirement is not necessarily an ERROR requirement for the caller. Don't mark it as such unless it also violates one of the *caller's* preconditions.

From the absence of a result

The previous requirements check whether the caller can handle each result of the subroutine. You should also check whether the caller can handle the absence of a result.

You needn't worry about preconditions: any test that satisfies them checks whether the caller can handle the absence of each precondition failure result.

Mutually exclusive postconditions are also not a problem. Executing one checks the absence of others.

When a postcondition is nonexclusive, there should be a specific requirement that it not be executed. (It might seem that any test that violates a precondition checks whether the caller handles the absence of each postcondition, including all the nonexclusive ones. However, code that checks for error results is often separate from code that handles normal results, so the test tells you only about error cases, not how the caller would handle the missing postcondition in a normal case.)

From returned data

The called routine may provide data to the caller. It might return a value in an Interval, or it might construct a global Collection. The IN requirements for that type may be useful, though they will often be redundant with requirements already found from other clues (such as the variable that stores the return value).

From the called routine's test requirements

Because the specification is often missing or incomplete, you may have to derive for yourself the different cases that the specification should spell out. (See Chapter 12.) If you're lucky, the called subroutine has been tested, and its test requirement checklist is available. That checklist should include the cases of interest (as well as others irrelevant to the caller). If the called routine is in the same subsystem as the caller, satisfying one of its test requirements can do double duty: testing the called routine and the calling routine's use of it.

3.10.1 An Example of Integration Testing Requirements

Suppose you have code that looks like this:

```
if (strncmp(argv[0], result_so_far, count)>0)
    printf("%s\n", argv[0]);
```

The integration testing requirements should exercise each of the function's distinct input and output cases. For strncmp, there are three output cases. When the first string is smaller, a negative value is returned. When it's larger, a positive value is returned. When they're identical, a zero is returned. There are two input cases for each of strncmp's string arguments, because strncmp ignores the tail of strings longer than count. So here are the test requirements:

strncmp
    result is positive
    result is negative
    result is 0
    argv[0] longer than COUNT characters
    argv[0] not longer than COUNT characters
    result_so_far longer than COUNT characters
    result_so_far not longer than COUNT characters

The negative and zero cases are tested separately, even though the program handles them identically. The reason is that perhaps the program shouldn't. Perhaps it should print argv[0] when it's identical to result_so_far—a typical off-by-one fault. Notice that the strncmp test requirements will thoroughly test the boundaries of the >. That's typical, and that's one reason such operators are ignored in the code. (The other is that a coverage tool should catch cases where boundaries are undertested.)

The two input cases are also useful. They provide requirements that probe whether strncmp is the right routine to call and whether count is the right boundary.

There could be test requirements for printf as well. printf can return either the number of characters printed or EOF, indicating failure. You don't need to write a test to discover that, if printf fails, this code won't notice. (This may or may not be a bug, depending on what the subsystem's requirements are.)

3.10.2 Another Example

Suppose a project began with a program, diff, that compares two files. The bulk of the work was done by a routine compare_files, which had this specification:

COMPARE_FILES(FILE1, FILE2)

PRECONDITIONS:
1. Validated: FILE1 can be opened for reading.
   On failure:
   "<FILE1> cannot be opened" is printed to standard error.
   The return value is 2.

2. Validated: FILE2 can be opened for reading.
   On failure:
   "<FILE2> cannot be opened" is printed to standard error.
   The return value is 2.

POSTCONDITIONS:
1. IF FILE1 and FILE2 are both directories
   THEN

   the output is "Common subdirectories: <FILE1> and <FILE2>"
   the return value is 0.

2. IF (FILE1 is a plain file and FILE2 is a directory
   OR FILE1 is a directory and FILE2 is a plain file)
   THEN
   the output is "Files are of different types"
   the return value is 1

3. IF FILE1 and FILE2 are identical plain files
   THEN there is no output and the return value is 0.

4. IF FILE1 and FILE2 are differing plain files
   THEN
   the output is "Files differ"
   the return value is 1.

The project adds a new front end to diff that allows it to compare two directories, file by file. That routine, called diff_dirs, calls compare_files to do the work. Part of the testing task must be to test their integration. compare_files presumably still works (and its tests can be rerun to check), but does diff_dirs call it correctly and handle the return value correctly?

compare_files has three postconditions and two preconditions, but only three distinct cases, corresponding to the three return values.

1. What happens when compare_files is given an unreadable file and returns 2? That question leads to this requirement:

    call to compare_files
        one of the files is unreadable (return value 2)

    This requirement doesn't specify which file is unreadable. It could be the first (violating Precondition 1) or the second (violating Precondition 2). The only difference is what's printed to standard error, which cannot affect diff_dirs. So there should be no need for two requirements.

2. Similarly, it should be enough to force a return value of 1 in a single way. It doesn't matter if the reason is two plain files that differ or the comparison of a file and a directory.

3. Finally, it shouldn't matter if the reason for a zero return value is common subdirectories or identical plain files. The former case raises an interesting thought, though: perhaps compare_files should optionally call diff_dirs when given two directories. That would allow comparing two entire directory trees instead of just the top level. This would be a change to the specification, and it would require changes to compare_files. Test requirements for that change could be gotten using the techniques of Chapter 14. Those requirements could be combined with the requirements from diff_dirs to get a single set of tests that test the new compare_files, diff_dirs, and their interaction.

3.10.3 A Final Example

Both of the previous examples had mutually exclusive postconditions. Here's one that doesn't:

PRECONDITIONS:

1. Validated: I > 0
    On failure: return -1.

POSTCONDITIONS:

1. IF I > GLOBAL
    THEN GLOBAL = I.
2. The return value is the previous value of GLOBAL.

That would have these requirements:

result is -1 (violated precondition)
GLOBAL is set to I (Postcondition 1 executed)
GLOBAL is left unchanged (Postcondition 1 not executed)

Since there were no function call clues for sreadhex, nothing is done in this step. There is a function call, memcpy, but I didn't write it down as a clue because it's always executed in exactly the same way. Any test requirements that might come from it would either always be satisfied or be impossible to satisfy.

3.11 Integration Test Requirements for SREADHEX

One of the dangers of catalogs is that they focus attention too effectively. In fact, you should be suspicious if all the clues in your checklist have requirements. That may mean you've become habituated to the catalog and only see clues you know you'll find there. Remember that the catalog is both general and inevitably incomplete; it can't be perfect for any particular program. You must augment it by thinking of new clues and requirements.

3.12 Error Guessing

❑ **Clear your mind**

Take a break—work on something else for a while, then come back and look at the problem with a fresh eye. You are about to try to be creative, and creativity comes best when immersion in a problem is followed by a rest. (See [Ghiselin55], especially the essay by Poincaré.)

❑ **Improve requirements**

Examine all the clues. Can you think of any new or better test requirements? If some clue has no test requirement, try to think of some way to test it.

❑ **Find new clues**

Think of your experience with similar subsystems. Can you draw any analogies that might lead to clues? If you know the bug history of the system, does that suggest particular buggy areas that deserve more attention? What could go wrong with this subsystem and, more importantly, what failures would be particularly serious?

In the sreadhex example, the specification and code were examined at the same time. That's not always the case. The MAX example (in Part 4) shows how the code can be examined later; look there for a concrete example of the topics discussed in this section.

If you don't look at the code until after you've generated all the test requirements from the specification, you probably don't know if an

3.13 Scanning the Code after the Specification

operation is implemented as inline code or by a subroutine call, so you don't know whether to include INLINE test requirements. Do include them, but mark them with a DEFER tag:

> when searching, single match in the first position   DEFER

This has two purposes:

1. When generating specification-based tests, you don't have to use this test requirement. However, you may if it's convenient.
2. When you finally do look at the code, the DEFER tag reminds you to check if the test requirement should be satisfied.

You need to be a bit careful where you put a deferred requirement. Never use a deferred requirement as the only refinement of an undeferred requirement. Don't create a structure like

> Some element in the list matches SOUGHT
> > The match is in the first position   DEFER

When building test specifications, a refinement is used instead of what it refines. But if you decide not to use the deferred requirement, the incorrectly refined requirement will never be used in the specification-based tests. If you later examine the code and decide the deferred requirement isn't worth satisfying and discard it, the requirement it refined would never be used at all.

In such a case, place the deferred statement at the same indentation level as the original:

> Some element in the list matches SOUGHT
> The match is in the first position   DEFER

Since it's not indented, it doesn't hide the original test requirement. It is as if you didn't notice the refinement, which rarely results in extra test specifications (especially when the two requirements are next to each other).

Of course, if there already was a refinement, there's no harm in adding a deferred requirement as another refinement at the same level:

> Some element in the list matches SOUGHT
> > The match is the DEFAULT argument
> > The match is in the first position   DEFER

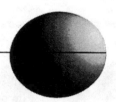

Test Specifications

At this point, you have a large number of test requirements. Ideally, they describe everything that needs to be tested. The thinking is done; now you mechanically combine requirements into test specifications. In practice, the process of building test specifications will often suggest new test requirements. These should be added to the checklist.

Test requirements should be converted into a small number of test specifications. Each test specification satisfies one or more test requirements. A test specification looks like this:

TEST 3:
    Global is initially 5
     setglobal(3, 7);
Expect
    return value is -1.
    Global is 3.

The first thing to notice is that, unlike test requirements, which are descriptions of sets of inputs, test specifications describe *exact, complete inputs*.

The inputs must be exact. Suppose you aren't precise during test design. You *must* be during test implementation because you can't give a test requirement as an argument to a function. If you delay the decision, you'll curse yourself when you come to implement the test specification and find the test isn't implementable (usually because you accidentally included contradictory test requirements). Undoing mistakes later is much harder than catching the problem early. Also, writing down a concrete test specification can trigger a moment when you say, "Wait a minute! What the specification says doesn't make sense." It's better to find such problems as early as possible.

The inputs must be complete for the same reasons. When the test runs, the Global has to have *some* value; why wait until implementation to decide which one? Even if the value is "irrelevant" to the test, specify it—you may discover it's not irrelevant at all. It may even suggest new test requirements that find faults.

The next thing to notice is that expected outputs are given. This is critically important. A test specification without the expected output is next to worthless. In that case, the tester must check the actual output when the test is run to "see if it looks reasonable". But studies have shown that testers looking at output for failures miss a high percentage of them; they're there to be seen, but testers don't see them.[1] To avoid this, tell them what they expect to see. (Better yet, tell a correctness-checking program what it expects to see. That's the topic of the next chapter.)

When you specify output, specify it as exactly as possible. At some point, an exact decision has to be made—is the actual output of the subsystem correct? The less precise the description of the expected output, the more likely that decision will be wrong.

Ideally, the description should be complete. If some global the subsystem uses is unchanged, say so. If some file is supposed to be untouched, say so. Failures where supposed-to-be-unchanged data are in fact changed are common enough—and missed often enough—that the extra reminder is worthwhile. Of course, it's usually impossible to specify the complete state of every variable the subsystem might conceivably touch. But every variable (global, file, and so forth) mentioned in the specification or code should have some expected post-test value specified.

In my experience teaching testing, the most common mistake is not specifying complete and exact expected output. It leads to a lot of missed bugs.

The rest of this chapter describes how to generate test specifications.

4.1 Marking the Requirements You Will Use

All of the most refined test requirements should be tagged with a zero in the left margin. That count will be incremented each time the test requirement is satisfied.

Precondition 2:
    There is at least one candidate
0   two identical candidates
0   There are no candidates.   ERROR

    a list of strings (the candidate list)
0   a single candidate
    more than one candidate
0   First candidate is largest (more than one) (DEFERRED)
0   Some other candidate is largest (more than one)
0   Last candidate is largest (more than one)

---

1. See [Myers78] and [Basili87].

These zero counts are the visual cues that identify which test requirements you need to look at. Note that even deferred test requirement are given counts. You might see an easy way to use them in a test specification you're writing anyway.

When converting requirements into exactly specified input values, the goal is to satisfy many requirements with a single test specification. Consider the following test requirement checklist. None of the test requirements have been used, so they all have a zero count.

```
0    arg1 = 0
0    arg1 = -1
0    arg1 = 1

0    arg2 even
0    arg2 odd
```

A single test specification can satisfy two test requirements, one for arg1 and one for arg2. I have no reason to favor any particular combination, so I'll pick arg1 = 0 and arg2=2 (even). After writing the test specification, I must update the checklist. First, I must note which test requirements are satisfied so that I know when I've satisfied them all. Second, I must note which test satisfies which test requirements. That's useful if I later discover the test is wrong. After I fix it, it might not satisfy some of the test requirements any longer. (Perhaps the problem was that two of them were contradictory.) I need to check that each of those test requirements is still satisfied by some other test or I must write a new test.

Here is the resulting checklist. The two requirements used have had their counts incremented and are annotated with the name of the test.

```
1    arg1 = 0       (test 1)
0    arg1 = -1
0    arg1 = 1

1    arg2 even      (test 1)
0    arg2 odd
```

I now need two more unsatisfied test requirements. I'll pick arg1 = -1 and arg2 = -1 (odd). Note that I'm picking a negative number for arg2. That's not a requirement, but I've already picked a positive one, and adding easy variety to the tests never hurts.

```
1    arg1 = 0       (test 1)
1    arg1 = -1      (test 2)
0    arg1 = 1

1    arg2 even      (test 1)
1    arg2 odd       (test 2)
```

Only `arg1=1` remains unsatisfied, so I must pick it. Since there are no more available test requirements for `arg2`, the choice of its value is arbitrary. In such a case, always pick the least-used test requirement. This prevents the common mistake of having many tests for one requirement and one test for each of the others. Overtesting one requirement underexercises parts of the subsystem and misses bugs.

I'll pick an even `arg2`. It would be a mistake to reuse `arg2=2` when there are millions of untried values. If the test requirement checklist is imperfect, it may be missing test requirements for `arg2`. I certainly won't satisfy them if I always use the same values. I'll pick the largest positive integer (which happens to be even on most computers). By doing that, I am adding additional variety to my test suite. Before, all the values were small (near zero). Now one of them is as large as it can be.

1	arg1 = 0	(test 1)
1	arg1 = -1	(test 2)
1	arg1 = 1	(test 3)
2	arg2 even	(test 1, test 3)
1	arg2 odd	(test 2)

This set of test requirements is now exhausted. If it hadn't been, the next choice for `arg2` would have been odd.

Here are the *standard combining rules*:

1. Each test specification should satisfy as many test requirements as is reasonable. There's no sense in doubling the amount of time you spend to squeeze in just one more test requirement, but more people make their tests too simple than too complex.

2. All test requirements should be satisfied.

3. If you must choose among a set of test requirements, pick the one that's been satisfied least.

4. Avoid repeating values; add variety where reasonable.

When there are many clues, each with several test requirements, combining many test requirements in each test specification produces complex tests. Always using the least-satisfied test requirements tends to make each test rather different than the others. The standard combining rules therefore increase the cost of writing the tests. The only justification for following them must be that they increase the effectiveness even more. Why?

❏ **simple bugs**

If each test satisfies only one test requirement, the tests will be simple. They will be more like the sort of informal "trying out the program" that developers typically do, and they will exercise the program in ways the developer anticipated. They won't find many bugs, because the developer has already found and fixed the ones they're suited for.

❏ **unsuspected requirements**

Simple tests are often implemented by writing the first one, then creating each new one by treating an earlier one as a template to be modified as little as possible. Such repetitive tests will exercise the same parts of the subsystem in the same ways. They won't accidentally test undiscovered test requirements or combinations of test requirements that can find unsuspected bugs.

❏ **marginal requirements**

Often, combining many test requirements allows the use of marginal test requirements that you couldn't justify if each test requirement were tested in isolation. The marginal requirements don't require whole new tests, just a little more work for an already-required test.

❏ **error-guessing**

Combining test requirements often suggests new test requirements; it acts as a spur to effective error-guessing. (These should be added to the checklist.)

In sum, you should design your tests around your imperfections as a tester. You won't think of everything, so enlist chance. In addition to finding bugs directly, part of the virtue of the catalog requirements is that they force more variety in your tests. You can't just reuse the same initialized array in every test; the Collection requirements won't allow it.

Another way of combining requirements would be more effective, but too expensive. Consider this example:

Whitespace
0   has spaces
0   no spaces

Case
0   uppercase
0   lowercase

The standard rules will produce two test specifications. The first might use an uppercase string with spaces, such as "A Z". The second would then use a lowercase string without spaces, like "az".

Why not add the other two combinations (an uppercase string without spaces and a lowercase string with them)? The tests would be just as complicated, and they would exercise the program in a greater variety of ways. The problem is that using all combinations generates many more test specifications without a corresponding increase in faults found.

The reasoning behind the standard combining rules is that, if there is an interaction, it can almost always be found without resorting to all combinations. Each of subsystem testing's different stages has a chance of finding the fault. If it escapes one stage, it can still be caught by the next. Here are the stages:

❏ **the specification**

If there's an interaction, the specification should have mentioned it, perhaps with a statement like

> if the string has spaces AND is uppercase

The normal processing would generate three of the four combinations:

> has spaces, uppercase
> has spaces, not uppercase
> doesn't have spaces, uppercase

(Probably another statement would have forced the remaining one.)

Of course, specifications don't always mention everything they should.

❏ **test requirements**

You may be suspicious that the specification is incomplete. If you think there *ought* to be an interaction, you should test for it. Do this by adding selected combinations to the checklist in the form of explicit combined test requirements, like "has spaces, uppercase", then use the standard combining rules. This is a form of error-guessing. It's often based on the bug history, your experience with similar systems, or suspicious-looking code.

Error-guessing based on the code can be made more rigorous, made into an explicit search for interactions. This is discussed in Part 5. This searching is not part of the basic technique because it's harder and takes more time. It's appropriate only for higher-risk subsystems.

❏ **test specifications**

Combinations can be free. In a realistic example, there would be more clues and requirements, so there would have to be more than four tests. Since each input would have to either have spaces or not, and be uppercase or not, you'd likely get all four combinations without ever thinking about them—provided you avoid falling into the trap of making all tests near-identical copies of each other.

❏ **coverage**

Ordinary coverage (described in Chapter 7) can often point out interactions not apparent from the specification. Chapter 25 discusses a type of coverage that targets interactions.

All of these stages are fallible, but their combination catches enough interaction faults that the further effort of doubling (or quadrupling, or worse) the number of tests has a tiny expected benefit. It's only cost-effective in high-risk subsystems or cases where tests are extraordinarily cheap. To get a more concrete feel for the cost of trying all combinations, try doing it for the sreadhex checklist. You'll quickly realize that it's not a practical alternative.

4.2.1 An Example of the Need for Complexity

In a large testing effort, it's easy to slip into overly simplistic tests no matter what your noble aspirations when you start. The first step down the slippery slope is usually when you begin semi-consciously patterning new tests after old ones.

The best way I've found of keeping the momentum toward complex tests is to think about bugs. When I see bugs that wouldn't have been found by simple tests, my enthusiasm for complex tests increases. Here's an example of a real bug found (too late) in real software. I will argue that both simple tests and code inspections would probably miss it, while complex tests would probably find it. The argument isn't meant to be definitive. The most convincing arguments will come from your own experience.

This subsystem takes commands, either from a terminal or a command file. There are many commands; we're concerned only with EXIT and INCLUDE. Their descriptions are adapted from the user's manual.

❑ **EXIT**

The EXIT command ends a session. Work started earlier may still be in progress. If so, the subsystem prompts you to specify whether it should finish and exit, cancel the work and exit, or not exit (ignoring the command). The prompt happens only if input is from the terminal; otherwise, the work is silently cancelled.

❑ **INCLUDE**

The INCLUDE command executes a series of commands contained in a file. It executes commands until it reaches the end of file, another INCLUDE command, or an EXIT command. You can nest INCLUDE files. When the subsystem reaches the end of an INCLUDE file, it returns to the next line of the file from which you executed the last INCLUDE command.

The bug happens when input is coming from a terminal, work is in progress, and an EXIT is found in an INCLUDE file. Would it be found by simple tests? Here's the test requirement checklist:

> source of input
> > terminal
> > file
>
> Exit command
> > No work in progress
> > Work in progress
>
> User response to work-in-progress prompt, a Case
> > Y (finish task)
> > N (cancel task)
> > I (ignore attempt to exit)
> > Some other response
>
> Include Depth, a count
> > 0
> > 1
> > > 1
>
> Include File, a stream of commands
> > Ends with EOF (that is, no EXIT).
> > Contains EXIT
> >
> > Contains INCLUDE (redundant with the Include Depth requirements)

Testing input from the terminal is more difficult than testing input from a file. It requires either manual testing or use of a tool that can capture and play back terminal input. Such tools, even if available, are harder to use than simply feeding a file to a program. The consequence is that terminal input will likely only be used for four simple tests of its unique requirements:

> Test 1A: (on terminal)
> > Start work
> > EXIT
> > Respond with 'Y'
> Expect: ...
>
> Test 1B: (on terminal)
> > Start work
> > EXIT
> > Respond with 'N'
> Expect: ...
>
> Test 1C: (on terminal)
> > Start work
> > EXIT
> > Respond with 'I'
> Expect: ...

Test 1D: (on terminal)
    Start work
    EXIT
    Choose something other than Y, N, or I.
Expect: ...

This set of tests will be completely separate from the other tests. In a simple testing strategy, there's no reason to complicate them with INCLUDE files, so the bug would not be found. Similarly, the INCLUDE tests would have no reason to take input from the terminal—that would just add work, and terminal input has already been tested.

So, it's quite plausible that simple tests would miss the bug. (After all, they did.) Given the above checklist, complex tests wouldn't. Each of the four user response requirements would be combined with one of the Include File requirements. Therefore, at least one of the complex tests would have an EXIT in the INCLUDE file, which would trigger the bug.

Here's the relevant part of the code that handles the EXIT command:

```
if (Input_from_terminal)   /* Global variable set at startup */
{
  if (work_in_progress)
  {
    ...
    note("Work in progress.");
    note("Y to complete work and exit.");
    note("N to cancel work and exit.");
    note("I to ignore the EXIT and continue.");
    readline(buffer);
    switch(buffer[0])
    {
      case Y: ...; break;
      case N: ...; break;
      default:                /* Note: anything else resumes */
        continue;
    }
  }
}
```

`Input_from_terminal` determines whether input originally came from the terminal. In the failing case, it's true, as is `work_in_progress`. The program prints the prompt to the terminal, then reads the answer *from the current input*. The current input is actually from an INCLUDE file, not—as it was originally—from the terminal. `readline` assumes the current input is a terminal and leaves `buffer` empty. (In the simple case, this results in the prompt being printed, no input being accepted, and the EXIT being ignored; in a more complicated case, it eventually results in an infinite loop.)

Since we have the advantage of knowing the failure, the error is obvious. There's an implicit assumption that

```
Input_from_terminal
```

means

```
Input_currently_from_terminal
```

instead of what it does mean, namely

```
Input_once_from_terminal_but_maybe_not_right_now.
```

In a real-life code review that incorrect assumption would be easy to miss. There is no code anywhere nearby to remind the reader of INCLUDE files, and the name of the variable cries out for misinterpretation (despite it being more clearly named than the vast majority of variables). I've seen lots of errors like this one slip past reviews, and I claim this one probably would too.

4.3
Error Test
Specifications

Normally, you attempt to use as many requirements per test specification as possible. When testing error handling, test each error in isolation. The reason is that errors often mask each other. As an example, consider this test requirement checklist for

```
                    FUN(int A, int B, int C):
```

A, an interval
  A=-1   ERROR
  A=0
  A=1
  A=2   ERROR

B, an interval
  B=5   ERROR
  B=6
  B=10
  B=11   ERROR

C, an integer
  C odd
  C even

A test where A=-1 and B=5 would not be a good one. The code might be written as

```
if (A < 0 || A > 1)
    exit_with_error("A is wrong");
if (B < 5 || B > 11)
    exit_with_error("B is wrong");
```

Since the program exits before it tests B, it will not discover that B is handled incorrectly.

Further, don't assume that an error test satisfies any other test requirements. Any test of FUN must provide a value for C, and that value must be either even or odd. But, since the incorrect call causes FUN to exit immediately, C is never used. It can hardly be said to be well tested. Therefore, an error test should increment the count for only its single error requirement.

This is not to say that the other requirements are irrelevant. In programs with more complicated error handling, variety is as important as it is for normal tests (perhaps more so). Use other test requirements in a varied way, just don't mark them as satisfied. For example, FUN's error tests might use these four calls:

Test 1: FUN(-1, 6, 1)   /* testing A error, requirement for B used, C is odd */
Test 2: FUN(2, 10, 100)   /* testing A error, different requirement for B used, C is even */
Test 3: FUN(0, 5, -1)   /* testing B error, requirement for A used, C is odd */
Test 4: FUN(1, 11, 0)   /* testing B error, different requirement for A used, C is even */

but the checklist would have its counts incremented like this:

A, an interval
1   A=-1   ERROR (test 1)
0   A=0
0   A=1
1   A=2   ERROR (test 2)

B, an interval
1   B=5   ERROR (test 3)
0   B=6
0   B=10
1   B=11   ERROR (test 4)

C, an integer
0   C odd
0   C even

Chapter 13 discusses some further refinements to error testing in Section 13.1.3.

4.4
Tips on Building Test Specifications

Here are some tips to use when building test specifications:

1. Test specifications are built by picking an unused test requirement, then adding in other requirements that are compatible with it. If your early tests use up all the easy test requirements, you're likely to end up with several incompatible ones, meaning that each requires its own test specification. One test specification per test requirement is not efficient, so start the design of each new test specification with a hard-to-combine requirement.

2. I find it most efficient to make the checklist online but print it out for test specification generation. Incrementing test requirements is easier with a pencil. When all the tests are finished, it's easy to update the online checklist.

3. Some requirements can be used in many tests. Once a requirement has been used in three or so tests, thinking about it further is probably not worthwhile. I just blacken the count into a solid bullet, which makes it easy to ignore that test requirement while there are still ones with small counts.

4. If all the test requirements for a particular input variable are blackened, start using typical, non-extremal values in preference to overusing the same test requirements. By using a different value for each new test, you increase the variety.[1]

5. Watch out for patterns in the way you pick test requirements. For example, I was once working with a checklist like this:

A, a collection
    0 elements
    1 element
    >1 elements

B, a collection
    0 elements
    1 element
    >1 elements
<many other test requirements>

My first test gave both A and B zero elements. My next gave A and B one element. My next gave A and B more than one element. There were still tests to write for the other requirements, so I reused the collection clues. My next test gave both A and B zero elements. My next test gave them both one. Unthinkingly, I was using the same combinations of A and B as before, because I was just cycling through the requirements round-robin. It would have been better to give A zero elements and B one, A one element and B many, and so on.[2]

4.5
Rules for Test Form

A well-formed test is more likely to be efficient and effective. Here's a checklist to match your tests against. It's also reproduced in Appendix F.

1. **Test inputs are specified exactly.**
2. **All test inputs are described.**
3. **Test specifications do not mention internal variables.**

To implement such a test, you'd have to find external inputs that force the internal variables to have the selected values. You might as well do that now. If you don't, you might discover it's impossible, which will require expensive rework.

---

1. Like similar techniques, subsystem testing tends to stress abnormal test specifications at the expense of typical user inputs. That's OK. More accurate simulations of actual use are the job of system testing, and the topic of another book.
2. My thanks to Mark Alan Brodie for pointing this out.

4. **Expected results are given exactly.**

   Imprecision is tolerable only when the specification is imprecise (as in the specification of, say, floating point routines). Even in those cases, you write something down as your expected result.

5. **All results are described, including variables that are not changed.**

   Without a list of what the subsystem should do, you can't tell if it did the right thing. Without a list of what it shouldn't do, you'll miss failures where it changed something it should have left alone. The next section has more on unchanged variables.

6. **Independent tests are best.**

   Be wary of writing test specifications that depend on each other. It may seem useful to have the results of one test be the initialization for the next, but this often causes the sort of problems that make maintenance so popular: Changes to one test break others in mysterious ways.

7. **Multiple tests per invocation are best.**

   When implementing tests, it is useful to run as many as possible per invocation of the subsystem. It sometimes happens that a subsystem only works the first time. If every test is with a fresh invocation of the subsystem, that failure will never be discovered. Typically, the subsystem is compiled into an executable. What this rule says is that this pattern is preferable:

   > Invoke the executable
   >> Set up test 1
   >> Run test 1
   >> Set up test 2
   >> Run test 2
   >> Set up test 3
   >> Run test 3
   >> ...

   as opposed to:

   > Invoke the executable
   >> Set up test 1
   >> Run test 1
   > Invoke the executable
   >> Set up test 2
   >> Run test 2

   > ...

This rule does not conflict with the previous rule so long as the second test is not designed to depend on the results of the first.

   (This is actually a test implementation rule rather than a test design rule, but it's convenient to include it in this checklist.)

4.6
Rules for Test Content

A single test requirement checklist can lead to many sets of test specifications. Not all will be equally good at finding bugs. A test's bug-finding power is increased if the following rules are followed. First, some terms need to be defined.

The *foreground* contains all the variables a particular test would change. sreadhex always sets *NREAD, so *NREAD is always part of the foreground. sreadhex sometimes sets *ODD_DIGIT and sometimes leaves it alone. In the tests where it's set, it's part of the foreground.

The *background* is everything that the subsystem should not modify in a particular test. (But a buggy implementation might, incorrectly). There are two parts to the background. The *immediate background* contains the variables a subsystem could modify in some test, just not this one. For a test that satisfies sreadhex's Postcondition 3, *ODD_DIGIT is in the immediate background because that postcondition doesn't change it. The *far background* contains all the variables the subsystem should never modify. A compiler shouldn't touch your mailbox (assuming none of the tests use your mailbox). A subsystem shouldn't modify a global variable its specification never mentions.

Given these definitions, here are the rules:

1. **Background modifications must be visible.**

    Before running a test, initialize the background to known values. If possible, use values different from those the subsystem uses. If the subsystem sets a particular field in a structure to either 0 or 1, initialize the other fields to 7. After the test, check that the background is unchanged. Are the other fields still 7?

    Or take a compiler that uses a source file to produce an executable, but isn't to touch the executable if the source has a syntax error. It might contain a fault because it first deletes the executable, then processes the source, then creates the new executable. If there's a syntax error, the executable will be deleted instead of being left alone. If all the error-handling tests are run without an executable, you'll never see a failure.

    Usually, you will only initialize the immediate background. In some applications, you might worry about parts of the far background. When testing a garbage collector, I went so far as to initialize and check the program's entire virtual memory.

    Failing to check for background changes is a common testing error.

2. **Foreground modifications must be visible.**

    For example, if the subsystem is to set a variable to 5, make sure it starts with some value other than 5. Otherwise, how do you know the subsystem actually did anything? This seems obvious, but you'd be surprised how often subtler versions of this mistake slip past.

It is especially important to make sure that a program's error handling code actually does something. If error handling might have to restore some correct state, ensure that the test causes state changes that have to be undone.

3. **Alternate effects should cause visible differences.**

Will your test detect a bug where the wrong postcondition is applied? This is a common error with special-case postconditions. Suppose you have two postconditions:

> Postcondition1: IF <trigger1>
> THEN result is A+A

> Postcondition 2: IF <trigger2>
> THEN result is A*A

Suppose you use a test that causes the subsystem to execute the action for Postcondition 2 when it should be executing the action for Postcondition 1. If A=2, you will not see the failure.

4. **Test requirements must be exercised.**

This is a generalization of the way error requirements are handled. Because error handling often prevents other requirements from having an effect, their counts are not incremented when they're used in error tests.

More generally, all test requirements describe some part of the subsystem's input. If, as a result of the rest of the input, that part is unused in the execution of a test, whatever's special about it—whatever caused you to think it was worth testing—has been untested. For example, if you put a special list element after an element the subsystem searches for and immediately returns, the special element is never processed.

Just asking the question, "will this requirement be exercised in this test?", catches most such mistakes. In some cases, it's hard to tell. Understanding the basic structure of the subsystem helps, as does the intuition that comes from programming experience. A detailed examination of the implementation can answer the question, but is expensive, prone to mistakes, and, in most cases, unnecessary. It's more efficient to enlist chance: using a test requirement in several tests increases the chance that it's really exercised in at least one. If chance fails you, coverage will sometimes detect the problem.

People sometimes worry whether a fault detected by one test requirement will cause others to be unexercised. This can happen. Suppose the program "dumps core" almost immediately. In order to exercise all requirements, you need to find the failure-provoking requirements and remove them from the test. This makes a simpler test that looks for faults masked by the first. Alternately, if the fault will be fixed quickly, you can just wait and run the original test again. Searching for the requirements that cause the failure may seem like excessive work, but it's work you may be doing anyway, to help the person fixing the fault.

5. **Make inputs distinct.**[1]

If a function takes two variables and the test requirements don't call for them to have the same value, make sure they have different values. Using the wrong variable is a common programming error, and you won't detect it if the wrong variable happens to have the right value. This rule applies to other kinds of "variable". If the subsystem uses one of two data files, make their contents as different as possible to increase the chance of detecting the fault where the subsystem uses the wrong one. Make elements of an array distinct. Make fields of a structure distinct. For example, suppose the program searches an array of these structures:

```
struct element
{
   int key;
   int count;
   int grade;
};
```

The search is performed by this routine, which is the subsystem being tested:

```
struct element *
find_one(int key, struct element *array)
```

If the search is for key=1, and there's a matching element in the array, neither its count nor grade field should contain 1. If one did, the subsystem would return the right element for the wrong reason. It would also be reasonable to have one of the other fields contain 1 in an earlier non-matching element, one whose key had some other value. That would catch the less plausible fault where the search was implemented as

```
if (elt->key == key || elt->count == key)
   return elt;
```

The fault isn't very likely, but it costs nothing to give the fields values that will catch it.

A test requirement is written in terms of the subsystem interface, but its real purpose is to exercise internal code in a way that might make it fail. The rules for test content increase the chance that the test

---

1. This trick is due to [Howden78].

requirement really does exercise the internal code as desired, rather than in the wrong way or not at all. They also increase the chance that any failure propagates to the external interface where it can be seen, and that the failure will be obvious enough when it gets there.

This book has concentrated on test requirements, not on their delivery to code or the propagation of failure. Later chapters will discuss those topics in more detail, but the emphasis remains the test requirement. The reason is cost. A thorough job of finding requirements doesn't cost much. Equivalent thoroughness in delivery or propagation is much more expensive.[1]

These rules for test content are also in Appendix F. When using them, remember that they are just specific ways of asking three general questions:

1. Will the test requirement be delivered to the appropriate code?
2. Will any failures propagate to the output?
3. Will the failures be visible?

If you first derive test specifications from the specification, then later add test requirements and specifications from the code, you have to do some extra work.

4.7.1 Processing the Requirements from the Specification

When working with the specification, you may mark test requirements with DEFER. If such requirements are convenient to use in a test, go ahead. For example, suppose you have this test requirement checklist:

```
A, a count
    0
    1

searching for A in LIST
    match not found
    match found (more than one element, exactly one match)
    found in first position        DEFER
```

---

1. [DeMillo78], [Morell90], [Offutt88], and [Richardson88] describe techniques with more explicit concentration on assuring delivery and propagation.

You may choose a test where A=0 and it's not found in LIST. Such a test might look like

TEST 1:
  A = 0
  LIST = 1, -2, 3334322
Expect: ...

The test requirements don't fully describe LIST—all they say is that it can't contain 0—so its contents are arbitrary. Then you may choose a test where A=1, which is in LIST. Again, LIST is underspecified. If it doesn't matter where the match is, it might as well be in the first position, satisfying the deferred requirement.

By deferring a test requirement, you're saying that it may be useful, but it's not so likely to be useful that you'll write a test specification just for it. Make the final decision about usefulness when you look at the code.

4.7.2 While Processing the Requirements from the Code

The easiest thing to do is to build a completely new checklist from the code, generating clues and test requirements in the usual way. Then examine all the test requirements you deferred earlier to see whether they should be discarded or used. If you want to use them, copy them into the new checklist.

Since you're looking at the specification checklist anyway, match the actual operations against those you'd expected. Are any expected operations missing? If so, perhaps that's a fault.

You must also decide whether to merge the new requirements into the old test specifications (where possible), or simply generate new test specifications for the new requirements. For example, suppose you've written a number of tests that use filenames, all shorter than 16 characters. When examining the code, you discover it handles filenames 16 characters or longer specially. Should you rework the old tests so that some use longer filenames, or should you add one new test that tests longer filenames?

Updating the old tests would be preferable, since it leads to fewer, more complex tests. However, it is usually harder than writing new tests, and there's some danger that adding new requirements will accidentally make the test fail to satisfy some old ones. Unless the old tests are easy to update, it's best to write new ones. But be sure to make them complex and varied. Generally, you'll have fewer requirements from the code than from the specification, so this will take a special effort. Use the old specification checklist to help.

Here's the complete set of test requirements for `sreadhex`. The most refined are marked with 0:

SREADHEX Test
Specifications

Checklist

Precondition 1
0   STR is a non-null pointer to an array that can hold RLEN bytes.

Precondition 7
0   RLEN is not 0
0   RLEN = 0   ERROR

Postcondition 1
     START+NUM_HEX_CHARS < RLEN*2, START+NUM_HEX_CHARS is even
0   START+NUM_HEX_CHARS = RLEN*2-2, START+NUM_HEX_CHARS is even
     START+NUM_HEX_CHARS >= RLEN*2, START+NUM_HEX_CHARS is even
0   START+NUM_HEX_CHARS = RLEN*2, START+NUM_HEX_CHARS is even
     START+NUM_HEX_CHARS < RLEN*2, START+NUM_HEX_CHARS is odd
0   START+NUM_HEX_CHARS = RLEN*2-1, START+NUM_HEX_CHARS is odd

Postcondition 2
     START+NUM_HEX_CHARS >= RLEN*2, START+NUM_HEX_CHARS is odd
0   START+NUM_HEX_CHARS = RLEN*2+1, START+NUM_HEX_CHARS is odd

Postcondition 3

Postcondition 4
     *ODD_DIGIT is initially >= 0
0   *ODD_DIGIT==0
     *ODD_DIGIT is initially < 0
0   *ODD_DIGIT==-1

STR, an array of bytes to be filled
0   a single element
0   more than one element

RLEN, a count
0   RLEN=1
0   RLEN=size of STR

NREAD, a pointer to a count
0   0

ODD_DIGIT, a pointer to an integer either -1 or [0..15]
0   15

S, a string
0   empty
0   a single element

hexadecimal character, in range ['0' .. '9', 'A'.. 'F', 'a' .. 'f']
0   /   (ASCII character before '0')
0   0
0   9
0   :   (ASCII character after '9')
0   @   (ASCII character before 'A')
0   A
0   F
0   G
0   `   (ASCII character before 'a')
0   a
0   f
0   g
0   All of 1-8, B-E, b-e

NUM_HEX_CHARS, a count of hexadecimal characters in S
0   0
0   1
0   all characters hexadecimal (more than one)

DIGIT, a location to be filled with an integer in range [0 .. 15]
0   0
0   15

number of unused hexadecimal characters in S, a count
0   >1

Searching for a value for an odd DIGIT.
0   all of several elements are hexadecimal (none filtered)
0   exactly one of several elements is not hexadecimal (one filtered)
     exactly one of several elements is hexadecimal (all but one filtered)
0   only hexadecimal character is first of several
0   only hexadecimal character is last of several
0   none of several elements are hexadecimal (all filtered)

Searching for a value for an even DIGIT.
0   all of several elements are hexadecimal (none filtered)
0   exactly one of several elements is not hexadecimal (one filtered)
     exactly one of several elements is hexadecimal (all but one filtered)
0   only hexadecimal character is first of several
0   only hexadecimal character is last of several
0   none of several elements are hexadecimal (all filtered)

4.8.1 Notes on the Design

Before designing any tests, you must decide how to handle the foreground and background.

1. STR, the destination, will always be 100 bytes long. RLEN, the amount of STR to fill, will always be less than 100, so that tests can check whether bytes beyond are touched. Tests will always specify the values of those background bytes, as well as the value of the byte before the beginning of STR.

   Notice that this means the RLEN=size of STR requirement will never be satisfied. Recall that I described it as a requirement that doesn't quite make sense; this is another reason why.

2. *NREAD, which holds the number of bytes filled in STR, will be initialized to 1000. Since this is larger than the length of STR, a failure to set *NREAD will always be detectable.

3. *ODD_DIGIT is both an input and output value. The tests should not cause it to be set to the value it already has.

4. S, the source string, is in the far background because no execution should ever change it. Tests will explicitly check that it's unchanged. (An unlikely failure, but easy to check.)

5. Tests could also check that decoder is unchanged. This would be harder to implement, since decoder is a static variable. (See the next chapter.) It's not worth the trouble, since the chance of a problem is infinitesimal.

Although test design is mostly mechanical, you must be alert for opportunities; for example, the design of the third test finds a specification bug. That's not unusual.

The first three tests are explained in great detail. The remaining tests are shown for completeness and because they illustrate a few remaining points.

4.8.2 Test 1

There is only one error requirement, RLEN = 0. It violates Precondition 7:

> Validated: RLEN is not 0
>> On failure:
>>> *NREAD is 0
>>> The return value is 0

Although the other arguments are picked to satisfy test requirements, those requirements are not incremented. Only the error requirement is satisfied by this test.

> TEST 1:
> STR, a 100-byte buffer, initialized to all 1's
> RLEN = 0
> *NREAD = 1000
> *ODD_DIGIT = 15

S = "a"   (note, distinct from the background of STR)
EXPECT
STR unchanged
*NREAD = 0
*ODD_DIGIT = 15
S unchanged
return value 0

Notice that the initialization of STR satisfies the rules for test content. Nothing should be put in STR. If the program incorrectly modifies it, the most likely values will be 15 and 10 (the value of 'a'). Therefore, neither of them should be used for initialization. (Ideally, some value that could never be a digit would be used, but there is no such value.)

Here's an excerpt of the updated checklist:

Precondition 1

0   STR is a non-null pointer to an array that can hold RLEN bytes.

Precondition 7
0   RLEN is not 0
1   **RLEN = 0**   **ERROR**   **(Test 1)**

NREAD, a pointer to a count
0   0   **(satisfied, but not incremented)**

ODD_DIGIT, a pointer to an integer either -1 or [0..15]
0   15   **(satisfied, but not incremented)**

S, a string
0   empty
0   a single element **(satisfied, but not incremented)**

The last step in designing a test is to double-check it against the Rules for Test Form and Rules for Test Design. This test conforms.

4.8.3 Test 2

The goal is to fill in the blanks in this test template:

TEST 2:
STR, a 100-byte buffer, initialized to all ___
RLEN = ___
*NREAD = 1000
*ODD_DIGIT = ___
S = ___
EXPECT
STR = ___
*NREAD = ___
*ODD_DIGIT = ___
S unchanged
return value ___

There are several very specific test requirements in the checklist:

        RLEN, a count
        0   RLEN=1

        ODD_DIGIT, a pointer to an integer either -1 or [0..15]
        0   15

        S, a string
        0   empty
        0   a single element

A single test could satisfy RLEN=1, *ODD_DIGIT 15, and S containing a single element:

        Test 2:
                STR, a 100-byte buffer, initialized to all ____
                RLEN = 1
                *NREAD = 1000
                *ODD_DIGIT = 15
                S = ____ (a string with a single hexadecimal character)

The test isn't complete. It doesn't specify which hexadecimal character is to be in S. The character '0' is a perfectly fine choice. The test also needs to specify STR's background. Anything other than 15 and 0 will satisfy the rules for test content. I'll pick 2.

These inputs satisfy Postcondition 3:

(Enough digits to fill STR; ignore any excess)
IF START + NUM_HEX_CHARS >= RLEN*2
THEN
A. The return value is 0.
B. *NREAD is RLEN.
C. For any hexadecimal character in S and index INDEX
        such that START + INDEX < RLEN*2
        DIGIT[START+INDEX] = HEX_CHAR[INDEX]
D. *ODD_DIGIT is unchanged.

So the complete test specification is:

TEST 2:
        STR, a 100-byte buffer, initialized to all 2's
        RLEN = 1
        *NREAD = 1000
        *ODD_DIGIT = 15
        S = "0"
EXPECT
        STR = 15 0 2 2 2...
        *NREAD = 1
        *ODD_DIGIT = 15
        S unchanged
        return value 0

(That *ODD_DIGIT doesn't change is not a violation of the rules for test content. The postcondition leaves it unchanged. The rule is only violated if the postcondition explicitly *sets* *ODD_DIGIT to the value it starts with.)

The next step is to see what other test requirements were satisfied along the way. Here are two:

Precondition 1

0   STR is a non-null pointer to an array that can hold RLEN bytes.

Precondition 7
0   RLEN is not 0

But the common pattern for all tests (STR 100 bytes, RLEN < 100) means every test will satisfy the first requirement. Indeed, every call to sreadhex must do that, because Precondition 1 is an assumed precondition. As promised in the previous chapter, this requirement is obviously always redundant. There's no point in incrementing its count once per test, so it will be removed.

Similarly, the second requirement is true of every non-error test. Repeatedly incrementing it would not be productive. It will also be removed.

This requirement is also satisfied:

0   START+NUM_HEX_CHARS = RLEN*2,
        START+NUM_HEX_CHARS is even

START is 1 in this test, because *ODD_DIGIT is not -1. NUM_HEX_CHARS is 1.

One of STR's requirements is satisfied, since a single element is filled:

STR, an array of bytes to be filled
0   a single element
0   more than one element

Since NUM_HEX_CHARS is 1, one of its requirements is satisfied:

NUM_HEX_CHARS, a count of hexadecimal characters in S
0   0
0   1
0   all characters hexadecimal (more than one)

Note that this is not redundant with the "S has a single element" requirement since that single element is not necessarily a hexadecimal character.

Both of the DIGIT requirements are satisfied:

DIGIT, a location to be filled with an integer in range [0 .. 15]
0   0
0   15

In fact, they are redundant with these requirements (among others):

> hexadecimal character, in range ['0' .. '9', 'A'.. 'F', 'a' .. 'f']
> 0   0
> 0   F

provided the rules for test content are followed. Those rules prohibit incrementing the counts for the hexadecimal character requirements if the characters weren't used, that is, put into STR. Without the rules, these two requirements could be "satisfied" by a test where RLEN was 1, S was "123456789ABCDE0F", and the tail of the string was completely untouched.

Since I intend to follow the rules, and since the DIGIT requirements have been satisfied, I'll drop them from the checklist.

No other requirements are satisfied by test 2. The updated checklist is on the next page. I've tidied up in one other way. It should be clear now that every test will involve deciding what value to give to *ODD_DIGIT, but its test requirements are spread the checklist. I'll group them together.

Checklist

Precondition 7
| 1 | RLEN = 0 | ERROR | (Test 1) |

Postcondition 1
    START+NUM_HEX_CHARS < RLEN*2, START+NUM_HEX_CHARS is even
| 0 | START+NUM_HEX_CHARS = RLEN*2-2, START+NUM_HEX_CHARS is even |

    START+NUM_HEX_CHARS >= RLEN*2, START+NUM_HEX_CHARS is even
| **1** | **START+NUM_HEX_CHARS = RLEN*2, START+NUM_HEX_CHARS is even (Test 2)** |

    START+NUM_HEX_CHARS < RLEN*2, START+NUM_HEX_CHARS is odd
| 0 | START+NUM_HEX_CHARS = RLEN*2-1, START+NUM_HEX_CHARS is odd |

Postcondition 2
    START+NUM_HEX_CHARS >= RLEN*2, START+NUM_HEX_CHARS is odd
| 0 | START+NUM_HEX_CHARS = RLEN*2+1, START+NUM_HEX_CHARS is odd |

STR, an array of bytes to be filled
| **1** | **a single element** | **(Test 2)** |
| 0 | more than one element | |

RLEN, a count
| **1** | **RLEN=1** | **(Test 2)** |

NREAD, a pointer to a count
0   0
ODD_DIGIT, a pointer to an integer either -1 or [0..15]
0   -1
0   0
1   **15**   **(Test 2)**

S, a string
0   empty
1   **a single element**   **(Test 2)**

hexadecimal character, in range ['0' .. '9', 'A'.. 'F', 'a' .. 'f']
0   /   (ASCII character before '0')
1   **0**   **(Test 2)**
0   9
0   :   (ASCII character after '9')
0   @   (ASCII character before 'A')
0   A
0   F
0   G
0   `   (ASCII character before 'a')
0   a
0   f
0   g
0   All of 1-8, B-E, b-e

NUM_HEX_CHARS, a count of hexadecimal characters in S
0   0
1   **1**   **(Test 2)**
0   all characters hexadecimal (more than one)

number of unused hexadecimal characters in S, a count
0   >1
Searching for a value for an odd DIGIT.
0   all of several elements are hexadecimal (none filtered)
0   exactly one of several elements is not hexadecimal (one filtered)
     exactly one of several elements is hexadecimal (all but one filtered)
0   only hexadecimal character is first of several
0   only hexadecimal character is last of several
0   none of several elements are hexadecimal (all filtered)
Searching for a value for an even DIGIT.
0   all of several elements are hexadecimal (none filtered)
0   exactly one of several elements is not hexadecimal (one filtered)
     exactly one of several elements is hexadecimal (all but one filtered)
0   only hexadecimal character is first of several
0   only hexadecimal character is last of several
0   none of several elements are hexadecimal (all filtered)

CHAP. 4 TEST SPECIFICATIONS

4.8.4 Test 3

Here's a test requirement that seems likely to be relatively incompatible with others.

S, a string
0   empty

I'll pick it, since I want to use up hard-to-combine requirements early.

*ODD_DIGIT needs a value. -1 hasn't been used. But suppose that's chosen. START will be 0. NUM_HEX_CHARS is 0. Since RLEN has to be at least 1 (by Precondition 7), this test would satisfy Postcondition 1:

> (An even number of digits that don't fill STR: use them all)
> IF START+NUM_HEX_CHARS < RLEN*2
>   AND START+NUM_HEX_CHARS is even
> THEN
>   A. The return value is 1.
>   B. *NREAD is (START + NUM_HEX_CHARS)/2
>   C. For any hexadecimal character in S at index INDEX,
>   DIGIT[START+INDEX] = HEX_CHAR[INDEX]
>   (For example, if character 0 is '9' and START is 0, 9
>   is placed as the 0th digit of STR.)
>   D. *ODD_DIGIT is -1.

So, in this test, sreadhex should set *ODD_DIGIT to a value it already has. That violates a rule for test content, since there's no way to tell if sreadhex actually obeys part (D) of the postcondition.

So *ODD_DIGIT should be some other value. The value 0 satisfies an as-yet-unsatisfied requirement. Now START is 1, so the test satisfies Postcondition 2:

> (An odd number of digits that don't fill STR: use them all)
> IF START+NUM_HEX_CHARS < RLEN*2
>   AND START+NUM_HEX_CHARS is odd
> THEN
>   A. The return value is 1.
>   B. *NREAD is (START + NUM_HEX_CHARS - 1)/2
>   C. For any hexadecimal character in S at index INDEX
>   except the final hexadecimal character,
>   DIGIT[START+INDEX] = HEX_CHAR[INDEX]
>   D. *ODD_DIGIT is set to the value of the last
>   hexadecimal character in S.

What does the postcondition do to *ODD_DIGIT? It sets it to the value of the last hexadecimal character in S. That doesn't make any sense—there is no such character. And what about Postcondition 4?

> IF *ODD_DIGIT is initially >= 0
> THEN
>   DIGIT[0] = the initial value of *ODD_DIGIT.

This puts *ODD_DIGIT as the first digit in byte 0. What goes in the second digit? This action is contrary to the purpose of *ODD_DIGIT, which is to avoid leaving bytes half-filled.

The specification is in error. The case where S is empty is special. Actually, it's not just the empty string that's special; it's any string that provides no digits. A correct solution would be twofold. First, a new postcondition is required:

> IF S has no hexadecimal characters
> THEN
> > A. the return value is 1.
> > B. *NREAD is 0
> > C. *ODD_DIGIT is unchanged.
> > D. STR is unchanged.

Second, old postconditions would have to be rewritten to avoid ambiguity. For example, Postcondition 4 would have to say:

IF *ODD_DIGIT is initially >= 0 AND S has hexadecimal characters
THEN
> DIGIT[0] = the initial value of *ODD_DIGIT.

These rewritten postconditions would have two effects. First, various old requirements would have "S has hexadecimal characters" added because of the AND rule. One of them would be:

START+NUM_HEX_CHARS = RLEN*2, START+NUM_HEX_CHARS even, **S has hex characters**

Second, there would be several refinements of NUM_HEX_CHARS, namely:

> NUM_HEX_CHARS, a count of hexadecimal characters in S
> > **NUM_HEX_CHARS=0**

0	**S an empty string**
0	**NUM_HEX_CHARS=0 and *ODD_DIGIT=-1**
0	**NUM_HEX_CHARS=0 and *ODD_DIGIT in [0,15]**
1	NUM_HEX_CHARS=1 (Test 2)
0	all characters hexadecimal (more than one)

The "empty string" is a refinement that was missed before, moved down from the "S, a string" clue. The other two come from Postconditions 1 and 2. (They're simplified forms of what the AND rule would give you.) I would probably also refine "NUM_HEX_CHARS=0" with "S contains only non-hexadecimal characters". That's the only other way NUM_HEX_CHARS can be zero. A specification omission justifies extra suspicion and extra test requirements.

The revision would be some work. (Changing a specification is always disruptive to both testing and coding.) You wouldn't learn anything new about subsystem testing from it, so I won't do it. Instead, I'll arbitrarily add a new precondition:

Assumed Precondition 8: S contains at least one hexadecimal character.

Some of the checklist requirements, like "S an empty string", are now unsatisfiable, so they're removed.

4.8.5 Test 3 (again)

*NREAD=0 looks like it might be hard to satisfy, so it's best to get it out of the way early. The only way to get *NREAD=0 is to satisfy Postcondition 2:

        IF START+NUM_HEX_CHARS < RLEN*2
            AND START+NUM_HEX_CHARS is odd
        THEN

                ...

            B. *NREAD is (START + NUM_HEX_CHARS - 1)/2

            ...

*ODD_DIGIT has to be -1 (to get START to zero) and NUM_HEX_CHARS has to be 1. That gives this test skeleton:

        STR, a 100-byte buffer, initialized to all ____
        RLEN = ___
        *NREAD = 1000
        *ODD_DIGIT = -1
        S = ____ (a string with a single hexadecimal character)

This happens to satisfy another requirement:

        ODD_DIGIT, a pointer to an integer either -1 or [0..15]
        0   -1
        0   0
        1   15   (Test 2)

RLEN is unspecified. If it's picked to be 1, it can satisfy

        0   START+NUM_HEX_CHARS = RLEN*2-1, START+NUM_HEX_CHARS is odd

Test 2 already had a single hexadecimal character, so I could use some non-hexadecimal characters, such as '/'. Why not use all the ones that have requirements: '/', ':', '@', 'G', and 'g'? The hexadecimal character should come after them (else they won't be exercised). The character '9' is an unused hexadecimal character. That portion of the checklist would then look like this:

hexadecimal character, in range ['0' .. '9', 'A'.. 'F', 'a' .. 'f']

1	/	(ASCII character before '0')	(Test 3)
1	0		(Test 2)
1	9		(Test 3)
1	:	(ASCII character after '9')	(Test 3)
1	@	(ASCII character before 'A')	(Test 3)
0	A		
0	F		
1	G		(Test 3)
1	`	(ASCII character before 'a')	(Test 3)
0	a		
0	f		
1	g		(Test 3)
0	All of 1-8, B-E, b-e		

All the test's inputs are specified, except for the background value of STR. It should be something other than 9. The value 11 will do. Here's the test:

TEST 3:
>   STR, a 100-byte buffer, initialized to all 11's
>   RLEN = 1
>   *NREAD = 1000
>   *ODD_DIGIT = -1
>   S = "/:@ G`g9"
> EXPECT
>   STR = 11 11 ...
>   *NREAD = 0
>   *ODD_DIGIT = 9
>   S unchanged
>   return value 1

As always, some test requirements were satisfied by accident. I'll only point out the more interesting ones. NUM_HEX_CHARS=1 is satisfied again:

NUM_HEX_CHARS, a count of hexadecimal characters in S

2	1	(Test 2, 3)
0	all characters hexadecimal (more than one)	

Some of the searching requirements might be satisfied, since there are several elements in the string. There are two groups of identical requirements. It's irrelevant which goes with which byte. I'll consider the first digit in the byte to be the odd digit. That's consistent with the variable name ODD_DIGIT (which points to what goes there), though it's not consistent with the usual C convention.

When searching for the odd digit, several non-hexadecimal characters are skipped over, looking for the only match. That satisfies one of the requirements.

Precondition 7
1   RLEN = 0   ERROR   (Test 1)

Postcondition 1
     START+NUM_HEX_CHARS < RLEN*2, START+NUM_HEX_CHARS is even
0   START+NUM_HEX_CHARS = RLEN*2-2, START+NUM_HEX_CHARS is even
     START+NUM_HEX_CHARS >= RLEN*2, START+NUM_HEX_CHARS is even
1   START+NUM_HEX_CHARS = RLEN*2, START+NUM_HEX_CHARS is even
          (Test 2)
     START+NUM_HEX_CHARS < RLEN*2, START+NUM_HEX_CHARS is odd
**1   START+NUM_HEX_CHARS = RLEN*2-1, START+NUM_HEX_CHARS is odd
          (Test 3)**

Postcondition 2
     START+NUM_HEX_CHARS >= RLEN*2, START+NUM_HEX_CHARS is odd
0   START+NUM_HEX_CHARS = RLEN*2+1, START+NUM_HEX_CHARS is odd

STR, an array of bytes to be filled
1   a single element   (Test 2)
0   more than one element

RLEN, a count
2   RLEN=1   (Test 2, 3)

NREAD, a pointer to a count
1   0   (Test 3)

ODD_DIGIT, a pointer to an integer either -1 or [0..15]
1   -1   (Test 3)
0   0
1   15   (Test 2)

S, a string
1   a single element   (Test 2)

hexadecimal character, in range ['0' .. '9', 'A'.. 'F', 'a' .. 'f']
1   /   (ASCII character before '0')   (Test 3)
1   0   (Test 2)
1   9   (Test 3)
1   :   (ASCII character after '9')   (Test 3)
1   @   (ASCII character before 'A')   (Test 3)
0   A
0   F
1   G   (Test 3)
1   `   (ASCII character before 'a')   (Test 3)
0   a
0   f
1   g   (Test 3)
0   All of 1-8, B-E, b-e

NUM_HEX_CHARS, a count of hexadecimal characters in S
2   1   **(Test 2, 3)**
0   all characters hexadecimal (more than one)

number of unused hexadecimal characters in S, a count
0   >1

Searching for a value for an odd DIGIT.
0   all of several elements are hexadecimal (none filtered)
0   exactly one of several elements is not hexadecimal (one filtered)
     exactly one of several elements is hexadecimal (all but one filtered)
0   only hexadecimal character is first of several
1   **only hexadecimal character is last of several   (Test 3)**
0   none of several elements are hexadecimal (all filtered)

Searching for a value for an even DIGIT.
0   all of several elements are hexadecimal (none filtered)
0   exactly one of several elements is not hexadecimal (one filtered)
     exactly one of several elements is hexadecimal (all but one filtered)
0   only hexadecimal character is first of several
0   only hexadecimal character is last of several
0   none of several elements are hexadecimal (all filtered)

4.8.6 Test 4

It now seems that the searching requirements are likely to be the hardest to satisfy, mostly because there's so many of them. I might as well plan how to use all of them right now. Doing this requires two decisions: whether the value of *ODD_DIGIT will be placed in the odd digit (thus which digit is searched for first), and what the pattern of hexadecimal and non-hexadecimal characters will be.

To begin, I will choose *ODD_DIGIT to be in [0,15]. I'll represent a hexadecimal character with 'H', a non-hexadecimal character with 'n'. 'H...' will mean repeating a hexadecimal character one or more times. That given, consider this pattern:

nHHHH...

The first search is for an even digit (since *ODD_DIGIT goes in the odd digit). What that search sees is "exactly one of several characters is not hexadecimal". The second search has consumed the first character. Therefore, the search for an odd digit works with "HHH...", that is "all of several elements are hexadecimal". After that character is consumed, the next search for the even digit sees "HH...", which satisfies the same requirement in the other search. So, three searching requirements can be satisfied by that pattern.

Given *ODD_DIGIT in [0, 15], another pattern "Hnn..." satisfies "only hexadecimal is first of several" for the even search and "none of several elements are hexadecimal" for the odd search.

If *ODD_DIGIT is -1, the same pattern satisfies the same requirements, starting with the opposite search.

Finally, "HnH", with *ODD_DIGIT -1, satisfies "exactly one of several elements is not hexadecimal" for the odd digit and then "only hexadecimal character is last of several" for the even digit.

This raises a question. The loop requirements (from subsetting a single collection) never seemed to match this two-loop program very well. Their use was justified in two ways: by the chance that they'd find interactions or faults of omission, and by the likelihood that they'd be satisfied in tests being written anyway. These patterns make the first seem less likely than ever, since the variety in S doesn't translate into a great deal of variety in processing. As for the second, it will turn out that these four patterns require 33 percent more tests.

So what of the justification? It doesn't hold well for such a small subsystem. In a larger subsystem, a much smaller proportion of tests will be created just to satisfy marginal requirements. There will still be a cost (primarily increased test design time, occasionally more tests), but it pays for itself in bugs found—both targeted bugs and completely unsuspected bugs discovered by variety.

Test 4 will begin with the first pattern. *ODD_DIGIT can be 0, which has not been used so far.

```
TEST 4:
     STR, a 100-byte buffer, initialized to all ____
     RLEN = ___
     *NREAD = 1000
     *ODD_DIGIT = 0
     S = nHHHH...
EXPECT
     STR = ___
     *NREAD = ___
     *ODD_DIGIT = ___
     S unchanged
     return value ___
```

This is a good opportunity to use up many hexadecimal characters. I should be careful to leave at least one value untouched, for use as the background of STR. I'll pick 9 as that value. Here's a string that matches the pattern:

S = "/12345678ABCDEFabcdef"

This leaves out 9, and it satisfies this postcondition requirement:

0   START+NUM_HEX_CHARS = RLEN*2+1, START+NUM_HEX_CHARS is odd

provided RLEN is 10. To satisfy the requirement, it also had to leave out one more hexadecimal character (to get an odd number). I chose '0', which is already satisfied. The effect will be to use all of the characters but the final 'f' to fill STR. Note that the 'f' requirement shouldn't be counted as satisfied, since it has no effect (its value isn't used anywhere).

Here's the test:

TEST 4:
        STR, a 100-byte buffer, initialized to all 9's
        RLEN = 10
        *NREAD = 1000
        *ODD_DIGIT = 0
        S = "/12345678ABCDEFabcdef"
EXPECT
        STR = 0 1 2 3 4 5 6 7 8 10 11 12 13 14 15 10 11 12 13 14 9 9...
        *NREAD = 10
        *ODD_DIGIT = 0
        S unchanged
        return value 0

The checklist is shown below.

Checklist

Precondition 7
1   RLEN = 0   ERROR   (Test 1)

Postcondition 1
     START+NUM_HEX_CHARS < RLEN*2, START+NUM_HEX_CHARS is even
0   START+NUM_HEX_CHARS = RLEN*2-2, START+NUM_HEX_CHARS is even
     START+NUM_HEX_CHARS >= RLEN*2, START+NUM_HEX_CHARS is even
1   START+NUM_HEX_CHARS = RLEN*2, START+NUM_HEX_CHARS is even
                        (Test 2)
     START+NUM_HEX_CHARS < RLEN*2, START+NUM_HEX_CHARS is odd
1   START+NUM_HEX_CHARS = RLEN*2-1, START+NUM_HEX_CHARS is odd
                        (Test 3)

Postcondition 2
     START+NUM_HEX_CHARS >= RLEN*2, START+NUM_HEX_CHARS is odd
1   START+NUM_HEX_CHARS = RLEN*2+1, START+NUM_HEX_CHARS is odd
     (Test 4)

STR, an array of bytes to be filled
1   a single element   (Test 2)
1   more than one element   (Test 4)

RLEN, a count
2   RLEN=1   (Test 2, 3)

NREAD, a pointer to a count
1   0   (Test 3)
ODD_DIGIT, a pointer to an integer either -1 or [0..15]
1   -1   (Test 3)
1   0   (Test 4)
1   15   (Test 2)

S, a string
1   a single element   (Test 2)

hexadecimal character, in range ['0' .. '9', 'A'.. 'F', 'a' .. 'f']
2   /   (ASCII character before '0')   (Test 3, 4)
1   0   (Test 2)
1   9   (Test 3)
1   :   (ASCII character after '9')   (Test 3)
1   @   (ASCII character before 'A')(Test 3)
1   A   (Test 4)
1   F   (Test 4)
1   G   (Test 3)
1   `   (ASCII character before 'a') (Test 3)
1   a   (Test 4)
0   f
1   g   (Test 3)
1   All of 1-8, B-E, b-e   (Test 4)

NUM_HEX_CHARS, a count of hexadecimal characters in S
2   1   (Test 2, 3)
0   all characters hexadecimal (more than one)

number of unused hexadecimal characters in S, a count
0   >1

Searching for a value for an odd DIGIT.
1   all of several elements are hexadecimal (none filtered)   (Test 4)
0   exactly one of several elements is not hexadecimal (one filtered)
     exactly one of several elements is hexadecimal (all but one filtered)
0   only hexadecimal character is first of several
1   only hexadecimal character is last of several   (Test 3)
0   none of several elements are hexadecimal (all filtered)

Searching for a value for an even DIGIT.
1   all of several elements are hexadecimal (none filtered)   (Test 4)
1   exactly one of several elements is not hexadecimal (one filtered) (Test 4)
     exactly one of several elements is hexadecimal (all but one filtered)
0   only hexadecimal character is first of several
0   only hexadecimal character is last of several
0   none of several elements are hexadecimal (all filtered)

4.8.7 Tests 5, 6, and 7

There are three more tests based on the searching patterns.
They're straightforward. Each test satisfies a different postcondition,
they each use different hexadecimal characters, and even the background character is varied from test to test.

TEST 5: (satisfies Postcondition 1)
    STR, a 100-byte buffer, initialized to all 3's
    RLEN = 2
    *NREAD = 1000
    *ODD_DIGIT = 15
    S = "AgG@"
EXPECT
    STR = 15 10 3 3 ....
    *NREAD = 1
    *ODD_DIGIT = -1
    S unchanged
    return value 1

TEST 6: (satisfies Postcondition 2)
    STR, a 100-byte buffer, initialized to all 7's
    RLEN = 1
    *NREAD = 1000
    *ODD_DIGIT = -1
    S = "f`:"
EXPECT
    STR = 7 7 7...
    *NREAD = 0
    *ODD_DIGIT = 15[1]
    S unchanged
    return value 1

TEST 7: (satisfies Postcondition 3)
    STR, a 100-byte buffer, initialized to all 8's
    RLEN = 1
    *NREAD = 1000
    *ODD_DIGIT = -1
    S = "F/a"
EXPECT
    STR = 15 10 8 8 ...
    *NREAD = 1
    *ODD_DIGIT = -1
    S unchanged
    return value 0

The complete set of test requirements is shown after Test 8.

---

1. Chapter 3, Section 3.8 (Intervals) mentioned two missing test requirements: that the result value of *ODD_DIGIT be both 0 and 15. This is the only test that accidentally satisfies one of them. Earlier tests did leave *ODD_DIGIT as both 0 and 15, but they didn't set it, so the test requirement can't be considered exercised. The rule for test content is only satisfied by this test.

4.8.8 Test 8

Only two requirements are unsatisfied:

NUM_HEX_CHARS, a count of hexadecimal characters in S
4 1 (Tests 2, 3, 5, 6)
0 all characters hexadecimal (more than one)

number of unused hexadecimal characters in S, a count
0 >1

Neither of these is very compelling. However, too many of the non-error tests use RLEN=1 (all but Tests 4 and 5), and too many of them have only a single hexadecimal character (all but Tests 4 and 7). These unsatisfied requirements can even up the balance with a test more typical of expected use.

I will choose *ODD_DIGIT=0 because the other two requirements have been used more often. Here is the test:

```
TEST 8:
     STR, a 100-byte buffer, initialized to all 14
     RLEN = 7
     *NREAD = 1000
     *ODD_DIGIT = 0
     S = "ddcbf967605DFCBA"
EXPECT
     STR = 0 13 13 12 11 15 9 6 7 6 0 5 13 15 14 14...
     *NREAD = 7
     *ODD_DIGIT = 0 (unchanged)
     S unchanged
     return value 0
```

The last three characters of S are unused, so their requirements are not incremented. I made sure to exercise all hexadecimal boundary characters that had only been exercised once. I added duplicate characters, just because no test had done that before and it's easy to do.

Precondition 7
1   RLEN = 0   ERROR   (Test 1)

Postcondition 1
    START+NUM_HEX_CHARS < RLEN*2, START+NUM_HEX_CHARS is even
1   START+NUM_HEX_CHARS = RLEN*2-2, START+NUM_HEX_CHARS is even
         (Test 5)
    START+NUM_HEX_CHARS >= RLEN*2, START+NUM_HEX_CHARS is even
2   START+NUM_HEX_CHARS = RLEN*2, START+NUM_HEX_CHARS is even
         (Test 2,7)
    START+NUM_HEX_CHARS < RLEN*2, START+NUM_HEX_CHARS is odd
2   START+NUM_HEX_CHARS = RLEN*2-1, START+NUM_HEX_CHARS is odd
         (Test 3,6)

Postcondition 2
    START+NUM_HEX_CHARS >= RLEN*2, START+NUM_HEX_CHARS is odd
1   START+NUM_HEX_CHARS = RLEN*2+1, START+NUM_HEX_CHARS is odd
                                      (Test 4)

STR, an array of bytes to be filled
3   a single element   (Test 2,5,7)
2   more than one element   (Test 4, 8)

RLEN, a count
2   RLEN=1   (Test 2, 3, 6, 7)

NREAD, a pointer to a count
1   0   (Test 3, 6)

ODD_DIGIT, a pointer to an integer either -1 or [0..15]
3   -1   (Test 3, 6, 7)
2   0   (Test 4, 8)
2   15   (Test 2, 5)

S, a string
1   a single element   (Test 2)

hexadecimal character, in range ['0' .. '9', 'A'.. 'F', 'a' .. 'f']
3   /   (ASCII character before '0')   (Test 3, 4, 7)
2   0   (Test 2, 8)
2   9   (Test 3, 8)
2   :   (ASCII character after '9')   (Test 3, 6)
2   @   (ASCII character before 'A')   (Test 3, 5)
2   A   (Test 4,5)
2   F   (Test 4, 7, 8)
2   G   (Test 3, 5)
2   `   (ASCII character before 'a')   (Test 3, 6)
2   a   (Test 4, 7)
2   f   (Test 6, 8)
2   g   (Test 3, 5)
1   All of 1-8, B-E, b-e   (Test 4)

NUM_HEX_CHARS, a count of hexadecimal characters in S

4	1	(Test 2, 3, 5, 6)
1	all characters hexadecimal (more than one)	(Test 8)

number of unused hexadecimal characters in S, a count

1	>1	(Test 8)

Searching for a value for an odd DIGIT.

2	all of several elements are hexadecimal (none filtered)	(Test 4,8)
1	exactly one of several elements is not hexadecimal (one filtered)	(Test 7)
	exactly one of several elements is hexadecimal (all but one filtered)	
1	only hexadecimal character is first of several	(Test 6)
1	only hexadecimal character is last of several	(Test 3)
1	none of several elements are hexadecimal (all filtered)	(Test 5)

Searching for a value for an even DIGIT.

2	all of several elements are hexadecimal (none filtered)	(Test 4,8)
1	exactly one of several elements is not hexadecimal (one filtered)	(Test 4)
	exactly one of several elements is hexadecimal (all but one filtered)	
1	only hexadecimal character is first of several	(Test 5)
1	only hexadecimal character is last of several	(Test 7)
1	none of several elements are hexadecimal (all filtered)	(Test 6)

---

sreadhex has eight tests. Given the appropriate support code, these can be implemented and executed without any further thought. After execution, the test's quality can be evaluated and improved.

Test design led to a specification bug. This is not uncommon. It's also not uncommon for the act of constructing test specifications to suggest new clues.

4.9
Where Do We Stand?

5

Test Drivers and
Suite Drivers

All the tests for a product should be collected into a *regression test suite*. Whenever the system changes, the relevant portions of the suite must be run again to see if what used to work still does. Unfortunately, there's no infallible way of finding all relevant tests. For this reason, it's useful to rerun the entire test suite periodically. The more often the entire suite is run, the quicker you'll find bugs caused by changes and the easier it will be to discover what change introduced the fault. On the smaller products I work on now, I run the entire test suite overnight. On larger products where the test suite took longer to run, I ran a fraction of it each night. In the morning, my first task was to check the log of the last night's run to see if any new failures had been discovered.

You cannot use a test suite effectively unless it's automated. Manual tests will not be run often enough. Further, manual testing means manual checking of correctness. This is simply too error-prone.

Tools for automating a regression test suite can be arbitrarily fancy, but there are two essential components.

1. Each test was designed with exact inputs and exact expected outputs. The *test driver* runs one or more tests. It presents the inputs to the subsystem and collects the actual outputs. It compares the actual outputs to the expected outputs. It clearly reports any discrepancy as a failure. It cleans up after itself (except when the test fails—in that case, the residue can help in diagnosing the problem).

2. The *suite driver* runs all or part of the regression test suite. It compares the result of this run to the record of a previous run. Are there any new failures? If so, a bug fix might have caused a new bug. Have any failures unexpectedly gone away? The fault probably wasn't fixed by accident; it's still present, but the failure is now obscured. You're now worse off because you have no clues to help you discover the fault.

Much of what a test driver does depends on the program under test. There are two design issues that apply to every test driver: delivering the inputs and comparing the expected and actual outputs.

5.1.1 Delivering Inputs to the Subsystem

There is little to say on this topic. You have to write code to do this, and that code is usually obvious from the test design, the subsystem you've chosen, and any tools other people have already written.

The driver should completely initialize the subsystem's environment before running the test. This avoids annoying problems like tests that only fail when a particular person runs them.

It is slightly preferable to separate the test inputs from the code that delivers them, typically by putting inputs in one or more separate data files. This simplifies test maintenance.

5.1.2 Comparing Actual and Expected Results

The driver compares actual and expected results. I prefer it to be quiet except when there's a failure. For example, here's the result of running one test in the test suite for the Generic Coverage Tool:

```
== multi3
```

The name of the test is printed. Any other output from the test is a test failure. This makes it quick and reliable to scan any collection of test output for failures (a line not beginning with an equal sign is a failure; the previous line with an equal sign identifies the test).

The means by which the comparison is done depends on the subsystem you're testing. If the subsystem produces text, comparison is simple. Create a file of expected output called the *reference file*. Capture the actual output in a *log file*. Use your system's file-comparison tools on the two files. If the subsystem doesn't produce text, consider ways that it might. For example, when testing some routines that manipulated a hash table, I modified a programmer's debugging routine to print the hash table to a file; that file was compared to an expected printout. This topic is discussed in more detail in Chapter 13.

Whenever possible, put the expected output into the reference file before running the test. Avoid running the test, checking the log file, then copying the log file into the reference file. By doing this, you stand a much greater chance of not noticing a failure, then "immortalizing" it by making it the reference output.

Sometimes it is impossible or very difficult to write the reference file in advance. For example, a subsystem's output may contain a lot of information other than what you're testing. Here are two tricks I use to reduce the chance of making errors in such a case.

1. I run the test and create the log file. I copy the log file to the reference file. Then I remove the essential part of the reference file without looking at it, leaving the part I'm not testing. I edit the reference file, adding my expected values. *Then* I compare the reference file

and the log file. The number of times there's a difference due to my predictions being wrong is sobering.

2. When testing the hash table, the location and order of entries in the hash table were irrelevant to correctness. Predicting them would have been a waste of time, but without such a prediction building a reference file in advance was impossible. I resigned myself to checking the log file and making it the reference file. But, to reduce the chance of missing a failure, the test prefaces the printout with expected values:

CHECK: Bucket 0 should contain (FIRST, FILE0_1_1, 1, 1)
CHECK: Its duplicate list should contain (FIRST, NULL, 0, -1)
CHECK: Bucket 0 should contain (FIRST2, NULL, 0, 2) (unchanged)
CHECK: Any primary with a non-empty duplicate list has allow_dups true
CHECK: All files in a duplicate chain have string-equal names
CHECK: All string-equal entries are linked together

Sometimes file comparisons will not work; it's too hard to translate the results of a test into text. In this case, the checking must be done by code.

Occasionally, you'll be lucky enough have an *oracle*, a program that can check correctness for you. For example, suppose you're testing a `sin` routine and you have an `arcsin` routine you trust. Rather than writing a large number of tests like

    expect(approx_equal(sin(0), 0));
    expect(approx_equal(sin(1), 0.841471));
    expect(approx_equal(sin(PI), 0));

where you have to calculate the correct result, you can simply write:

    expect(approx_equal(arcsin(sin(0)), 0));
    expect(approx_equal(arcsin(sin(1)), 1));
    expect(approx_equal(arcsin(sin(PI)), PI));

This is better because you do not have to generate the expected result. Indeed, in this case, a sensible testing approach would be to try designed tests and then try a few million random inputs. Beware, though: If `arc-sin` and `sin` were written by the same person, they might contain complementary mistakes.

These tests use a couple of typical utility routines. The macro `expect` prints a failure message and line number if its argument is false. The macro `approx_equal` is used to test approximate equality, which is always useful in numerical tests.

Another type of oracle is the *gold program*, which you assume to be correct, perhaps because it's the system this system is to replace. Beware, though, that some studies have shown that common-mode failures can cause independently developed programs to fail identically [Knight86].

Most often, you'll have to write code that explicitly checks the correctness of the subsystem's result. Take care that when your checking code discovers a failure, it reports it clearly, so that people scanning the test log do not miss it.

The suite driver runs the entire test suite or some part of it. It records the result of each test (usually by simply passing along the test driver's output). This record is called the *history file*. Here's a part of an old history file for one of my programs:

```
==== routine/
====== routine
====== routine2
====== rout-comb1
====== rout-comb2
====== rout-comb3
====== rout-comb4
====== rout-bug
====== call
====== call2
====== call-comb
call-comb.c:74: Couldn't create 'T' file.
call-comb.c:74: Failed:   cp /usr/tmp/gcta20173 Tcall-comb.c
==== race/
====== race1
====== race2
====== race3
```

The lines not beginning with "==" are a failure. As long as that fault remains unfixed, it will show up in the history file. The history file is thus not a record of what running the test suite *should* look like, but a record of what it actually looks like. By comparing a saved history file with the history file from the latest test suite run, you can track the status of the system to see if failures that were supposed to have been fixed have been fixed, whether new failures have been introduced, and whether old failures have mysteriously disappeared or changed symptoms.

In order to emphasize that the complete test development process is analogous to the software development process, Bill Hetzel speaks of "testware engineering" [SQE85]. The term is a good one because it encourages you to plan what you'll do before you do it. Because testware is not the same as deliverable product, your plans will be different.

The tests themselves are the major component of testware. This book is mostly about how the engineering of tests is different from the engineering of software. But for substantial subsystems, test drivers and suite drivers can be significant software in their own right, and they should be developed using a conventional software engineering process. However, one difference may be the extent to which drivers are themselves tested. All software is tested (or inspected) when the expected benefit justifies the work. Since the purpose of drivers is different than the purpose of customer-visible software, you need to think separately about how much testing is justified. I claim drivers should often be tested less thoroughly than product.

What are the risks of undertesting drivers?

1. A fault in the drivers may mask a fault in the subsystem by transmuting failures into apparent successes. This will result in the ultimate harm (a subsystem fault being passed onto the customer) only if it masks every failure the subsystem fault causes in the test suite, and if the driver's fault isn't discovered for another reason. The odds of a fault escaping by that route are usually low—but they depend on your subsystem and drivers, so you should think about the risk.

2. Finding a driver fault during use is more expensive than finding it while testing the driver. But the differential is probably much smaller than the folk theorem ratio that "faults found after shipping product are ten times as expensive as faults found during test." The smaller differential argues for less thorough testing. How much less depends on how the drivers are to be used now and on the likely future maintenance. Drivers to be used throughout a world-spanning organization need thorough testing. Drivers to be used by people in the same hallway need less.

The problem with simple, straightforward, general answers is that they're always wrong. Better answers come from situation-specific questions: Will you find more subsystem faults by testing the drivers or by spending that time using them? In the short term? In the long term?

5.4
The SREADHEX
Driver

Normally, I would test `sreadhex` via Ghostscript or some major subsystem. That would save me the expense of writing scaffolding code, and it would exercise other parts of the program. For this example, `sreadhex` is tested directly. The tests invoke it, collect its results, and compare them to the expected results.

5.4.1 Directory and File Structure

Despite testing a routine directly, I try to keep it in its natural environment. That means placing the tests in a subdirectory of the source directory, where they are less likely to get lost and more likely to be run after changes. This also means the routine is not extracted from its original source file; rather, the entire file is compiled into the test using a compilation such as:

```
cc ../source.c tests.c utilities.c
```

That's a little more work when the tests are created, and changes to *../source.c* are more likely to cause problems compiling the test (usually trivial problems, such as a new reference to a global that's defined in some other file and now has to have a dummy version defined in *utilities.c*). This extra work pays off because there are no problems keeping extracted copies up to date. It also makes it easier to use functions called by the function under test, rather than having to separately extract them or write special-purpose stubs.

Many tests are run by the same executable. This catches bugs due to incorrect changes to the program state. The skeleton for the `sreadhex` test file looks like:

```
main()
{
    run test 1...
    run test 2...
    ...
}
```

In the first test, `sreadhex` will run its initialization code; in the remainder, it won't. If every test were in its own executable, we'd have no evidence `sreadhex` works more than once. But Ghostscript (the product that contains it) will certainly call it more than once, so we'd like some.

5.4.2 Drivers and Stubs

A single test looks like this:

```
printf("=== TEST 1\n");
init_bytes(str, STRLEN, 1);
odd_digit=15;
nread=1000;
s_orig = "a";
strcpy(s, s_orig);
retval = sreadhex(str, 0, &nread, &odd_digit, s);
expect(strcmp(s, s_orig)==0);
expect(nread==0);
expect(odd_digit==15);
expect(retval==0);
check_digits(str, STRLEN, nread, 1);
```

Test output is printed to standard output. Any line not beginning with an equal sign is a failure. Failure messages also begin with the string "FAILURE".

A few utility routines are used:

1. `init_bytes` initializes the entire `str` to the value specified in the test design. It also initializes the byte before `str` to the same value.

2. `expect` is a C preprocessor macro that will print the following sort of message unless its argument is true:

   FAILURE (line 29): odd_digit==1 was false.

3. `check_digits` takes a byte array, its maximum length, the amount actually filled by `sreadhex`, the background value for the remaining bytes, and the value for each of the digits that was filled in. Here's its call for test 6:

   check_digits(str, STRLEN, nread, 5, 0, 10, 15, 9);

   The first four digits are expected to be 0, 10, 15, and 9. All the remaining digits are expected to be 5.

5.4.3 Running the Tests

Here are the results of invoking *run-suite*:

```
% run-suite
== Tcomplete
=== TEST 1
FAILURE: Background byte 0 (of a total of 100) is incorrect.
FAILURE: Expected 0x11, got 0xFA.
STR array has nread 0 (total length 100), contents:
FA1111111111111111111111111111111111111111111111111111111111111111
1111111111111111111111111111111111111111111111111111111111111111111
1111111111111111111111111111111111111111111111111111111
=== TEST 2
=== TEST 3
=== TEST 4
=== TEST 5
=== TEST 6
=== TEST 7
=== TEST 8
```

Precondition 7, where `rlen==0`, is not handled correctly. The program overwrote the first byte when it should have done nothing. The fault is only detectable if you think to check the background (which, in this case, is all of STR). It's interesting to note that the failure would have been more obvious if ODD_DIGIT had been -1. Here's the test with that change to the input (and the corresponding required change to ODD_DIGIT's expected output value):

```
printf("=== TEST 1\n");
init_bytes(str, STRLEN, 1);
odd_digit=-1;              /* Changed from 15 */
nread=1000;
s_orig = "a";
strcpy(s, s_orig);
retval = sreadhex(str, 0, &nread, &odd_digit, s);
expect(strcmp(s, s_orig)==0);
expect(nread==0);
expect(odd_digit==-1);     /* Changed from 15 */
expect(retval==0);
check_digits(str, STRLEN, nread, 1);
```

Here's the result of running the test:

```
% run-one Talt-test1
== Talt-test1
=== TEST 1
FAILURE (line 29): odd_digit==-1 was false.
FAILURE (line 30): retval==0 was false.
```

In these results the return value is wrong and odd_digit is overwritten. When I used `sreadhex` as a homework assignment in a testing class, six of fourteen students detected the fault. They had all tested Precondition 7 with ODD_DIGIT -1. The remaining eight students had also tested Precondition 7, but they used another value for ODD_DIGIT. All of them failed to check the background, so all of them missed the failure.[1]

5.5 Where Do We Stand?

A log file contains the actual results of a particular test. A reference file contains the expected results. If they are different, there's a bug in either the program, the specification, or the test.

A test driver executes a test and reports on success or failure. A suite driver does the same for an entire set of tests. In most cases, a run of the suite driver will reveal some failures. None of them should be surprises, since they should have been reported when the test was originally written. New failures are bad news. So are unexpected successes. You know when they've happened by comparing a new run of the test suite to the history file, which contains a record of which tests are known to pass and which are known to fail.

---

1. Needless to say, I emphasize the rules for test content much more strongly now. Also, I'd given them a different sort of utility routine to check the str array. The version of check_digits described above makes it obvious that you should check the background; the one they got didn't provide that hint.

Inspecting Code with the Question Catalog

Some types of faults are very difficult to detect with testing. For example, suppose your program allocates memory but fails to release it, or opens files but fails to close them. Such "resource leaks" are often visible only when the program runs for many hours or days. Inspections are the best way of finding them (though there are specialized tools that can move certain types of memory-use faults into the realm of the testable).

Therefore, you must inspect your code. You have to test as well because there are some kinds of faults that escape inspections. People are too good at adopting the assumptions of the designer, for example, by believing that a library routine does what it "obviously" does. The computer, executing a test case, is immune to assumptions, so it can reveal those errors. People also miss subtle interaction faults because they can't keep enough detail in their heads. (That's why they make them, too.) Computers have no trouble with detail.

And there are many faults that both inspections and testing will find. The question, then, is which to favor. I believe in using inspections for what testing cannot do and relying on testing for the bulk of bug-finding.[1] The reason is that testing builds a safety net. You can be sure that many maintenance changes to the subsystem will contain subtle faults. You'll either test or inspect for them—the techniques given in Chapter 14 are suitable for either approach. But you'll inevitably miss some. If you've built a thorough automated test suite that exercises the entire subsystem, there's hope that some test not designed for the change will nevertheless catch the bug. If you don't have a thorough test suite, no one will catch it but a customer.

---

1. Of course, some faults, such as "variable used before set," are best found by static analysis tools or smart compilers. Those should be run, and any faults they discover fixed, before either inspections or testing.

A Question Catalog for Inspections (Appendix D) gives an inspection checklist. It is intended to be used as a supplement to whatever style of inspections, code reviews, or walkthroughs you use now. If you don't use any, I recommend [Freedman90].

The procedure for using the question catalog is simple. For each procedure (or other chunk of code), scan the catalog. First check whether the question applies anywhere, next whether the answer is yes. A yes answer means a probable fault.[1]

You shouldn't rely solely on the question catalog. During design, development, and testing of the subsystem, build your own subsystem-specific question catalog to help you target likely faults in the subsystem. Concentrate especially on faults you predict might happen during maintenance. As an example, here's the question catalog at the head of the *gct-strans.c* file in the Generic Coverage Tool. (In this case, "no" means a fault.)

```
* 1. Have only copies of temporaries been used?
* 2. Has the original value of temporary_id been freed?
* 3. Does the instrumented tree have the same type as the original tree?
* 4. If locals are set pointing to parts of a tree, is the tree still the same when
*     the locals are used (else they might point to the wrong place)?
* 5. Are locals set to values derived from the root of an instrumented tree?
* 6. Do the mapfile entries read from left to right?
* 7. Is SELF built into the resulting instrumented tree?
* 8. Is any temporary_id that is an initialized non-static declared
*     OUTERMOST? (See gct-temps.c.)
*/
```

Keeping such code-specific checklists with the code increases the chance that they'll be used (and used before the fault is created).

6.1 Obligations

One useful way to build such a code-specific checklist is to think of obligations [Perry89]. Obligations are a third part of the specification, related to preconditions and postconditions. A precondition says what the caller must do before the call. A postcondition says what the called subsystem must do during the call. An obligation says what must happen at some point after the call. A specification for the standard C library routine `malloc(size)` might read:

Postcondition 1:
    IF SIZE bytes of memory are available
    THEN a pointer to a block of at least SIZE bytes is returned
    ELSE 0 is returned and ERRNO is set to ENOMEM.

Obligations:
    The memory must be freed with free() or realloc().

An obligation can also say what mustn't happen. On UNIX, information about a user can be gotten with the `getpwnam(name)` function. Its specification would look something like this:

---

1. This style of inspections was inspired by [Parnas85].

Precondition 1:
>Validated: NAME must be in the password file.
>On failure: ...

Postcondition 1:
>A pointer to the corresponding password file entry is
>returned. The password entry is a `struct passwd`
>and has the following form: ...

Obligations:
>The entry is contained in a static area, not
>dynamically allocated memory. Therefore it must not be freed.
>Do not access the return value after the next call; it will
>be overwritten.

Preconditions and postconditions can be tested at a single point (just after the subsystem produces results). Obligations usually cannot. If an obligation is satisfied along one path through the program, it may not be satisfied along any other. The difficulty is compounded because obligation failures are often not very observable. Failure to free memory may have no external effect for many hours, until the system runs out of memory. For these reasons, obligations lend themselves to inspections.

I find it valuable to carefully document the obligations of every routine. When a routine calls another, it either fulfills the obligations, or it documents them as obligations for its own caller. The simplest way for a routine that calls `malloc` to fulfill the obligation is to call `free`. The simplest documentation is simply to repeat the obligation:

Obligations:
>Global permanent_name is assigned storage. That
>storage must be freed with free() or realloc().

But other ways of fulfilling or documenting obligations are acceptable, as long as the programmer's intent is documented well enough that another person reading the calling code will ask the right questions. (Those being questions that will reveal a fault, if one exists.) For example, suppose `malloc` is called to obtain storage that is never to be freed. In that case, the caller might change the documentation:

Obligations:
>Global permanent_name is assigned storage. That
>storage must never be freed.

The subsystem could also simply not pass the obligation along to its caller, instead handling it like this:

```
permanent_name = (nametype) malloc(size);
/* Malloc obligation is ignored—this is permanent storage */
```

Which of the two is most appropriate depends on the chance that a caller might incorrectly call `free(permanent_name)`. (Since `permanent_name` is a global, every routine called after its allocation *could* free it, even those that don't use it at all. It would be unreasonable to pass the obligation along to all those routines. At some point, the obligation would have to be dropped from the documentation.)

Inspecting a routine means double-checking:

1. Reading the headers for every called subroutine
2. Listing all the obligations
3. Checking whether the routine in question either fulfills or documents them

I have prevented many faults by writing down obligations, and caught a few in the inspections.

The inspection can be done without the benefit of documentation by discovering the obligations in the code. It is then best to add them as documentation.

6.2 Inspecting SREADHEX

The procedure for inspections is to prop the source up on one side, open the *Question Catalog for Code Inspections* on the other side, firmly plant the coffee cup in the middle, and step through the catalog. You can refer to the code in Fig. 6–1 (on page 144).

The first match in the catalog is "Buffers".

- Are there always size checks when copying into the buffer?
- Is this buffer ever too small to hold its contents?

> ➡ *For example, one program had no size checks when reading data into a 12-character buffer because the correct data would always fit. But when the file it read was accidentally overwritten with incorrect data, the program crashed mysteriously.*

The sreadhex tests do a good job of checking for overflow. Not all tests can do that, which is why the question is in the catalog. It doesn't hurt to check again. limit points past the last byte to be filled. Values are placed into str *before* the bounds check on line 69. If ptr is initially equal to limit, as it would be if rlen were 0, the background will be overwritten. This is the same bug already discovered in testing.[1]

decoder is also a buffer. It looks correctly sized.

None of the other catalog entries show problems.

---

1. When I used this program as a homework assignment in a testing class at the University of Illinois, none of the people who failed to find the fault through testing discovered it in inspections. Since then, using different homeworks, I've been continually surprised by how bad people can be at finding relatively simple faults through inspections. In industrial settings, I've also seen wide variations in success at using inspections (using various different inspection techniques).

Fig. 6-1
The SREADHEX
code

```
41   sreadhex(str, rlen, nread, odd_digit, s)
42     byte *str;
43     uint rlen;
44     uint *nread;
45     int *odd_digit;
46     register byte *s;
47   {   byte *ptr = str;
48       byte *limit = ptr + rlen;
49       byte val1 = (byte)*odd_digit;
50       byte val2;
51       register char *decoder = (char *)(decode_hex + 1); /* EOFC = -1! */
52
53       if ( decoder[-1] == 0 )              /* not initialized yet */
54       {   static char hex_chars[] = "0123456789ABCDEFabcdef";
55           int i;
56           memset(decoder - 1, hex_none, 257);
57           for (i = 0; i < 16+6; i++)
58             decoder[hex_chars[i]] = (i >= 16 ? i - 6 : i);
59           decoder[0] = hex_eofc;
60       }
61       if ( val1 <= 0xf ) goto d2;
62   d1:  while ( (val1 = decoder[sgetc(s)]) > 0xf )
63         {   if ( val1 == hex_eofc ) { *odd_digit = -1; goto ended; }
64         }
65   d2:  while ( (val2 = decoder[sgetc(s)]) > 0xf )
66         {   if ( val2 == hex_eofc ) { *odd_digit = val1; goto ended; }
67         }
68       *ptr++ = (val1 << 4) + val2;
69       if ( ptr < limit ) goto d1;
70       *nread = rlen;
71       return 0;
72   ended:*nread = ptr - str;
73       return 1;
74   }
```

Using Coverage
to Test the Test Suite

A good test suite should thoroughly exercise the code. This thoroughness can be measured. Four useful measures are branch coverage, multicondition coverage, loop coverage, and relational operator coverage.

Branch Coverage

In branch coverage, you measure whether every branch in the subsystem has been taken in every possible direction. For example, in

```
func(count)
{
    if (count % 2 == 0)
        printf("count is even.\n");
    for(; count < 5; count++)
        printf("count %d\n", count);
}
```

the `if` statement would need `count` both even and odd. The test of the `for` loop must evaluate true at least once and false at least once. Full coverage could be achieved in two tests:

```
func(4);
func(13);
```

Branch coverage is one widely used measure. Three other types of coverage are also useful.

Multicondition Coverage

Multicondition coverage [Myers79] is stronger than branch coverage. It requires that every logical operand take on all possible values. For example, for

if (A && B)

multicondition coverage requires that A be both true and false and that B be both true and false. Notice that branch coverage is satisfied with the two inputs (A=1,B=1) and (A=0, B=1), but multicondition coverage is not. In the C language, it would require these cases:

A true, B true
A true, B false
A false, B irrelevant

(B is irrelevant because of short-circuit evaluation of &&—if A is false, the value of B is unevaluated and may be meaningless, as in if (p && p > field == 3).)

Multicondition coverage provides a good illustration of how coverage can indirectly reveal faults. Consider this common C fault:

if (A > 0 && B = 1)

The second clause is incorrect. Branch coverage will be satisfied by

A == 1, B == *anything*
A == 0, B == *anything*

so it won't force fault-revealing inputs. However, multicondition coverage is impossible to satisfy because of the fault—a fact that will be revealed when coverage results are examined. A similar observation was made by [Holthouse79].

Loop Coverage

Neither of the two coverage measures above force the detection of bugs that exhibit themselves only when a loop is executed more than once. For a loop like

while (test)
body

loop coverage requires three conditions:

1. that the test be false on its first evaluation so the body is not executed.
2. that the test be true the first time, then false, so the body is executed exactly once.
3. that the test be true at least twice, forcing at least two executions of the loop.

There are some kinds of faults that can be detected only in one of these three cases. For example, incorrect initialization is not done if the loop is never entered, and its effects may be obscured if the loop executes twice.

Or consider a test-at-the-top loop that is intended to sum up the elements of an array:

```
sum = 0;
while (i > 0)
{
    i -= 1;
    sum = pointer[i];      /* Should be += */
}
```

This program will give the wrong answer only when the loop is executed more than once.

Of the three conditions, taking the loop exactly once seems to find the fewest faults. I have, however, seen one rather embarrassing fault that could only be discovered by a single execution of a loop. As it happened, the first user of that software—me—tried it out the first time on exactly such a case, saw the failure, and concluded the program didn't work at all.

You may have noticed that some catalog entries, such as Collections, contain "none," "one," and "more than one" requirements. Loop coverage helps you discover when you missed these clues.

Relational Coverage

Relational coverage checks whether the subsystem has been exercised in a way that tends to detect off-by-one errors. A typical cause of these errors is using < instead of <=. In such a case,

```
if (A < 5)
    return 0;
else
    return 1;
```

should have been

```
if (A <= 5)
    return 0;
else
    return 1;
```

Simply exercising the branch true or false may not detect the fault. Suppose your two test cases are

```
A=0
A=100
```

The program produces the correct results for both tests—the fault is not found. The only case that can detect the fault is when A=5. Relational coverage requires this boundary condition.

It also requires the other side of the boundary. Suppose the programmer made an off-by-one error in choosing the constant so that the correct program would be:

```
if (A < 4)
     return 0;
else
     return 1;
```

A=4 detects this fault, whereas A=5 would not, so you need both values. (If you look in the catalog, you'll find test requirements for relational operators that force these values.)

7.2
Infeasible
Coverage

If a branch has never been taken in the true direction, a coverage tool could print out

"lc.c", line 271: if was taken TRUE 0, FALSE 28 times.

This could be considered a test requirement. For reasons explained later, it's called a *coverage condition* instead.

A coverage condition may be impossible to satisfy. For example, the loop

```
for (i = 0; i < 100; i++)
{
     printf("%d\n", i);
}
```

can never be executed zero times or exactly once.

As another example, "sanity checking" a code like this is not unusual:

```
if (<something "impossible" happens>)
  panic("Program internal error: ...");
```

Most often, these sanity checks are correct and no test can force the branch in the true direction. (Of course, they're also sometimes wrong. You have to think hard before accepting a sanity check.)

Coverage conditions of these two types are called *infeasible coverage conditions*.

7.3
Using
Coverage
Information

(The discussion in this section assumes you had enough time for complete subsystem testing. If you didn't, or if the subsystem is inherently hard to exercise (which really amounts to the same thing), you use coverage differently. (See Part 3.)

You should expect nearly 100 percent feasible coverage. Anything less represents a deficiency in your tests. Surely you'd rather not have a customer be the first person in history to exercise the code in the else part of an if?

Let's assume you get 95 percent coverage, a typical number. How should the remaining 5 percent be handled? A few conditions will probably be test implementation mistakes—the test doesn't do what you intended. Those are usually easy to fix. But there will still be some design mistakes or omissions. The wrong way to fix them is to treat the list of missed coverage conditions as test requirements. Writing a set of tests that satisfies each condition will reach 100 percent coverage, but it probably will not repair all the deficiencies. The reason is faults of omission. Consider this code:

```
a = b / c;
```

which should read

```
if (c != 0)
  a = b / c;
```

Since you are testing the incorrect program, a coverage tool can't tell you that you need a test where c is zero. It can't measure the coverage of a branch that doesn't exist.

What a coverage tool can tell you is where to find weak areas in your test design. That is, coverage can provide clues.

Suppose your coverage tool produces this line:

"lc.c", line 271: if was taken TRUE 0, FALSE 28 times.

In a program that processes C source, line 271 might be this if:

```
if (close_quote_not_seen)
{
  error("Unterminated character constant");
}
```

That tells you that you've never tested an error case like this:

```
main()
{
  putchar('X);          /* No closing quote */
}
```

It is also likely that you failed to test handling of other incorrect characters, such as quotes containing nothing, characters too big to fit in a byte, and so on. Those are all requirements for an undertested clue:

incorrect quoted characters
    unterminated
    empty
    too big for a byte
    containing unquoted quote mark

You'll find bugs if the programmer forgot the same special cases you did.

When examining missed coverage, follow this procedure:

1. Ask if the coverage condition is impossible (as, for example, in a sanity check or automatically generated code). If so, ignore it.
2. Find existing clues corresponding to the condition. What preconditions or postconditions would have to be triggered to exercise it? Is it part of any clichéd operation, such as a searching loop or streaming operation? What variables are involved? For example, if a loop has never been taken once, you may realize the loop operates on some input Stream and a Collection that's being filled.
3. Try also to think of new clues, not just underexercised old clues.
4. Find new test requirements for underexercised clues. Use all of the normal techniques, especially the catalogs and error guessing.
5. Measure coverage again and repeat until you reach 100 percent feasible coverage.

The 100 percent rule, like any other, can occasionally be broken. If you convince yourself (better, someone else) that exercising a coverage condition would not be cost-effective, you can substitute a careful code review. Consider code that handles hardware errors by immediately shutting down the system:

```
if (<strange transient error happens>)
    shutdown_now();
```

Assuming that you've tested shutdown_now, and that you're convinced that the if's test-expression correctly identifies the transient error, testing this might be of little use. Suppose, on the other hand, that the error is handled by a complicated recovery procedure. Faults in such procedures are fairly common, in large part because the programmer may inadvertently depend on assumptions that the original error invalidates. Such faults are hard to find in inspections, because the reader tends to make those same inadequate assumptions. Testing works better: the computer doesn't make assumptions, it just executes code.

Even if you decide to "satisfy" coverage by reviewing the code, you should still think of undertested clues and requirements. Use those in the inspection.

How much does all this cost? It's more work than blindly forcing coverage. But, in my own testing, adding tests to satisfy coverage this way adds about 4 percent to the total testing cost. If I simply forced 100 percent coverage the easy way, I might spend only 2 percent. The cost difference is negligible, but the chance of finding extra faults is not.

If you reach much less than 100 percent feasible coverage, that's not just a clue to improve the test suite, it's also a clue to improve the test *process*. If you don't get nearly 100 percent by the normal means, fix the normal means. Special-purpose catalogs might help, as might more training. Or perhaps subsystem testing itself needs to be improved.

7.3.1 An Example of the Cost of Coverage

I spent roughly a month testing a critical 2600 line module. The overall coverage of those tests was 86 percent. The feasible coverage was

96 percent. Of the 129 uncovered coverage conditions, 74 were impossible, 17 were from deliberately untested temporary code, 24 were due to a major feature that had never had repeatable tests written for it, and 14 corresponded to 10 untested minor features.

Completely testing the major feature required four hours of work for design and implementation. This testing discovered one fault. A test designed solely to achieve coverage would likely have missed it. (That is, the uncovered conditions could have been satisfied by an easy and obvious—but inadequate—test.)

Testing the minor features required two hours. Branch coverage discovered one pseudo-fault: dead code. A particular special case check was incorrect. It was testing a variable against the wrong constant. This check could never be true, so the special case code was never executed. However, the special case code turned out to have the same effect as the normal code.

After fixing the faults, I reran the entire test suite to see if all expected coverage conditions had been satisfied. I found that one had not. A typo caused the test to use the wrong inputs. Finding this test error and correcting it took a half hour. (Running the test suite took none of my time, since it's completely automated.)

This work—six and one half hours—was a small part of the total testing effort. Of the two faults, one could never cause a failure, and the other would cause a failure only in rather obscure C programs, so the effort of finding them was arguably not worth it. However, the knowledge that I had a thorough test suite increased my confidence considerably. No faults have since been found in that module.

7.3.2 An Example of the Need for Careful Use of Coverage

As an illustration of the dangers of simplistic interpretations of coverage, recall the bug in Chapter 4 that involved exiting within an INCLUDE file when the input was from the terminal. Here's the code again. It handles the EXIT command.

```
if (Input_from_terminal)        /* Global variable set at startup */
{
    if (work_in_progress)
    {
        ...
        note("Work in progress.");
        note("Y to complete work and exit.");
        note("N to cancel work and exit.");
        note("I to ignore the EXIT and continue.");
        readline(buffer);
        switch(buffer[0])
        {
            case Y: ...; break;
            case N: ...; break;
            default:                /* Note: anything else resumes */
                continue;
        }
    }
}
```

The failure happened only when both `ifs` were taken true and the EXIT was in an INCLUDE file. A simplistic test suite that misses the failure can easily achieve perfect coverage.

Suppose, though, there was no test where case Y was taken. Because the code nowhere mentions INCLUDE files (a fault of omission), coverage provides no hint that they should be used in a test. The obvious simple test to satisfy coverage would not use INCLUDE files. It would look like this:

> Input from the terminal.
> Start work.
> EXIT
> Answer 'Y'

That test will find no failure.

The only hope of causing the failure is to use coverage as a signal that the general area of exiting with terminal input has been undertested. This gives you a second chance to write more complex tests, ones that might use INCLUDE files. You're unlikely to do that unless you design your coverage-based tests as you did the original tests. That means using the original test requirement checklist to help you make the tests complex, even though all the requirements have already been satisfied.

Because even the most careful tester would probably write only a few additional tests, the chance of stumbling over the right combination is much reduced. Coverage-driven tests added to an incomplete test suite are no substitute for a complete one.

7.4 A Larger Example

The `sreadhex` test suite gets too high coverage to be a good example, so a different program will be used first.

7.4.1 The Program

NAME

lc—count lines of code and comment in a C program

SYNOPSIS

lc [-{] [-}] [-number] [file...]

DESCRIPTION

lc counts the number of lines of code, lines of comment, and blank lines in a C program. The output looks like this:

% lc lc.c

	Pure Code	Pure Comment	Both Cod&Com	Blank	Total Code	Total Comment	Total Lines	Pages
lc.c	311	437	62	117	373	499	927	28

"Pure Code" means lines of code with no comments, "Pure Comment" means lines with only comments; "Both Cod&Com" means lines containing both. "Blank" lines contain neither code nor comments.

If no *file* arguments are given, input is taken from standard input.

OPTIONS

-{ -} These options instruct `lc` to count lines containing only brackets as blank lines.

-number
The number argument tells `lc` how many lines fit on a page.

7.4.2 Using the Generic Coverage Tool (GCT)

This section is here for two reasons. First, you may be curious about how a coverage tool is used. Second, Chapter 14 on testing changes uses a fault in GCT as an example. The example will be clearer if you've seen a use of GCT.

The first step is to tell GCT what to measure. That information is kept in the file *gct-ctrl*. For this example, it contains:

```
(coverage branch multi loop relational)
(options instrument)
```

The first line tells GCT we want branch, multicondition, loop, and relational operator coverage. Other types of coverage are possible, but aren't described in this book.

This command initializes GCT:

```
% gct-init
```

GCT acts just like a C compiler. All that is normally required is to tell your system-building tools to use GCT instead of the default C compiler. Using the standard UNIX make command, this would be done like this:

```
% make CC=gct
```

When invoked, make executes the following commands:

```
gct -c lc.c
gct -c get.c
gct -o lc lc.o get.o
```

The first command results in an object file, *lc.o*. Although GCT appears to be a C compiler, what it is actually doing is modifying the source from *lc.c* so that it measures its own execution, placing the result into a temporary file, calling the system's C compiler to compile that file, and leaving the result in *lc.o*.

7.4.3 Coverage

The test suite for `lc` was developed using an earlier version of subsystem testing [Marick91b]. A few tests were removed for this example. The modified test suite achieved 96 percent coverage.

The greport command shows a detailed listing of missed coverage. (Summary reports are also available.)

```
% greport GCTLOG
"lc.c", line 137: operator > might be >=. (L==R)
"lc.c", line 137: condition 1 (argc, 1) was taken TRUE 43, FALSE 0 times.
"lc.c", line 139: condition 1 (<...>[...], 1) was taken TRUE 0, FALSE 14 times.
"lc.c", line 153: if was taken TRUE 0, FALSE 29 times.
"lc.c", line 162: loop zero times: 0, one time: 19, many times: 10.
"lc.c", line 172: if was taken TRUE 0, FALSE 43 times.
```

The first two lines of greport output refer to line 137, which is the program's option processing loop. The line in question is highlighted below.

```
while (--argc > 0 && (**++argv == '-'))
    {
        if ( (*argv)[1] == LCURL || (*argv)[1] == RCURL)
        {
            white_bracket = TRUE;
        }
        else if (sscanf (*argv + 1, "%d", &page_size) == FALSE)
        {
            fprintf (stderr, "lc: Bad page size argument: %s\n", *argv);
            exit (BAD_FLAG);
        }
    }
```

The first greport line,

"lc.c", line 137: operator > might be >=. (L==R)

is from relational coverage. The parenthetical remark (L==R) is a reminder that the boundary where the two sides of the relation operator are equal has never been tested. GCT is asking to see at least one test where --argc==0. To force that, the call to lc must have no nonoption arguments. It must look like one of these:

```
% lc < INPUT
% lc -} < INPUT
% lc -34 < INPUT
```

That is, lc was never tested when it took its input from standard input. "Input from standard input" should be added as a clue to the test requirement checklist.

The next line of greport output is from the same line of the program.

"lc.c", line 137: condition 1 (argc, 1) was taken TRUE 43, FALSE 0 times.

This is from multicondition coverage. Line 137's while loop test has two components:

--argc > 0

and

```
**++argv == '-'
```

The first of them was always true in every test, never false. (Because the second component evaluated to both true and false, greport doesn't show it by default.)

This condition means the same thing as the last one. To get --argc equal to zero in the option-processing loop, there can be only arguments beginning with a dash -- that is, lc must take its input from standard input. It's not unusual for two different coverage types to yield the same clue. It's certainly not inevitable, so none of the coverage types are redundant.

The next line,

"lc.c", line 139: condition 1 (<...>[...], 1) was taken TRUE 0, FALSE 14 times.

corresponds to this code:

```
while (--argc > 0 && (**++argv == '-'))
{
    if ((*argv)[1] == LCURL || (*argv)[1] == RCURL)
    {
        white_bracket = TRUE;
    }
    else if (sscanf (*argv + 1, "%d", &page_size) == FALSE)
    {
        fprintf (stderr, "lc: Bad page size argument: %s\n", *argv);
        exit (BAD_FLAG);
    }
}
```

It is also an example of multicondition coverage.[1]

This line says that *argv[1] is never LCURL. That is, the -{ option was never tested. It should be added as a clue to the checklist.

The next line,

"lc.c", line 153: if was taken TRUE 0, FALSE 29 times.

tells that this if has never been taken in the true direction:

```
if (argc == 0)
{
    tally_file (stdin, &file_tally);
    show_header ();
    show_tally ("", &file_tally);
}
```

Again, this is redundant information. The program never reads from standard input.

---

1. The message looks peculiar. What does (<...>[...], 1) mean? This parenthetical information uniquely identifies a part of what may be a deeply nested expression, like (A && (B || C) || D). The details aren't relevant to this book.

The next line,

"lc.c", line 162: loop zero times: 0, one time: 19, many times: 10.

is the first example of loop coverage. This particular loop traverses all of lc's non-option arguments.

```
for (index = 1; index <= argc; index++)
{
    if ((fp = fopen (*argv, "r")) == NULL)
    {
        status = FILE_NOT_FOUND;
        fprintf (stderr, "lc: can't open %s\n", *argv);
    }
    else
    {
        tally_file (fp, &file_tally);
        if (fclose (fp) == EOF)
            panic (PANIC, "Fclose error.");
        show_tally (*argv, &file_tally);
        if (argc > 1)
            make_total (&total_tally, &file_tally);
    }
    argv++;
}
```

The loop is always entered at least once; the loop test is never false on the first try. But this coverage condition is infeasible. The loop is in the else branch of the if(argc==0) on the previous page. So, argc must be greater than zero, and the loop can't be taken zero times.[1]

The rest of the greport line means that lc was given a single argument 19 times and more than one argument 10 times.

The next greport line is:

"lc.c", line 172: if was taken TRUE 0, FALSE 43 times.

which corresponds to this line:

```
if (fclose (fp) == EOF)
    panic (PANIC, "Fclose error.");
```

Evidently, the programmer thinks an EOF return from fclose() is impossible (but is checking anyway, just in case). Of course, what a programmer thinks and what is true may be two different things. (In fact, the original testing of lc found a case where a similar "impossible" return value was in fact possible.) You as a tester would want to think hard about

---

1. Actually, this conclusion is only valid if argc can't be less than zero. It certainly starts out non-negative, since there can't be a negative number of arguments to a program. Some of the code decrements it. Since you can't see all the code, you'll have to trust me that argc can't be decremented below zero.

how to generate EOF returns, because error handling is a fertile source of serious faults caused by mistaken assumptions. (But, for this book, assume you think of nothing.)

7.4.4 New Tests

The two new clues should be used to generate new test requirements. Do they suggest anything else missed in test design? If not, there are only two new test requirements:

1. input from standard input.
2. Use the -{ option.

They can be satisfied with a single test, such as

% echo 'main(){printf("hello, world\n");}' | lc -{

That's a bad test, though, because it violates a rule for test content. The – { option only has an effect when applied to lines containing nothing but a brace. A better test would be

% echo "{" | lc -{

Having a test with more variety—a more typical C program—would be better yet.

This section examines the coverage of the sreadhex test suite. Here is what GCT shows:

```
% greport GCTLOG
"stream.c", line 57: loop zero times: 0, one time: 0, many times: 2.
"stream.c", line 61: operator <= needs boundary L==R+1.
"stream.c", line 62: loop zero times: 18, one time: 0, many times: 2.
```

The first line refers to the loop that sets up the decoder array. It executes a fixed number of times, so the "zero" and "once" conditions are impossible.

```
56      memset(decoder - 1, hex_none, 257);
57      for ( i = 0; i < 16+6; i++ )
58          decoder[hex_chars[i]] = (i >= 16 ? i - 6 : i);
59      decoder[0] = hex_eofc;
```

The second line refers to line 61:

```
61      if ( val1 <= 0xf ) goto d2;
62 d1:  while ( (val1 = decoder[sgetc(s)]) > 0xf )
63          {   if ( val1 == hex_eofc ) { *odd_digit = -1; goto ended; }
64          }
65 d2:  while ( (val2 = decoder[sgetc(s)]) > 0xf )
66          {   if ( val2 == hex_eofc ) { *odd_digit = val1; goto ended; }
67          }
68      *ptr++ = (val1 << 4) + val2;
69      if ( ptr < limit ) goto d1;
```

It is asking for a case where val1 (initialized with *odd_digit) is 0xf+1 (16). However, that would violate assumed Precondition 5:

Assumed: *ODD_DIGIT is in the range [-1, 15].

There is no point in providing such a value. (I considered it when looking at the Intervals section of the catalog and deliberately omitted it because of the assumed precondition.)

The final coverage condition says that the first while loop was never taken exactly once. What does that say about test design? The clue for the loops (taking subsets) emphasizes the entire substring given to a loop. That provides variety in interactions with the other loop, but under-tests the loop's own processing. That processing works on a sequence of nonhexadecimal characters ending in either a hexadecimal character or end-of-string. Coverage says that both ways to end the sequence have been exercised, but the sequences themselves haven't been. They should be treated as Collections.

Here are the new clues:

nonhexadecimal characters for odd loop, a collection
nonhexadecimal characters for even loop, a collection

The Collection clue from the catalog says:

- empty   IN/OUT
- a single element   IN/OUT
- more than one element   IN/OUT
- full   IN/OUT
- duplicate elements   IN/OUT
(may be an error case, or impossible)

Most of these were already satisfied by existing tests. ("Full" means the rest of the string is all nonhexadecimal.) Here are the ones that aren't:

nonhexadecimal characters for odd loop, a collection
    one
    duplicate elements
nonhexadecimal characters for even loop, a collection
    duplicate elements

That's the original coverage condition, together with two "duplicate element" requirements that I originally decided not to use. Since I have to write a new test anyway, I'll use them this time.

Another clue that comes to mind is the larger loop, constructed with the goto on line 69. The coverage tool can't detect that loop, so it can't determine how many times it's been iterated. That doesn't mean that the loop coverage requirements don't apply. The loop tests at the bottom, so it's impossible to iterate it zero times. A quick scan of the tests shows that it iterates once and more than once.

The loop has two entry points. Has it been iterated once from each entry point? More than once? This amounts to checking all possible combinations of these requirements:

clue: *ODD_DIGIT
    a digit value
    -1

clue: main loop iteration
    1 time
    more than once

That could be done by multiplying the *ODD_DIGIT requirements and using them to refine the loop iteration requirements. That multiplication produces:

main loop iteration
    1 time
        1 time, with a digit value for *ODD_DIGIT
        1 time, with a -1 value for *ODD_DIGIT
    more than once
        more than once, with a digit value for *ODD_DIGIT
        more than once, with a -1 value for *ODD_DIGIT

These requirements aren't likely to be valuable, but I have to write a test anyway. If one of them wasn't satisfied, I might as well use it instead of repeating one of the others. Only the last one wasn't satisfied.

(Chapters 25 and 26 will discuss this case further and show how it can be better analyzed, but at greater expense. If coverage had given me more to work with, I wouldn't be considering this multiplication at all. I'm only trying to add as much as possible to the single test I need to write.)

The test might as well also satisfy one of the two postcondition requirements that have only been satisfied once:

1   START+NUM_HEX_CHARS = RLEN*2+1, START+NUM_HEX_CHARS is odd

I'll also reuse all the interior hexadecimal elements, since some of them have only been used once. I'll use duplicate hexadecimal characters, as well as nonhexadecimal. Here's the test:

TEST 9:
    STR, a 100-byte buffer, initialized to all 10's
    RLEN = 11
    *NREAD = 1000
    *ODD_DIGIT = -1
    S = "9111:2@@3"44:gg5eG5Ge68cBCD7Ebdf"
EXPECT
    STR = 9 1 1 1 2 3 4 4 5 14 5 14 6 8 12 11 12 13 7 14 11 13 10 10...
    *NREAD = 11
    *ODD_DIGIT = -1
    S unchanged
    return value 0

As expected, this test satisfies the coverage condition. It doesn't find a bug.

There's a surprising omission in the GCT output. In developing Test 3, I discovered a specification problem. The specification makes no sense when S contains no hexadecimal characters. Rather than fix the problem, I ignored this part of the test requirement checklist:

NUM_HEX_CHARS, a count of hexadecimal characters in S
    NUM_HEX_CHARS=0
0   **S an empty string**
0   **NUM_HEX_CHARS=0 and *ODD_DIGIT=-1**
0   **NUM_HEX_CHARS=0 and *ODD_DIGIT in [0,15]**
1   NUM_HEX_CHARS=1   (Test 2)
0   all characters hexadecimal (more than one)

Coverage gives no clue those requirements were skipped. Why not? The code treats strings without any hexadecimal characters the same as strings ending in nonhexadecimal characters. Because there's no code for the special case, coverage can't detect that it's untested.

This special case is an artifact of the specification, which could be rewritten to make it disappear. The general point holds, though: Even if you use coverage conditions as clues, not requirements, you won't catch all test omissions. Coverage is not so reliable that you can afford to skimp on test design.

<table>
<tr><td>

7.6

**Where Do
We Stand?**

</td><td>

`sreadhex` doesn't show off coverage very well.

1. There is one unsatisfied coverage condition. But it doesn't seem likely there's a fault that would only be caught when exactly one nonhexadecimal character is skipped. The code behaves the same way no matter how often it loops, and it certainly seems that's the way it should be.
2. Using coverage in a search for missed clues didn't do much good. The obvious clue led back to the original coverage condition, plus two others that had already been considered and discarded. Stretching for other requirements, I found an untested interaction.

Other times that I've used coverage, I've been surprised and pleased at how it points to a bad design or implementation error. Sometimes the error is obvious; sometimes it's found after thinking hard about what coverage implies. Here, `sreadhex`'s test design was missing only a little variety, and coverage adds it back.

That means writing another test to add variety to an area (the looping requirements) that already appeared overtested—which hardly seems worth the effort. However, don't forget that `sreadhex` is artificially small. In real life, tests wouldn't be written for it alone. Rather, it would be tested along with the rest of its subsystem. (See Chapter 13.) Measuring coverage for the whole subsystem test suite would lead to several new test requirements, some clearly valuable. `sreadhex`'s coverage could be satisfied by tests that would be written anyway.

`sreadhex` is a worst case scenario for coverage. It illustrates the procedure, not the typical results.

</td></tr>
</table>

▎▎▎▎▎▎▎▎ CHAP. 7 USING COVERAGE TO TEST THE TEST SUITE

Cleaning Up

The last part of any task should be tidying up to make later tasks easier. For subsystem testing, these later tasks are:

1. discovering you missed a requirement in your original test design. What you'll want to do is find all related tests, ones where you might be able to change to satisfy your test requirement. You'll need to know the old test requirements for the tests to make sure you don't stop satisfying any of them.

2. maintaining the test suite along with the subsystem. Changed code means new test requirements. They may already be satisfied, or perhaps existing tests could be updated to satisfy them. If new tests have to be written, they should still have variety. That can mean making use of old test requirements.

3. finding all tests for a feature so that you can examine them or rerun them. For example, this can be useful when planning changes to a feature. Tracing from features to tests or from tests to features is harder in subsystem testing. When a testing technique calls for each test to test only one feature, it is (usually) easy to go from a feature to its tests or in the reverse direction. With subsystem testing, every test tests several features and the complete set of tests for a feature may be widely dispersed.

The information you need is available and written down during test design. What you must do is make sure it will still make sense to you (or someone else) months from now. Consider the checklist a first draft; now polish it.

1. Are the descriptions of the clues clear? Can they be related back to features in the external interface, when appropriate?
2. Can the test requirements be understood by someone else? (They tend to be rather terse and cryptic.)
3. Each test requirement has a list of test specifications that satisfy it. Is the list accurate? Are the test names given there adequate to find the implemented test?
4. Have the test specifications been saved? They're usually easier to understand than their implementations.

Even with good documentation, it's often easier to write a new test than to find old relevant tests and update them. But beware of writing new tests without variety and complexity.

Miscellaneous Tips

The catalog scanning rules described how you might reject a test requirement if you thought it not worthwhile. There's another option: Add it, but mark it as LOW priority. When building test specifications, use it if it's convenient, but otherwise ignore it.

As an example, consider a subroutine call with three postconditions. Suppose the three different actions are "indistinguishable" as far as the caller is returned. "Indistinguishable" is in quotes because, of course, many bugs happen when seemingly identical cases turn out to have important differences. You can add the three requirements to the checklist, but mark two of them LOW.

Two low priority requirements that can often be used are those that the AND rule and OR rule ignore. Those requirements are unlikely to find bugs directly, but they may add additional variety to the tests. Suppose you're building test specifications and you have a checklist like this:

Postcondition 2 (A AND B):
6   A true, B true
5   A true, B false
7   A false, B true

It's better to use the `A false, B false` case than to use one of the others yet again. You'd have this checklist:

Postcondition 2 (A AND B):
6   A true, B true
5   A true, B false
7   A false, B true
1   A false, B false

9.2
Indeterminate
Limits

Subsystems sometimes have unspecified or unspecifiable limits. For example, a multiuser game may not define how many users can play at once, but it should behave well when one too many users try to enter it. Programs that use system resources (most particularly virtual memory) may simply accept work until resources run out. How much work can be done depends on what other programs are contending for resources, but resource exhaustion should always be handled correctly.

The simple case is when there is a single variable associated with the limit:

> number of users, a count
> > 0
> > 1
> > >1
> > maximum possible value
> > one larger than maximum possible value   ERROR

Even though the maximum possible value is unknown, the error test is easy to write. It is a simple test that continues to add users until the program fails. When it does, the failure should be graceful. Note that this is an error test, so it only increments the count on the ERROR requirement even though all values of "number of users" were exercised on the way to the maximum.

Now that the maximum is known, it can be used as a way of adding variety to other, non-error, tests. This can cause problems in test suite maintenance, because simple changes to the program may change the limit. Using the maximum often may not be worthwhile, but some reasonable large value should be used to add variety to some of the tests.

The harder case is when there's no single limit variable. There may be a pool of resources used by several different operations. Exactly when the subsystem runs out depends on what mix of operations was used. This is typically the situation when allocating virtual memory.

One thing you can do is to find every place where more of the resource is requested, then arrange for the program to fail at that location. For example, find every `malloc` in the program. For each one, discover what causes it to be executed. Then repeat that operation until the `malloc` fails. The problem is that most paths to the `malloc` in question will also allocate memory, and it may be those allocations that fail. You can discover this with coverage. If the code is written as

    if (NULL == malloc(...))

coverage will tell you that your test didn't do what you wanted. Knowing that doesn't solve the problem, though.

A solution is to write a `malloc` stub that fails on command, so that you can induce a failure exactly when you want it. (See also the discussion of testing software that reuses in Chapter 20.)

Having an error-handling version of malloc may or may not help. For example, GCT uses a routine called xmalloc to allocate memory. It is the only routine that calls malloc directly. If no memory is available, xmalloc prints an error message, calls a standard cleanup routine, and exits. Because error handling is simple, I feel no need to test what happens when each xmalloc fails. If it were more complex, and the program did more that might require recovery, I would wonder whether each use of xmalloc was appropriate. Perhaps the cleanup or recovery would not be adequate for a failure at a particular location.

Part 2

ADOPTING SUBSYSTEM TESTING

The next chapter describes an easy path to full adoption of the subsystem testing technique. Based on my experience teaching this technique, I present a plan for gradual adoption, where at no time are you changing your current practice very much. This generally works better than changing everything all at once. If you do that, you'll invariably run into problems, and the temptation to abandon the new way and go back to what you're used to becomes irresistable. Gradual adoption means small and surmountable problems that don't jeopardize getting that all-important next release out the door.

Even after gradually adopting the whole process, you should expect to spend some months in serious testing before you're completely comfortable and (especially) as efficient as you want to be. The second chapter contains some tips to speed you on that path.

10

Getting Going

Here is how I recommend you adopt subsystem testing.

10.1
Use Coverage

The first step is to understand what your current tests do. You don't change the way you design tests, you merely measure them and then spend some additional time (however much is available) making improvements that the measurements suggest.

Coverage is a good place to start because the results are concrete and easy to understand. The measurements are often startling, thus convincing people that their testing really isn't thorough enough.

Developers testing their own code usually react well to the idea of measuring coverage. They're rarely very enthused about testing, so they're happy that coverage provides a concrete goal. If they're getting fairly good coverage already, it's not unreasonable to just set a 100 percent feasible coverage goal (with, perhaps, a liberal interpretation of "not worth testing"). As developers get used to coverage, they'll want to know how to get better coverage numbers faster, so that they can get testing over with as soon as possible. The rest of the technique, including the use of coverage to provide clues about weak test design, now becomes more appealing.

When the existing tests have low coverage (which is typical for larger subsystems), using coverage as a goal is counterproductive. The time spent taking a list of coverage results and adding tests for them one by one would be better spent focusing on simple, cheap, broad brush tests. In any case, getting low coverage results and then plodding through test after test toward an unattainable goal is demoralizing. In such a case, avoid getting bogged down in details. Scan the coverage results relatively shallowly: Look for large bodies of code that are poorly exercised, or try to discover some obvious pattern of missing tests (such as weak testing of error handling). Having identified those areas, forget about coverage while you improve testing of those features or bodies of code. Measure coverage only to confirm that the new tests are behaving as expected.[1]

Partial coverage goals (such as 65 percent) seem appealing in such situations, but in practice they often shift the emphasis onto making the numbers no matter what. You'll get worse tests. The goal should be some unspecified improvement in coverage, but only because of better tests. For the same reason, I discourage too much monitoring of coverage during the initial testing. Coverage can too easily become the only goal.

After a particular testing task is over, take some time to think about what coverage told you about your test design and implementation. Are there easy ways to improve it?

10.2 Improve Test Specifications

Most people are used to going directly from the subsystem to test specifications or implemented tests. It takes time to become comfortable with test requirements. In the interim, concentrating on test specifications is a good next step. There are four ways to gradually improve your tests.

Enlist chance and variety

You must build your tests to increase the chance of finding unexpected failures by accident. A really good tester will always think about introducing variety, and will often stumble on new and powerful test requirements as a result. But substantial improvement requires only simple things:

1. Don't test features independently. If you need to test feature A and also feature B, consider doing it in a single test rather than two simpler tests. You may discover interaction faults you didn't think to test for.

2. Don't create a set of tests by writing the first and then making every new test a minimal variation on the previous one. Your chance of finding unplanned faults is small. Spend a few minutes thinking about how to introduce variety. If the new test is to be a copy of an old one—because writing one from scratch is above some threshold of "too much work"—spend a few seconds thinking about how to change the copy in some seemingly unnecessary ways.

3. Choose unforced values randomly. Whenever I had a free choice for a filename, I used to use "foo". Now, instead of using that one

---

1. If your coverage is low, and the system is large, you may want to use a coarser granularity of coverage. For example, you may measure only which routines were not entered, giving you a very general overview of what parts of the system you're exercising. If that granularity is too coarse, measure also which function calls were made by the entered routines. (Both of these measures are implemented in GCT; they may not be measured by other tools.)

name for every test, I use a new name for each test, and I make sure to use absolute pathnames, pathnames with directory components, and so on.

Remember that getting stuck in a rut makes for bad tests, and that complex tests are worth the trouble. Spend a little extra effort on complexity and variety.

Use the Design Checklists

The checklists for test form and content, summarized in Appendix F, mostly apply to any style of test design. Since they're checklists, they're simple to use. Quickly running through the checklists will help you discover ineffective tests.

Use the Question Catalog

The Question Catalog for code reviews can also be used in any situation and takes little time. (Adopt it at the same time as coverage if you already do code reviews.)

Move toward Test Requirements

As your tests start to have more variety, separating the decision about what needs testing from the writing of tests begins to feel more natural. Instead of writing tests for a particular feature, then moving to the next feature, write test requirements for several features before designing any tests. Use the longer lists of what to test as the main source of variety.

10.3 Improve Test Requirements	At this point, you begin using the essence of subsystem testing: gathering test requirements everywhere you can and combining them into high-yield test specifications. But until the mechanics of generating tests becomes second nature, it's best not to work with too many test requirements too early. Here's a ranked listing of sources of test requirements; add the later sources as you feel comfortable with the technique in practice.

1. The subsystem's external specification (user's manual, etc.) is the most important source. This is convenient, since most people find testing based on the specification natural and obvious.

   If the subsystem has a user interface, the standard catalog's Parsing and Syntax section is both easy to understand and useful. You will want to read Chapter 16 first.

2. Next, derive test requirements from the individual routines, beginning with the most important ones. Use whatever per-routine documentation is available. If there is no external description of the routine, you'll need to look at the code.

3. Add variable, operation, and integration (subroutine call) clues last. Until you get experience, you'll be slow at finding them. Stay below your level of frustration, but push yourself to be more

thorough every time you test. Concentrate on finding the most important and obvious requirements first.

These test requirements are deferred until last because they're the hardest. Your frustration will be reduced if everything else is rote first. Integration clues are easy to find, but hard to analyze—that's why integration faults happen. Catalog clues are harder to find (though the requirements are easier). It takes experience to understand all the catalog's entries well and to see how the more abstract entries correspond to real programs. The easiest way to find catalog clues (both operations and data types) is to look for loops.

10.4 Improve Analysis of Specifications in Parallel

In parallel with the above process, you'll be improving your analysis of specifications. In the early stages, you'll take whatever specifications you are given and treat them as you always have. As you improve your test specifications, you'll simultaneously improve your skill at finding the preconditions and postconditions hidden within whatever style of specification you've been given. As you continue to improve, you'll become more efficient, and you'll start finding definitions within specifications. Of course, in both cases, you may be working from the code, rather than from a separate specification.

Using other styles of specification is the topic of Chapter 12. Skill development will also be discussed in that chapter.

Getting Good

There are two parts to getting better: becoming more efficient and becoming more effective. Efficiency means writing the same tests in less time, and it comes naturally with practice. Effectiveness means missing fewer clues and requirements, using the requirements to produce better test specifications, and using coverage information correctly. Effectiveness is harder to increase. Conscious attention to feedback helps.

There are three sources of feedback: coverage, bug reports, and reflection on your own decisions.

Coverage

Coverage should always be used to point to missed clues and test requirements. More than that, you should compare coverage between testing tasks. The raw numbers are not so useful, though it's interesting to see whether you're generally getting better over time. What is more important is looking for patterns of missed coverage. Do you often undertest loops and their contents? Perhaps that's a clue that you need to look harder for Collections or Streams when making the test requirement checklist. Do you often undertest error handling? Next time, you can focus on that.

Bug Reports

Whenever a bug is found, you should ask why the fault slipped past testing and how it could be caught next time. (This is in addition to the important question of what error happened and how it could be prevented next time.) A useful response to a bug report is to think of a clue and test requirement that would have forced the bug's discovery. Do they match anything in the catalog? If so, you now know how to use the catalog better. If not, perhaps they should be added to the catalog. (This was, in fact, how much of the catalog was built.) Perhaps a new catalog, specific to an application or application area, should be created. Over time, such a catalog can become a powerful tool.

Could the bug have been found by some other combination of existing test requirements? If so, this is a situation where an interaction existed and was missed. Could it somehow have been discovered? (Recall that the basic technique considers test requirements independent unless there's specific evidence of an interaction, typically through the use of an AND or an OR. Part 5 gives other sources.)

Was there a test requirement for the fault that for some reason didn't cause a visible failure? Perhaps one of the rules for test form or content would have prevented that. Or perhaps those rules are incomplete. Can you learn anything about avoiding that sort of problem next time, either by changing the tests or the subsystem?

Bugs are immensely valuable data. Don't waste them. When I teach subsystem testing, part of my pay is the chance to look at interesting bugs. I've learned a lot that way.

When a bug is found by your tests, take note of which clues and requirements led to it. Over time, you'll develop a sense of the relative value of different clues.

Reflection

Because coverage is an indirect measure of quality, it's an incomplete source of feedback. And you hope that there won't be so many faults in the subsystem that your every testing mistake will be exposed. To learn more than what they tell you, you have to take the time to think about your testing. The patterns you notice in what you do can help you do better. Here are a few examples:

1. Do you find yourself with many free choices for inputs when designing test specifications? Perhaps you're missing clues in the catalog, especially those, like Collections and Streams, that can be combined with many others. Perhaps you're being too strict when deciding that test requirements aren't worth adding to the checklist. You could satisfy them at little additional cost.

2. Do you end up with "straggler" test specifications, ones created just to satisfy leftover test requirements? Perhaps this is a problem during design. You may not be looking hard enough for combinations, or you may not be starting with the hardest requirements to combine. Or you may be including too many requirements. A requirement with low expected value does no harm if it can be combined into a test being written anyway, but writing a special test for it is another matter. Perhaps you're making too many combination requirements because of a fear of interactions. Instead of

>   variable A, a count
>   0
>   1
>   >1
>   variable B, a collection
>   empty
>   one element
>   full
>   duplicates

you're writing a checklist like this, which is harder to satisfy:

```
interaction of A and B
      A=0, B empty
      A=0, B full
      A=1, B empty
      A=1, B full
variable A, a count
      A>1              (other requirements covered above)
variable B, a collection
      one element      (other requirements covered above)
      duplicates
```

3. In teaching subsystem testing, I've discovered that some people are very good at seeing operation clues, but miss variable clues. Some people are just the opposite. Which are you? You need to be good at both.

4. Expect most of the clues to be found from the specification. Obviously, this depends on how thorough the specification is and how much of the internals are irrelevant to the users and thus hidden. But if you consistently discover a lot of new clues when searching the code, you may be missing them in the specification. That's bad, since the code won't provide clues for faults of omission.

5. If you rarely find clues in the code, that may be a problem too. Perhaps you haven't learned to abstract the detail of the code into clues. When all else fails, look for loops. Where there are loops, there are probably Collections and Streaming operations of some sort. (Loop coverage will usually point this out more directly.)

6. All parts of the technique should yield their share of clues. It's easy to overemphasize what you're most comfortable with. Watch for that. In particular, make sure that the methodical parts of subsystem testing don't blind you to the need to finish it up by stepping back and trying to guess test requirements based on intuition and experience.

Part 3

SUBSYSTEM TESTING
IN PRACTICE

The `sreadhex` example in Part 1 was a small, well-specified example. Real life rarely offers those kinds of examples. This section describes how to cope with more realistic situations.

▲ Chapter 12 discusses how to extract precondition, postcondition, and definition information from specifications written in a different style (or, when there is no specification, from the code).

▲ Chapter 13 discusses what must be done when the subsystem is large, perhaps thousands of lines of code. How do you cope with the complexity of testing such a subsystem? What implementation dangers are there? How large a subsystem should be tested at once?

▲ Chapter 14 discusses testing bug fixes and other changes. Ordinary subsystem testing is not appropriate in that case; you must narrow your focus in certain ways and expand it in others.

▲ Finally, Chapter 15 describes what parts of subsystem testing to abandon when you don't have enough time for the full technique, together with how the remaining parts should be tailored to the situation.

Using More Typical Specifications

(Including None at All)

In Part 1, there were a variety of clues: operations, variables, preconditions, postconditions, and definitions. The first two required detective work. You had to find them and then discover test requirements for them. In contrast, the latter three were given to you, and their requirements came directly from IF-THEN-ELSE statements.

Real specifications are rarely that helpful. Clues and test requirements corresponding to preconditions, postconditions, and definitions have to be discovered. This chapter is about how to do that systematically and efficiently. "Systematically" means writing some form of abbreviated specification. If you try to go directly from a typical specification to test requirements, you'll miss special cases. The easiest ones to miss are, of course, the same ones the programmer already missed. "Efficiently" means putting nothing in the abbreviated specification that can be found just as well in the original.

Here's part of an abbreviated specification (from `sreadhex`):

IF START + NUM_HEX_CHARS >= RLEN*2
THEN use as much as fits

The THEN part has been abbreviated into a shorthand *effect*. The effect is used in two ways:

1. You find it in the original specification, then work out what IF expression would cause it.
2. It's a clue for the test requirement checklist. The requirements come from the IF expression:

    using as much as fits
        START + NUM_HEX_CHARS >= RLEN*2
        START + NUM_HEX_CHARS < RLEN*2

Because the effect omits detail, only a few operation and variable clues can be found in the abbreviated specification. You'll have to refer to the original specification for the rest. You'll also need the original specification to get the complete expected results that a test specification requires.

Adding detail to the effect would be more work than it's worth. There are other efficiency tricks when abbreviating a specification; they'll be discussed at the appropriate points.

Terminology

The terminology of Part 1 distinguished between preconditions, postconditions, and definitions. Their essential similarity was glossed over because the differences were more important. For this chapter, the similarities are more important. For that reason, it will treat all three constructs as being of the form:

IF <defining term>
THEN <effect>

or

IF <defining term>
THEN <effect>
ELSE <another effect>

The effect is anything the subsystem does. It can be a precondition failure effect, a postcondition effect, or part of a definition. The *defining term* is an expression, perhaps using AND or OR, that describes what inputs cause the effect. Each boolean component of the defining term is called a *cause*. The entire IF-THEN or IF-THEN-ELSE statement is called the *cause-effect statement*.

Code

This chapter also discusses what to do if there's no specification at all. That might seem a ridiculous situation: if there's nothing that says what the subsystem must do, how can you tell whether what it does do is correct? Deriving a specification from the code seems meaningless: the result will just be an alternate description of the code, and what's the point of testing the code against that?

In fact, the situation is not so dire. By examining the subsystem, you can determine its intent more or less exactly. Testing then becomes the process of comparing what a subsystem does against the programmer's intent as summarized in a specification. You can still find lots of faults, though you must be specially wary of faults of omission.

Improving Your Skill

Learning to abbreviate specifications is a skill that will take time to develop. The basics are finding effects, finding causes, and relating them with defining terms. That's not difficult. What is difficult is writing the cause-effect statements so that they won't cause extra or redundant work later. There are two parts to that:

1. Avoiding effects that will lead to no new test requirements.
2. Knowing how to create definitions.

The first time you read this chapter, you can skim over those topics. When you first try summarizing specifications, start with simple precondition and postcondition effects, and don't worry about definitions at all. As you discover sources of extra work, you can reread the relevant sections of the chapter.

There are two exercises in this chapter. They illustrate some of the finer points. The MAX example, from Chapter 17, gives you a simpler opportunity to practice.

12.1 An Example: GREPORT

The following specification will be used in the detailed explanation of the procedure. It's a simplified version of the manual page for one of GCT's component tools. sreadhex will be used to show how the procedure applies to code.

The first part of the specification describes the syntax. Square brackets [ ] denote optional elements. Vertical bars | separate alternatives. Elements in bold font must be given exactly as written. Elements in italic font should be replaced with appropriate text.

SYNOPSIS

greport [-n] [**-test-dir** *master_directory*]
       [**-test-map** *map_file_name*] [**-all**]
       [[**-visible-file** | **-vf**] *source_file_regex*]
       [[**-visible-routine** | **-vr**] *source_routine_regex*]
       [*log_file_name*]

DESCRIPTION

greport uses the mapfile and the logfile to produce a report on the test execution that resulted in the logfile. The report contains information about conditions that have not yet been fully tested. The mapfile is created during the instrumentation of the source code by **gct**. The logfile is written during a test run. The mapfile is named *gct-map* by default. The logfile is given as the single argument. If no logfile is given, **greport** reads from standard input. **greport** will report an error if the logfile and mapfile come from different programs.

Example:

% greport GCT_LOG
"lc.c", line 247: if was taken TRUE 0, FALSE 3 times.
"lc.c", line 568: loop zero times: 1, one time: 0, many times: 1551.

This report shows that a branching statement was never taken true and that a loop was never executed exactly one time.

If another test is run that causes the if to be taken in the TRUE direction, a later report will not display the first line. If that test also causes the loop to execute one time, the second line will not be shown.

OPTIONS

-all
    greport will display the values for all coverage conditions, satisfied

or no. Such a display might look like:

> "test.c", line 3: operator < might be <=. (L==R) [0]
> "test.c", line 4: while was taken TRUE 1, FALSE 1 times.
> "test.c", line 4: loop zero times: 0, one time: 1, many times: 0.

For output lines that don't normally include counts, the number of times a condition has been satisfied is given in trailing brackets.

-n

This option causes **greport** to show only those lines with counts greater than zero. This is most useful in a pipeline like this:

> % gnewer -logical log later-log | greport -n

which gives a detailed report on what new coverage was added between *log* and *later-log*. The output format is the same as **-all**.

-visible-file
-vf

These two options are synonyms. They may be repeated to name several files. If given, **greport** reports only on coverage conditions within the named files.

-visible-routine
-vr

greport reports only on coverage conditions within the named routines. These options may also be repeated, and they can be combined with **-vf**. In that case, a line in either a visible file or a visible routine is shown.

-test-dir *master_directory*

The *master directory* is the directory where all of **gct**'s data files are kept. By default, it is the current directory. This option changes the default.

-test-map *map_file_name*

By default, information about coverage conditions is found in the file *gct-map* in the master directory. This option changes the default. Unless the argument is an absolute pathname, it is taken to be in the master directory. (An absolute pathname is one that begins with a slash. If you're a DOS user, think of an absolute pathname as something like C:\gctests.)

12.2
The Procedure

Listing Effects

The most efficient time to look for effects is while you're already looking for variable and operation clues. Here's a partial result of a search of the **greport** specification. The lines in bold type are effects. You should check back in the specification to make sure you understand where each effect came from.

> the opened mapfile, a collection of mapfile entries
> -test-map argument, a pathname
> command line syntax, a syntactic statement[1]
> **printing a line of output**
> **line shows appended [number]**
> **logfile and mapfile mismatch error message (error effect)**

If the effect is an error effect (caused by violating a precondition), identify it as such. If you don't, you might forget to add ERROR tags to its test requirements. You may have trouble deciding whether a particular effect should be an error effect. Decide by considering its interaction with test requirements from other sources. If it stops further processing, as with

```
function(a, b, c);
{
    if (some_condition)
        return 0;  /* Is this an error effect? */
    <much more processing>
}
```

other test requirements won't be exercised when it happens. In that case, it should be *treated* like an error effect, even if you're not sure it means the inputs were wrong. Its test requirements should be exercised in isolation. The decision is not always so clearcut—sometimes an effect will mask some requirements but not all. Treating it as an error effect will reduce the risk of incrementing the counts on unexercised requirements, but it will also reduce the chance of finding interactions between the effect and requirements it doesn't mask.

Omit Redundant Effects from the List

The Procedure

While searching for operation and variable clues, also list effects
> Note error effects
> Avoid effects with redundant information

Separately write defining terms
> Every effect clue must have a defining term
> Some operation or variable clues might also
> Create definitions as convenient
>> They have defining terms that yield test requirements
>> They may be variable clues as well

Check your work
Create test requirements in the normal way

---

1. This is shorthand for applying the catalog syntax rules to all the different optional arguments of the syntax. There's no need to write separate clues for each optional argument.

Don't write down effects that you know will lead to requirements you'd also get from other sources. In particular, avoid syntax error effects or effects that depend only on whether some syntactic element is used or not used. As an illustration, consider the optional -test-dir argument from the **greport** syntax:

greport [*-test-dir master_directory*] other options omitted for example

The Syntax Alternatives catalog entry gives these two requirements:

> -test-dir option
>   -test-dir option used
>   -test-dir option omitted

The POSIX catalog gives a further requirement

> "-test-dir" is last word on command line (its argument is omitted)

(Chapter 16 gives more details about testing syntax, and the MAX example in Chapter 17 shows how command-line syntax is tested.)

This syntax could also be described in cause-effect statements. One effect would be this:

> message about missing argument to -test-dir (error effect)

Then you'd write its defining term:

> IF -test-dir is given without an argument
> THEN message about missing argument to -test-dir (error effect)

That would lead to these requirements:

> -test-dir is given without an argument   ERROR
> -test-dir is given with an argument

But the first of these is already in the checklist (in a slightly better version). The second will be satisfied in any normal test that uses the -test-dir option. The checklist already requires such a test.

The syntax and the cause-effect statement are two different ways of describing the same subsystem behavior. Since the descriptions are redundant, the requirements will be too. While you're learning subsystem testing, you can expect to miss redundant effects. That's annoying, because it causes extra work, but you'll quickly get better at it.

Building the Defining Term

You now have a test requirement checklist with clues—effects, operations, and variables. Write defining terms for all the clues that need them. Do this separately from the test requirement checklist. Having the checklist contain both test requirements and defining terms for the same clues is confusing.

To write a defining term for an effect, first find all of its causes, then combine them with ANDs and ORs. For example, here is an incomplete list of the causes of the "printing a line of output" effect:

-all argument given
    (in which case, a line is always shown)
-n argument given
    (shows lines that have some count > 0)[1]
some count for line > 0
    (shown if -n argument given)
-n argument not given
    (shows lines that have some count = 0)
some count for line = 0

And here is a defining term that uses those causes:

Postcondition LINE SHOWN:
    IF (-all given
        OR (-n given AND some count for line > 0)
        OR (-n not given AND some count for line = 0))
    THEN that line is shown in the output.

Notice that I labelled the cause-effect statement as a postcondition and gave it a name. That isn't necessary, but I find such labels make the list of cause-effect statements more readable.

Ignore Error Causes Except when Defining Error Effects

Unless you're writing the defining expression for an error effect (violated precondition), ignore any causes of errors. For example, do not write a postcondition like this

Postcondition LINE SHOWN:
    IF (-all given
        OR (-n given AND some count for line > 0)
        OR (-n not given AND some count for line = 0))
        AND the logfile and mapfile come from the same program
        AND the mapfile entry exists
        AND the mapfile entry is syntactically valid
        AND the logfile entry exists
        AND the logfile entry is syntactically valid
    THEN that line is shown in the output.

Preconditions should handle all error cases. All other cause-effect statements can assume no preconditions are violated. If you wrote such a defining term you'd do additional work without any improvement in your testing. If you apply the AND and OR rules to this example, keeping in mind that a test can only violate one precondition at a time, you'll see that the new clauses add only trivial refinements.

---

1. Actually, the wording in the manual page is ambiguous. The text "show only those lines with counts greater than zero" could be interpreted as "show only those lines with *all* counts greater than zero". The ambiguity didn't occur to me until I wrote this chapter. One of the benefits of rewording the specification is that it finds such ambiguities, which can confuse both the developer and the customer.

Convenience Definitions

The LINE SHOWN postcondition is not complete. It only applies if none of the "visibility" options are given (-vf, -vr, -visible-file, or -visible-routine). The defining term could be upgraded as follows:

Postcondition LINE SHOWN
    IF (**none of the visibility options are given**
       OR the line's file is named in a -vf option
       OR the line's file is named in a -visible-file option
       OR the line's routine is named in a -vr option
       OR the line's routine is named in a -visible-routine option)
       AND
    (-all given
    OR (-n given AND some count for line > 0)
    OR (-n not given AND some count for line = 0))
    THEN that line is shown in the output

This is getting to be large and awkward. It would be better to separate out the new terms as a definition:

Postcondition LINE SHOWN:
    IF a line is potentially visible
       AND
    (-all given
    OR (-n given AND some count for line > 0)
    OR (-n not given AND some count for line = 0))
    THEN that line is shown in the output

Definition POTENTIALLY VISIBLE
    IF   none of the visibility options are given
    OR the line's file is named in a -vf option
    OR the line's file is named in a -visible-file option
    OR the line's routine is named in a -vr option
    OR the line's routine is named in a -visible-routine option
    THEN the line is potentially visible.

When the ANDs and ORs are treated independently, as described in Chapter 3, the two alternatives produce exactly the same test requirements. In each case, the OR expression describing the visibility options generates its own independent set of test requirements. According to the

multi-way OR rule, they'd be:

none of the visibility options are given	(true, false, false, ...)
line's file is named in a -vf option, named nowhere else	(false, true, false, ...)
line's file is named in a -visible-file option, named nowhere else	(false, false, true, ...)
...	
some visibility option given, neither line's routine nor file named in it	(all false)

You may recall from Chapter 3 that treating ANDs and ORs independently is not always the right choice. In practice, you will usually use the Requirements for Complex Booleans catalog (Appendix E). Using it produces different requirements for these two alternatives. The alternative with the definition has fewer requirements. While you're learning subsystem testing, pretend the difference does not exist: make convenience definitions whenever they're convenient, and don't worry that you'll lose a few test requirements. They're seldom necessary. When you are more comfortable with the entire process, read Chapter 25, which will tell you when definitions should not be used. Multicondition coverage should point out most test omissions in the meantime.

A third version of LINE SHOWN might be even clearer:

Postcondition LINE SHOWN
    IF   (a line is potentially visible)
          AND
          (-all given OR **the line has an interesting count**)
    THEN that line is shown in the output.

Definition POTENTIALLY VISIBLE
    IF   none of the visibility options are given
       OR the line's file is named in a -vf option
       OR the line's file is named in a -visible-file option
       OR the line's routine is named in a -vr option
       OR the line's routine is named in a -visible-routine option
    THEN the line is potentially visible.

Definition INTERESTING COUNT
    IF
       EITHER (-n given AND some count for line > 0)
       OR (-n not given AND some count for line = 0)
    THEN the line has an interesting count.

The requirements follow. Some simplification is possible, but it is omitted so you can see where the requirements come from. ANDs and ORs are treated independently, as per Chapter 3.

There's more that can be done. Different types of output lines have different numbers of counts. For example, the lines for an if and a generic

LINE SHOWN

line potentially visible true,	(-all given OR line has interesting count) false
line potentially visible false,	(-all given OR line has interesting count) true
line potentially visible true,	(-all given OR line has interesting count) true
-all given true,	line has interesting count false
-all given false,	line has interesting count true
-all given false,	line has interesting count false

POTENTIALLY VISIBLE
none of the visibility options are given
line's file is named in a -vf option, named nowhere else
line's file is named in a -visible-file option, named nowhere else
line's routine is named in a -vr option, named nowhere else
line's routine is named in a -visible-routine option, named nowhere else
some visibility option given, neither line's routine nor file is named in it

INTERESTING COUNT

(-n given AND some count > 0) true,	(-n not given AND some count = 0) false
(-n given AND some count > 0) false,	(-n not given AND some count = 0) true
(-n given AND some count > 0) false,	(-n not given AND some count = 0) false
-n given true,	some count > 0 false
-n given false,	some count > 0 true
-n given true,	some count > 0 true
-n not given true,	some count = 0 false
-n not given false,	some count = 0 true
-n not given true,	some count = 0 true

loop look like this:

"lc.c", line 247: if was taken TRUE 0, FALSE 3 times.
"lc.c", line 568: loop zero times: 1, one time: 0, many times: 1551.

The first has two counts; the second has three. Therefore, "some count for line = 0" should itself have a defining term, one that looks like

Definition ZERO COUNT
IF   the line is from an "if" AND (the TRUE count is 0 OR the FALSE count is 0)
    OR the line is from a loop AND
        (the "zero iterations" count is 0
    OR the "exactly one iteration" count is 0
    OR the "more than one iteration" count is 0)
    OR ...

This definition would clearly lead to useful test requirements. You want to know that **greport** doesn't miss the zero count in either of these:

"test.c", line 4: if was taken TRUE 1, FALSE 0 times.
"test.c", line 4: if was taken TRUE 0, FALSE 1 times.

Every convenience definition's name should be listed in the checklist. That's where you'll put the test requirements gotten from the defining term. (List the effect if you don't bother giving the definition a name.)

Non-Boolean Convenience Definitions

All the convenience definitions seen so far define causes, that is, boolean variables. They don't have to. For example, consider the START variable in sreadhex:

```
START
    IF (*ODD_DIGIT == -1)
    THEN
        START is 0
    ELSE
        START is 1
```

That's a convenience variable. It allows three simple postconditions like

(An even number of digits that don't fill STR: use them all)
IF (START+NUM_HEX_CHARS < RLEN*2) ...

instead of three more complex postconditions like

IF (NUM_HEX_CHARS < RLEN*2 AND *ODD_DIGIT = -1)

    OR

(NUM_HEX_CHARS < RLEN*2-1 AND *ODD_DIGIT in [0,15])...

You should be aware, though, that using START alters the checklist. The more complex form will give rise to more test requirements. You have three options:

1. Read Chapter 25. It describes how you can make the simplification, then multiply test requirements where appropriate.
2. Assume the worst and use the more complex form. Remember, you can always mark the excess test requirements with DEFER, then use as many of them as you can in the tests you have to write anyway.
3. Use your intuition. In this case, START seems justified because the calculation of when to stop (NUM_HEX_CHARS < RLEN*2) is independent of where the first character came from (*ODD_DIGIT or S). Remember, mistakes at this stage might be caught by other test requirements, by the way test requirements are combined into test specifications, or by coverage.

Definitions for Operation and Variable Clues

Effects aren't the only clues that have defining terms. Operation and variable clues might as well. For example, one of the **greport** clues is "the opened mapfile". It should have a defining term that describes how the -test-map and -test-dir arguments are combined to name the file that's opened.

Convenience Definitions without Defining Terms

As you write defining terms, you'll probably think of shorthand variables that are useful but hard to define. In sreadhex, NUM_HEX_CHARS was one. It's a useful notion, but writing a defining term for it doesn't seem productive. Such definitions should still be written as clues. NUM_HEX_CHARS is a count and leads to useful test conditions (in fact, better test conditions than you'd get from a more precise definition).

Remember not to worry about whether convenience definitions have any analogue in the code. A definition can give good test requirements whether or not it really "exists".

Checking Your Work

When you're finished, you should check your work to make sure you haven't missed anything. Scan the original specification again, asking these questions:

▲ Have I missed any effects?

▲ Have I found all the causes for each effect?

▲ Are there any unused causes, ones that don't seem to affect any effect?

Don't forget to check the specification for common errors:

❏ **incompleteness**

Are there any possible inputs whose handling is not described? These are often assumed preconditions. That is, the designer assumed they could never happen. Make sure they really can't.

❏ **ambiguity**

Is there any input that could cause two contradictory effects?

Creating Test Requirements

Process all the defining terms as in Part 1. Search the catalog for variable and operation clues. Guess errors.

12.3 Exercises	Skill at searching for cause-effect statements requires practice. There are three exercises in this book. The easiest is in Chapter 17, where you summarize the MAX specification. You might want to try that now. The following two are a bit subtler. The second of them shows how summarizing a specification interacts with catalog requirements. If you don't yet have experience using the standard catalog (particularly the Syntax entries), you'll have trouble getting the right answer. The POSIX catalog is also used.

1. Write the postcondition for "line shows appended [number]".
2. Write the definition for the opened mapfile. This will be a little more awkward because it's not a boolean, but a Collection. You will need to write a definition that describes the name of the file that's opened. You should begin by writing down one or more effects like this:

the master directory is X

Don't be afraid to use intermediate effects.

Here are two solutions:

APPENDED_NUMBER

Postcondition APPENDED_NUMBER:
    IF (-all option given OR -n option given)
        AND the line does not normally show a count
        AND the line is to be shown in the output
    THEN the line shows an appended [number]

Notes

1. The "line is to be shown in the output" cause could be omitted without harm. Its purpose is to prevent you from writing a test like this:

    Test 1:
        -n option given
        -all not given
        all counts = 0
        line normally shows a count
    Expect:
        Line isn't shown

and thinking that you've tested the results of APPENDED_NUMBER. Since nothing is printed, you can't tell whether it would have had an appended number or not. The rules for test content should catch that mistake, as would coverage, but it doesn't hurt to get it right in the first place.

2. There are several types of lines that "do not normally show a count", but the specification doesn't describe them. Other parts of the GCT documentation do. Those types are:

    operator line
    operand line
    call line
    routine line
    race line

Certainly each of these cases should be tried. They could be written in a definition:

    IF a line is one of these types:
        operator line
    OR operand line
    OR call line
    OR routine line
    OR race line
    THEN it normally does not show a count

However, it would be better to think of "line type" as a Case variable, which would lead to refining APPENDED_NUMBER test requirements with the different type of lines that show or do not show counts. (This example will also be discussed in Chapter 25.)

The Opened Mapfile

When calculating which file to open, there are first two intermediate effects:

1. the master directory can be changed from its default of the current directory.
2. the mapfile name can be changed from its default of *gct-map*.

Then there are two possible final effects:

1. the mapfile name is used as the file to open (if it's absolute).
2. the mapfile name in the master directory is used (in all other cases).

The first two effects could be defined as follows:

> IF the -test-dir option is given
> THEN its argument becomes the master directory

> IF the -test-map option is given
> THEN its argument becomes the mapfile name

However, neither of these is necessary. The catalog's syntax rules will guarantee that both the true and false cases will be tried. (For optional syntax, the catalog requires that the optional element be both given and omitted.) For the same reason, the effects of syntax errors don't need defining terms.

Since the two final effects are mutually exclusive, they can be the THEN and ELSE clauses of a single IF:

> IF the mapfile name is absolute
> THEN it's used as the file to open
> ELSE the file to open is the mapfile name in the master directory

That cause-effect statement assumes that the mapfile exists and is readable. Were that assumption not made, two statements would be required:

> IF the mapfile name is absolute AND it exists AND it's readable
> THEN it's used as the file to open

> IF the mapfile name is not absolute AND it exists AND it's readable
> THEN the file to open is the mapfile name in the master directory

However, the assumption is reasonable because all error causes (such as unreadable files) should be handled in separate preconditions. Moreover, the catalog contains these requirements under "Opening a File for Reading":

> file does not exist
> file is readable
> file exists, but not readable

That eliminates the need to add this detail in a separate explicit precondition.

Actually, even the "IF the mapfile name is absolute" defining term isn't required. The reason is the Pathnames clue in the POSIX catalog, which includes this entry:

IIII➤ • Absolute   IN, OUT
            Example: "/tmp/X"
        • Relative   IN, OUT
            Examples: "../tmp/X", "tmp/X", "X"

That would result in this checklist entry:

    -test-map argument, a pathname
        absolute
        relative

which is exactly what would come from the defining term.

Therefore, the final result of all this analysis is that no definition is needed. The checklist clue can remain in its original form:

    the opened mapfile, a collection of mapfile entries

Note that it does no harm to use one of the redundant defining terms, it just wastes effort. Expect to miss simplifications while you're learning.

12.4 Deriving Specifications from the Code

Effects and causes can be derived from the code as well as from the specification. Fig. 12–1 shows an abbreviated version of the sreadhex code once more for easy reference. The code header will be used for reference only since this is an example of using the code. The results will not be identical to the specification in Part 1.

If, as sreadhex does, a routine contains two separate return statements, it's a safe bet that each corresponds to a different effect. In this case, the statement on line 71 is the effect of running out of STR: there's no more room for digits, though there may be more hexadecimal characters in S. The statement on line 73 is the effect of running out of S: There are no more hexadecimal characters. Those two effects can be listed as clues:

    returning "ran out of STR" indication
    returning "ran out of S" indication

There are two different ways to reach line 73—either from line 63 or line 66. Each sets *ODD_DIGIT differently, in ways that have visible external effect. Those two effects are refinements of one of the previous effects:

    returning "ran out of STR" indication
    returning "ran out of S" indication, with odd character left over in *ODD_DIGIT
    returning "ran out of S" indication, with no character left over

There have been two types of effects: the return value and the setting of an externally-visible variable (*ODD_DIGIT). Are any other variables set? *NREAD is, but that setting doesn't have its own distinct cause (since it's always set just before a return). So it can be considered part of the "returning" effects.

Fig. 12–1
The·
SREADHEX code,
abbreviated

```
29   /* Read a hex string from a stream. */
30   /* Answer 1 if we reached end-of-file before filling the string, */
31   /* 0 if we filled the string first, or <0 on error. */
32   /* *odd_digit should be -1 initially: */
33   /* if an odd number of hex digits was read, *odd_digit is set to */
34   /* the odd digit value, otherwise *odd_digit is set to -1. */
39
40   int
41   sreadhex(str, rlen, nread, odd_digit, s)
42     byte *str;
43     uint rlen;
44     uint *nread;
45     int *odd_digit;
46     register byte *s;
47   {   byte *ptr = str;
48       byte *limit = ptr + rlen;
49       byte val1 = (byte)*odd_digit;
50       byte val2;
51       register char *decoder = (char *)(decode_hex + 1);   /* EOFC = -1! */
52
53       if ( decoder[-1] == 0 )        /* not initialized yet */
54         {   static char hex_chars[] = "0123456789ABCDEFabcdef";
55             int i;
56             memset(decoder - 1, hex_none, 257);
57             for ( i = 0; i < 16+6; i++ )
58               decoder[hex_chars[i]] = (i >= 16 ? i - 6 : i);
59             decoder[0] = hex_eofc;
60         }
61       if ( val1 <= 0xf ) goto d2;
62   d1: while ( (val1 = decoder[sgetc(s)]) > 0xf )
63         { if ( val1 == hex_eofc ) { *odd_digit = -1; goto ended; }
64         }
65   d2: while ( (val2 = decoder[sgetc(s)]) > 0xf )
66         { if ( val2 == hex_eofc ) { *odd_digit = val1; goto ended; }
67         }
68       *ptr++ = (val1 << 4) + val2;
69       if ( ptr < limit ) goto d1;
70       *nread = rlen;
71       return 0;
72   ended:*nread = ptr - str;
73       return 1;
74   }
```

What about the setting of the decoder/decode_hex array? That
effect is not visible outside of sreadhex, so it's not relevant to an ordinary user. It does need to be tested, though, so it could be listed as an
effect:

sreadhex initialized

Assume that's all of the effects. (There's at least one missing.) They are listed in the test requirement checklist along with variable and operation clues. Now they need defining terms. One of the postconditions could be written as

IF there are too few characters in S to fill STR AND that's an odd number of characters THEN returns "ran out of S" indication, with odd character left over

Remember, this cause-effect statement is not intended to be a precise description of what the program does—only under what circumstances it does it. Still, that defining term is not precise enough. How many, exactly, is too few? The length of STR is easy to know: 2*RLEN. So, any number less than 2*RLEN is too few, provided *ODD_DIGIT didn't provide an extra one. If *ODD_DIGIT did, the boundary is 2*RLEN-1.

*ODD_DIGIT provides a digit if it's in the range [0,15]. This is checked on line 61. (Recall that the lower boundary is created by putting a possibly negative number into an unsigned byte.) According to the code, -1 is not the only value that causes *ODD_DIGIT to be ignored. The value 16 would work just as well; the program would produce exactly the same results. The only thing that forces the use of -1 is the convention established in the code header:

32   /* *odd_digit should be -1 initially: */

combined with the convention of using the *ODD_DIGIT result from the last call as its value in the next one. That convention, nowhere enforced in the code, is an assumed precondition, an assumption about what the caller will do:

Assumed: *ODD_DIGIT is in the range [-1, 15].

In this particular case, the effects of violating it are harmless. (Omitting it produces a less restrictive specification than the one in Part 1—a less restrictive specification that happens to be satisfied by exactly the same code.)

Now that RLEN's and *ODD_DIGIT's roles have been defined, a more precise postcondition could be written like this:

NUM_HEX_CHARS is number of hexadecimal characters in S.

IF (NUM_HEX_CHARS < RLEN*2 AND *ODD_DIGIT not in [0,15]
        AND NUM_HEX_CHARS is odd)
            OR
    (NUM_HEX_CHARS < RLEN*2-1 AND *ODD_DIGIT in [0,15]
        AND NUM_HEX_CHARS is even)
THEN returns "ran out of S" indication, with odd character left over

That looks overly complicated. The other two postconditions will have the same pattern of complication: two exclusive cases that depend on the value of *ODD_DIGIT. They can be simplified by using the value of *ODD_DIGIT in the length calculation:

```
START
     IF (*ODD_DIGIT in [0,15])
     THEN
          START is 1
     ELSE
          START is 0

IF START+NUM_HEX_CHARS < RLEN*2 AND START+NUM_HEX_CHARS is odd
THEN returns "ran out of S" indication, with odd character left over
```

This simplification is justified, roughly speaking, by observing that the complication in the specification has no counterpart in the code. *ODD_DIGIT's initial value is used on line 61, and running out of characters is independent of whether it was used or not. (See Chapter 25 for more discussion.)

This analysis leads to abbreviated versions of three of the Part 1 sreadhex postconditions. The abbreviations leave out detail about the effects. The remaining clue can be handled easily:

> IF sreadhex has not been called before
> THEN sreadhex is initialized

That seems to finish the abbreviated specification, but I made a mistake. Checking my work revealed that not all of the effects had been accounted for. The filling of STR from S was, as was the setting of *ODD_DIGIT, but putting the initial value of *ODD_DIGIT into STR wasn't. That leads to this postcondition:

> IF *ODD_DIGIT is initially in the range [0, 15]
> THEN it becomes the first digit of STR.

But the defining term is identical to START's, so this postcondition doesn't add new requirements.

Thinking about possible specification incompleteness is another part of checking your work. Particular values of some of the variables are not handled: NREAD a null pointer, ODD_DIGIT a null pointer, a STR too short to hold RLEN bytes, and so on. These are clearly illegal inputs, as far as the code is concerned, so they are assumed preconditions:

> Assumed: NREAD is a non-null pointer to an integer.
> Assumed: ODD_DIGIT is a non-null pointer to an integer.
> Assumed: STR is a non-null pointer to an array that can
>   hold RLEN bytes (hence 2*RLEN digits).

Whether the assumptions are *correct* is another matter. Remember that assumed preconditions are assumptions about what the caller does. They should be checked when calling routines are inspected. Is there ever a way NREAD could be null?

These particular unhandled inputs can be found in the test requirement catalog (for the first two) and the inspection catalog (for the last). You should also be alert for subsystem-specific special cases.

If you look at the original sreadhex specification, you'll notice Precondition 7:

> Validated: RLEN is not 0
>   On failure:
>   *NREAD is 0
>   The return value is 0.

Why wasn't it found? The reason is that it's completely artificial. If you check, the specified results of violating this precondition are identical to those that satisfying Postcondition 3 would give if RLEN were 0. Precondition 7 exists only because I needed an example of a validated precondition, not because it corresponds to anything in the code. (The test requirement RLEN=0, from Precondition 7, finds a fault. But the same requirement is redundantly gotten by considering RLEN a count, so the precondition is not needed. Not using a precondition means RLEN=0 won't be considered an ERROR requirement. That's appropriate, because it should be a perfectly valid input.)

Working with Large Subsystems

13.1 Coping with Complexity

Ideally, you would design tests for a 10,000 line subsystem just as you would for `sreadhex`. You would derive test requirements from all sources, including the subsystem's external specification, internal routine specifications, and the code within the routines. Then you would combine them all into test specifications.

If you try this in practice, you'll be swamped by complexity. You won't be able to handle that many test requirements all at once. You'll spend too much time, especially time correcting many design and book-keeping errors. You must break the problem down. Create all the test requirements, but build test specifications from subsets of them. I find that I can handle about five pages of test requirements comfortably. (This varies, of course, according to the complexity of the requirements and subsystem.)

How should these subsets be selected? If the test requirements are all from related routines, the tests will be easier to design and write, but they'll have less variety. In particular, they'll be weak at finding interaction faults between those routines and the rest of the subsystem. In my own testing, I use the following procedure, which is also given in the checklists of Appendix F:

1. Derive all the test requirements from the subsystem's external interface.
2. Derive the test requirements from all internal routines.
3. Select a manageable group of test requirements. One half to three fourths should be from internal routines. (Use requirements from related routines, ones which often call each other. That means that the interface requirements serve double duty—they test both the

calling and called routine. It also allows more combinations of test requirements, thus more complex tests.) The remainder of the test requirements are from the external interface. Use ones that will force variety into the tests.

4. Build test specifications from those requirements. Stop when you find yourself unable to satisfy more than one or two unsatisfied requirements per test. Merge those unused test requirements into the next group.

5. The tests can be implemented now or after all test specifications are written. To catch design or implementation problems as soon as possible, I usually implement immediately. I'll also usually check coverage after each set of tests, but I don't examine it in detail. I just verify that I'm getting the sort of coverage I expect, and I scan the coverage reports to see if my test design is missing anything obvious that I can include in the next batch of tests.

6. Repeat, starting with Step 3, continuing until all requirements are used.

7. Measure coverage of the entire test suite and look for missed clues in the usual way. If that results in too many clues to work with all at once, pick subsets that will increase the variety of coverage-based tests.

I find this an efficient approach. The external interface requirements are used more often than the internal requirements, which is appropriate. They're more important.

13.1.1 Scheduling Testing

Remember that the process of test design can reveal specification bugs. These are cases where the specification does not handle some plausible inputs or where it clearly does not match customer needs. Since those bugs are often terribly hard to fix, and of great importance to customers, it makes sense to design some tests early.

When possible, develop the first test requirement checklist along with the specification. Use it during specification reviews. Write some of the test specifications at the same time. Those tests may lack some variety, because they won't make use of internal test requirements, but they will force you to think hard about the subsystem's interface and specification.

When the code is finished, find the internal requirements and use them as described in the previous section. First combine them with any unused external requirements. Then reuse already-satisfied external requirements. You'll probably end up with more tests than if you'd waited until you had all the requirements before building the first test. Some of the external requirements will be "overused". That's fine. It will make doubly sure that the external interface is well exercised.

13.1.2 Routine Requirements

When generating clues and requirements from a routine, tag them with the routine's name. Do this by building one checklist per routine. When building test specifications, you'll work with groups of requirements. Some will be from the external interface; others will be from internal routines. Such a combined checklist would look like this:

> External interface NOTIFY command
> > carbon copy effect
> > > CC given, BCC not given
> > > CC not given, BCC given
> > > CC not given, BCC not given
>
> > ...
>
> requirements from the open_network_connection routine
> > hop_count, a count
> > > hop_count=0
> > > hop_count=1
> > > ...
>
> > ...

The `hop_count=0` requirement means "use the external interface to force `open_network_connection` to be called with `hop_count` zero". It is usually fairly easy to work backwards from a routine name to the part of the external interface that exercises it. Sometimes it's hard.

An important reason for tagging clues with their source is that it forces more thorough testing of global variables. Suppose you have a global count called `clients`. If five routines use `clients`, you will have five sets of requirements:

> trial1() clues
> > clients, a count
> > > 0
> > > 1...
>
> trial2() clues
> > clients, a count
> > > 0
> > > 1...
>
> > ...

instead of a single global clue

> clients, a global count
> > 0
> > 1...

The larger set of clues forces all the users of `clients` to exercise it thoroughly. The single clue might never give a zero value to `trial1()`, missing the bug when that function tries to divide by `clients`.

You've perhaps noticed an oddity here. When a variable is used in several functions in the subsystem, it is to be well exercised in each. When a variable is used in several places in a function, it needn't be. That is, suppose we were testing this function:

```
a_function(int which, int arg)
{
    switch(which)
    {
    case trial1:
        arg = arg/clients;
        break;
    case trial2:
        arg = arg + clients;
        break;
    ...
    }
}
```

Subsystem testing would require only that `clients` take on the value 0, 1, >1, and so on. There's a single `clients` clue, not one per `case`, so the bug in `trial1` (possible division by zero) could be missed. How can this be right?

Let me name the two situations. Call the one where each global's requirements are satisfied separately for each routine the *global reachability rule*. The more thorough situation is that every variable (local as well as global) is fully exercised at every use of that variable (every statement where the program refers to the value of the variable). This is the *complete variable reachability rule*. There are three reasons for not using that rule as part of basic subsystem testing:

❏ **Global reachability is much cheaper.**

There will be many variables, but few of them will be global. There are many fewer routines that use globals than statements that use variables. Complete variable reachability would have vastly more requirements than global reachability.

❏ **Global reachability has associated errors.**

Many faults are caused when the writer of a routine either completely forgets about a global or fails to anticipate one of its possible values. Other than global reachability, there is no mechanism to create test requirements to find those faults. Global reachability is necessary.

❏ **Complete variable reachability is adequately covered otherwise.**

Global reachability is also usually sufficient. That is, most or all of the important complete reachability requirements will be satisfied by tests you'd write anyway. ("Important" means those associated with likely faults.) In this respect, complete reachability is like coverage: there's no reason to think about requirements that will be automatically satisfied. Unlike coverage, there's no safety net—there's no way to measure when the requirements aren't satisfied.

For this reason, you may want to be explicit about the more important complete reachability requirements. Doing this is a topic of Chapter 25.

13.1.3 ERROR Requirements in Larger Subsystems

The rules for error tests given in Part 1 were:

1. Every test satisfies exactly one ERROR test requirement.
2. Only the ERROR requirement's count is incremented. Non-ERROR requirements are never considered satisfied by an error test specification. Two ERROR requirements are never satisfied by the same test.

These rules are a simpler restatement of the general rule for test content that test requirements must be exercised. The simplification is based on two assumptions:

1. Error checking is the first thing a subsystem does.
2. Error checking leads to an immediate exit.

The rules generally work well for small subsystems, even when the assumptions are not completely true (they sometimes aren't). In larger subsystems, ERROR requirements are sometimes better handled in a less simpleminded way. That is, the general rule is applied differently.

Delayed Error Handling

Suppose that a great deal of processing takes place before the error is detected. There are three cases.

1. The results of the earlier processing affect the way the error is detected or handled. If so, the ERROR requirement should be satisfied several times with several combinations of the requirements from the earlier processing. The procedure is described shortly.
2. The error wipes out all the effects of the processing. Further, the results of the processing have no effect on error handling. In this case, the traditional handling of ERROR requirements is perfectly appropriate. The non-ERROR requirements have no visible effect, so their counts should not be incremented. (Be wary: What may seem to have no effect may actually have one. If suspicious, treat this case like the previous one.)
3. The earlier processing has visible effects, but they are independent of the error handling (have no effect on it). If so, it may be more efficient to test the earlier processing and an ERROR requirement together in the same test. In this situation, you do increment the counts for non-ERROR test requirements, because you know they are exercised and have visible effects.

High-Risk Error Handling

Until now, each error requirement was tested exactly once, whereas most non-error requirements were satisfied by several tests. If there is a fault, you only get one chance to see it. That may be reasonable, since error handling faults are often not too important. (There's usually a simple workaround for the user: don't cause the error.) It's especially reasonable if you make the single test complex. A complex test avoids testing what the programmer already tested (though programmers generally skimp on error handling tests). More importantly, complexity forces you to think, so you may think of an unhandled error requirement.

But error handling is not always unimportant. An undetected error may lead to a catastrophe. If an error requires recovery (rather than just detection and exiting), faults are likely and probably severe. If error handling is high risk, you should test it thoroughly while still ensuring that all non-ERROR test requirements are exercised in non-error tests.

Do the following for each distinct error effect.

1. In a separate checklist, list each of the error requirements that can cause that error effect.
2. Select all non-error test requirements that might be relevant. Include any that the error-checking or error-handling code might depend on. Copy them to the new checklist.
3. Double check. Consider the error effect carefully. If it is underspecified (error effects often are), derive or guess more test requirements. Also make sure no test requirements for operations or variables were missed. Pay special attention to OUT variables. Their test requirements will force diverse and stressful execution of the error handling code.
4. Design error handling tests from the new checklist. Every test specification should satisfy one (but only one) of the error requirements and as many of the other requirements as possible. Finish when all the requirements (of both kinds) have been satisfied at least once.
5. When the error checklist is used up, the error requirements can be marked as satisfied in the original checklist. The other requirements are left unchanged. Each of them must still be satisfied in a non-error test, if possible.

Error-Checking Routines

Some routines in a subsystem may have the job of checking for errors. Such a routine might look like this:

```
/* Returns 1 if the file is available. Returns 0 if it is unavailable
 * for any reason, including network outage, another user has it
 * locked, it doesn't exist, and so on.
 */

int
check_file_availability(char *filename)
{
  ...
}
```

Scattered throughout the subsystem would be code like this:

```
some_function()
{
    ...
    if (!check_file_availability(file))
    {
        return ERROR;
    }
    ...
}
```

The test requirement checklist for some_function should look like this:

```
some_function checklist
    file is not available              ERROR
    some other requirement
    ...
```

It also might contain error requirements for the different possible causes of unavailable files, if they might have an effect on some_function.

What of the separate checklist for check_file_availability? It will look like this:

```
check_file_availability checklist
    file is available
    there's a network outage
    ...
```

The first question is whether these requirements should be marked with ERROR. On the one hand, a network outage is not an error from check_file_availability's point of view, it's just a condition it reports. On the other hand, check_file_availability has no purpose other than to find error conditions for other parts of the subsystem. I recommend adding ERROR markers to reduce the chance that these requirements will incorrectly be satisfied in tests not intended to be ERROR tests.

Whether or not the check_file_availability requirements are marked as ERRORs, satisfying some_function's "file is not available" requirement must also satisfy one of them. Its count should be incremented. It is certainly exercised with visible effects, so the rule for test content is satisfied. Thus, the very first ERROR test specification might increment these two requirements:

```
some_function checklist
1   file is not available              ERROR (Test 1)
0   some other requirement
...

check_file_availability checklist
0   file is available
1   there's a network outage           ERROR (Test 1)
...
```

The preceding discussion skimmed over some of the dangers of testing a large subsystem. That testing works with a list of test requirements, many of which are particular to certain routines. To satisfy them, you must find inputs to the subsystem that deliver appropriate values to those routines. To discover a fault, any incorrect internal results must propagate to the boundary of the subsystem, where they're compared to the expected results.

As subsystems grow larger, certain problems grow as well. First, you may see no way to satisfy a test requirement for an internal routine through the subsystem interface. In this case, you have several options:

1. You can test the routine in isolation. This requires writing a driver that delivers input to the function. You may also have to write *stub* functions to replace the subroutines the function calls. Other times you may be able to extract those subroutines as well, but it's often the case that they call other subroutines, which call other subroutines, and so on. You end up having to extract nearly everything.

    As mentioned in the introduction, writing such drivers and stubs is expensive. It becomes especially expensive during maintenance. If you use stubs, any change to the subsystem may require that corresponding changes be made to stubs, or that new stubs be written. Drivers also often have to be changed. This multiplies the cost of changes, and increases the chance that drivers and stubs will be abandoned.

    In my own testing, I seldom test routines in isolation.

2. Another alternative is to ignore the test requirement. This is appropriate if you believe it can *never* be satisfied while the routine is in the subsystem. (That is, test requirements can be infeasible, just like coverage conditions.) For example, the routine may do some validation of its input, but the subsystem always passes it correct input. There is some danger here: even if the error case cannot be exercised in this system today, it might be exercised in the same system tomorrow. Or the code might be reused under the assumption that it's been completely tested.

3. You can use the test requirement in a code inspection. Be sure to keep the test requirement and use it in reinspections when the code changes.

4. My preference is to modify the subsystem to make it more easily testable, by adding "minidrivers" to the system itself (usually controlled by a combination of compile-time and run-time flags). These drivers deliver the appropriate value to the function under test. Because they're very specific, they're usually simple. This approach is discussed below.

A more serious problem is when you *think* you've satisfied an internal routine's test requirement, but your test is incorrect. This can happen even in unit testing, of course, but it's a more common problem in subsystem testing because there's so much code between the subsystem interface and the routine you wish to exercise. Perhaps some of that code handles your chosen input as a special case and never delivers it to the targeted routine. Coverage often points to such testing mistakes. It's not infallible, though, because many test requirements check for faults of omission, and coverage is poor at detecting the absence of such requirements. Internal mini-drivers make the problem less likely.

The most serious problem is that incorrectness in the interior routine may not reveal itself in the subsystem output. For example, suppose the internal routine produces a complicated linked list structure and the subsystem produces 0 or 1. Information is lost in that transformation ([Voas91a], [Voas91b]). A correct and incorrect linked list structure may both produce 1, so you can't test the interior routine well via the subsystem.

The possible solutions to this problem are to switch to unit testing, hope that all failures do propagate, or modify the subsystem to reveal its internal state (by printing the linked list structure, for example). The last possibility is usually not too difficult; I prefer it.

13.2.1 Internal Test Drivers

The difficulties mentioned in the previous section arise because systems are not designed to be testable—they are not designed to be easy to force into known states, and they do not provide internal results in a way that allows them to be compared to expected results. Of course, redesigning systems for testability is usually too big a job to attempt at any particular time—there's always a release to get out.

What needs to be done is to add testing code at those points in the subsystem where inputs are hard to force (to give you external control) and at those points where information is lost (to make that information available). This needs to be done gradually, within existing time constraints. What is needed is a way of "growing" the testability of the system, so that every month you have a better prototype of a truly testable system.

Fortunately, programmers in the course of debugging have the same needs as testers, and they often write debugging code that can be adapted to testing.

Consider the GNU Make program. It maintains an internal hash table of files. The programmer wrote debugging code to print out the entries in the hash table. The output looks like this (edited for brevity):

```
# Files

a::
# Command-line target.
# Implicit rule search has not been done.
# Implicit/static pattern stem: ' '
# Last modified Mon Jul 27 10:37:55 1992 (712251475)
# File has been updated.
# Successfully updated.
# 18 variables in 23 hash buckets.
# average of 78.3 variables per bucket, max 2 in one bucket.
```

This is almost what you would need to check the results of the hash table manipulation routines, but there are several problems:

1. The file's location in the hash table is not printed (in particular, we want output that shows how hash table collisions have been handled).
2. Variable values are translated into text useful to the person (such as "successfully updated"). For testing, we'd prefer to see the exact values, especially if several distinct values are merged into one message.
3. The date in the output will cause spurious differences when expected output is compared to actual output. (This problem can be avoided by "smart differencing" programs that can be told to ignore fields that are expected to change between runs of a test.)

Revising the routine to solve these is simple. An example of testing output is:

```
aa:: (at bucket 194, bucket pos 0, duplicate pos 0)
#  (update_status = 1) (allow_dups = 1)
aa: (at bucket 194, bucket pos 0, duplicate pos 1)
#  (update_status = 2) (allow_dups = 0)
aa: (at bucket 194, bucket pos 0, duplicate pos 2)
#  (update_status = 3) (allow_dups = 0)
# 2 files in 1007 hash buckets.
# average 0.2 files per bucket, max 1 files in one bucket.
```

The hash table routines are now testable at very little expense.

Surprisingly, some organizations discourage the inclusion of debugging code in the finished product. The code may then be unavailable for testing; at best, it will be less useful (because it's "throwaway" code in the first place). Eliminate this policy.

The same organizations probably also resist "cluttering up the code with testing crud." You often don't want testing code in the executable, usually for performance reasons. (However, if the testing code is modified debugging code, that inclusion may save a lot of time when answering phone calls from customers.) But there is rarely a reason not to include testing code in the source and compile it out in the delivered version. There are three arguments you may face:

❐ **"We should test what we ship"**

This is absolutely true—for the last two runs of the test suite. During earlier development, there is very little risk in using a testing version. The small risk of the testing code obscuring a fault and causing it to be discovered late is counterbalanced by the other faults that will be found because more tests are feasible. ("Last two runs" instead of "last run" because the last run is just before delivery. If the testing code does obscure a fault, that's a terrible time to discover it.)

❒ **"Too much testing code makes the system unmodifiable."**

If your testing modifications cause every third line to be

#ifdef TESTING

you should certainly rethink them. Testing changes should be as modular as any other enhancement.

❒ **"This will break the development schedule."**

Internal test support code does add to maintenance costs. For example, changing the definition of a structure may require fixing the testing code before the subsystem will compile. If the fix is wrong, many tests will fail spuriously and the reason will have to be discovered. Even if much of the work is done by the tester, there is schedule impact.

The important thing to emphasize is that the total workload is reduced. Subsystem changes always wreak havoc with test support code; it's just that the developers never saw it before. (Only testers did.) Grow testability slowly to minimize disruption—and give the time saved back to the developers.

As converting debugging code to testing code becomes more common, make it simpler by providing conventions, support code, and examples. Keep in mind that the purpose is not to make the debugging code harder to write, but to make it more adaptable for testing. As low-cost efforts prove their worth, move toward a more complete in-system debugger and test driver. I'll discuss an example.

I was the leader of a team of programmers porting a version of Common Lisp from an obscure workstation to an obscure minicomputer. The workstation was of the now unfashionable type that allowed user-programmable microcode. That is, it did not exactly have a "native" instruction set; instead, each high-level language compiler could assume a machine language tailored to its requirements. The Common Lisp compiler assumed an instruction set much like that of the MIT Lisp Machines. For example, the Lisp "cons" instruction was also a machine language instruction, implemented in microcode. The garbage collector was also implemented in microcode.

The first step of the port was to emulate all the microcoded instructions by C and assembly code on the minicomputer, turning it into a Lisp machine emulator. Garbage collection was the hardest instruction; I began with it. I implemented debugging code that allowed me to initialize the state of the imaginary Lisp machine, take a snapshot, garbage collect, take another snapshot, and compare the two states. For testing, all that was required was to allow the garbage collector debugger to be driven by a script. The remaining instruction emulations were debugged and tested using extensions of what I'd already done for garbage collection, mainly by adding more flexibility in setting up the starting state. As the system grew closer to completion, more debugging features were added as needed. (In particular, after every difficult bug fix, I asked myself what new debugging command would have made the problem more obvious. Then I added that command.) Because this increasingly capable driver was designed to be script-driven, each new debugging feature could also be a new testing feature.

Of course, in other systems, such an elaborate test driver is not required. Almost all of the Generic Coverage Tool's tests use special testing code, but most of them depend on only one 10-line segment. Some of the others use relatively simple subsystem-specific routines that print out a portion of GCT's internal state.

At some point, a gradual approach may be insufficient; eventually, you may find that you need an overhaul of the system to test as thoroughly as you like. But the costs are modest, the benefits immediate, and success at small changes can give you the experience you'll need to justify a more designed, less "grown," internal test driver.

13.2.2 External Debuggers

A good programmable debugger can also be used. Instead of building an internal debugger, customize an external one. There are some drawbacks, though. The testing code is outside the system and easy to invalidate accidentally. The invalidation is less noticeable than in a test driver written in the system's source language (where the invalidation usually takes the form of a driver that will no longer compile). Programming the debugger is a rarer skill than programming in the source language, and the customizations are usually not very maintainable. The debugger's language is probably not very powerful, making it harder to suppress unnecessary detail in the output. The input and output will likely not look very much like the way you design your tests, making an extra mental translation necessary when writing them.

Nevertheless, the writer of the debugger has done a lot of work that you might have to redo, so this is certainly an option to consider.

13.2.3 Doing Without

It's important to note that you can still write tests even if you don't yet have a good internal debugger. Consider the case of the system that returns 1 or 0. You can design and implement all the tests now, even though the lack of revealed state means you'll miss some bugs. In the future, the implementation can be upgraded to check correctness of internal state.

If you know you can't satisfy a test requirement without an internal test driver, you shouldn't write a test specification that satisfies it. You'll have to save that test requirement and create a test for it later.

In practice, testing usually tracks development, and the subsystems you test are the subsystems that the development team produces. Choosing a subsystem amounts to deciding whether a development subsystem is the right size to test. Should it be subdivided? Should it be tested together with another small subsystem? Here are some considerations:

13.3 Choosing Subsystems

1. Your first priority is making test implementation easier. Select a body of code whose test driver will be simple to write. Implementation is easiest if the subsystem can be tested through the whole-system interface.

2. Testability is nearly as important. Will you be able to satisfy internal test requirements? Will failures propagate to the output?
3. Ideally, there should be a single programmer responsible for a subsystem. If the code belongs to several programmers, too many bugs will have ambiguous ownership, and time will be wasted assigning responsibility. A single "owner" of the subsystem also means that the tester always knows who to go to for advice.
4. A disadvantage of subsystem testing is that faults are harder to track down than when units are tested in isolation. (The corresponding consolations are that less time is spent implementing tests, and that more faults are found. It may be harder to debug a subsystem test failure, but it beats debugging a customer's failure over the phone.) Don't combine subsystems if that will make debugging much harder.
5. Larger subsystems mean that more must be complete before testing can begin. They also mean that there's less opportunity to schedule testing tasks in parallel.

13.3.1 Who Tests?

An important part of planning testing is matching the tester to the subsystem. A tester who knows compilers well can test a compiler better and faster. That tester can deal with larger subsystems, largely because testability problems are more obvious and their solutions clearer. The logical extension of this is to have a programmer test his or her own subsystem.

The conventional wisdom is that programmers can't test their own code. This is broadly true, but you can optimize your testing by considering the details of how it's true. Most programmers have no training in testing, so a trained tester of course does better. Even if the programmers are trained, independent testers will find more—and more serious—faults, especially those caused by mistaken assumptions. The programmers won't find those because they're the people who originally made the mistaken assumptions, and they're likely to cling to them.

However, programmers do test much more cheaply because they have less to learn about the system. It is this that accounts for the widespread practice of having individual programmers test their own code, and only involving independent testers when an integrated system (or large subsystem) is available. The additional benefit of the independent tester does not outweigh the additional cost. (Especially if the independent tester doesn't finish "coming up to speed" until after the system is shipped.)

I recommend a strategy that assigns parts of testing to those who can do them most cost-effectively. Most programmers, with training, can test their own small subsystems perfectly well—especially if they measure their testing with coverage. Such small subsystems offer less scope for mistaken assumptions, and the type of mistaken assumptions they contain are the sort the catalogs target.

As subsystems grow larger, an independent point of view becomes more important. When developers create their test requirement checklists—during, not after, design and coding—they begin to need occasional consulting from testing experts. A skilled tester can sit down with the developer, get a quick guided tour of the subsystem, and efficiently help improve the text requirements. Detailed knowledge is not required. The developer writes the test specifications, but the testing expert should review them for two reasons. The first is that such a review reveals undiscovered test requirements. The second is to check the rules for test form and (especially) test content; the person writing the tests is much more liable to overlook the testing mistakes these target.

Developers implement the tests, but testing experts should provide implementation support techniques and tools. It is more efficient to have a few experts than to expect everyone to know everything. This implementation support will also help developers create tests that are truly repeatable and maintainable.

The independent tester as test consultant can serve many programmers. As subsystems become still larger—and more prone to serious assumption errors—the independent tester does more of the testing work. System testing is where such errors dominate, and it is there that an independent testing team is critical. They target particular system risks and write special tests for them.

With appropriate guidance, review, and coverage, most programmers can detach themselves enough from their product to catch almost all the faults. Some cannot; some people are just lousy testers. The economic fact of life is that those programmers are anachronisms. They're less valuable in a quality-conscious world.

14

Testing Bug Fixes and Other Maintenance Changes

This chapter discusses applying subsystem testing during maintenance. [1]

Maintenance can either be enhancements or bug fixes; both cases are tested the same way.

[Basili81] reports that 6 percent of changes to a system were to correct or complete a previous change. [Weiss85] reports that between 2.5 percent and 6.1 percent of all changes result in a fault. I have heard of failure rates as high as 10 percent for bug fixes. Clearly, testing changes is important.

It's also expensive. As a very rough rule of thumb, I estimate that it's three times as much work to test a later change than it would be to test the same code as part of the original system. As always there's a tradeoff between effort and thoroughness. Testing during maintenance is much easier if you have a good automated test suite. You can build on that previous work. Unfortunately, changes must often be tested without one. This presents new problems: you cannot afford to generate a large set of test requirements, form test specifications, then throw all those tests away because you have no test suite to put them in. You need a lower cost solution that loses as little effectiveness as possible. (A great deal will inevitably be lost.)

Bugs in Changes

There are several ways a change can be inadequate. First, it can simply be wrong (a bug fix does not fix the reported bug). More likely it is a change that isn't general enough. It correctly handles some inputs, such as those that caused a reported failure, but continues to fail on related inputs.

---

1. This way of looking at changes was partly inspired by [Hamlet92] and [Morell91], and by discussion with Dick Hamlet.

As an example, consider a nutrition analysis program that miscalculates the number of calories. The program's calculation is

```
calories = 4 * (grams_of_fat + grams_of_protein + grams_of_carbohydrates);
```

An alert customer notices that the number of calories reported for a 42-gram scone is wrong and reports the bug. The programmer fixes the fault with this code:

```
if (food == SCONE)
    calories = 150;
else
    calories = 4 * (grams_of_fat + grams_of_protein + grams_of_carbohydrates);
```

The program now gives the right answer for scones. It's still wrong, though, because it miscalculates the number of calories due to fat. The correct formula is

```
calories = 9 * grams_of_fat + 4 * (grams_of_protein + grams_of_carbohydrates);
```

Finding that the program is wrong requires testing more than just that the original failure went away. Other inputs should also be tried, "nearby" inputs that exercise the changed code in different ways. Not just any nearby input will do—in this case, testing on nonfat foods would not reveal the bug. The nearby inputs should be those likely to reveal faults; that is, they should satisfy test requirements.

This particular example seems silly. Surely, no programmer would make such a fix? In fact, programmers do every day, usually because they're under heavy time pressure, don't understand the application area, and are afraid a more general change will break something else in a system they don't know well. When fixing faults in an unfamiliar system, I easily become obsessed by the overwhelming fragility of the whole thing, the feeling that any change could bring the whole house of cards crashing down. It's hard to force myself to make a change more general than is absolutely required, especially when the backlog of unfixed bugs keeps growing.

Another reason to test nearby inputs is that changes can be too general. When the original change was made to handle a special case, the test of which cases are special can be incorrect. If so, ordinary cases are incorrectly treated specially. As an example, this divide-by-zero error

```
a = b / c;
```

might be fixed with

```
if (c > 0)   /* Should be == */
then
    a = b / c;
else
    signal_error("Input value C should not be zero.");
```

**Questions
Maintenance Testing
Should Answer**

▲ Was the change
correct?

▲ Was the change
general enough?

▲ Did the change break
something else?

▲ Should the change
be made somewhere
else?

A test of c==0 would confirm that the change "fixes the reported bug". That it was in fact incorrect won't be found until c is given a value less than zero.

Ordinary subsystem testing, slightly modified and with a restricted focus, is good at finding such problems. Other incorrect changes are harder to find. The worst are the "house of cards" problems, those where the change disturbs some delicate relationships assumed by distant code. In one system, a global queue could be in one of two states. A bug fix changed subsystem A so that, in one circumstance, the queue was placed in the second state. Unknown to the person fixing the bug, distant subsystem B assumed that the queue was always in the first state. The now violated assumption had catastrophic results. But there was no clue about that assumption in any of the source for subsystem A. (There wasn't really much of a clue even in subsystem B.) This type of fault will be called a *propagation fault*.

A final type of incorrect fix is another lack of generality problem. The same fault might exist in several places, but it's often fixed in only one. How are those other *similarity faults* identified?

Subsystem testing during maintenance has two parts. The first concentrates on exercising the changed code to discover the simpler problems. The procedure is roughly the same as always, but the focus is restricted to particular parts of the subsystem. Because of that tight focus, special vigilance is required to avoid adopting the same (possibly mistaken) assumptions that the code does. And, even with it, you will likely end up with more test requirements than you can afford, especially if you must test manually. In that case, some will have to be ignored, or used in code reads rather than tests. (Because simply noticing a test requirement often makes you think of a fault, it's better to discover them and discard them than restrict the focus even further.)

The second part of maintenance testing concentrates on propagation and similarity faults. The test requirements for these faults are often hard to implement, so this step is usually done in a code read or design review, or as a part of the analysis before the change is made.

14.1
An Example

The following code is similar to some in the coverage tool, GCT, described in the chapter on coverage. The code in bold face fixes a fault.

```
if (strcmp(argv[i], "-test-cc")) {
    char *new_dir = safe_concat(GCT_DIR, "/", argv[++i]);
    if (strlen(new_dir) > max_dir_name)
        max_dir_name = strlen(new_dir);
    names[0] = new_dir;
}
```

GCT operates by preprocessing C source, adding code to measure coverage, then invoking a C compiler to compile the instrumented source. The -test-cc option is used to name a nondefault compiler.[1] In addition to telling GCT what compiler to use, the name also identifies a directory

---

1. In UNIX, options conventionally begin with a '-'. They're used like DOS options, which begin with a '/'.

where compiler-specific include files are stored. That directory is a subdirectory of GCT_DIR, a constant pathname selected when GCT is first installed. A typical compiler-specific directory would be */usr/local/lib/gct-include/gcc*. It would contain the GNU C compiler's versions of *<varargs.h>* and *<stdarg.h>*, to be used in preference to the versions in */usr/include*.

This code, then, calculates the compiler's directory (new_dir) and stores it as the zero-th entry in the names array, ensuring that it will be searched before any other system include files. But the variable max_dir_name stores the maximum length of the directories in the names array. In the original program, names[0] was replaced without updating max_dir_name. Too little space might later be allocated, leading to a buffer overflow and catastrophic failure. The solution was to update max_dir_name when necessary. (Note that this is a classic fault of omission.)

This particular example is of a single, small change. Larger changes will be discussed later.

Subsystem testing is applied, focusing on the new text and nearby text. A checklist in Appendix F summarizes this procedure.

14.2 The Basic Procedure for Testing Changes

The Size of the Change

Focusing only on the new text will make you miss some faults, especially ones caused by not enough generality. From now on, the "changed code" will be all the new text and all the text within one or two enclosing blocks. (Curly braces, { }, delimit blocks.) In the GCT example, all the code shown is part of the changed code.

Variables

In practice, test requirements from variables are very effective at finding bugs in changes. Concentrate on them. Write down all the variables in the changed code as clues, omitting only those that are redundant with other variables. Do *not* omit variables that are handled the same as before the change—perhaps they should be handled differently, and the only way to detect that is to exercise their test requirements.

The changed code from the example leads to these clues:

-test-cc argument, a string
program's argument list, a collection (from argv and argc)
GCT_DIR, a pathname[1]
max_dir_name, a count
names[], a collection of strings

---

1. GCT_DIR is a constant, set at installation time. Treating it as a clue would result in the "relative pathname" requirement from the POSIX catalog. It makes no sense to install GCT with GCT_DIR as a relative pathname. When I wrote the installation instructions, it never occurred to me that someone might. Of course, someone did. My attitude toward such misunderstandings is that they're documentation bugs to fix. So I did, essentially making an assumed precondition explicit. But it would have been better to have used the catalog during installation testing and found the problem then.

You need still more variable clues. When making a change, a common error is forgetting some variables. Here is an example. Device error handling was improved in a device driver. The improved code checked for a particular status, using code like this:

```
if (status_word & ERROR_FLAG)
    <handle this error>
```

But in fact that error bit wasn't the only one. The code should have looked like this:

```
if (status_word & (ERROR_FLAG | OTHER_ERROR_FLAG))
    <handle this error>
```

The "forgotten variables" were the other bits in the status word.

To discover such problems, discover and list variables related to those variables that are handled differently by the changed code. "Handled differently" means either that their values are used differently, or that they can have a different value as the result of the change. Good types of variables to consider are unchanged fields in a changed structure, variables with a similar purpose, or variables that are commonly used together with changed variables. At best, such variables will directly find faults. At the worst, they will serve as sources of variety in test specifications. (Concentrating on variety is, if anything, even more important when testing small changes. There aren't as many easy sources of variety as when testing entire subsystems.)

In summary, the following variables should be listed:

▲ variables used or set differently by the changed code.

▲ any variables used or set by the changed code, even if they're handled just the same.

▲ variables unmentioned in the changed code, but related to variables used or set differently.

The Demonstration Requirement

The demonstration requirement is a test requirement describing those inputs that cause a failure. For the example, the test requirement would be

-test-cc is given AND the new name is longer than the current default

This is the situation in which max_dir_name has the wrong value. Demonstration requirements have two parts. The first part causes the changed code to be executed. The second part causes it to be exercised such that it has a different effect than the unchanged code did.[1]

---

1. Those who read the Overview of Subsystem Testing will recognize these as the reachability and necessity conditions, respectively.

The demonstration requirement is listed as a clue. Because the requirement uses AND, it will lead to at least three test requirements:

1. one in which the changed code is not executed.

   (-test-cc is not given)

2. one in which the changed code is executed, but the results are as before.

   (-test-cc given, new name is not longer than the default)

3. one that is the demonstration requirement itself.

   (-test-cc given, new name is longer than the default)

The first is of little use. At best, it reminds you to think of whether any other code should have the same change made. (Might other options that change names also forget to change max_dir_name?) The second test requirement is used in tests that check whether the change is too specific. The final requirement checks whether the change does what it's supposed to do.

The Specification

The routine and subsystem specifications are two other sources for clues. Each of them may have preconditions or postconditions which, when satisfied or violated, cause the changed code to be executed. They should be written down as clues and processed in the ordinary way (including the AND/OR rules). Some of the resulting test requirements will not exercise the changed code; those can be discarded, but all should at least be considered.

If there are no preconditions and postconditions for the routine, treat the changed code as if it were a function you were testing without a specification. That is, derive the relevant effects and their defining terms, as described in Chapter 12.

For the example, three postcondition requirements that apply to the -test-cc option seemed relevant:

the named directory does not exist
the named directory is empty
the named directory has include files in it

(Just what happens in each case is not important for this example.)

I'm embarrassed to admit that, at this point in testing the fix, I stumbled across another fault. Here again is the code, this time with the new fault in bold font:

```
if (strcmp(argv[i], "-test-cc")) {
    char *new_dir = safe_concat(GCT_DIR, "/", argv[++i]);
    if (strlen(new_dir) > max_dir_name)
        max_dir_name = strlen(new_dir);
    names[0] = new_dir;
}
```

This code assumes that when -test-cc is given, its argument is always given. This is not the case in an invocation like

```
% gct -test-cc
```

`safe_concat` is given `argv[++i]`, which is a null pointer in this case. The result, on most machines, is a crash. This is particularly embarrassing because this situation is explicitly mentioned in the POSIX test requirement catalog. Since I wrote that catalog, I should know about this type of mistake, and I shouldn't make it. Instead, my knowledge allowed me to catch it after I did.

Notice that I wasn't looking for this kind of fault at all; I was looking to see how postconditions exercised the changed code. But I was looking at the code in a different way, in the right frame of mind to see faults. Having faults jump out at you is a normal experience in those circumstances.

The Operations

The operations that affect the changed code should be listed. These are

▲ any cliches contained in the changed code

▲ any cliches containing the changed code

▲ any function calls in the changed code.

The example contains no cliches. It is, however, enclosed in a cliche, the large loop that processes all of GCT's options. The POSIX catalog contains test requirements for option processing. One of them calls for the invocation that catches the embarrassing second fault. This is an example of how a focus wider than just the new code can find faults. In this case, it was a fault unrelated to the change, but it could as well have been a side effect of the change.

The Bug Report as a Clue

It is very important to ask why the existing tests failed to detect the bug. A bug report points to under-exercised or missing clues, just as coverage conditions do. Use the bug report as a spur to error-guessing.

Test Requirements

As already noted, test requirements are derived in the usual way. It is reasonable to ignore test requirements that never exercise the changed code. Pay special attention to variables; in particular, treat them as Cases whenever possible. Bug fixers are forever being presented with bug reports that say, in effect, "when variable X has this value, the code must do such-and-so". Too often the fix causes a failure when the variable has some other type of value. For example, an integer-valued variable might have a special value meaning "default". Any change to code using that variable should test it with both the default and nondefault cases, *especially* if one of them is not mentioned in the code. As another example, linked lists often have distinguished elements (such as the head or the tail). Code that manipulates list elements should be tested with both distinguished and ordinary elements, even if the code doesn't appear to change the list structure (which is when those distinguished elements normally have to be handled differently).

Test Specifications (with an Existing Test Suite)

You've identified relevant test requirements. You now merge these into your existing test suite.

1. Rerun the old tests for this subsystem. When changed code corresponds to changed specification, expect some of those tests to fail.
2. Find old tests that exercise the changed code. Consider whether they satisfy the test requirements already. (Coverage tools are good for this.) Consider whether any can be easily modified to satisfy the test requirements, especially if you have to change the tests because they failed in the previous step.
3. Satisfy the remaining test requirements in the normal way. Most tests should satisfy the demonstration requirement (that is, they should be tests that cause the changed program to behave differently from the unchanged one). Not all will. Since you likely have fewer test requirements than you do when developing the initial test suite, pay special attention to ensuring that tests have variety and complexity.
4. Don't forget to use the Question Catalog. Some of the questions in it are directed toward changed code, such as this one:

▥▶ Sometimes, variables are used as caches for other values or must otherwise be updated in synchrony. If a value changes, are all synchronized variables updated?

5. The augmented test suite should reach 100 percent coverage.

Test Specifications (with no Test Suite)

It is when testing small changes or bugfixes that you are most likely to have to test without an automated test suite. When testing larger amounts of code, you can justify creating one, but the expense will not seem worthwhile for a single small change. In such a case, the following procedure works reasonably well:

1. Using all the test requirements is probably impossible: Without a test suite, you can't justify writing all the tests just to throw them away. I recommend generating all test requirements anyway. The act of searching for them often reveals faults.
2. Write the basic tests for the demonstration requirement, even if those tests are manual tests that are later discarded. For example, make sure the input from the bug report no longer fails.
3. Write as many more tests as you can. If you then have unused test requirements, use them in code reads. Ask if the program handles each of them correctly. In addition to that, I often find it useful to design the test specifications, even if I don't implement them. Designing a test specification forces me to be concrete. Selecting values to satisfy several test requirements at once can make me notice bugs that slip past me when I'm thinking only about abstract test requirements.
4. Don't forget the Question Catalog.
5. Expect 100 percent coverage of the changed code. Think carefully about missed coverage in the changed routine; there may be interac-

tions between that code and the changed code. The discussion of interactions in Part 5 may be of use.

Often, you'll have a repeatable *system* test suite, but one that has poor coverage of the subsystem containing the change. Think about whether you can add system tests that do. Most likely, you'll not design those new tests from a detailed analysis of the changed code, but the change may still provide a specification-level clue that you can use during system testing. Certainly you should track bug reports so that you know which are the most fault-prone parts of the system; concentrate your system testing there.

14.3 Propagation Faults

Under the demonstration requirement, the changed code has a changed effect on some variables. Will this effect break other, distant code? There are five steps in answering this question.

1. Deciding whether propagation faults are a risk—or would you be better off spending your time on other testing?
2. Finding the code that might be broken. This is hard.
3. Finding how the effect can propagate to that code. This is usually not too hard—in principle.
4. Implementing a test that really does cause the effect to propagate. The practice is often quite a bit more difficult than the principle.
5. Measuring whether you tested what you intended.

The Risk

The risk is, in general, dependent on the system, the application area, and the change. However, the larger the effect, the larger the risk. For example, the -test-cc bug fix has a simple effect on a single count (max_dir_name). Not surprisingly, later code is unaffected by the change. If, instead, the change were to rearrange a complex data structure, there'd be a much greater chance that the subtle assumptions of later code would be violated. So, when evaluating risk, pay attention to the complexity of the data structures affected.

This is true—perhaps especially true—when only part of a data structure is changed. In particular, beware of this situation: A changed routine affects a data structure, and you examine the callers of that routine and discover that they pass it only a small part of larger data structure. Because the programmer may not realize how the part relates to the larger whole, violated consistency relationships and other assumptions are likely. (The programmer will likely know how *one* caller uses the results, that being the caller that called the changed routine in the original bug report. But other callers may use the results in different ways.)

The Users

The code affected by the changed results can be hard to find. A reasonable approach begins by listing all the changed variables (those used or set differently because of the change). Together with each variable, list its purpose and how it is affected by the change. The latter notations are particularly important, because they help identify the relationships you'll be searching for throughout the rest of the system. Here are some examples:

▲ C_runq, the current element of run queue rque, used to be first one, now the one with highest priority.

▲ current file's parse tree now contains multiple pointers instead of duplicate subtrees.

▲ declaration list for this compound statement (in current Contour_record). Now includes typedefs.

Notice that the names are not as important as the purpose. The names can change, such as when a list is assigned to different variables in turn, but the purpose remains relatively constant: A queue of processes remains a queue of processes, no matter what its name.

After listing the variables that are changed, spend some time thinking about related variables that you might list. For example, if the changed variable is part of some larger data structure, perhaps the whole data structure should be listed, together with its purpose.

Sometimes, the actual change is only to set a flag that causes some larger change later, when some event happens. Include in your list of variables those that will be differently affected if that event happens. Mention the event in the variable's purpose.

Now you must find the uses of these variables in the rest of the subsystem or larger system.[1] There are two practical ways:

☐ **search**

Although the purpose is most important, you can't search for it. You can use text searches to find all uses of the same name (such as a global variable, a field name, or a type used in a declaration). For example, search for

```
Process_queue;         /* A global */
struct *process_queue  /* Type of state we changed. */
->current_process      /* Field we changed. */
```

☐ **ask**

The second way is to send electronic mail to everyone who works on the system, describing the variables affected by the change and how the change affects them, and asking if they know of code that uses those variables. You might even get a reply that says, "No! No! You can't do that! "from someone you would have never thought to include in a design or code review.

Don't be surprised if you find many routines that use a variable, especially in old systems that have decayed away from whatever modularity they once had. You may not even be able to examine each routine in detail, much less test them all. The dilemma, of course, is that such systems are

---

1. But don't forget that some of the most important users of the changed results may be in the changed routine itself. Some of the discussion in Part 5 may be of use.

exactly those most prone to propagation faults. But if you have to filter out some uses because of lack of time, apply these rules:

1. Many of the using routines will use the variable in roughly the same way. Concentrate on uses that seem atypical.
2. Favor routines that use more than one changed variable; these routines are more likely to depend on subtle relationships between variables.
3. Scan the using routine; if what it does with the variable intersects the description of how the change affected that variable, test that routine.

Example: Suppose a change modifies the contents of a string, perhaps changing its length. Code that uses those contents is higher risk than code that simply calls `strlen` to count the length of the string.

Example: A routine picks the next value of a list to process. Before the change, the element returned was always the first element of the list. After, it's the one with the largest priority field. The change affects the relationship between the selected element and the list, so it probably will not induce bugs in distant code that only increments a field in the selected element. If the distant code removes the selected element, you'll need more testing.

Tests
Having identified the code that might be broken by the change, you need to exercise it correctly. Such a test would have three parts:

❏ **demonstration requirement**
The changed code must have a changed effect.

❏ **user reachability requirement**
The effect must reach the using code.

❏ **user demonstration requirement**
The using code should be exercised in cases where its use of the changed variables is affected by the change. This can be hard. Failing that, use the IN variable test requirements for the changed results that reach the using code.

For example, if a tree is converted to have multiple pointers to common subexpressions, cycles might be possible. Suppose the routine in question searches the tree. A single test might have the following:

1. A tree with cycles has been created.
2. That tree is given to the searching routine.
3. No match is found on a branch with a cycle.

The third entry is suggested by the "search fails" test requirement from the catalog. The hope is that a missing match on a newly-cyclic structure might lead to an infinite loop. This is a case where the searching routine might have to handle the changed tree differently than before.

Each of these requirements could be chosen from several alternatives. There may be several requirements that demonstrate the change, there may be several ways to reach the using code, and there may be several user demonstration requirements. In such a case, you might build a test requirement checklist like this:

        demonstration requirements
            demonstration-1
            demonstration-2
            demonstration-3

        user-reachability requirements
            user-reachability-1
            user-reachability-2
            user-reachability-3

        user-demonstration requirements
            user-demonstration-1
            user-demonstration-2
            user-demonstration-3

Three tests could satisfy all nine requirements. If you can't afford more than one propagation test for the using code (not uncommon), you might just write it immediately, not bothering with the checklist.

In practice, even a single test can be hard to write. In large systems, it can be hard to force a changed variable to reach a distant user. In such a case, a careful code review is appropriate.

Coverage

If you do decide to implement a test, you need to check whether it does what you intended. The most likely problem is in getting to the using code: either it is never executed, or the effect of the demonstration requirement has been lost by that time. (For example, intervening code could simplify a carefully constructed complicated list structure.) Coverage easily rules out the first. The second is harder; check whether the way the code executed is consistent with the values you intended to deliver to it.

Examining coverage may also suggest new interactions between the using code and the changed code.

14.4 Similarity Faults

If a misunderstanding caused one fault, it may cause several. If there is one place in the code where creating a new directory failed to update max_dir_name, there might be others. A basic step in any bug fix should be a systematic search for similar bodies of code. If any are found, ask if they contain the same fault. If the answer is a clear "no," there's no need for tests. If the answer is "yes," the fault must be fixed and tested. In doubtful cases, writing a test may be the easiest way of answering the question.

Finding that similar code is, of course, the problem. Here are three ways:

1. Conduct a search like the one for users of changed results. Write down the changed variables (those used or set differently) together with their purpose and how they were affected by the change. Search for code that uses variables for the same purpose. Remember that you're not looking for just the same variables, but perhaps for different variables used the same way. That makes the search harder.
2. Look for code that calls the same functions. This is easy to do with a cross-reference listing tool.
3. Find code with similar postconditions (perhaps with a quick scan of code headers, perhaps by asking people).

The original demonstration requirement exercises the original buggy code in a particular way. Ask whether exercising the similar code in the same (or analogous) way would cause a failure. Most often, the answer will be obvious. When it's doubtful, you can write a test.

In the case of the -test-cc fault, I took this approach:

1. I was first worried about other cases where max_dir_name was not updated. max_dir_name should be updated whenever the names array is set, so I searched for all code that changed that array. They were all obviously correct and, indeed, well tested.
2. Since that was simple, I decided to worry about all cases where too little memory might be allocated. Although I use a tool that warns when a program copies into an allocated buffer that's too small, it can tell me nothing if no test ever causes such a copy. (That's why the original fault wasn't found before GCT was released.) I searched the program for all occurrences of "len", "max", and the memory allocation routines. I found no problems.

14.5 Testing Larger Changes

Changes are not necessarily contiguous. The following is a simple example:

Noncontinuous changes

old	new

if (update)
{
    cumulative += current;
    last_match = this_match;
}
	if (update)
	{
	    cumulative += current + 1;
	    last_ match = this_match;
	    update_count++;
	}

In this case, the rule about considering the entire enclosing block to be changed code means that both changes are merged into one. That's often the situation. In other cases, the changes are more widely separated. I recommend considering the changed code to be the smallest block that includes all the new code. The alternative is to treat each changed block independently. This is more dangerous, since the changes likely interact.

At the very least, make sure that you use test requirements from each change in all your tests. (Build a single test requirement checklist.)

If much of the function has changed, pretend that it's new code and test it completely. If most of sreadhex were changed in a later version of Ghostscript (as indeed happened), the entire process followed in Part 1 would be followed again.

If a function's specification changes, that is a change to all calls of the function. The function behaves differently given the same arguments, so all users of that behavior must be tested. In this example, the call has "changed" even though the text has not been touched.

old	new	
t = build_tree(source);	t = build_tree(source);	***Specification Changes in a Called Subroutine***

Such a change may require a lot of testing. That's as it should be—changes to the behavior of a widely used function are dangerous.

Even if a function's specification does not appear to change, it's wise to run some tests that exercise users of that function. It's not unknown for callers to depend—perhaps unintentionally—on undocumented behavior.

A major worry is gradual degradation of the test suite during maintenance.

14.6 Test Suite Decay

▲ Changes to the code may result in old tests that no longer satisfy the test requirements for which they were originally designed. The lovingly crafted complex data structure delivered to a routine deep within the subsystem may now be intercepted by new code. (Coverage might catch that, but it might not.)

▲ Updating old tests can cause them to lose test requirements. You need to test a special case, so you add it to a collection used in an existing test. But that was the only one-element collection. Again, coverage might catch this mistake.

▲ If the system evolves by a series of small changes, the tests for those changes will tend to be more simplistic than old tests, and thus less good at finding unexpected faults. Eventually, those tests will form a major proportion of the test suite—which will then be generally weak.

To avoid test suite decay, pay close attention to decreases in coverage. It is too easy just to patch up the tests to regain the coverage. That restores only some test requirements, but not the all-important ones that check for omission faults. Use missing coverage as a pointer to missing clues.

The second way to avoid test suite decay is to insist on tests with variety and complexity. Go beyond what is minimally required to check if the maintenance change worked.

15

Testing Under Schedule Pressure

15.1 Testing Without Enough Time

Having too much to do in the time allotted is a fact of the tester's life. When I don't have enough time to test a subsystem properly, I approach the task in one of two ways. Which I choose depends mainly on how unfamiliar the implementation is. If I understand the subsystem but don't have enough time, I choose broad but shallow testing. If I don't understand the subsystem's internals and don't have time to learn them, I let coverage guide my testing.

Shallow Testing

1. I rely most on the external specification and routine specifications. For the latter, I use existing design documents, code headers, or the code itself to summarize a specification (using the techniques from Chapter 12). I spend some time, but not much, scanning the code for cliches. I concentrate on loops: The operation and variable cliches they suggest seem to cause the most variety in the smaller number of tests I'll be able to write. I use the most obvious integration requirements (from subroutine calls), and I spend a little extra time considering test requirements for globals.

2. If the error-handling code is of the "report it and quit" variety, I usually leave it untested until more time is available. (But it's important to test "recover and continue" error-handling code.)

3. I expect these tests to evenly exercise the subsystem. That is, no part of it should have an unusually high proportion of unsatisfied coverage conditions. That expectation may be wrong: there may be a few underexercised sections of code caused by either design mistakes or implementation mistakes. There may also be a few systematic

design shortcomings, such as an untested special case that affects many routines within the subsystem. And there will certainly be individual coverage conditions that are obviously worth exercising.

So, although I look at coverage, I handle it differently than in full-scale subsystem testing. I first look at the percentage of coverage conditions satisfied for "components" of the subsystem. Depending on the size of the subsystem, a component could be a routine, a file, or a directory full of files. If a component has low coverage, I ask what that component does in terms of the external interface. That part of the specification should be tested more thoroughly. I'll next quickly scan all unsatisfied coverage conditions (starting with those from the underexercised components). My goal is not to translate each into clues, but to get a general sense of where my testing was weak. I'll also find individual coverage conditions to satisfy. Those are usually due to localized but important test design omissions or simple test implementation mistakes. This quick scan is not as effective as using coverage to find clues. But it's much faster if there's 30 percent missing coverage (not atypical).

4. Having found broad weaknesses in my tests (as well as some specific details), I improve the test suite as time allows.
5. I always apply the Question Catalog. If there's time, I think about the remaining coverage conditions during that inspection.

Coverage-Driven Testing

This is an even faster approach, and it doesn't require much understanding of the internals.

1. I derive test requirements only from the interface specification and a few very important routines.
2. After that, I run the tests and measure coverage of the entire subsystem. I interpret the coverage of the important routines in the usual way.
3. Because I barely looked at the internals when designing tests, coverage will be uneven. I use coverage summaries to find underexercised components (typically files). Each component is handled separately. That's more efficient, but reduces the chance of finding interaction bugs. The order in which components are handled is based more on their importance than on the amount of coverage they've gotten.
4. For each component, I ask what kinds of test would exercise it, then improve those kinds of tests. They are typically tests of a certain part of the external interface. I'll usually ask a developer for some help, but only for general background. I'm more likely to ask "what does routine swizzle_frob do?" or "what does the code in *fall-back.c* do?" than "what's the purpose of this if on line 344?" If I look at individual coverage conditions at all, it will be quickly, to see if a systematic error jumps out at me.
5. I have no particular coverage goal for the improved tests. I'll measure coverage again to check whether coverage is now roughly in line with other parts of the subsystem and perhaps to check if systematic mistakes remain.

6. By concentrating on testing where coverage clusters, I eventually end up with a residue of coverage conditions that have little to do with each other. (Or, more likely, I run out of time first.) I stop then.

This approach relies heavily on coverage to guide testing. Because internally-derived test requirements are underemphasized, it tends to miss omission faults. I have, however, used this technique to good effect (tested quickly and found bugs).

This approach is particularly useful for testers who don't know the internals of the system and don't have time to learn. It requires a developer's help to relate coverage to parts of the specification, but that usually doesn't consume much time. In some cases, such as special cases for complicated internal data structures, it does.

15.2
Testing Without *NEARLY* Enough Time

If you don't have enough time for either of the previous two techniques, abandon subsystem testing. Pool the time saved and try to do a good job of system testing, the topic of another book.

Part 4

EXAMPLES AND EXTENSIONS

`sreadhex` does not have a user interface. Most user interfaces can be described with a rigorous syntax. Chapter 16 explains the standard catalog's requirements for syntax testing in detail.

Chapter 17 gives another complete example, MAX, that illustrates some points `sreadhex` did not, including syntax testing. It also gives you an opportunity to build your own test requirement checklists and test specifications, then compare them to the solution given here.

The remaining chapters discuss extending the technique to other situations. As you'd hope, the extensions are straightforward: They build on the basic technique and previous extensions.

Chapter 18 covers testing consistency relationships between variables.

Chapter 19 considers testing software that uses state machines in either its design or implementation. It also discusses statecharts

(Harel87), which are an extension of classical state machines. This chapter is the first one to consider the implications of systems that take sequences of inputs, rather than all inputs at the same time.

Reusing software reduces development costs. It can also reduce testing cost, provided test design and coverage focus on likely faults in the software that reuses. This is the topic of Chapter 20.

Object-based programming organizes subsystems around data types, rather than around functions. Object-based subsystems contain persistent state (globals in an encapsulated form), sometimes are designed using state machines or statecharts, and make reuse more tractable. Chapter 21 discusses how the general techniques of earlier chapters can be specialized to such subsystems.

Object-oriented programming adds inheritance and dynamic binding to object-based programming. Chapter 22 considers the effects of inheritance on testing. Generic components (templates in C++) have much the same effect, so they are also discussed in this chapter. Chapter 23 works through an example of inheritance. Chapter 24 discusses dynamic binding.

Syntax Testing

The input of many programs can be described by a rigorous language (typically regular expressions or context-free grammars). The MAX program, in the next chapter, is an example. Because they have a clichéd structure, the statements in a syntax are clues that can be mechanically turned into test requirements. The standard catalog explains how. The POSIX catalog has some extensions for command-line arguments. This chapter describes those catalog entries in more detail.

Syntax testing, like all subsystem testing, is based on two rules:

1. Derive test requirements from likely programmer errors and program faults.
2. Assume test requirements are independent unless there's explicit evidence to the contrary.

The notation used in the catalog is derived from [Beizer90]. Some of the test requirements are from [Beizer90]; others are from [Papagiannakopoulos90].

A simple syntactic statement looks like this:

**16.1
Notation**

    this is a statement

That statement requires four elements ("this", "is", "a", and "statement") to be given in exactly that order. Anything else is an error.

Optional elements are surrounded by square brackets:

    this is required [but this can be omitted]

Such a syntax statement can be satisfied by either of two inputs:

> this is required
> this is required but this can be omitted

Anything else is a syntax error.

Alternatives are separated by vertical bars:

> this | that

That statement is satisfied by either of two inputs:

> this
> that

Alternatives can be made optional by surrounding them with square brackets:

> [this | that]

In this case, no input (the empty input) is also allowed.

Curly brackets are used for grouping:

> [{ yet another } | { one more }] statement

This statement is satisfied by

> yet another statement
> one more statement
> statement

Ellipses are used for repetition:

> repeat...

is satisfied by

> repeat
> repeat repeat
> repeat repeat repeat
> ...

At least one repetition is required. Square brackets allow zero repetitions:

> [repeat]...

There is almost always a maximum repetition. Often, it's not explicitly specified. Sometimes even the designer doesn't know what it is.

Syntax statements can be named, then referred to by other statements. The names and references are written in bold font.

> **input:**   { put | retrieve } [**option**] **file**...
> **option:** -f | -g | -m

The syntax is satisfied by inputs such as these:

> put file1
> put -m file1 file2
> put -g file1 file2 file3
> retrieve -f file53

The definition of a syntactically valid **file** is presumably given elsewhere.

Syntax statements can contain references to themselves either directly or indirectly as in the following:

> **alternate:**   [first **tail**]
> **tail:**   second **alternate**

If you know about parsing, you know that adding such self-reference complicates the implementation. It has little effect on testing.

The syntactic statements are usually not complete descriptions of valid inputs, especially if they come from a user's manual. Here are some examples:

1. The program may be case-insensitive. Rather than writing syntax like

    { put | PUT | pUT | PUt | pUt ...}

   there's a single statement somewhere in the document like "all commands are case-insensitive". That would lead to requirements like these:

    a command is all uppercase
    a command is all lowercase
    a command is mixed-case

   Those three test requirements would be combined round robin with syntax-derived test requirements to keep the commands varied.

2. The syntax of a variable name in C does not include the fact that it must be defined before use. That information is elsewhere in the specification. It would lead to (at least) these test requirements:

    variable name is previously defined
    variable name is undefined   ERROR

3. Syntactic elements are usually separated by arbitrary "white space". The definition of allowable white space is separate from the syntax. The standard catalog contains some test requirements for common situations. Others can be handled by considering the definition of white space as a syntax in its own right and independently applying the syntax catalog entries. (This corresponds to the traditional division of syntax processors into a parsing phase and a lexical analysis phase.)

16.2
Test
Requirements

A specification may contain several syntactic statements, and each statement may have several syntactic elements. Here's an example:

> **input:**   {put | retrieve } [**option**] **target**...
> **option:**   -f | -g | -m

Subsystem testing by default assumes independence. That means that both statements produce their own test requirements. Further, the test requirements for the {put|retrieve} construct are independent of those for the target... construct. The independent requirements are combined in the normal way when test specifications are built. They're not combined in the checklist unless:

1. Something else in the specification describes an interaction, such as a statement beginning "If the command is put AND there is exactly one target".
2. The code shows an interaction. (Chapters 25 and 26.)
3. You have historical evidence of interactions that aren't stated explicitly (from general knowledge of this application, its bug history, or similar applications). (This is error guessing.)

The code that checks whether inputs conform to the syntax is called the "parser." In some cases, the parser is ordinary code written by hand. In other cases, the syntax description is given to a program (a "parser generator") that writes the parser for you. A generated parser doesn't need to be tested as thoroughly. It does still need to be tested because the syntax description might be wrong. In what follows, INLINE requirements apply to code written by hand. They needn't be used for code produced by a parser generator.

16.2.1 Nearby items

Some of the test requirements are ERROR requirements. Many of these say to use a "nearby item." Those are items that are incorrect according to the syntax, but differ only slightly from correct items. Here are a couple of examples. If the syntax requires the token "put", pick an alternative that satisfies the catalog's String Comparison requirements, such as

> pu
> puy
> putt

The latter is probably the most likely to be incorrectly accepted. Also use your knowledge of the particulars of the system. For example, suppose some of the system ignores case but this subsystem should not. Then a good nearby alternative would be to use

> PUT

You can spend arbitrarily large amounts of time trying nearby items. Clearly, that effort quickly stops being worthwhile. I try only one or two unless the program is critical. But I try to be clever about the one or two that I choose. Rather than trying simple misspellings, I try to guess likely programmer errors.

16.2.2 Sequences

All of the requirements for sequences check whether the parser rejects incorrect input.

- Last item missing   INLINE
- Extra item   INLINE
- Items in wrong format

➥*(Try one wrong format for each item in the sequence.)*

Here's a sample test requirement checklist. The syntax is listed as a clue and the requirements are given below it.

PUT **sourcename device**

PUT **sourcename**	ERROR (last item missing)
PUT **sourcename device device**	ERROR (extra item)
P **sourcename device**	ERROR (first item in wrong format)
PUT **device device**	ERROR (second item in wrong format)
PUT **sourcename sourcename**	ERROR (third item in wrong format)

Each of the last three requirements tries a nearby incorrect item. The choice of "P" instead of "PUT" would be reasonable if similar commands allow abbreviations but this one should not. If it does, that's a bug (more likely a specification or documentation bug than an implementation bug).

16.2.3 Alternatives

The alternative test requirements look for two types of programmer errors: failure to accept one of the alternatives and accepting too many alternatives.

- Each of the legal alternatives
- None of the alternatives (may be an ERROR)
- An illegal (but nearby) alternative.   INLINE

For the example, I'll use a style of writing syntax-derived test requirements that's often convenient. In a test requirement, a hyphen (-) means that any legal element is allowed. (It's a "don't care" entry.) A • means that an optional element is omitted.

Here's the syntax:

{A | B}   [C]   [D | E]

First, I'll give the non-ERROR test requirements:

```
A       -       -
B       -       -
-       •       -
-       C       -
-       -       •
-       -       D
-       -       E
```

This notation emphasizes the independence of test requirements. This set of test requirements could be satisfied by many different sets of tests. Here are two:

Test Set 1   Test Set 2

A C D   B D
B   A C
A C E   A E

Which combination you choose would depend on how the requirements combine with those from the rest of the checklist.

Here are the ERROR requirements:

```
•   -   -       ERROR (because either A or B must be given)
C   -   -       ERROR (C chosen because it's a nearby alternative to A and B)
-   c   -       ERROR (another nearby alternative, if lowercase is illegal)
-   -   DE      ERROR
```

Here I've made an explicit choice about what nearby item to use. I could have just noted the need for a nearby item, as in

```
-   -   <near>
```

But there's no advantage to that. Non-error test requirements are made as general as possible to increase the chance they can be combined with others. Error test requirements are never combined with others, so they might as well be made specific immediately.

16.2.4 Simple Repetition

The test requirements for repetitions should look familiar. They're derived from those for Counts and Intervals. They will also satisfy most of the Collection requirements if, as is usually the case, the repetition creates a Collection.

- The minimum number of repetitions
- One less than the minimum number of repetitions
- 1 repetition
- > 1 repetition
- The maximum number of repetitions (if known)
- One too many repetitions
- Incorrect but nearby item as last   INLINE
  Example: "09:" given syntax "numeral..."

The "1 repetition" case is redundant if the iteration is of the form
repeat..., but not if it's of the form [repeat].... The rules also apply
to repetitions with other minimum counts. The ">1 repetition" requirement is redundant if the maximum number of repetitions is known. However, even if the maximum is known, it may be hard enough to test that
you decide to satisfy it only once. The ">1 repetition" requirement will
then help you keep your tests varied.

The specification often doesn't give the maximum number of repetitions. Sometimes it's easy to find, by either asking the programmer or
looking in the code. (In this case, consider documenting it.) Other times,
it's hard to find. In that case, it is reasonable to write a single test that continually increases the number of repetitions until the subsystem rejects the
input (typically because it has run out of resources). That test should
answer these questions:

1. Does the subsystem fail catastrophically instead of rejecting the
   input cleanly?
2. Does it reject the input when the repetition count is too small?
   Although you might not know the exact maximum, perhaps you
   know it must be at least 10.

There should be a test where an incorrect item is used in the repetition. It is best to make that item the last in the repetition. If a collection is
built and then checked, the last element is probably the most likely to be
left unchecked. So, given the syntax

   numeral...

I'd prefer

   039:

to

   :039

(The colon is used because it's the next character after '9' in the ASCII character set.)

16.2.5 Repetition and Alternatives

Sometimes syntax descriptions combine repetition and alternatives.
For example, you might see

   [A | B]...

or

   {A | B}...

The first test requirements come from treating repetition and alternatives
independently. For each example, there are three from the alternative and

---

up to seven from the repetition. The only difference between the two statements is which is an ERROR requirement.

> A used
> B used
> C used   ERROR (nearby value)
> {A | B} zero times   ERROR (for the second example)
> {A | B} once
> {A | B} maximum number of times
> ...

These requirements can, of course, be combined in the normal way.
Some additional requirements are useful:

- Each element is omitted in at least one test
- Everything is used in reverse order from that given in the description.

The first requirement makes sure that each alternative is unused in at least one non-ERROR test. Without it, the non-ERROR requirements for "{A | B}..." could be satisfied by these tests:

> A
> ABABABABABAB

In neither test was A unused, so there's no evidence the program will work in that case. The requirement for zero repetitions doesn't satisfy these requirements because zero repetitions is an ERROR for this syntax. It is not an ERROR for "[A | B]...", so a separate requirement to omit each element is not necessary. (It may be desirable, especially if you suspect the subsystem may handle "no elements given" as a special case.)

Another useful requirement is to use all the alternatives in a single repetition. Perhaps that hits some resource limit. That is, given this syntax statement:

> {A | B | C | D | E | F | G | H | I | J | K | L | M | N}...

Perhaps

> N M L K J I H G F E D C B A

will fail when three tests like

> N M L K J
> I H G F E
> D C B A

wouldn't. (Notice that I tried the items in the reverse order from the syntax description. That's just because the programmer probably tried them in the forward order. Variety never hurts.)

Don't forget that test requirements are independent. Here is some syntax:

> **input:** {put | retrieve } [**option**] **target**...
> **input2:** check [valid] **option**
> **option:** -f | -g | -m

Here are the non-ERROR test requirements:

> syntax of input
> > put used
> > retrieve used
> > option used
> > option not used
> > one target
> > more than one target
> > the maximum number of targets
> syntax of input2
> > valid used
> > valid not used
> syntax of option
> > -f used
> > -g used
> > -m used

Interactions between the different options and the command chosen (put, retrieve, or check) are possible. But it's not the job of the syntax to reveal interactions; it's the job of the rest of the specification and the techniques in Part 5. Given only the syntax, there's no reason to test the -f option with put, given that it's already been used once with check. (If there will have to be more than three tests anyway, attention to variety and the standard combining rules will lead to tests of more combinations.)

There are two exceptions.

Self-Reference

The first is in syntax statements that contain either direct or indirect references to themselves.

For example, C structures can contain structures. Some relevant syntax statements might look like

> **structure-def:** struct **identifier** '{' **component**... '}' ;
> **union-def:** union **identifier** '{' **component**... '}' ;
> **component:** **variable_def** | **union_def** | **structure_def** | ...

(The quotes around the curly brace indicate they are part of the structure, not grouping symbols in the syntax statement.)

The danger is that the code that parses structures won't be reentrant. Suppose the code is organized like this:

1. When the opening curly brace is noticed, a *global* list of components is initialized to NULL.
2. As each component is seen, it is added to the front of the list.
3. When the closing curly brace is noticed, the list is reversed and space for the structure is allocated.

What happens with this code?

```
struct
{
  int j;
  struct { int x; int y; };
  int k;
};
```

The internal structure will overwrite the global. For this reason, such recursive references should be tested. That wouldn't be guaranteed if component could be used in other contexts. For example, if it could also be used in unions, you might end up with these tests:

```
union { struct { int j; }; };
struct { union { int j; }; };
```

which would not trigger the bug. So be sure to write explicit test requirements for self-references:

```
a structure_def that contains a structure_def
a union_def that contains a union_def
```

Repetition and Alternatives

Repetition and alternatives can be disguised, as in this syntax:

input: check {**option**}...
option: -f | -g | -m

This syntax accepts the same input as

input: check {-f | -g | -m}...

so the special catalog requirements for repetition and alternatives should also apply:

- Each element is omitted in at least one test
- Everything used in reverse order from that given in the description.

A Second Complete Example: MAX

MAX is a simple complete program with several contrived bugs. It illustrates these points:

1. Summarizing a specification.
2. Deriving tests from the specification alone, later adding tests based on the code.
3. Testing based on syntax.
4. Successful use of the Question Catalog for Code Inspections.
5. How new tests derived from the code may fail to increase coverage—but find a fault nevertheless.
6. A test driver suitable for simple filters. It checks for failure by comparing reference files to the program's output.
7. How subsystem testing is robust. Mistakes in one stage can be caught in later stages.

This example requires that you know (or be willing to learn) a little about UNIX command-line argument handling and a couple of standard C library routines. It uses both the standard catalog and the POSIX catalog.

Instead of passively reading this section, you should build your own specifications, checklists, and test specifications, then compare them to the solution given here. The discussion will not be as detailed as it was for sreadhex.

17.1
The Specification

MAX is a program that prints the lexicographic maximum of its command-line arguments. For example:

```
% max 1 3 3
3
% max foo bar baz
foo
```

There is only one option:

-ceiling

This provides a ceiling: if the maximum would be larger than this, this is the maximum.

```
% max -ceiling 2 1 3
2
```

The program gracefully handles one likely user error: misspelling the -ceiling argument. Suppose the program were invoked as

```
% max -cieling 2 1 3
```

MAX might interpret -cieling as just another argument, in which case it would print "3" instead of the intended "2". That's harmless in such a trivial program, but in general "garbage in, error message out" is preferable to "garbage in, garbage out". So the program will print an error message in this case. Arguments beginning with dashes that should not be interpreted as options have to be in an unambiguous location, as with:

```
% max 2 1 3 -not-an-option
```

In summary, the syntax is `max [-ceiling arg] candidate....`
The normal exit status is 0. Any error causes an exit status of 2.
Create an abbreviated specification now by writing cause-effect statements. Fig. 17–1 contains one solution.

Fig. 17–1 The abbbreviated specification	ERROR EFFECTS (preconditions): E1. IF the word after "max" begins with a '-' AND it is not "-ceiling" THEN an error message. POSTCONDITIONS: P1. IF the -ceiling option was given and its ARG is > any of the candidates THEN MAX prints the largest candidate. P2. IF the ceiling option was given and its ARG is <= some candidate. THEN MAX prints the ceiling ARG.

Notes for Fig. 17–1:

1. There are no preconditions for syntax errors. The catalogs will produce the test requirements.
2. There could be a postcondition for what MAX does when no ceiling option is given. However, that would just lead to two test requirements that will also come from the syntax: "-ceiling not given" and "-ceiling given".
3. The two postconditions I did list will give redundant test requirements. There are three distinct classes of inputs:

   -ceiling not given

   -ceiling given, ARG > any candidate

   -ceiling given, ARG <= some candidate

Both of the postconditions will lead to all three. That's typical of postconditions that neatly partition the inputs. With a little experience, you can recognize those cases.

Next search for clues.

17.2.1 The Clues

The precondition and postcondition clues are straightforward:

Precondition E1:

Postcondition P1:
Postcondition P2:

There are some variables in the specification. There's the ceiling, which is a string. There's a list of candidates, each of which is a string. Those two types of variables, the list and what it contains, are separate clues.

the ceiling, a string
a candidate, a string
a list of strings (the candidate list)

The specification talks about the "largest" candidate. There must be searching involved:

searching candidate list for maximum.

Finally, there's command line syntax. Here is the final list:

Precondition E1:
Postcondition P1:
Postcondition P2:
the ceiling, a string
a candidate, a string
a list of strings (the candidate list)
searching candidate list for maximum
command line syntax

Now add test requirements from the defining terms.

17.2.2 Requirements from the Preconditions and Postconditions

Test requirements from the first precondition are a straightforward application of the AND rule:

Precondition N1:

Word after "max" begins with '-', is not "-ceiling". ERROR	(true, true)
Word after "max" begins with '-', is exactly "-ceiling".	(true, false)
Word after "max" does not begin with '-'.	(false, nonsensical)

Notice that the last requirement is simplified.

Postcondition P1's defining term also uses AND. The AND rules yield:

The -ceiling option was given, arg > any candidate	(true, true)
The -ceiling option was given, arg <= some candidate	(true, false)
The -ceiling option was not given.	(false, nonsensical)

These all refine previous requirements.

Postcondition P2 will give the same test requirements.

Precondition E1:
- Word after "max" begins with '-', is not "-ceiling".   ERROR
- Word after "max" begins with '-', is exactly "-ceiling".
- -ceiling given, arg <= some candidate
- -ceiling given, arg > any candidate
- Word after "max" does not begin with '-'.
- The -ceiling option is not given.

the ceiling, a string
a candidate, a string.
a list of strings (the candidate list)
searching candidate list for maximum.
command line syntax

Now add test requirements from the catalogs. I recommend using the student catalog augmented with the SYNTAX section from the standard catalog and the COMMAND LINES section from the POSIX catalog.

17.2.3 Scanning the Catalog

As with the earlier sreadhex example, the left-hand page will contain catalog entries and explanations, while the facing page will show how the checklist is modified.

I will deliberately avoid noticing the Other Comparison Operators entry, which could refine the requirements that use <= and >. (That will give coverage something to do.)

The first match is General Collections, which has this set of test requirements:

• empty	IN/OUT
• a single element	IN/OUT
• more than one element	IN/OUT
• full	IN/OUT
• duplicate elements	IN/OUT
(may be an error case, or impossible)	

This matches the "list of strings" clue. The empty list is an error according to the syntax. Although that requirement should also be discovered by the syntax section of the catalog, it might as well be listed now. "A single element" and "more than one element" are also new, but not errors. The notion of "a full command line" has no real meaning in POSIX commands: such cases are handled by the shell, so this requirement can't be added. I choose not to add duplicate entries. (Note that the omitted Comparison Operator requirements would force duplicate entries, so I am compounding the mistake.)

The next match is STRINGS. The main entry here is

• The empty string.	IN, OUT

That could certainly apply to the candidates or the ceiling, so it's listed. (At this point, I should have noticed that MAX prints a string and listed "printed result, a string" as a clue with "the empty string" as a test requirement. But I didn't. As with sreadhex, I didn't think hard enough about output variables.)

There are also test requirements for comparing strings:

• V1 and V2 same length, differing in last element.	INLINE
Example: "abc" and "abd"	
• V1 has same elements as V2, but one element shorter.	INLINE
Example: "ab" "abc"	
• V2 has same elements as V1, but one element shorter.	INLINE
Example: "abc" "ab"	

but they're all INLINE. MAX most likely uses the standard library routine strcmp, so I DEFER the whole category.

Precondition E1:

> Word after "max" begins with '-', is not "-ceiling".   ERROR
>
> Word after "max" begins with '-', is exactly "-ceiling".
>> -ceiling given, arg <= some candidate
>>
>> -ceiling given, arg > any candidate
>
> Word after "max" does not begin with '-'.
>> The -ceiling option is not given.

the ceiling, a string
- **ceiling as empty string**
- **compared to maximum candidate, same length, differ in last element   (DEFER)**
- **compared to maximum candidate, same elements, one element shorter   (DEFER)**
- **compared to maximum candidate, same elements, one element longer   (DEFER)**

a candidate, a string
- **candidate as empty string**
- **compared to current maximum, same length, differ in last element   (DEFER)**
- **compared to current maximum, same elements, one element shorter   (DEFER)**
- **compared to current maximum, same elements, one element longer   (DEFER)**

a list of strings (the candidate list)
- **no candidates   ERROR**
- **a single candidate**
- **more than one candidate**

searching candidate list for maximum.
command line syntax

SEARCHING is the next match. Here are the requirements:

- Match not found
- Match found (more than one element, exactly one match)
- More than one match in the collection
- Single match found in first position   INLINE
  (it's not the only element)
- Single match found in last position
  (it's not the only element)

Here, the search is one where MAX keeps searching for a maximum larger than the current maximum. It doesn't make sense for there to be no maximum if there's any candidate, so I omit "match not found". "Exactly one match" would mean that the first candidate (the first current maximum) is the final maximum. "More than one match" would mean that some other candidate was largest. Both of these can be listed.

Since for this particular searching operation, "single match found in first position" is the same as "exactly one match", it needn't be written down. The other, "single match found in last position", is a refinement:

> First candidate is largest (more than one)
> Some other candidate is largest (more than one)
>   Last candidate is largest

Notice that these test requirements also satisfy the "more than one element" requirement invented earlier and they are more refined. They can be listed under that one.

The next match is "CONTINUED SEARCHING", where the search resumes after a match is found. That applies to MAX since the search continues to the end of the candidate list. The catalog gives this test requirement:

> Further match immediately adjacent to last match

In MAX, this would be a case where the maximum is found, and then the very next element is larger.

Precondition E1:

    Word after "max" begins with '-', is not "-ceiling".   ERROR

    Word after "max" begins with '-', is exactly "-ceiling".

        -ceiling given, arg <= some candidate

        -ceiling given, arg > any candidate

    Word after "max" does not begin with '-'.

        The -ceiling option is not given.

the ceiling, a string

    ceiling as empty string

    compared to maximum candidate, same length, differ in last element   (DEFER)

    compared to maximum candidate, same elements, one element shorter (DEFER)

    compared to maximum candidate, same elements, one element longer   (DEFER)

a candidate, a string

    candidate as empty string

    compared to current maximum, same length, differ in last element   (DEFER)

    compared to current maximum, same elements, one element shorter   (DEFER)

    compared to current maximum, same elements, one element longer   (DEFER)

a list of strings (the candidate list)

    no candidates   ERROR

    a single candidate

    more than one candidate

- **First candidate is largest (more than one)**
- **Some other candidate is largest (more than one)**
- **Last candidate is largest (more than one)**

searching candidate list for maximum.

- **Further match immediately adjacent to last match**

command line syntax

The Syntax entry (in the standard catalog) applies to MAX in two ways. First, there's an optional argument, "-ceiling". It should be both given and not given. Both of those are already in the checklist under precondition E1. The catalog also calls for an illegal alternative, such as a misspelling. There's already a requirement for that, also under precondition E1.

The candidate list is a simple repetition of the form A.... However, most of the requirements were already found by considering the candidate list to be a collection. One remains: that a "nearby" element be the last element of the repetition. However, MAX accepts any candidate except a first one beginning with a '-', which is already in the checklist. So this requirement is impossible to satisfy.

The POSIX catalog describes command line options:

⮕ For multicharacter option names, consider the Comparing Strings rules and Syntax. (Some of these requirements are redundant with Syntax requirements; they're repeated here to make sure they're not missed.)
- All options present (in reverse order from syntax description)
- No options present
- Repeated option
  (If the option takes an argument, it should take a different value the second time.)
- Option with missing argument as last option
  Example: "tar -f"
  (You often get a null-dereference core dump in this case.)
- Missing option argument followed by option
  Example: "tar -f -e"
  (This usually exposes not coding errors, but nonrobustness in the specification: POSIX programs don't generally do a lot of sanity checking of arguments.)
- Partial option
  Example: "cat -"
- Unknown option

The comment is relevant. It refers to deferred comparisons like checking whether "-ceilin" or "-ceilingg" is mistaken for "-ceiling". These could be used to refine the error requirement of Precondition 1, but I don't want to commit to them yet. So I place them with the other precondition requirements, but not indented. (Because I'm lazy, I didn't copy the three test requirements given in the catalog. If I decide to use them, I'll spell them out then.)

"All options present" and "no options present" are already covered, since there's only one option. "Repeated option" is an interesting requirement:

    max -ceiling X -ceiling Y

Here, the first "-ceiling" identifies X as the ceiling. The second "-ceiling" is itself a candidate. This refines "more than one candidate". (It would do no harm to not notice the refinement and list it under "command line syntax".)

There's more about this catalog entry on the next page.

Precondition E1:
>   Word after "max" begins with '-', is not "-ceiling".   ERROR
- **Nearby misspellings of "-ceiling"   DEFERRED ERROR**
>   Word after "max" begins with '-', is exactly "-ceiling".
>>   -ceiling given, arg <= some candidate
>>   -ceiling given, arg > any candidate
>   Word after "max" does not begin with '-'.
>>   The -ceiling option is not given.

the ceiling, a string
>   ceiling as empty string
>   compared to maximum candidate, same length, differ in last element   (DEFER)
>   compared to maximum candidate, same elements, one element shorter   (DEFER)
>   compared to maximum candidate, same elements, one element longer   (DEFER)

a candidate, a string
>   candidate as empty string
>   compared to current maximum, same length, differ in last element   (DEFER)
>   compared to current maximum, same elements, one element shorter   (DEFER)
>   compared to current maximum, same elements, one element longer   (DEFER)

a list of strings (the candidate list)
>   no candidates   ERROR
>   a single candidate
>   more than one candidate
>>   First candidate is largest (more than one)
>>   Some other candidate is largest (more than one)
>>>   Last candidate is largest (more than one)
- **max -ceiling X -ceiling Y**

searching candidate list for maximum.
>   Further match immediately adjacent to last match

command line syntax

There are still more test requirements for command line options.

➡ • Option with missing argument as last option
  Example: "tar -f"
  (You often get a null-dereference core dump in this case.)
• Missing option argument followed by option
  Example: "tar -f -e"
  (This usually exposes not coding errors, but non-robustness in the specification: POSIX programs don't generally do a lot of sanity checking of arguments.)
• Partial option
  Example: "cat -"
• Unknown option

The first test requirement calls for

  max -ceiling

One could make a case that this is a refinement of the "There are no candidates" test requirement. However, I believe these are really independent input errors that will be handled by two different chunks of code. POSIX C programs typically check and consume options first, then the rest of the program works on the remaining command line arguments. One of the criteria for refinement is not met:

> (3) You predict that the inputs excluded by the refinement wouldn't find any bugs that the refinement won't also find.

If "max -ceiling" is handled correctly, the program will probably exit before the code that handles missing candidates is ever executed. Faults in that code would be unexercised. So I put this requirement under the "command line syntax" clue. (Note: If I did fail to use "no candidates", coverage of MAX would signal the omitted test. That doesn't always happen, though.)

Precondition E1:

    Word after "max" begins with '-', is not "-ceiling".   ERROR

    Nearby misspellings of "-ceiling"   DEFERRED ERROR

    Word after "max" begins with '-', is exactly "-ceiling".

        -ceiling given, arg <= some candidate

        -ceiling given, arg > any candidate

    Word after "max" does not begin with '-'.

        The -ceiling option is not given.

the ceiling, a string

    ceiling as empty string

    compared to maximum candidate, same length, differ in last element   (DEFER)

    compared to maximum candidate, same elements, one element shorter   (DEFER)

    compared to maximum candidate, same elements, one element longer   (DEFER)

a candidate, a string

    candidate as empty string

    compared to current maximum, same length, differ in last element   (DEFER)

    compared to current maximum, same elements, one element shorter   (DEFER)

    compared to current maximum, same elements, one element longer   (DEFER)

a list of strings (the candidate list)

    no candidates   ERROR

    a single candidate

    more than one candidate

        First candidate is largest (more than one)

        Some other candidate is largest (more than one)

            Last candidate is largest (more than one)

    max -ceiling X -ceiling Y

searching candidate list for maximum.

    Further match immediately adjacent to last match

command line syntax

- **No option argument: max -ceiling   ERROR**

▐▶ • Missing option argument followed by option
   Example: "tar -f -e"
   (This usually exposes not coding errors, but non-robustness
   in the specification: POSIX programs don't generally do a
   lot of sanity checking of arguments.)
• Partial option
   Example: "cat -"
• Unknown option

"Missing option argument followed by option" is an interesting
case:

max -ceiling -ceiling X

Presumably -ceiling is here taken to be the actual ceiling to be
compared to X. This is a refinement of "a single candidate". (Note: Even
though this test requirement is clearly targeted toward faults in programs
that have multiple options, I'll use it for this program where such a fault
could hardly exist. Odd requirements often find faults other than those
they're designed to find. That seems unlikely in this case, but I'm nearing
the end of the catalog and probably won't find any other refinements for
"a single candidate", so I might as well use this one.)
   There are still a couple of other test requirements. "Unknown
option" is redundant. "Partial option" would seem to be a refinement of
"unknown option". They're both listed because the two requirements target different faults (in different parts of a typical implementation—you'll
see an example of this in MAX).
   All the requirements for ARGUMENTS, the next entry in the catalog, are redundant.
   Here's the final checklist, ready for test specification generation:

Precondition E1:
0   Word after "max" begins with '-', is not "-ceiling".   ERROR
0   Nearby misspellings of "-ceiling"   DEFERRED ERROR
      Word after "max" begins with '-', is exactly "-ceiling".
0   -ceiling given, arg <= some candidate
0   -ceiling given, arg > any candidate
      Word after "max" does not begin with '-'.
0   The -ceiling option is not given.

the ceiling, a string
0   ceiling as empty string
0   compared to maximum candidate, same length, differ in last element   (DEFER)
0   compared to maximum candidate, same elements, one element shorter   (DEFER)
0   compared to maximum candidate, same elements, one element longer   (DEFER)

a candidate, a string
0   candidate as empty string
0   compared to current maximum, same length, differ in last element   (DEFER)
0   compared to current maximum, same elements, one element shorter   (DEFER)
0   compared to current maximum, same elements, one element longer   (DEFER)

a list of strings (the candidate list)
0   no candidates   ERROR
      a single candidate
0   **max -ceiling -ceiling X**
      more than one candidate
0   First candidate is largest (more than one)
              Some other candidate is largest (more than one)
0   Last candidate is largest (more than one)
0   max -ceiling X -ceiling Y

searching candidate list for maximum.
0   Further match immediately adjacent to last match

command line syntax
0   No option argument: max -ceiling   ERROR
0   **Partial option ("-")**   **ERROR**

17.2.4 Test Design

The four undeferred error cases are simplest. Here they are:

TEST 1: (for no argument to option)
  max -ceiling
Expect
  Some message about missing ceiling argument to standard error.
  Exit status 2.

The specification doesn't say what happens in the case of a syntax error. (That's pretty common.) Some error message seems like a reasonable expectation; the expected results will have to be refined when I see what the program actually does. (If there were a programmer available, I'd ask.)

  This test contains two errors. In addition to the option without an argument, it also contains no candidate (violating Precondition 1). This is generally undesirable, but in this case it's unavoidable since the partial argument must be the last word on the command line. However, only the first test requirement has its count incremented.

TEST 2: (for partial option)
  max - x
Expect
  Some message about incorrect option to standard error.
  Exit status 2.

TEST 3: (for misspelling of "ceiling")
  max -ceilin arg candidate
Expect
  Some message about incorrect option to standard error.
  Exit status 2.

Note that x, arg, and candidate are the exact arguments to the function, not placeholders. I chose those names because I have no reason to prefer any particular names. Notice that both tests have a candidate so they don't violate two preconditions at once.

  Test 3 was inspired by these two requirements:

0 Word after "max" begins with '-', is not "-ceiling." ERROR
0 Nearby misspellings of "-ceiling" DEFERRED ERROR

The misspelling of -ceiling was inspired by the deferred requirement. I had to pick some misspelling, and there was no reason not to use a deferred one. This does not violate the rule against testing two error test requirements at once since -ceilin is a refinement of the other.

TEST 4: (for no candidates)
  max
Expect
  Some message about missing candidates to standard error.
  Exit status 2.

The first normal test specification begins with a very specific test requirement:

max -ceiling X -ceiling Y

One of the precondition test requirements can be used in this test:

-ceiling given, arg > any candidate

The string "}}}" is a nice large ASCII string to use as the ceiling ('}' is almost the largest ASCII character). It also has the virtue of detecting the (very unlikely) fault where a strange character like '}' is not allowed. This doesn't satisfy any test requirement, but the only test requirement that gives a specific string is "ceiling as empty string", and the empty string is smaller than "-ceiling", so it can't be used in this test.

The test can satisfy another test requirement:

First candidate is largest (more than one)

This requires that Y be a string smaller than "-ceiling". The empty string is such a string, and it satisfies one more test requirement.

The inputs are now completely specified:

TEST 5:
     max -ceiling }}} -ceiling ""
Expect
     Max prints "-ceiling"
     Exit status 0.

The next test begins with another specific requirement:

max -ceiling -ceiling X

The requirement that the ceiling has to be less than or equal to some candidate can be satisfied by this test. The empty string can't be used for X, since "-ceiling" is greater than it. The empty string is the only specific string in the checklist. Since there's no better choice, one of the deferred string comparison requirements can be reused. The string "-ceilin" was already used (in the error tests), so it would be better to use another one. The string "-ceilinh" has not been used yet.

TEST6:
     max -ceiling -ceiling -ceilinh

Expect
     Max prints "-ceiling"
     Exit status 0.

Of the remaining requirements, the one least compatible with others is probably "ceiling as empty string". Since the ceiling is thus the smallest possible string, it must be max's result. (It was at this point that I noticed that I'd missed using "the value printed" as a String clue. The only test requirement from it is "empty string," which is already satisfied by this test.)

Using some of the "candidate list" or "searching candidate list" test requirements to help design an argument list would be incorrect. It would violate the rule that each test requirement should be exercised. Suppose the requirement that the second of two candidates be largest were satisfied. Since the result is to be the ceiling, there'd be no way of knowing that the program correctly identified the second candidate as largest.

Nevertheless, at least one candidate must be given an exact value. The deferred string comparison conditions can help, since the candidate must be compared to the ceiling. Picking a candidate slightly larger than the empty string satisfies one of them.

> TEST7:
> > max -ceiling "" a
> Expect
> > Max prints the empty string.
> > Exit status 0.

All the tests so far use the `-ceiling` option. A test that doesn't will satisfy "the -ceiling option is not given". The remaining unsatisfied test requirements can also be used:

> Last candidate is largest (more than one)
> Further match immediately adjacent to last match

as well as a test requirement for the candidate:

> > compared to current maximum, one element longer   (DEFER)

Here's the test specification:

> TEST8:
> > max " " z
> Expect
> > Prints "z"
> > Exit status 0

The "candidate as empty string" was reused.
> Here, for reference, is the checked off checklist:

Precondition E1:

1	Word after "max" begins with '-', is not "-ceiling". ERROR	(Test 3)
1	Nearby misspellings of "-ceiling" DEFERRED ERROR	(Test 3)
	Word after "max" begins with '-', is exactly "-ceiling".	
2	-ceiling given, arg <= some candidate	(Test 6, 7)
1	-ceiling given, arg > any candidate	(Test 5)
	Word after "max" does not begin with '-'.	
1	The -ceiling option is not given.	(Test 8)

the ceiling, a string

1	ceiling as empty string	(Test 7)
0	compared to maximum candidate, same length, differ in last element	(DEFER)
1	compared to maximum candidate, same elements, one element shorter	(DEFER) (Test 7)
0	compared to maximum candidate, same elements, one element longer	(DEFER)

a candidate, a string

2	candidate as empty string	(Test 5, 8)
1	compared to current maximum, same length, differ in last element	(DEFER) (Test 6)
0	compared to current maximum, same elements, one element shorter	(DEFER)
1	compared to current maximum, same elements, one element longer	(DEFER) (Test 8)

a list of strings (the candidate list)

1	no candidates ERROR	(Test 4)
	a single candidate	
1	max -ceiling -ceiling X	(Test 6)
	more than one candidate	
1	First candidate is largest (more than one)	(Test 5)
	Some other candidate is largest (more than one)	
1	Last candidate is largest (more than one)	(Test 8)
1	max -ceiling X -ceiling Y	(Test 5)

searching candidate list for maximum.

1	Further match immediately adjacent to last match	(Test 8)

command line syntax

1	No option argument: max -ceiling ERROR	(Test 1)
1	Partial option ("-") ERROR	(Test 2)

17.3
Deriving
Tests
from the
Code

This is the code for MAX. What clues can you find?

```
11      #include <stdio.h>
12
13      #define BUFSIZE   20
14
15      main(argc, argv)
16        int argc;
17        char **argv;
18      {
19       char result_so_far[BUFSIZE];     /* Largest value to date. */
20       char ceiling[BUFSIZE];
22
23       result_so_far[0] = '\0';                /* Start as smallest possible string. */
24       result_so_far[BUFSIZE-1] = '\0';/* Ensure always null terminated. */
25
26       ceiling[0]='\177';                      /* Start as largest possible string. */
27       ceiling[1]='\0';
28       ceiling[BUFSIZE-1]='\0';                /* Ensure always null-terminated. */
29
30       /* Handle options. */
31       for(argc--, argv++; argc > 0 && '-' == **argv; argc--, argv++)
32         {
33           if (!strcmp(argv[0], "-ceiling"))
34             {
35               strncpy(ceiling, argv[1], BUFSIZE);
36               argv++;                  /* Skip argument. */
37               argc--;
38             }
39           else
40             {
41               fprintf(stderr, "Illegal option %s.\n", argv[0]);
42               exit(2);
43             }
44         }
45
46       if (argc == 0)
47         {
48           fprintf(stderr, "Max requires at least one argument.\n");
49           exit(2);
50         }
51
52       for (;argc > 0; argc--, argv++)
53         {
54           if (strcmp(argv[0], result_so_far)>0)
55               strncpy(result_so_far, argv[0], BUFSIZE);
56         }
57       printf("%s\n", strcmp(ceiling, result_so_far) <0 ? ceiling : result_so_far);
58       exit(0);
59      }
```

`ceiling` and `result_so_far` are buffers to be filled. They can be used as clues. But there's something else going on here—nothing in the specification says there's a limit on the length of arguments. The code enforces one, though. This is a bug in the specification. It is fixed by adding a new effect.

IF any string longer than 19 characters is entered
THEN only the first 19 characters are used

This postcondition yields four new test requirements (two when applied to the ceiling string and two when applied to a candidate string):

New postcondition
    ceiling string longer than 19 characters.
    ceiling string 19 characters or less
    candidate string longer than 19 characters.
    candidate string 19 characters or less.

There's an option-checking operation (the whole loop), but it was already used in the checklist (as the "command line syntax" clue).

These subroutines are used: `strcmp` and `strncpy`. They are clues.

All the deferred requirements in the specification checklist are either used or refer to non-inline operations (`strcmp`). They needn't be copied into the code checklist. The new checklist looks like this:

ceiling, a buffer
result_so_far, a buffer
New postcondition
    ceiling string longer than 19 characters.
    ceiling string 19 characters or less.
    candidate string longer than 19 characters.
    candidate string 19 characters or less.

strcmp (of candidates)
strcmp (of candidates to ceiling)
strncpy (into ceiling)
strncpy (of result_so_far)

The catalog's Comparison Operators entry applies to the new postcondition. It adds boundary conditions. For example, "longer than 19 characters" provides two requirements: 19 characters exactly and 20 characters exactly. These same requirements are also gotten from "19 characters or less".

The Container entry is in the standard catalog, not the student catalog. It will be used here because MAX provides an example of an entry people sometimes find hard to understand. MAX overwrites an existing stored string with another. Here are requirements:

- New contents have 1 more element than will fit.
- New contents just fit.
- New contents leave room for exactly one element   INLINE
  (can catch unchecked "small harmless" additions)
      Example: putting "abcd" in an array of six characters
- 0 elements added (is container emptied?)
- Some elements added, but fewer than in original   INLINE
  container (are old contents cleared?)
      Example: putting "ab" in an array containing "abc"

The first two requirements seem applicable. A 19-character string will just fit (remember the trailing null at the end of C strings), and a 20-character string is one more than will fit. For `ceiling`, these two requirements are exactly the same as the boundary conditions just found. For the candidate, they're actually more refined, since they apply only to candidates actually copied into `result_so_far`. So they're written as a refinement. (The rules for test content would also force this.)

The third test requirement doesn't apply because MAX never adds any more to the container. The fourth and fifth are omitted because I trust `strcpy` to handle zero-length copies and to correctly null-terminate what it copies.

Here are the new requirements. The ones in bold are the most refined.

> ceiling, a buffer
> result_so_far, a buffer
> New postcondition
> > ceiling string longer than 19 characters.
> > > **20 characters**
> > ceiling string 19 characters or less
> > > **19 characters**
> > candidate string longer than 19 characters.
> > > **20 characters**
> > > > **candidate is result_so_far**
> > candidate string 19 characters or less.
> > > **19 characters**
> > > > **candidate is result_so_far**

> strcmp (of candidates)
> strcmp (of candidates to ceiling)
> strncpy (into ceiling)
> strncpy (of result_so_far)

The next step is to find integration test requirements.

The `strcmp` user documentation says that it has three possible return values: less than zero, zero, and greater than zero. Normally, all three of those cases should be tested for both calls. However, the program considers two of the cases identical by checking the result with an inequality. I will make a testing mistake by believing the program and considering only success or failure. (In this particular case, the program happens to be correct, but that doesn't invalidate the general principle.) You'll be able to see the effects of that mistake on coverage.

> strcmp (of candidates)
> > New candidate larger than result_so_far
> > New candidate not larger than result_so_far

> strcmp (of candidates to ceiling)
> > Ceiling less than result_so_far
> > Ceiling not less than result_so_far

In the case of `strncpy`, there are two cases: where it null-pads (<`BUFSIZE` characters) or truncates (>= `BUFSIZE` characters). But the 19-character and 20-character requirements already written down satisfy those two cases with the added benefit of being boundary conditions. So nothing need be written down.

The finished checklist is shown below.

ceiling, a buffer
result_so_far, a buffer
New postcondition
    ceiling string longer than 19 characters.
        20 characters
    ceiling string 19 characters or less
        19 characters
    candidate string longer than 19 characters.
        20 characters
          candidate is result_so_far
    candidate string 19 characters or less.
        19 characters
          candidate is result_so_far

strcmp (of candidates)
    New candidate larger than result_so_far.
    New candidate not larger than result_so_far
strcmp (of candidates to ceiling)
    Ceiling less than result_so_far.
    Ceiling not less than result_so_far

strncpy (into ceiling)
strncpy (of result_so_far)

Existing tests satisfy some of the new requirements just by chance:

Ceiling less than result_so_far   (6,7)
Ceiling not less than result_so_far   (5)
New candidate larger than result_so_far   (8)
New candidate not larger than result_so_far (5)

So these needn't be used in test specification generation, except to provide variety, just like any other satisfied requirements. The four boundary requirements are all that need new tests.

They have to be handled a bit carefully. The rules for test content require that they have some visible effect. One appropriate effect is that the twentieth character not appear in the output (that it be truncated correctly). The nineteenth character should appear in the output. Moreover, if two strings differ in the 19th character, that character should make a difference in which one is considered larger.

Because of visibility, it would not be right to have a single test with four strings that satisfy all four requirements. Instead, three tests will be used.

The first test satisfies the requirement that the candidate be twenty characters:

TEST 9:
     max -ceiling 123456789012345678f   123   12   1   123456789012345678a0
Expect
     123456789012345678a
     exit status 0

I added some smaller candidates just for variety. The ceiling is 19 characters, and it is the 19th character that makes the ceiling higher than the maximum candidate. However, it's something of a weak test of the 19th-character boundary because the 19-character string is only used in a comparison; it does not appear in the output.

The next test just reverses the strings to exercise the ceiling's 20-character boundary:

TEST 10:
     max -ceiling 123456789012345678a0   123456789012345678f
Expect
     123456789012345678a
     exit status 0

The extra candidates have been removed for variety.

Because the 19-character requirements haven't been well tested, one more test is added to show that a 19-character string can be printed as well as used in comparison:

TEST 11:
     max -ceiling ===================M + ===================D   ""
Expect
     ===================D
     exit status 0

In this case, the candidate is printed. Another test, one that printed a nineteen character ceiling, could also be written, but I won't bother. In this case, adding another test is trivial. A real program would likely be complex enough that adding a new test would be significant work. That work would not be justified for a requirement that's actively used twice in comparisons, if never in printing. The printing of the ceiling is unlikely to fail in ways that printing of the candidate didn't.

Refer back to the text of *max.c* (see page 260) given in the previous section. One relevant question is:

⇒ • Can this string ever not be null-terminated?

`result_so_far` and `ceiling` are strings printed as output. They must be null-terminated. The program makes an attempt to ensure that by initially setting the last element to null.

`ceiling` is filled by copying from the argument list using `strncpy`:

```
20    char ceiling[BUFSIZE];
...
35        strncpy(ceiling, argv[1], BUFSIZE);
```

`strncpy` copies at most `BUFSIZE` characters. But the buffer is only `BUFSIZE` characters long. That means that it could be completely filled with characters, and the trailing null might be overwritten. This is a fault. The correct argument to `strncpy` should be `BUFSIZE-1`.

The same thing happens in the `strncpy` that fills `result_so_far`—another fault.

Tests 9 and 10 will exercise this fault. They will certainly fail, since at least 20 characters will be printed out, whereas the specification calls for 19. Exactly what is printed depends on what comes after the buffers, which depends on how the compiler lays out local arrays; but it cannot be the correct result. The failure might be as small as a single character difference in a long string. Such a small failure is easy to miss if you just run the test and see if the output "looks right." Writing precise expected output before the test makes you much less likely to miss it.

The fault is readily visible because it's so close to the external interface. Had it been buried deep within a larger subsystem, it would have been less visible. That's why this question is in the Question Catalog.

This question in the BUFFERS section should lead to the discovery of the same two faults:

⇒ • Is this buffer ever too small to hold its contents?

For example, one program had no size checks when reading data into a 12-character buffer because the *correct* data would always fit. But when the file it read was accidentally overwritten with incorrect data, the program crashed mysteriously.

The POINTERS section of the catalog asks this question:

⇒ • When dereferenced, can a pointer ever be null?

argv[X] is a pointer that can only be null when the argument list has been exhausted. Can the argument list be exhausted at a point where argv[X] is dereferenced? Here's the relevant code:

```
31    for(argc--, argv++; argc > 0 && '-' == **argv; argc--, argv++)
32      {
33        if (!strcmp(argv[0], "-ceiling"))
34          {
35            strncpy(ceiling, argv[1], BUFSIZE);      /* Make this result-so-far */
36            argv++;                                  /* Skip argument. */
37            argc--;
38          }
39        else
40          {
41            fprintf(stderr, "Illegal option %s.\n", argv[0]);
42            exit(2);
43          }
44      }
```

1. *argv is dereferenced in the loop test on line 31, but only when argc>0. That test ensures that *argv is not null.
2. Within the for loop, argv[0] can never be null since argv[0] is the current argument and the loop is entered only if there's a current argument.
3. However, what about argv[1] on line 35? There's no guarantee that there's anything after "-ceiling". Indeed, there's a test specification in which there wasn't. It's now clear that test will cause a failure. There should be a check before the strncpy—omitting such a check is a very common error, which is why the requirement is in the catalog.
4. argv[0] in the second for loop will never be null, because that code is protected by the argc>0 test. (This loop isn't shown. It's on line 52, if you want to refer to the complete code.)

The catalog asks this question of functions:

⯈ • Is this function correct? Should it be a different function with a similar name? (E.g., strchr instead of strrchr?)

The strncpy calls are the right functions. The calls to printf look right—the program doesn't use printf when it should be using fprintf, for example.

The call to strcmp in the second for loop looks suspicious:

```
52    for (;argc > 0; argc--, argv++)
53      {
54        if (strcmp(argv[0], result_so_far)>0)
55            strncpy(result_so_far, argv[0], BUFSIZE);
56      }
```

Should MAX be using strncmp? It may have truncated the string put into result_so_far, so shouldn't it also use a truncating comparison? That's suspicious, but the suspicion doesn't pay off. The program will give the right answer in this case (assuming the BUFSIZE fault has been fixed). Suppose the arguments are

XXXXXXXXXXXXXXXXXXX5
XXXXXXXXXXXXXXXXXXX4

In the first iteration of the loop, result_so_far will get

XXXXXXXXXXXXXXXXXXX

This will be compared to the second argument, which will compare as larger. That argument will be copied into result_so_far, but it will be truncated, so that result_so_far will still be the same value. Thus the answer is correct (although the program did some work that could have been avoided).

Nothing else in the catalog looks significant. The catalog has found two faults that will be found again by testing. The tests should still be written: They might find other faults, they'll test that the faults are fixed correctly, and they're easy to run after maintenance changes (whereas code reads are hard to repeat and often aren't done with as much diligence the fifth time as the first).

17.5 The Test Driver and Running the Tests

MAX prints a value (to either standard output or standard error) and exits with a particular status. It requires only a simple driver, one that can capture those two outputs and compare them to the expected outputs. The driver will be named doit. A call to doit looks like this:

doit Test1 2 -ceiling

The first argument is the name of the test. The expected standard output is stored in *Test1.ref*. The expected standard error is stored in *Test1.ref2*. The next argument is the expected return status. The remaining arguments are given to MAX.

That use of doit implements this test specification:

TEST 1:
        max -ceiling
Expect
        Some message about missing ceiling argument to standard error.
        Exit status 2.

Test1.ref will be empty since no normal output is expected. Initially, *Test1.ref2* will contain "<Some message about missing ceiling argument>" because the specification doesn't detail the actual error message. The first time the test is run, doit should report that the actual error message differs from the expected. If the actual message is reasonable, it will be made the reference message.

All the calls to doit—all the implemented tests—can be collected into a single shell script called `run-suite`. It looks like this:

```
doit Test1  2 -ceiling
doit Test2  2 - x
doit Test3  2 -ceilin arg candidate
doit Test4  2
doit Test5  0 -ceiling }}} -ceiling ""
doit Test6  0 -ceiling -ceiling -ceilinh
doit Test7  0 -ceiling "" a
doit Test8  0 "" z
doit Test9  0 -ceiling 123456789012345678f 123 12 1 123456789012345678a0
doit Test10  0 -ceiling 123456789012345678a0 123456789012345678f
doit Test11  0 -ceiling ==================M + ===================D""
```

This is the output from the first run of the test suite:

```
% run-suite
== Test1 ====== ( max -ceiling )
doit: 1019 Memory fault—core dumped
Status was 139; should have been 2.
FAILURE: Actual error output (marked with ACT) differs from expected (EXP).
0a1
EXP:  <Some message about missing ceiling argument>
```

➡ *This is caused by a fault found during the inspection.*

```
== Test2 ====== ( max - x )
FAILURE: Actual error output (marked with ACT) differs from expected (EXP).
1c1
ACT:  Illegal option -.
---
EXP:  <Some message about incorrect option>
```

> ➡ *The error message is reasonable, so it's put in Test2.ref2.*
> *The same is true for Test 3 and Test 4.*
> *(The next time the suite runs, no differences will show up.)*

== Test3 ====== (max -ceilin arg candidate)
FAILURE: Actual error output (marked with ACT) differs from expected (EXP).
1c1
ACT: Illegal option -ceilin.

EXP: <Some message about incorrect option>
== Test4 ====== (max)
FAILURE: Actual error output (marked with ACT) differs from expected (EXP).
1c1
ACT: Max requires at least one argument.

EXP: <Some message about missing candidates>
== Test5 ====== (max -ceiling }}} -ceiling)
Status was 2; should have been 0.
FAILURE: Actual standard output (marked with ACT) differs from expected (EXP).
0a1
EXP: -ceiling
FAILURE: Actual error output (marked with ACT) differs from expected (EXP).
1d0
ACT: Max requires at least one argument.

➥*Test 5 is peculiar—there was no standard output, just an unexpected error message.*
That's because the option-processing loop shouldn't have been a loop, but a simple if *test. This is a new fault.*

== Test6 ====== (max -ceiling -ceiling -ceilinh)
Status was 2; should have been 0.
FAILURE: Actual standard output (marked with ACT) differs from expected (EXP).
0a1
EXP: -ceiling
FAILURE: Actual error output (marked with ACT) differs from expected (EXP).
1d0
ACT: Illegal option -ceilinh.

➥*This is a slightly different manifestation of the same fault.*

== Test7 ====== (max -ceiling a)
== Test8 ====== (max z)

➥*The program passes Tests 7 and 8.*

== Test9 ====== (max -ceiling 123456789012345678f 123 12 1 123456789012345678a0)
FAILURE: Actual standard output (marked with ACT) differs from expected (EXP).
1c1
ACT: 123456789012345678a0

EXP: 123456789012345678a
== Test10 ====== (max -ceiling 123456789012345678a0 123456789012345678f)
FAILURE: Actual standard output (marked with ACT) differs from expected (EXP).
1c1
ACT: 123456789012345678a0123456789012345678f

EXP: 123456789012345678a
== Test11 ====== (max -ceiling ==================M + ==================D)

> ➥*The program fails Tests 9 and 10, as expected. It passes Test 11.*

run-suite is the essence of a suite driver. In order to compare old and new runs of a test, its output can be saved and compared with the output from later runs:

```
% run-suite > release1.hist
### Do lots of development.
% run-suite > release2.hist
% diff release1.hist release2.hist
### The output shows what's changed between releases.
```

17.6 Using Coverage

This is what the MAX test suite misses:

"max.c", line 52: loop zero times: 0, one time: 3, many times: 1.
"max.c", line 54: operator > needs boundary L==R+1.
"max.c", line 57: operator < might be <=. (L==R)
"max.c", line 57: operator < needs boundary L==R-1.

The first line refers to the second while loop, the one that actually processes candidates. The loop has never executed zero times. Zero iterations is impossible since the immediately preceding if exits in the case that would cause it.[1]

The second line says that no test has explored a boundary condition for the result of strcmp. It requires

strcmp(argv[0], result_so_far)>0

to be true, but just barely. In general, there are two reasons for testing such a condition. First, to check that the expression is correct. Second, boundaries for that expression can reveal faults in the rest of the code (either

---

1. Actually, that's not true for this *incorrect* program, though it would be for a correct one. There's a case in which the loop might be executed 0 times. On machines that treat a dereferenced null pointer as a zero, the strncpy in the option-processing loop (line 35) will succeed, and argc will be decremented. If there are no further arguments, the loop will terminate with argc -1, which would escape the check (line 46), cause the second loop to be skipped, and make the program exit with status 0. Note that even on such machines the test would fail since the expected exit status is 2.

before or after the expression). Perhaps the same boundaries are less obvious special cases elsewhere in the program.

In this particular case, a higher boundary is obviously incorrect, the boundary case has no effect on the rest of the code, and it seems very unlikely that it should. (It would be a fault of omission if the boundary should have been handled specially but wasn't.) Further, the strcmp documentation only says that it returns 0, a number greater than 0, or a number less than 0. There is no documented way to force a return value of 1 (though it can be easily done for most strcmp implementations). So this coverage condition can safely be ignored.

The third line shows the return value of the strcmp on line 57 is never exactly 0; that is, the ceiling is never identical to result_so_far in this code:

```
57   printf("%s\n", strcmp(ceiling, result_so_far) <0 ? ceiling : result_so_far);
58   exit(0);
```

In this case, it doesn't matter if the relational expression is wrong. Either of the two variables can be printed, since they have identical contents. It also seems unlikely that the rest of the program will go wrong in this case. Certainly code after the expression can't, since the program immediately exits. So this coverage condition needn't be satisfied. Satisfying it would have been simple, though:

```
TEST 12:
     max -ceiling 1 1
Expect
     1
     Exit status 0
```

The fourth greport line is similar to the second; it would require strcmp to return -1. It can be ignored for the same reason.

At this point, you should be alarmed. I have apparently drifted into the trap of thinking of coverage conditions as test requirements, not clues. I should be thinking that this coverage points out that I missed things in test design (the Other Comparison Operators entry and the "duplicate elements" requirement from the Collections entry) and also that perhaps I should reconsider the unused deferred test requirements. That's true. But because this is a simple program, thinking of coverage conditions as clues will have the same effect as thinking of them as test requirements. It's in testing larger, harder programs that the difference becomes critically important.

Suppose the test suite had been written without reference to the code. The *greport* output would have been the same as above. The two code-based tests, those that explored long strings, added no coverage. All they do is find a bug. This is an instance of how 100 percent coverage is not enough, and how coverage will not uncover all weaknesses in a test suite, only some of them.

Testing Consistency Relationships

State variables are usually interdependent. The allowable value of one variable may depend on the value another has. If this is the case, there's a *consistency relationship* between the two variables, and it can lead to test requirements. It's worth discussing the process in detail, because it's a nice example of finding test requirements through an analysis of possible faults. (Of course, because consistency checking is a clichéd operation, the analysis only needs to be done once.)

As a simple example, consider two variables, LEFT and RIGHT. LEFT can have the value 0 or 1. RIGHT can be in the range [0-10]. There are three *dependency statements*:

Statement 1: LEFT=0 requires RIGHT in the range [0-5]
Statement 2: LEFT=1 requires RIGHT in the range [6-10]
Default: Any other value of LEFT is an error

In this particular case, the default statement doesn't describe a dependency. Instead, it's a precondition on the values of LEFT alone. It's still convenient to list it. In other cases, the default may be a true dependency, as in:

Default: Any other value of LEFT requires RIGHT to be even

Notice that a particular value of LEFT is classified into exactly one statement. RIGHT values can overlap. For example, RIGHT=2 could be described by either Statement 1 or the new default.

A subsystem can treat dependency statements in one of three ways:

1. The subsystem's caller must never attempt to violate consistency. (This is like an assumed precondition for every operation in the subsystem interface.)
2. The caller has no direct access to the variables, so it is impossible to give inputs that violate consistency.
3. The subsystem detects attempts to violate consistency and fails them as an error. (This is like a validated precondition.)

The latter two are typical of user interfaces; all three are common in programmatic interfaces.

No matter what the approach, implemented tests should check that consistency is not violated. This is especially true if one of the variables is in the foreground. But you'll find even more bugs if you check consistency after every test, including those where the variables are in the background or even far background. Consistency violations happen in unexpected ways often enough that it's worth the effort. The effort can be low when tests are automated.

The following discussion of test design will assume the third approach (the subsystem must reject inconsistent changes). Designing tests for the two simpler cases follows the same procedure except that ERROR test requirements are omitted.

Suppose there are two routines to change the variables, change_LEFT and change_RIGHT. For the moment, assume that the code for change_LEFT should look like this:

```
change_left(int new_LEFT)
    {
        switch(new_LEFT)
        {
          case 0:   /* Enforce dependency statement 1 */
            if (RIGHT < 0 || RIGHT > 5) { print_error(); return; }
            break;
          case 1:   /* Enforce dependency statement 2 */
            if (RIGHT < 6 || RIGHT > 10) { print_error(); return; }
            break;
          default:   /* Default is always an error */
            print_error(); return;
            break;
        }
        LEFT = new_LEFT;
```

The code for change_RIGHT could have almost the same structure. Only the variable names are changed as shown in bold font. (The implications of a different structure are discussed later.)

```
switch(LEFT)
    {
       case 0:
         if (new_RIGHT < 0 || new_RIGHT > 5) { print_error(); return; }
         break;
       case 1:
         if (new_RIGHT < 6 || new_RIGHT > 10) { print_error(); return; }
         break;
       /* No default needed: LEFT is guaranteed to be 0 or 1. */
    }
    RIGHT = new_RIGHT;
```

(The case where there's a single consistency checking routine, called by both functions, will be considered later.)

Plausible Implementation Errors
What are plausible implementation errors, and what test requirements would detect them?

One of the routines doesn't enforce consistency
One of the routines is missing the switch statement. This fault is detected by any test requirement that violates the consistency relationship. The following test is an example:

```
INITIALLY:   LEFT=0, RIGHT=5
TEST:        Change_LEFT(1)
EXPECT:      Error message, LEFT and RIGHT unchanged
```

Note that both routines must be tested with inputs that violate consistency. Note also that the targeted fault is a fault of omission. If you only tested the consistency relationship using change_LEFT, and there was no consistency checking in change_RIGHT, you'd miss the bug and coverage would give you no clue that you had.

One of the dependency statements isn't enforced
The incorrect code might look like

```
if (new_LEFT == 0 && (RIGHT < 0 || RIGHT > 5))
    { print_error(); return; }
/* Omitted checking of new_LEFT == 1 */
```

Catching such faults requires that each dependency statement be violated. That should produce an error indication. If the dependency statement is unchecked, it won't.

The consistency check does not stop processing
A consistency check might detect an error, but fail to stop the state change. Here's an example:

```
switch(new_LEFT)
{
    case 0:                    /* Enforce dependency statement 1*/
        if (RIGHT < 0 || RIGHT > 5) print_error();  /* return missing */
        break;
    case 1:                    /* Enforce dependency statement 2 */
        if (RIGHT < 6 || RIGHT > 10) { print_error(); return; }
        break;
    default:                   /* Default is always an error */
        print_error(); return;
        break;
}
LEFT = new_LEFT;
```

This fault is easily detected provided all your tests check the background (that what shouldn't be changed isn't changed). Other variants of this error would result in multiple error messages, which are even easier to detect.

Consistency of the current value is checked, not that of the proposed value

Here are two instances of this fault:

```
switch(LEFT)                            /* new_LEFT should be used. */
{
   case 0:                              /* Enforce dependency statement 1*/
     if (RIGHT < 0 || RIGHT > 5) { print_error(); return; }
     break;
   case 1:                              /* Enforce dependency statement 2 */
     if (RIGHT < 6 || RIGHT > 10) { print_error(); return; }
     break;
   default:                             /* Default is always an error */
     print_error(); return;
     break
}
LEFT = new_LEFT;


switch(LEFT)
{
   case 0:                              /* Tests RIGHT instead of new_RIGHT */
     if (RIGHT < 0 || new_RIGHT > 5) { print_error(); return; }
     break;
   case 1:
     if (new_RIGHT < 6 || new_RIGHT > 10) { print_error(); return; }
     break;
}
RIGHT = new_RIGHT;
```

The first can be found by any violation of the consistency relationship. Since it tests the old variable—which was initialized to a consistent value—the violation will go undetected. The expected error message will not appear.

Finding the second requires more tests. Each dependency statement must be violated, and each reason for a violation must be exercised. That is, there must be a test like this:

```
Test 1: Test statement 1 violation
       INITIALLY:      LEFT=0, RIGHT=3
       TEST:           Change_RIGHT(6)
       EXPECT:         Error message, LEFT and RIGHT unchanged
```

and another like this

```
Test 2: Another test for Statement 1 violation
       INITIALLY:  LEFT=0, RIGHT=3
       TEST:       Change_RIGHT(-1)/* This will catch the fault */
       EXPECT:     Error message, LEFT and RIGHT unchanged
```

The best way to ensure such tests is to treat RIGHT as an interval variable clue:

➡ [A, B] (Both A and B are in the interval)
 • V1 = A - epsilon   IN
 • V1 = A   IN, OUT
 • V1 = B   IN, OUT
 • V1 = B + epsilon   IN

Note that these requirements must be exercised when LEFT=0. The type of test design described below will ensure that. Mistakes in test design will lead to unsatisfied multicondition and relational operator coverage (provided the required code wasn't omitted).

Other wrong variables are used
There could be a variety of misused variables. Here is an example:

```
switch(new_LEFT)
{
   case 0:            /* Enforce dependency statement 1*/
      if (RIGHT < 0 || LEFT > 5) { print_error(); return; }
      break;
   case 1:            /* Enforce dependency statement 2 */
      if (RIGHT < 6 || RIGHT > 10) { print_error(); return; }
      break;
   default:           /* Default is always an error */
      print_error(); return;
      break
}
LEFT = new_LEFT;
```

Finding such faults is a type of weak mutation testing [Howden82]. In my experience, most such faults are caught by tests designed for other reasons [Marick91b].

RIGHT is misclassified
This would be a situation like the following:

```
switch(LEFT)
{
   case 0:            /* Wrong test for 0 boundary */
      if (new_RIGHT <= 0 || new_RIGHT > 5) { print_error(); return; }
      break;
   case 1:            /* Wrong test for 10 boundary */ .
      if (new_RIGHT < 6 || new_RIGHT > 9) { print_error(); return; }
      break;
}
RIGHT = new_RIGHT;
```

In the first case, new_RIGHT=0 is rejected when it should be accepted. In the second, new_RIGHT=10 is rejected when it should be accepted. These are caught in the same way as the fault of using RIGHT rather than new_RIGHT: new_RIGHT is treated as an interval clue.

LEFT is misclassified

To illustrate this fault, let's use a slightly more complicated dependency statement. The change is in bold face:

Statement 1: LEFT=0 requires RIGHT in the range [0-6]
Statement 2: **LEFT in [1, 2]** requires RIGHT in the range [6-10]
Default: Any other value of LEFT is an error

Correct code for processing this would look like this:

```
switch(new_LEFT)
{
  case 0:                 /* Enforce dependency statement 1 */
    if (RIGHT < 0 || RIGHT > 6) { print_error(); return; }
    break;
  case 1:                 /* Enforce dependency statement 2 */
  case 2:
    if (RIGHT < 6 || RIGHT > 10) { print_error(); return; }
    break;
  default:                /* Default is always an error */
    print_error(); return;
    break;
}
LEFT = new_LEFT;
```

There are several possible errors: leaving out case 2, adding an extra case 3, mistyping case 2 as case 3, putting case 2 in the wrong place. To find these, you must first exercise case 2. Again, the catalog provides the requirements with the Cases entry:

➠ V1 might be any of (C1, C2, ... Cn).
Specification only.

• V1 = each possible case.	IN, OUT
• V1 = some impossible case.	IN

But there's a little more complexity. If there is a fault, you must make sure the failure is visible. For example, suppose the code were incorrectly written as

```
switch(new_LEFT)
{
  case 0:
    if (RIGHT < 0 || RIGHT > 6) { print_error(); return; }
    break;
  case 1:                       /* Case 2 omitted */
    if (RIGHT < 6 || RIGHT > 10) { print_error(); return; }
    break;
  default:                /* Default is always an error */
    print_error(); return;
    break;
}
LEFT = new_LEFT;
```

It is not enough to exercise case 2. Consider this test:

INITIALLY:	LEFT=0, RIGHT=3
TEST:	Change_LEFT(2) /* This will miss the fault */
EXPECT:	Error message, LEFT and RIGHT unchanged

The problem is that both the correct and incorrect programs call `error`. A rule for test content ("Alternate actions should cause visible differences") has been violated. To guarantee discovery, you must ensure that the correct results are different from the results of misclassifying LEFT into any of the other dependency statements.

As another example, consider this misclassification of `case 1`:

```
switch(new_LEFT)
{
  case 0:
  case 1:            /* Case 1 in the wrong place */
    if (RIGHT < 0 || RIGHT > 6) { print_error(); return; }
    break;
  case 2:
    if (RIGHT < 6 || RIGHT > 10) { print_error(); return; }
    break;
  default:           /* Default is always an error */
    print_error(); return;
    break;
}
LEFT = new_LEFT;
```

This test will miss the fault:

INITIALLY:	LEFT=0, RIGHT=6
TEST:	Change_LEFT(1)
EXPECT:	LEFT=1, RIGHT=6

The problem is that **RIGHT=6** is consistent according to both the second dependency statement (the correct one) and the first (where LEFT=1 is misclassified). This test will detect the fault:

INITIALLY:	LEFT=0, RIGHT=5
TEST:	Change_LEFT(1)
EXPECT:	Error, LEFT and RIGHT unchanged.

Finding such faults, then, involves this process:[1]

1. Find values of LEFT to test.
2. For each value of LEFT, pick a value of RIGHT and calculate the expected results.
3. For each other dependency statement, including the default, assume LEFT is misclassified into it. Check whether the value of RIGHT causes a different expected result for that statement.

---

1. This process can be justified by considering all the plausible misclassification faults. If you want to do so, make sure you've read the section on "Subsystem Testing and the Theoretical Ideal" in An Overview of Subsystem Testing. It will help you organize your approach.

4. If the expected result for some misclassification is not distinct, an additional value of RIGHT has to be chosen. Repeat until every misclassification has given a distinct result.
5. If there is completely different code for change_LEFT and change_RIGHT, the process must be applied to both.

How hard all this is depends on the consistency relationship. In practice, checking each dependency statement may be too much work. In that case, only the most likely misclassifications are checked. These are usually the adjacent dependency statements. The default is also a likely misclassification, because it's applied whenever the programmer forgets a case.

The previous discussion can be boiled down to the rules in this section. They'll seem complex at first, but the example should make them clear.

18.1.1 The Basic Checklist

1. Each routine that changes a variable is a clue. (The case where a routine can change two variables at once is discussed later.)
2. Each dependency statement, including the default, leads to a test requirement. The requirement is that the dependency statement be exercised.
3. Refinements are found by treating the LEFT variable as a catalog entry. Use each requirement to refine the dependency statement it exercises.
4. Annotate each LEFT requirement with the dependency statement the subsystem is most likely to incorrectly apply to it. If two statements are

Statement 1) LEFT in [0-3] requires RIGHT in range [0-4]
Statement 2) LEFT in [4-10] requires RIGHT in range [10-40]

here are the annotations:

Statement 1 exercised:
    LEFT=0   (default)
    LEFT=3   (statement 2)
Statement 2 exercised:
    LEFT=4   (statement 1)
    LEFT=10   (default)
Default exercised:
    LEFT=-1   (statement 1)
    LEFT=11   (statement 2)

"Mostly likely misclassifications" are easy for Intervals, not so easy for Cases. Given these dependency statements:

1: Disaster FIRE requires action WATER
2: Disaster HURRICANE requires action FLEE
3: Disaster TORNADO requires action COWER
4: Disaster EARTHQUAKE requires action RUSH_OUTDOORS

what is the most likely misclassification for "HURRICANE"? It will be one or both of the two adjacent ones (since programs usually use the specification ordering). It's convenient to use "adjacent" as the annotation for Case variables.

5. Each dependency statement describes allowable values of RIGHT. Generate test requirements by treating that group of values as a variable. If values are an Interval, you will get boundaries both within and outside it. The latter are ERROR requirements. If the values are a Case, you'll get all possible cases and one illegal case. If a single value is allowed, there are two requirements: that the single value is used, and that some other value is used.

Place the resulting requirements as refinements of the dependency statement they came from. Remember to mark ERROR requirements.

The rules will be explained by applying them to part of a user interface description for a program that modifies the configuration of a machine. The syntax is:

update device type {tape | disk | optical | net}
update device address NUMBER

The consistency relationship is:

TAPE statement:	type tape requires address to be 0 or 1.
OPTICAL statement:	type optical requires address in the range [1,10].
DISK and NET statement:	type disk or net requires address to be any non-negative integer.
Default statement:	Any other type signals an error.

The first clue will be for update device type consistency checking. The first step is to list the dependency statements. The next step is to place the requirements for the type as refinements. To avoid confusion, it's important to make clear that the requirements apply to the new (proposed) value of the type, not the existing value. (Many faults in subsystems like this are caused by programmers confusing the old and new values, and you don't want to repeat their mistakes.) Next, likely misclassifications are added as annotations to the device type test requirements.

consistency checking: update device type
    Note: "type" is the value given in the command;
       "address" is the current value
    Tape dependency exercised
       type=TAPE   (adjacent)
    Optical dependency exercised
       type=OPTICAL   (adjacent)
    Disk and net dependency exercised
       type=DISK   (adjacent)
       type=NET   (adjacent)
    Default dependency exercised   (gives an error)
       type=some illegal name   (adjacent)   ERROR

Now the RIGHT requirements are added. Notice they are indented to the same level as the LEFT requirements, meaning LEFT and RIGHT requirements can be combined in any way that exercises the dependency statement.

```
consistency checking: update device type
        Note: "type" is the value given
        in the command; "address" is the current value
        Tape dependency exercised
                type=TAPE               (adjacent)
                address=0
                address=1
                address=neither 0 nor 1                    ERROR
        Optical dependency exercised
                type=OPTICAL            (adjacent)
                address=0                                  ERROR
                address=1
                address=10
                address=11                                 ERROR
        Disk and net dependency exercised
                type=DISK               (adjacent)
                type=NET                (adjacent)
                address=-1                                 ERROR
                address=0
                address=some very large number
                        (from Counts Catalog entry)
        Default dependency exercised (gives an error)
                type=some illegal name  (adjacent)  ERROR
```

18.1.2 Annotations to Increase Failure Visibility

Faults due to misclassifications of the LEFT variable must be made more visible. This is the job of the Rules for Test Content. But, because they apply in a specialized way to consistency checking, it's convenient to write them directly into the checklist. Each LEFT variable requirement (including those listed under the default) is given two refinements.

1. The first requires that the expected result of the correct program be different from the expected result of incorrectly applying the most likely misclassification. The latter result is calculated by pretending the LEFT value matches an incorrect dependency statement, then checking if the RIGHT value is consistent with that statement.
2. The second requires that the expected result be different from that of the default dependency statement. This refinement is not used for variables listed under the default case since the expected result can't be different from itself.

The two refinements can often be satisfied with the same test. Note that "different result" does not necessarily mean one has to be successful and the other an error. If both fail, but the error messages clearly describe the dependency statement that was violated, the results are different enough. (In general, the more information the subsystem reveals, the easier testing is.)

The refinements are treated like other test requirements except in one way. It doesn't matter whether they're satisfied by an ERROR or non-ERROR test. This is indicated by annotating the requirement with EITHER. If the test violates consistency, two requirements will have their counts incremented: the ERROR requirement and an EITHER requirement.

Here is the refined example. I've continued to use the "adjacent" shorthand to save typing. For type=OPTICAL, there are two adjacencies: the tape dependency and the disk-and-net dependency. For type=TAPE, there's only one: the optical dependency.

This pattern is used for all consistency relationships. Only the names and the values differ.

Fig. 18-1
A typical consistency
checking checklist
	consistency checking: update device type
	    Note: "type" is the value given
	        in the command; "address" is the current value
	    Tape dependency exercised
	        type=TAPE (adjacent)
	            different from misclassification as default EITHER
	            different from misclassification as adjacent EITHER
	        address=0
	        address=1
	        address=neither 0 nor 1 ERROR
	    Optical dependency exercised
	        type=OPTICAL (adjacent)
	            different from misclassification as default EITHER
	            different from misclassification as adjacent EITHER
	        address=0 ERROR
	        address=1
	        address=10
	        address=11 ERROR
	    Disk-and-net dependency exercised
	        type=DISK (adjacent)
	            different from misclassification as default EITHER
	            different from misclassification as adjacent EITHER
	        type=NET (adjacent)
	            different from misclassification as default EITHER
	            different from misclassification as adjacent EITHER
	        address=-1 ERROR
	        address=0
	        address=some very large number
	    Default dependency exercised (gives an error)
	        type=some illegal name (adjacent) ERROR
	            different from misclassification as adjacent ERROR

Notice that the misclassification requirement for the default dependency is marked as ERROR, rather than EITHER. That's because it's the refinement of an ERROR requirement. It wouldn't matter if it were listed as EITHER since it could only be used in an error test.

It's worth showing how a few tests are created. Here are the dependency statements and some test requirements:

TAPE statement:	type tape requires address to be 0 or 1.	
OPTICAL statement:	type optical requires address in the range [1,10].	
DISK and NET statement:	type disk or net requires address to be any non-negative integer.	
Default statement:	Any other type signals an error.	

consistency checking: update device type
    Tape dependency exercised

	type=TAPE (adjacent)	
0	different from misclassification as default	EITHER
0	different from misclassification as adjacent	EITHER
0	address=0	
0	address=1	
0	address=neither 0 nor 1	ERROR

A tape dependency test must be of the form

INITIALLY:	Type is **X**, address is **Y**
TEST:	update device type TAPE
EXPECT:	<...>

I will choose to satisfy "address=0", which means there will be no error. The "foreground modifications must be visible" test design rule says that it would be unwise to have the initial device type be TAPE, so it needs to be some other type compatible with an address of 0. NET will work. Here's the test:

Test 1

INITIALLY:	Type is NET, address is 0
TEST:	update device type TAPE
EXPECT:	Type is TAPE, address is 0

If the adjacent optical dependency were incorrectly used instead, the expected result would be an error. If the default were applied, it too would be an error. So each of the requirements that the result be different than a likely misapplication is satisfied. The incremented checklist looks like this:

consistency checking: update device type
    Tape dependency exercised

	type=TAPE (adjacent)		
1	different from misclassification as default	EITHER	(Test 1)
1	different from misclassification as adjacent	EITHER	(Test 1)
1	address=0		(Test 1)
0	address=1		
0	address=neither 0 nor 1	ERROR	

The previous example satisfied each of the misapplication require-

ments, but required no thought to do it. Indeed, once 0 was selected, there was no freedom of choice. That's not always the case, as this example will show.

TAPE statement:	type tape requires address to be 0 or 1.		
OPTICAL statement:	type optical requires address in the range [1,10].		
DISK and NET statement:	type disk or net requires address to be any non-negative integer.		
Default statement:	Any other type signals an error.		

consistency checking: update device type
    Tape dependency exercised
        type=TAPE   (adjacent)

1	different from misclassification as default	EITHER	(Test 1)
1	different from misclassification as adjacent	EITHER	(Test 1)
1	address=0		(Test 1)
0	address=1		
0	address=neither 0 nor 1	ERROR	

This time, I will satisfy the "neither 0 nor 1" requirement, which leads to an error. Two obvious possibilities are -1 and 2. However, note that -1 also violates all other dependency statements including the adjacent one. The address 2 does not. If the optical dependency statement is mistakenly applied, 2 will be accepted, giving no error. Therefore, 2 is a better choice than -1.

Here's the test:

Test 2
    INITIALLY: Type is OPTICAL, address is 2
    TEST: update device type TAPE
    EXPECT: Error message, TYPE remains OPTICAL, address remains 2

Note that the background is explicitly checked. Here's the updated test checklist. Observe that the EITHER requirement is incremented, even though the test is an ERROR test.

consistency checking: update device type
    Tape dependency exercised
        type=TAPE   (adjacent)

1	different from misclassification as default	EITHER	(Test 1)
2	different from misclassification as adjacent	EITHER	(Test 1, 2)
1	address=0		(Test 1)
0	address=1		
1	address=neither 0 nor 1	ERROR	(Test2)

As a final example, consider another dependency statement.

TAPE statement: type tape requires address to be 0 or 1.
OPTICAL statement: type optical requires address in the range [1,10].
DISK and NET statement: type disk or net requires address to be any non-negative integer.
Default statement: Any other type signals an error.

```
disk-and-net dependency exercised
    type=DISK        (adjacent)
        different from misclassification as default        EITHER
        different from misclassification as adjacent       EITHER
    type=NET         (adjacent)
        different from misclassification as default        EITHER
        different from misclassification as adjacent       EITHER
    address=-1                                             ERROR
    address=0
    address=some very large number
```

There is no way to set up the starting state with an `address=-1`, so that can be discarded as an impossible requirement.

`address=0` gives little freedom for action. Fortunately, the adjacent optical dependency statement yields an error if `address` is 0. The default does as well. So a single test can satisfy both misclassification requirements for `type=DISK`.

`address=some very large number` gives different results from the optical dependency (and, indeed, both other dependencies) provided "very large" means "greater than 10," which certainly seems reasonable. So, a second test can satisfy both of the NET requirements.

In this case, the misclassification requirements didn't force new tests, just additional checking during design. If any of the misclassification requirements couldn't have been satisfied with the given requirements for `address`, other values for `address` would have to be chosen.

Here are the two tests:

Test 2
    INITIALLY: Type is TAPE, address is 0
    TEST: update device type DISK
    EXPECT: TYPE is DISK, address is 0

Test 3
    INITIALLY: Type is DISK, address is 2147483647
    TEST: update device type NET
    EXPECT: TYPE is NET, address is 2147483647

The code for `update device address` is, for the moment, assumed to be completely independent from the `update device type` code. The structure of the consistency checking code is assumed to be the same, except that the changed variable is the address, not the type. So, the pattern of the requirements is the same, as is the way test specifications are built. The only difference is that the new address is used:

consistency checking: update device **address**
> **Note: "type" is the current value; "address" is the value given in the command**
> Tape dependency exercised

type=TAPE	(adjacent)	
different from misclassification as default		EITHER
different from misclassification as adjacent		EITHER
address=0		
address=1		
address=neither 0 nor 1		ERROR

Optical dependency exercised

type=OPTICAL	(adjacent)	
different from misclassification as default		EITHER
different from misclassification as adjacent		EITHER
address=0		ERROR
address=1		
address=10		
address=11		ERROR

disk-and-net dependency exercised

type=DISK	(adjacent)	
different from misclassification as default		EITHER
different from misclassification as adjacent		EITHER
type=NET	(adjacent)	
different from misclassification as default		EITHER
different from misclassification as adjacent		EITHER
address=-1		ERROR
address=0		
address=some very large number		

Default dependency exercised (gives an error)

type=some illegal name	(adjacent)	ERROR
different from misclassification as adjacent		ERROR

One minor difference occurs when building test specifications. The `update device type` tests changed the type so they could satisfy the default's `type = some illegal name` requirement. For `update device address`, the type is an existing value; it isn't changed by the routine. But a pre-existing illegal type name is not allowed by the consistency relationships, so this requirement should be impossible to satisfy and can be dropped.

That raises a question. If the default case is impossible for the correct subsystem, what is the expected result of a fault that incorrectly exercises it? Here's a possible implementation of update device address:

```
switch(type)
{
case TAPE:
     if (new_address != 0 && new_address != 1)    FAIL;
     break;
case OPTICAL:
     if (new_address < 1 | | new_address > 10)    FAIL;
     break;
case DISK:
case NET:
     if (new_address < 0) FAIL;
     break;
default:
     Is there a default case? What happens?
     break;
}
```

In the previous command, where the type was changed, the default had to cause a failure. In this command, though, the default should never be taken. A trusting programmer would believe that and leave the default out of the switch. A suspicious programmer would write the default as:

```
default:
     panic("Program error: impossible type in change device address.");
     break;
```

The two implementations have a different result. Consider this test and suppose the DISK case was forgotten:

INITIALLY:	Type is DISK, address is 0
TEST:	update device address -1
EXPECT:	?

The first implementation would accept the change and set the program to an inconsistent state. The second would print the error message. The second way is obviously preferable, but tests have to find the fault no matter what the implementation. This can be done by following this more specific rule:

> When changing a LEFT variable, "different from misclassification as default" means specifically that the test requirement must be used in an ERROR test.

An error message is distinct from both results (assuming that the error message about a program failure is distinct from one about a user failure).

For the tape dependency, satisfying this requirement is automatic, since type=TAPE must be used when the ERROR requirement "address=neither 0 nor 1" is satisfied. The optical dependency's requirement is also automatic. Satisfying this requirement will require one extra test for the disk and net dependency. The single error requirement (-1) has to be used for both `type=DISK` and `type=NET`. Without the need to discover misclassifications into the default, it would be used with only one.

18.1.3 Testing this Example

So how well does all this work? This checklist produces 11 tests. I ran the tests against the assumed implementation. As expected, they yield 100 percent feasible branch, loop, multicondition, and relational coverage. More importantly, they catch plausible faults. All nine boundary errors are caught, as well as six errors in the formation of && and || expressions (using the wrong operator and leaving one of the terms out). All five cases where the old address is checked instead of the new one are caught. Further, any use of one variable for another is also, as is any use of a constant where a variable is required. The only misuse that isn't caught is one use of a variable for a constant:

```
case TAPE:
        if (new_address != 0 && new_address != type)  /* should be 1 */
            FAIL;
        break;
```

which is not a very likely fault. All omitted dependency statements are caught. Of the nine possible cases where the wrong dependency statement was applied, one fault was missed.

```
case TAPE:
case DISK:          /* This case should be moved down two levels. */
        if (new_address != 0 && new_address != 1)   FAIL;
        break;
case OPTICAL:
        if (new_address < 1 || new_address > 10)    FAIL;
        break;
case NET:           /* DISK should be here. */
        if (new_address < 0)                        FAIL;
        break;
```

This was missed because the requirements only call for different results for the adjacent cases, and TAPE is not adjacent to DISK. Catching this fault would require an extra test, and doesn't seem worthwhile. (If both NET and DISK were misclassified, which seems more likely, the fault would be caught.)

Of course, you'd expect tests designed assuming a certain type of implementation to exercise that implementation thoroughly. But what about alternate implementations? Suppose the code used a case analysis of the new address rather than of the old type. That code would look like this:

```
if (new_address < 0) FAIL;
if (new_address == 0 && type == OPTICAL)     FAIL;
if (new_address > 1 && type == TAPE)         FAIL;
if (new_address > 10 && type == OPTICAL)     FAIL;
```

The tests again achieve 100 percent coverage, and they even do slightly better at finding faults. The only one that's missed is a very implausible one where the variable new_address is used instead of the constant OPTICAL:

    if (new_address == 0 && type == **new_address**)   FAIL;

Of course, not every possible variant implementation will be fully tested. In most such cases, though, coverage will detect mismatches.

The previous section described the basic approach. This section addresses varying the approach in response to some common situations.

18.2.1 More than Two Variables

Consistency needn't involve only two variables. A dependency statement simply has the form left-hand-side requires right-hand-side. The contents of the two sides are arbitrary. Here's an example:

Statement 1:   A=0 or B in [0-5] requires C in [0,3] and D=65
Default: C must equal D.

Applying the OR rule to the left hand side of Statement 1 gives

    Consistency checking
        Statement 1 exercised
            A=0, B not in [0-5]
            A!=0, B in [0-5]
        Default exercised
            A!=0, B not in [0-5]

The catalog provides refinements: -1, 0, 5, and 6. The out-of-range values apply to two requirements. Should they be listed independently, or should they each be listed under each requirement they could refine? The general rule remains that requirements should be independent unless there's evidence they should be multiplied. There's no such evidence here. In fact, the consistency checking code most likely looks like

    if (A==0 | | (B => 0 && B <= 5))
        {if (D!=65 | | C < 0 | | C > 3)   FAIL;}
    else
        if (C!=D)   FAIL;

so the checking of B is only done once. (See Chapter 25 for more on multiplying test requirements.)

The updated checklist looks like this:

Consistency checking
B=-1
B=6 .
Statement 1 exercised
A=0, B not in [0-5]
A!=0, B in [0-5]
B=0
B=5
Default exercised
A!=0, B not in [0-5]

Statement 1's right-hand side can be processed by the AND rule and the catalog. The default's right-hand side is a simple boolean expression that gives two test requirements. Here is the updated checklist:

Consistency checking
B=-1
B=6
Statement 1 exercised
A=0, B not in [0-5]
A!=0, B in [0-5]
B=0
B=5
C in [0,3], D=65
C not in [0,3], D=65   **ERROR**
C=-1   **ERROR**
C=4   **ERROR**
C in [0,3], D!=65   **ERROR**
C=0
C=3
Default exercised
A!=0, B not in [0-5]
C==D
C!=D   **ERROR**

Finally, the annotations to increase failure visibility are added:

```
Consistency checking
    B=-1
    B=6
    Statement 1 exercised
        A=0, B not in [0-5]
            different from misclassification as default      EITHER
        A!=0, B in [0-5]
            different from misclassification as default      EITHER
            B=0
            B=5
        C in [0,3], D=65
        C not in [0,3], D=65                                 ERROR
            C=-1                                             ERROR
            C=4                                              ERROR
        C in [0,3], D!=65                                    ERROR
        C=0
        C=3
    Default exercised
        A!=0, B not in [0-5]
            different from misclassification as statement 1  EITHER
        C==D
        C!=D                                                 ERROR
```

Statement 1 can be exercised in two distinct ways (because of A and because of B), and each of those must be distinct from the default at least once.

After this, test specifications can be created in the usual way.

18.2.2 Exercising the Rest of the Subsystem

These test requirements are targeted to faults in the consistency checking code. They will also find later faults, faults in the code that uses the variables. Adding two more types of requirements will do an even better job.

LEFT Variable Requirements

Consider this dependency statement:

Statement 2:   address in [5,10] requires priv=off.

Requirements from that might be

Statement 2 exercised:
    address=5

different from misclassification as statement 1	EITHER
different from misclassification as default	EITHER

    address=10

different from misclassification as statement 3	EITHER
different from misclassification as default	EITHER

    priv=off
    priv=on   ERROR

Suppose these requirements, including the misclassification requirements, could be satisfied with these two tests:

INITIALLY:	address is 7, priv is off
TEST:	set address to 5
EXPECT:	address is 5, priv is off

INITIALLY:	address is 20, priv is on
TEST:	set address to 10
EXPECT:	Error message, address remains 20, priv remains on

That would mean the rest of the subsystem has never been executed with address=10. Missing that boundary seems dangerous. It's especially dangerous if the specification was wrong and the boundary should be 9, not 10. Perhaps the system will crash when the address is 10 and priv is off.

The solution is to add a "consistency satisfied" requirement for each LEFT value:

Statement 2 exercised:
    address=5

different from misclassification as statement 1	EITHER
different from misclassification as default	EITHER
consistency satisfied	

    address=10

different from misclassification as statement 3	EITHER
different from misclassification as default	EITHER
consistency satisfied	

    priv=off
    priv=on   ERROR

Often, the requirements are automatically satisfied. That's the case when there's exactly one LEFT value for a dependency statement.

RIGHT Variable Requirements

Consider this consistency relationship:

Statement 1: A=0 requires B in [10,20]
Default: B is in [1,100]

That gives this checklist:

```
statement 1 exercised
    A=0
            different from misclassification as default    EITHER
        B=9                                                ERROR
        B=10
        B=20
        B=21                                               ERROR
default exercised
    A!=0
            different from statement 1 misclassification   EITHER
        B=0                                                ERROR
        B=1
        B=100
        B=101                                              ERROR
```

There are two overlapping ranges for B. That should raise suspicions. The range [10,20] is special when A is zero—but might it not also be special when A is not zero? The specification doesn't mention it, but specifications are often wrong. The test specifications for the default will never try values within that range. If they have an effect in the default case, the tests will not find it. Even if the subsystem specification is correct, the range [10-20] might be a manifestation of implementation detail that should also be exercised in the default case.

The checklist could be augmented as follows:

```
statement 1 exercised
    A=0
            different from misclassification as default    EITHER
        B=9                                                ERROR
        B=10
        B=20
        B=21                                               ERROR
default exercised
    A!=0
            different from misclassification as statement 1   EITHER
        B=0                                                ERROR
        B=1
        B=100
        B=101                                              ERROR
        B=10        DEFER
        B=20        DEFER
        B=9         DEFER (even lower priority)
        B=21        DEFER (even lower priority)
```

The requirements have been marked with DEFER because it's probably not worthwhile to use them all. One of the two interior values (10 and 20) is probably sufficient, but there's no reason not to use both if it's conve-

nient. The values outside the special range would probably reveal nothing that the undeferred outside values (1 and 100) don't. But they might be usable in tests being written anyway.

More rigorously:

1. The basic technique was to find values from the way the RIGHT variable is used in dependency statement X, then add them as refinements of "statement X exercised".
2. If the RIGHT values can also satisfy dependency statement Y, think about adding them as deferred refinements of "statement Y exercised". This is a form of error guessing.
3. Don't limit yourself to dependency statements within the same consistency relationship. Suppose there's also a relationship between variables C and B that contains this statement:

    Statement 1: C>0 requires B in [30,40]

Adding B=30 and B=40 to the original relationship's "default exercised" requirement might be worthwhile. (It would be less useful to add it to "statement 1 exercised" because it would be an ERROR requirement there.)

18.2.3 When Checking Is Done by a Library Routine

The requirements discussed so far assume each routine has its own consistency-checking code. But that code could also be gathered in one routine called in every place that a variable could change. That routine needs to be tested with the full set of requirements, but each caller does not. What are the likely faults in the callers?

1. The consistency checking routine is not called. This is detected by any attempted change that violates consistency.
2. The old value of the changed variable is used. The update device type code might call

    check_consistency(**type**, address);

    instead of

    check_consistency(**new_type**, address);

    This is also caught by any attempted violation.
3. The variable arguments are switched. This is caught by applying one of the Rules for Test Content: "Make inputs distinct". It applies to all test specifications, so needn't be mentioned specifically here.

So, a complete checklist for such a situation would look like this:

check_consistency routine
> Note: "type" and "address" are the routine's arguments;
> whether they're the existing or proposed values is irrelevant

➡ *Consistency requirements, following pattern of Fig. 18–1.*

update device type
> type changed to inconsistent value   ERROR

➡ *other test requirements from whatever else the command does*

update device address
> address changed to inconsistent value   ERROR

➡ *other test requirements from whatever else the command does*

check_consistency is most likely tested via the two commands, so each of them will actually violate consistency several different ways. You will most likely divide the exercising of check_consistency evenly between its two callers. (Recall from Chapter 13, Section 13.1.3, that the duplicate ERROR notations are not a problem.)

18.2.4 Unchecked or Impossible ERROR Requirements

Perhaps the subsystem doesn't validate consistency: It's up to the user to set variables correctly. Or perhaps the user has no direct access to the variables involved, so consistency cannot be violated. Nevertheless, the different ways consistency can be maintained are still useful as test requirements. Create the test requirements in the normal way, but omit the ERROR requirements. The "different from misclassification" require-ments are still useful, because they probe what's special about each depen-dency statement. They must be satisfied by non-ERROR tests.

18.2.5 When More than One Variable Can Change at Once

User interfaces often allow several variables to change in the same command. The same subsystem that correctly handles

    update type OPTICAL
    update address 5

may break on

    update type OPTICAL address 5

The safest implementation for such code is to maintain two copies of the variables. The first contains the existing values (known to be consistent). The second contains the proposed values. The code has the following framework:

    Copy the existing values into the proposed values
    While there's more input
        Update the appropriate proposed value with the input value
    Check the consistency of the proposed values
    If consistent
        Copy the proposed values into the existing values

In this case, the standard approach to testing consistency checking works fine. The checklist follows the pattern of Fig. 18–1, but the type and address refer to the proposed values. That is, "type" will mean the input value, if given; otherwise, it will be the existing type.

Unfortunately, programmers are likely to write more complicated code that does exactly the consistency checking required, avoiding unneeded use of unchanged variables. Such code is likely to be a maze of if statements:

```
if variable A has changed
     check A
     if variable B has also changed
          Check the consistency of new_A and new_B
     else
          Check the consistency of new_A and B
else
     B can't be inconsistent, so don't check A and B.
```

This complicated code is far more likely to contain faults. Because the consistency checking is carefully tailored to the exact consistency relationship, it's not a cliché that can be analyzed in the same way as the change of a single variable. But the situation is not hopeless. There are four combinations for two variables:

LEFT changed,	RIGHT unchanged
LEFT unchanged,	RIGHT changed
LEFT changed,	RIGHT changed
LEFT unchanged,	RIGHT unchanged

(The last is not useful.) The Rules for Test Content say that alternate actions should make a visible difference. In this code, a likely alternate action is checking the wrong value (the existing value rather than the new value). The tests must reveal this. For the three useful combinations, this can be done as follows:

LEFT changed, RIGHT unchanged
     Result different from that gotten using current value of LEFT
          (Since the current LEFT and RIGHT are consistent, the result
          must be an ERROR.)
LEFT unchanged, RIGHT changed
     Result different from that gotten using current value of RIGHT
LEFT changed, RIGHT changed
     Result different from that gotten using current value of LEFT
     Result different from that gotten using current value of RIGHT

It is safest to satisfy each of these requirements at least once per dependency statement. This is unneeded for some implementations, but it probably will not require too many extra test specifications. The checklist would look like:

consistency checking: update device type and address

Note: type and address are proposed values; either or both may be given

Tape dependency exercised

only type changed, to inconsistent value	**ERROR**
only address changed, to inconsistent value	**ERROR**
both changed, unchanged type would have different result	**EITHER**
both changed, unchanged address would have different result	**EITHER**
type=TAPE (adjacent)	
different from misclassification as default	EITHER
different from misclassification as adjacent	EITHER
address=0	
address=1	
address=neither 0 nor 1	ERROR

Optical dependency exercised

only type changed, to inconsistent value	**ERROR**
only address changed, to inconsistent value	**ERROR**
both changed, unchanged type would have different result	**EITHER**
both changed, unchanged address would have different result	**EITHER**
type=OPTICAL (adjacent)	
different from misclassification as default	EITHER
different from misclassification as adjacent	EITHER
address=0	ERROR
address=1	
address=10	
address=11	ERROR

and so on

This checklist will probably exercise the implementation thoroughly, but be sure to check coverage. Multicondition coverage will be particularly useful.

It will probably be easy to find bugs if the programmer implemented consistency checking this way for more than two variables. There should be no need to try all combinations of changed and unchanged variables. Try all pairs, as below:

A changed, B unchanged
> Result different from that gotten using current value of A

A unchanged, B changed
> Result different from that gotten using current value of B

A changed, B changed
> Result different from that gotten using current value of A
>
> Result different from that gotten using current value of B

A changed, C unchanged
> Result different from that gotten using current value of A

A unchanged, C changed
> Result different from that gotten using current value of C

A changed, C changed
> Result different from that gotten using current value of A
>
> Result different from that gotten using current value of C

B changed, C unchanged
> Result different from that gotten using current value of B

B unchanged, C changed
> Result different from that gotten using current value of C

B changed, C changed
> Result different from that gotten using current value of B
>
> Result different from that gotten using current value of C

You will be able to satisfy more than one of these with each test. Be sure to check coverage.

State Machines and Statecharts

State machines and statecharts are often used for subsystems that communicate with the outside world, including people (user interfaces, especially graphical ones) and other subsystems (networking protocols). They play an important role in object-oriented design; every object in an object-oriented system may contain its own state machine or statechart.

A state machine or statechart can serve two purposes: as a model of subsystem behavior and as an implementation framework. The model will be only a portion of the subsystem specification, and the implementation framework will be a small part of the subsystem's code.

As a tester, you may find any combination of model and framework:

▲ Both the model and framework are present.

▲ Only the model is present. There is no explicit framework in the code; rather, the implementation is spread throughout the rest of the subsystem. This is referred to as an *implicit implementation*.

▲ There's a readily identifiable framework, but no model in the specification. (Most likely, a model was used in design then thrown away.) The model can easily be derived from the framework.

▲ Neither a model nor a framework was used, but either could have been. This chapter is most valuable in such a situation.

The chapter has these sections:
1. Classical finite state machines and their implementation.
2. Statecharts, an extension of state machines that makes them both more powerful and more concise.
3. Creating a model when you weren't given one.
4. Inspecting models and implementations.
5. Testing based on the models.
6. Testing independent and communicating state machines.

Inspections and testing work together, but inspections are more important.

All discussions are organized so that people who are working only with state machines can easily ignore statecharts.

Parts of this discussion draw on [Beizer90], though our approaches are substantially different. Beware: I have only had personal experience testing state machines. I have not tested statecharts. While I believe the approach here is reasonable, I also believe it can be refined and extended, especially when it comes to inspecting statechart models for specification errors.

19.1 State Machines

A state machine model is a useful way to describe certain types of programs. These programs respond to a small number of distinct *events*. The exact response depends on the type of the event and the value of some internal *state*. A response may change the state. Responses can also include arbitrary actions, typically including some sort of output. Because a state machine's actions depend on two variables, the state and the event, they are often represented in a table. In the table below, the states run across the top and the events run down the side.

	state1	state2
eventA	state1 / "A in 1"	state2 / "A in 2"
eventB	state2 / "B in 1"	state1 / "B in 2"
eventC	state2 / "C in 1"	state2 / "C in 2"

Each entry is a *state transition*. A transition names the next state, followed by a summary of the action. In the case of this state machine, the action prints the message in quotes.

One of the states is usually designated the starting state. Let's suppose that it's state1. That given, the response to the input sequence eventB, eventA, eventB, eventA, eventC will be this output:

B in 1
A in 2
B in 2
A in 1
C in 1

State machines can also be represented graphically, as in Fig. 19–1. The boxes represent states. The arrows represent state transitions. They are labeled with the event that causes the transition and the action that happens as part of the transition. They point to the next state. (In examples where the action is irrelevant, it is sometimes left off to avoid clutter.) The arrow that comes from no state points to the starting state. Think of it as coming from outside the state machine. The graphical form is usually easier to understand, but the tabular form is easier to work with systematically.

19.1.1 Implementation

This section will show three typical frameworks. There are many variations on these basic themes. In particular, an intermediate language is sometimes used to hide the framework. In other cases, a tool creates the framework directly from the model. The only code a human writes is that which implements the action.

Fig. 19-1

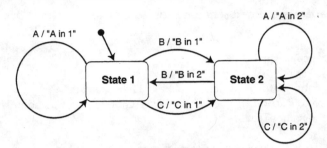

A state machine framework is often implemented as a collection of routines. Each routine corresponds to a single event. Here's an implementation for one event of the sample state machine:

```
/* The state is a global variable with two values, state1 and state2. */

void
eventB()
{
    switch(State)
    {
        case state1:
            printf("B in 1");        /* Perform action */
            State=state2;            /* Select next state */
            break;
        case state2:
            printf("B in 2");
            State=state1;
            break;
        default:
            program_error("eventB");
    }
}
```

The other events follow the same pattern.

The framework can also be a more direct translation of the tabular form into code. Each transition's action is a separate routine:

```
void Cin1(event, state)[1]
    enum eventT event;
    enum stateT state;
{
    printf("C in 1");
}
```

The action and the next state are bundled up into a transition data structure:

```
typedef struct
{
  enum stateT next_state;        /* The next state */
  void (*action)();              /* Action during transition */
} transitionT;
```

And the complete set of transitions is stored in a state table:

```
transitionT State_table[NUM_EVENTS][NUM_STATES] =
{
/*                      state1          state2 */

/* eventA */            {{state1, Ain1},    {state2, Ain2}},
/* eventB */            {{state2, Bin1},    {state1, Bin2}},
/* eventC */            {{state2, Cin1},    {state2, Cin2}}
};
```

There is an event handling function that uses the state table:

```
void
handle_event(event)
    enum eventT event;
{
  static enum stateT state = state1;                      /* Initial state */

  (*(State_table[event][state].action))(state, event);/* Process the event */
  state = State_table[event][state].next_state;        /* Update the state */
}
```

Less common is an implementation where individual routines correspond to states. Such a routine might look like this:

---

1. It's conventional to pass the state and event to the transition function. If nothing else, it helps with debugging.

```
void
state2()
{
    enum eventT event = get_event();

    switch(event)
    {
    case eventA:
        printf("A in 2");
        state2();
        break;
    case eventB:
        printf("B in 2");
        state1();
        break;
    case eventC:
        printf("C in 2");
        state2();
        break;
    default:
        program_error("state1");
    }
}
```

This function fetches the next event, performs the required action, then invokes the function that represents the next state.[1]

19.1.2 Sparse State Machines

The earlier description gives the impression that every state/event pair in a state machine invokes a meaningful transition. In fact, it's typical for the model to declare many events illegal in many states. This declaration can be validated or assumed (like preconditions). If validated, there will be error transitions for the illegal combinations, as in this model:

	state1	state2	errorstate
eventA	errorstate / "error"	state1 / "A in 2"	errorstate / "error"
eventB	state2 / "B in 1"	errorstate / "error"	errorstate / "error"
eventC	state2 / "C in 1"	state1 / "C in 2"	errorstate / "error"
resetevent	errorstate / "error"	errorstate / "error"	state1 / "reset"

---

1. You might have noticed that this implementation will lead to unlimited stack growth unless the compiler optimizes away function calls immediately followed by returns. A implementation might invoke the next state with a call like next_state(state1), where next_state is a "magic" function that avoids stack growth, perhaps by using longjmp. A less fancy implementation would set a global State and return to the caller, which would be a simple control loop of the form for(;;)(*State)();

A global is used because a function returning a pointer to a state function won't work in C (without casting).

If the illegal combinations incorrectly occur, the result is a transition to the error state. Once in the error state, the subsystem remains there until a reset event occurs, whereupon it returns to the initial state (state 1).

If the illegal combinations are impossible or solely the caller's responsibility, the state machine would look like this:

	state1	state2
eventA	—	state1 / "A in 2"
eventB	state2 / "B in 1"	—
eventC	state2 / "C in 1"	state1 / "C in 2"

The dashes represent impossible combinations. If such a combination does happen, the results are undefined. (If the developer programs defensively, the result is a message about a program error; if not, it's likely to be a mysterious failure.)

The effect on testing is like that of validated vs. assumed preconditions. Error transitions should be tested. Faced with a transition claimed to be impossible, you should think about whether it really is. If it's not, you've found a bug.

19.1.3 Duplicate Transitions

It's not unusual for two transitions to perform the same action. If the state machine is implemented as a two dimensional array, several elements of the array will point to the same function. The action may be slightly different for different transitions: In that case, the transition function can use the `state` and `event` variables that are passed to it to implement the differences.

Consider the example with error states. The `State_table` array would look like this:

```
{
/*                  state1              state2              errorstate */

/* eventA */        {{errorstate,notify},  {state1,Ain2},      {errorstate,notify}},
/* eventB */        {{state2,Bin1},        {errorstate,notify},  {errorstate,notify}},
/* eventC */        {{state2,Cin1},        {state1,Cin2},      {errorstate,notify}},
/* resetevent */    {errorstate,notify},   {errorstate,notify},  {state1,reset}}
};
```

and `notify` can be implemented as

```
void notify(enum eventT event, enum stateT state)
{
    fprintf(stderr, "Illegal transition: event %s in state %s.",
        event_name(event), state_name(state));
    fprintf(stderr, "Issue RESET.");
}
```

(You might have already noticed that all the different XinY functions could be implemented by a single function, since they all simply print the state and event.)

For many applications, state machines grow large and cumbersome. Statecharts extend state machines to deal with those problems. They were originally described in [Harel87]. The description in [Harel88] is briefer and less complete, but it's in a journal that's easier to find. (The original paper is worth tracking down if you can—it's wonderfully clear and persuasive.) [Rumbaugh91] and [Booch93] also describe statecharts, though Booch omits some features.

This discussion also omits a few features. The only nontrivial omission is orthogonal states. They are covered separately at the end of the chapter.

19.2.1 State Actions

In state machines, processing happens as part of a transition. Suppose, though, that the subsystem is the central controller for an expensive copy machine, one of 3000 owned by Largcorp, Inc. This copy machine automatically notifies a central repair center whenever it detects a fault in itself. The key word is "whenever": Some action takes place on any entry to the ERROR state regardless of the event that causes the entry. There are three ways to handle this:

1. Ignore the common action. The state machine model is an abstraction, after all, and the commonality could be considered just one of many unimportant details. This would be a poor choice if the common action is critical to an understanding of the subsystem.
2. Duplicate the common action in each transition. But duplicating information increases the chance of errors.
3. Localize the common action in the state. A section of a model might look like this:

Fig. 19-2

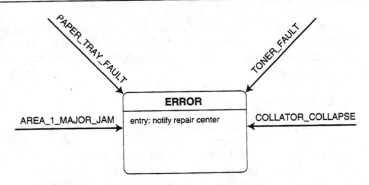

The model shows that calling the repair center is a part of any entry to the error state. The use of the word "entry" implies that there can also be an action that happens on any exit from the state. That action might call Largcorp's vendor monitoring center and tell it how long the repair took. Finally, there might be an action that takes place continually while the copier is in the error state (that is, an action that's started on entry and stopped on exit). Such an action might flash a "repair service called" light on the copier's front panel. The updated model would look like this:

Fig. 19–3

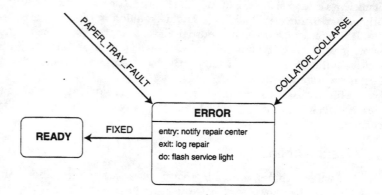

In a tabular model, state actions can be summarized at the head of the column devoted to the state. An example is given in Section 19.2.2.

Actions that take place during the state are sometimes called "activities". They typically take significant time to execute, whereas entry and exit actions are supposed to be effectively instantaneous. In the discussion that follows, "state actions" will be used to refer to entry actions, exit actions, and activities.

Activities can summarize a lot of processing. That processing might itself be modelled by a state machine. See "Nested States", below. Often, the end of that processing is treated as an event itself. If the activity is "get input", a transition from the state might be labeled "input gotten". There also might be an "input request timed out" event that leads to an error state.

When entering a state, the transition action is performed first, then the entry action, then the activity is started. When leaving a state, the activity is stopped, the exit action is performed, then the transition action is performed.

19.2.2 Conditional State Transitions

Suppose version 1.0 of the fault-detection software is detecting spurious faults. As a result, version 1.0a lets the customer tell the copier to ignore all faults. How can this be economically represented?

The 1.0 statechart might look like this, in part. (The action has been left out for most of the transitions, since it's not relevant to this example. Impossible transitions are marked with a dash.)

	WARMING	READY	COPYING	ERROR **entry:** call repair **exit:** notify repair done **do:** notification light
IS_WARM	READY	-	-	-
START	WARMING	COPYING	COPYING	ERROR
STOP	WARMING	READY	READY	ERROR
TRAY_FAULT	-	ERROR / switch to other tray	ERROR / switch to other tray	-

One way to represent the override is this machine, where the states ending in "NF" ignore faults:

	WARMING	READY	**READY_NF**	COPYING	**COPYING_NF**	ERROR
IS_WARM	READY	-	-	-	-	-
START	WARMING	COPYING	**COPYING**	COPYING	**COPYING**	ERROR
STOP	WARMING	READY	**READY**	READY	**READY**	ERROR
TRAY_FAULT	-	ERROR	**READY**	ERROR	**COPYING**	-

This seems wrong. A global change (adding new states) has been made because of a feature that affects only error events. An alternate solution, adding events like PAPER_TRAY_FAULT_NO_FAULT, has the same problem: The state machine will become much larger.

A better solution is to allow conditional state transitions. Here is what they might look like.

	WARMING	READY	COPYING	ERROR
IS_WARM	READY	-	-	-
START	WARMING	COPYING	COPYING	ERROR
STOP	WARMING	READY	READY	ERROR
TRAY_FAULT	-	**ERROR [faults obeyed] / switch to other tray**	**ERROR [faults obeyed] / switch to other tray**	-

The conditions are in brackets. A condition is checked after the event occurs. If it is true, the transition is made. Otherwise, the state machine stays in the same state and no action takes place.

The graphical notation also adds the bracketed condition to the transition:

Fig. 19-4

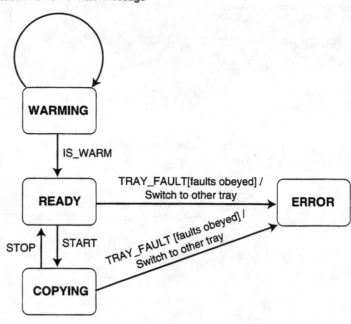

Notice the notation START | STOP, which indicates that the transition applies to either of the two events. Notice also that some transitions are left out of the graph. This is appropriate because graphical models are intended more to clarify than to include every detail. Of course, the program must handle every detail, and every detail should be tested.

19.2.3 Nested States

Nested states are another way of avoiding overly large state machines. They allow individual states to be treated as state machines themselves.

Fig. 19-5

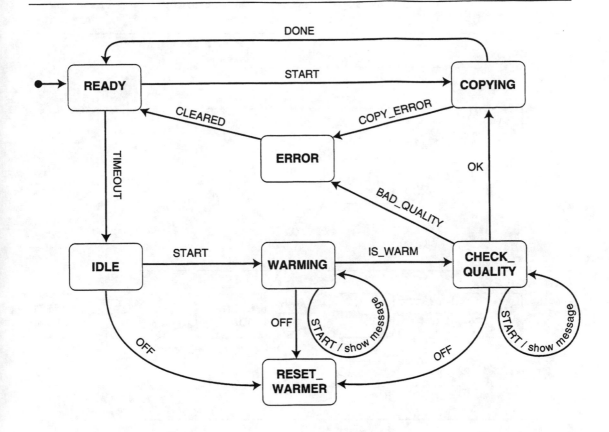

Many copiers will switch into a power-saving mode after they've not been used for a while. The procedure for making copies is the same in either mode: you put the originals in the copier and press START. Fig. 19-5 shows the state machine for a copier that implements this feature. That state machine is a mess. If you're trying to figure out the overall operation of the copier, all the detail is irrelevant and potentially confusing. The lack of clear boundaries between parts of the graph makes understanding the power-saving mode harder.

Fig. 19–6 encapsulates the power-saving states into their own state machine named POWERSAVE. This state machine is called a *superstate*.

Fig. 19–6

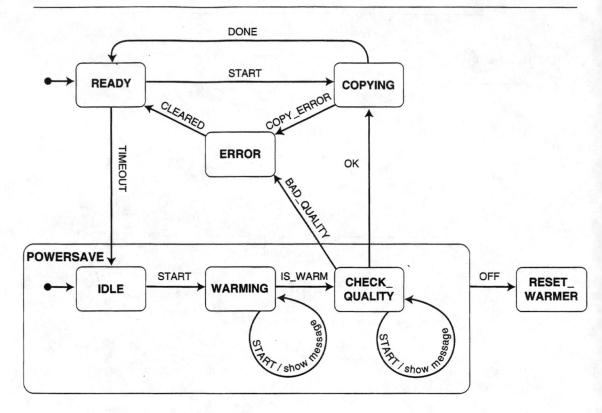

Transitions can be between *substates* of the superstate (as between WARMING and CHECK_QUALITY) or from a substate out of the superstate (as between CHECK_QUALITY and COPYING). Notice also that all the transitions for the OFF event are represented by a single arrow. All of the states within POWERSAVE respond to OFF by making that transition.[1]

This encapsulation helps somewhat, but still clutters up the graph with substates irrelevant to someone who wants only an overview. A second graph can be drawn that would ignore the details of the substates. This would look like Fig. 19-7.

---

1. This violates the encapsulation a bit, since RESET_WARMER should really be part of the POWER_SAVE state machine. Adding another enclosing box, containing POWER_SAVE and RESET_WARMER, would solve that problem, but doesn't seem worthwhile.

CHAP. 19 STATE MACHINES AND STATECHARTS

Fig. 19-7

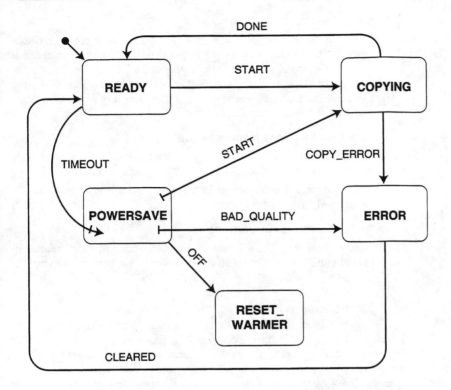

Arrows with bars indicate transitions to or from particular hidden substates. Tools could allow you to select how many levels of detail to show, thus avoiding the trouble of drawing separate graphs. (Note that I chose to label the transition from POWERSAVE to COPYING with START, rather than the more correct OK. START is more meaningful from this abstract perspective.)

Here are the different types of transitions. They may be from any state at any level to any state at any level.

❏ **Transitions between normal states at the same level**

These are the same as in ordinary state machines. Examples: In Fig. 19–6, WARMING to CHECK_QUALITY, READY to COPYING.

❏ **Transitions downward to substates**

A transition may be downward to a particular substate. Examples: READY to IDLE in Fig. 19–6

If the transition crosses several state boundaries, state entry actions are performed in the order the arrow crosses the boundaries. (That is, from the outside in.)

❑ **Transitions to superstates**

A transition to a superstate might not specify any particular substate. In that case, the starting state of the nested state machine is used. Example: In Fig. 19-7, the transition from READY to POWER_SAVE is actually a transition to IDLE. In Fig. 19–6, the arrow to IDLE could have stopped at the boundary of POWER_SAVE and meant the same thing.

❑ **Transitions upward from substates**

A substate may have an arrow to a state outside the nested state machine. Example: CHECK_QUALITY to ERROR in Fig. 19–6.

If the transition crosses several state boundaries, the exit actions are performed from the inside out.

❑ **Transitions from superstates**

A transition from the superstate, but not from any particular contained substate, applies to all the states in the superstate. Example: The OFF arrow in both Fig. 19–6 and Fig. 19-7.

Statecharts in Tabular Form

Statecharts exist to suppress and organize detail. The clarity they provide is largely lost if they are written in tabular form, so it is probably best to keep them graphical. In tabular form, each superstate would have its own table. Transitions could refer to superstates, or to substates with a notation like *superstate::substate*. Events that cause the same transition for every state could be described separately from the other events, or the transition could be repeated for each state.

19.2.4 History

Our copier was designed for high-volume environments where deadlines are met at the last minute, the sort of businesses that send more documents by next-day delivery than by regular mail. A complete copier failure would cause the business to collapse, so a faulty copier can switch to a low-resolution backup mode and function haltingly until it is repaired. The switch is made by this state machine:

Fig. 19-8

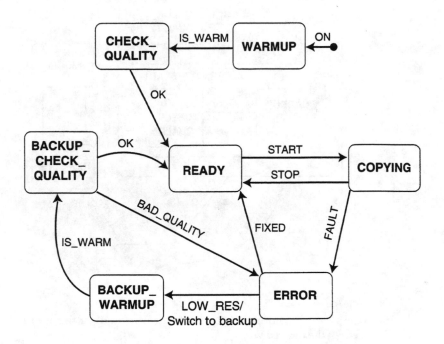

This solution is not complete. When the copier is turned off and then back on, it should start in low-resolution mode. There is no way to model that with a state machine. Statecharts solve the problem by allowing superstates to have history. History is indicated by the letter *H* in a circle. A transition to a superstate with history goes to the starting substate the first time. Thereafter, a transition to the superstate goes to the last substate, not necessarily the starting substate. (Note: The history applies only when the arrow points at the superstate, not within it to a substate.) Consider this statechart:

Fig. 19-9

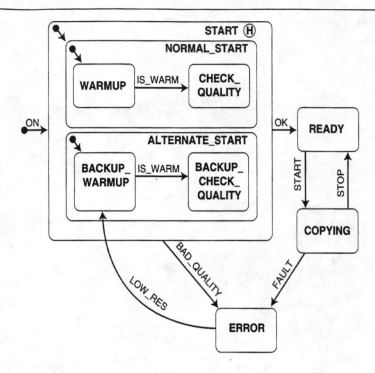

It has the same behavior as the previous statechart, and it also handles the ON event in the desired way.

1. First consider what happens when the state machine is turned on the first time. The START state has two nested substates, NORMAL_START and ALTERNATE_START. NORMAL_START is the initial substate. It is itself a superstate with initial substate WARMUP. That's the starting state, followed by CHECK_QUALITY, followed by READY.

2. Suppose the copier is turned off before any fault is discovered. The START superstate has history, so the last substate is revisited. That last substate, NORMAL_START, happens to be the initial substate, so the whole sequence occurs again. Note that history does not apply to the nested NORMAL_START; otherwise, CHECK_QUALITY would be entered.

3. Now suppose a fault is discovered while COPYING. The ERROR state is entered, then the BACKUP_WARMUP state, then BACKUP_CHECK_QUALITY, then back to READY.

4. Now the copier is again turned off and on. Since the START superstate has history, the last substate entered is reentered. Of the two substates, NORMAL_START and ALTERNATE_START, ALTERNATE_START is the last, so it is reentered. ALTERNATE_START does not have history, so its last substate (BACKUP_CHECK_QUALITY) is not reentered. Instead, the start state (BACKUP_WARMUP) is entered. Thereafter, the state machine proceeds to BACKUP_CHECK_QUALITY and then to READY.

19.2.5 Statechart Implementation Frameworks

Simple statecharts can use minor variations on any of the three state machine frameworks. For example, this event function contains a conditional transition:

```
event1()
{
    switch(State)
    {
        case STATE_A:
            stateA_event1_action();
            State = stateA;
            break;
        case STATE_B:
            if (condition)
            {
                stateA_event2_action();
                state = stateB;
            }
            break;
    }
}
```

More complicated statecharts don't fit the state machine frameworks well at all. To convince yourself, try to implement the following statechart. (This will also be a good way to make sure you really understand the statechart features.)

Fig. 19–10

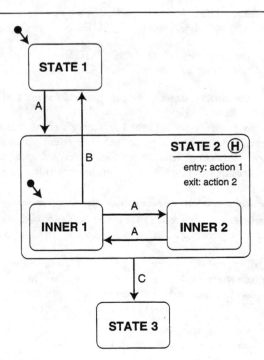

Be sure that STATE2's exit action happens on the transition from INNER2 to STATE3. Consider whether the two substates can be prevented from having to know about the C event, which should really be handled in a single place by STATE2. Don't forget to implement the history.

An ad hoc implementation, where you write special code that exactly implements a particular statechart, would be quite error-prone. A better solution is to implement a state chart engine that operates on a data structure that corresponds to the model. Such a data structure would be built by code like this:

```
/* Create the events. */
event_ptr A = event("A"), B = event("B"), C = event("C");

/* Create the states.  By default, they're simple states. */
state_ptr state1 = state("state1", START_STATE);
state_ptr state2 = state("state2", NOT_START_STATE);
state_ptr inner1 = state("inner1", START_STATE);
state_ptr inner2 = state("inner2", NOT_START_STATE);
state_ptr state3 = state("state3", NOT_START_STATE);

/* Add entry and exit actions for state2.*/
add_entry_action(state2, action1);
add_exit_action(state2, action2);

add_history(state2);                /* Turn on history for state 2. */
add_substate(state2, inner1);    /* Place substates within state 2. */
add_substate(state2, inner2);

transition(state1, A, state2, NO_ACTION);
transition(state2, C, state3, NO_ACTION);
transition(inner1, B, state1, NO_ACTION);
transition(inner1, A, inner2, NO_ACTION);
transition(inner2, A, inner1, NO_ACTION);
```

Tools that implement statecharts can generate such a statechart framework directly from the model.

Of course, it's possible that there may be no structural correspondence between the statechart and the subsystem. The only correspondence may behavioral. This is especially likely when a statechart is used to model the behavior of an existing implementation.

19.3
When and How
to Build Models

If the subsystem has behavior that could be described with a state model but doesn't have one, create it. It will help you find faults in two ways:

1. Building and then inspecting the model will sometimes help you realize that the subsystem does not do what the user requires.
2. You can use the model to find test requirements you might overlook in all the detail of the larger specification or code.

This discussion assumes an implicit implementation. If there's an explicit framework, reconstructing the model is trivial.

CHAP. 19 STATE MACHINES AND STATECHARTS

19.3.1 When Models are Useful

Before embarking on the effort of building a model, check whether one seems reasonable. State machines or statechart models are useful parts of a larger specification when:

☐ **the inputs can be categorized into a reasonable number of distinct events**

Each of these events is a name that may hide a lot of detail. For example, in a communications protocol, the name ACKNOWLEDGE-MENT may represent an incoming packet that contains much data. However, from an abstract, external viewpoint, all acknowledgements are handled the same way.

☐ **the event history matters**

Earlier events affect the handling of later events. If no event can affect any later event, the machine has no state that's useful to model.

☐ **the event history can be abstracted into a reasonable number of states**

The important point here is that how you got to a state should be irrelevant. Any event sequence that reaches it has the same effect as any other. Just as an event may summarize many inputs, a state may summarize many combinations of values of several internal variables.

In the above, "reasonable" is relative to the size of the subsystem. The model should be substantially smaller and easier to understand than the subsystem whose behavior it describes.

19.3.2 Building a Model

This section describes a systematic method for building a model. It is not the only method. Use a less systematic approach if you prefer, but be sure to apply the inspection checklist, given in Section 19.4, to your results.

Try some scenarios

First get comfortable with the operation of the subsystem. Build some scenarios (sample sequences of inputs) and step through them. Your set of scenarios should be typical of the most common uses of the subsystem. With some subsystems, you will have little idea of which scenarios are common. Guessing wrong is better than not guessing at all.

Decide on the scope and number of state machines

Some inputs to the subsystem have nothing to do with state. Their effect is independent of what inputs came before, and they can have no effect on any later inputs. Leave them out of the model, though other parts of the specification should describe what they do.

Some groups of inputs may be independent of each other. Perhaps commands A and B affect each other, but never affect or are affected by commands C and D. Considering them all as events in a single model may result in an explosion of state/event pairs. Independent state machines solve this problem. Handling completely independent state machines is a special case of handling communicating state machines, which is discussed at the end of the chapter.

Decide on events

From the user's point of view, the events are real, while the states are abstractions invented to explain behavior. Events come from externally visible input; the states are hidden. Since you're trying to model the external behavior of the subsystem, the place to start is with the input.

Events should partition the total input into a small number of distinct categories. Often the partitioning is obvious, as when the subsystem accepts a small number of distinct commands. Most likely, each command is a distinct event.

In some systems, internal state is more obvious than the events. In that case, feel free to start with state, but keep in mind that it's part of an implementation you're provisionally assuming is faulty. Don't allow it to force a categorization of inputs that doesn't make external sense.

Decide on state variables

List those variables that are both changed by events and can affect the response to later events. The "variables" you list may not actually be present in the subsystem. Fictional variables are fine, so long as they can be used to build an accurate model of external behavior. There will often be only one variable.

You should be able to divide each variable's possible values into a small number of groups. Values to group together are those that have the same effect on all events.

Decide on states

At this point, you might have two state variables:

variable 1

> group 1A
> group 1B

variable 2

> group 2A
> group 2B

The possible states are all possible combinations of all the groups of all the variables:

> variable 1's value is in group 1A, variable 2's value is in group 2A
> variable 1's value is in group 1A, variable 2's value is in group 2B
> variable 1's value is in group 1B, variable 2's value is in group 2A
> variable 1's value is in group 1B, variable 2's value is in group 2B

Often, some of the combinations will be redundant. That is, two of them might have the same effect on later events. If so, group them together as the same state.

Be suspicious if you can't describe a combination with some meaningful name. That might be a sign that the two state variables are really part of independent state machines.

Use the common scenarios to add transitions

Take the scenarios you developed in the first step, translate them into sequences of state transitions, and add those transitions to your model. You now have a model that handles typical user scenarios.

It's easy to concentrate on the next state and forget about the actions. Don't. Make sure to say what each transition does. (Again, the full specification of the action will be elsewhere; the model only contains the name or some other brief description.)

Add remaining transitions

Typical user operations won't cover all possible transitions. Error transitions are the most likely to be missing. For each state, consider which events are possible, and add transitions for them.

Adding superstates (statecharts)

Superstates are a tool to reduce complexity. They group together states whose differences are irrelevant at some level of abstraction. Here are a couple of structural clues that superstates are appropriate:

1. If there are events that are possible in only a few states, you might collect those states together into a superstate. You can then ignore that event outside those states.
2. If some event provokes the same response from a group of states, perhaps it should be a transition away from a superstate containing those states.

Adding other statechart features

1. You may find that a particular subsystem variable should have an effect, but only in a few state/event combinations. Treating it as a state variable will cause an explosion of new states, which mostly behave just like old states. Similarly, a particular state/event combination's behavior may depend on the fine detail of the event. Again, splitting the event into two or more events leads to a growth in the model out of proportion to the benefits. Conditional transitions can solve this problem. Be wary, though, of using conditions to patch up state machines that really need more states or events. Especially

dangerous are conditions that use variables set by actions. These can be misused to produce a second, hidden, state machine.

The focus of the statechart should be the events and states. Too many conditions can be a symptom of straining to squeeze a subsystem into an inappropriate formalism.

2. History is a good way to represent initialization that must be performed the first time a superstate is entered, but which should be skipped thereafter.

3. If several transitions from or to a state have the same action, ask whether entry actions, exit actions, or state activities are appropriate. Be especially suspicious if all but one of the transitions share actions. Perhaps its uniqueness is a mistake.

19.4 Inspecting State Machines and Statecharts

Whether or not you built the state machine or statechart model yourself, you should systematically inspect it. Expect to find faults of two kinds. The implementation may not correspond to the model. (Note that it can be the model that's wrong, not the implementation.) Or the model may not satisfy user requirements. (Declare the user wrong at your peril.)

More faults in the model and framework will be found by inspections than by test requirements. Test requirements from the model mainly strengthen test requirements from other sources.

19.4.1 Check the Model

Completeness

You already performed this step if you build the model yourself.

Is every state/event pair described by the model? If a pair is not described, is it *really* impossible? Or if there is some default transition, such as to an error state, is that appropriate for this pair?

Statecharts often claim particular events can happen only within particular superstates. Ask if this is true. (This is a special case of the previous check.)

If a statechart has a transition that applies to an entire superstate, make sure it really does make sense for each substate.

If a statechart has some conditional transitions, ask if the conditions can apply to other transitions, especially transitions with the same event. Also ask if the variables mentioned in the conditions might be relevant in any way to other transitions.

Ambiguity

Incorrect abstraction can hide relevant detail. A transition that seems perfectly sensible in terms of abstract events and states may be clearly wrong if you think about real inputs. For each transition, try to think of any real input for which the action or next state is inappropriate. Finding one probably means two states or two events were incorrectly lumped together. (If you are allowing statecharts, it may mean a missing conditional transition.)

Contradictions

In a graphical model, two transitions from the same state should not be labeled with the same event.

Contradictions are more likely in statecharts. Consider this example:

Fig. 19-11

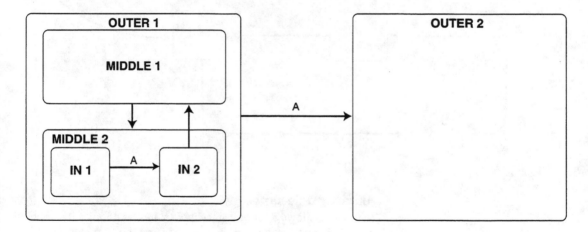

What is the effect of the A transition in the IN1 state? The arrow attached to IN1 says the next state is IN2. The arrow attached to OUTER1 says it's OUTER2.

Fig. 19–12

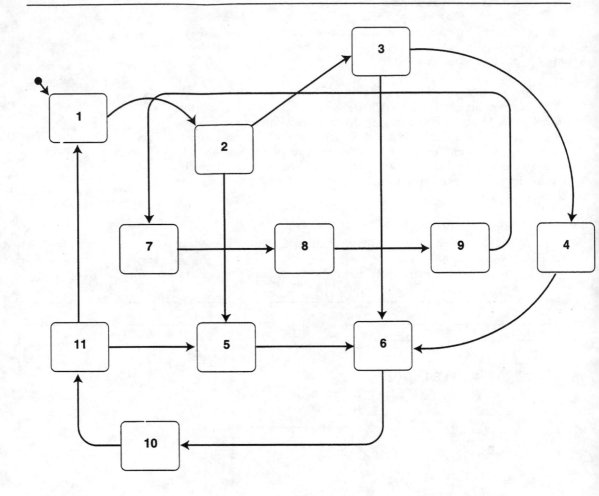

Unreachable states

Fig. 19–12 shows a set of unreachable states. Although it's not obvious, states 7, 8, and 9 can never be reached from the start state, 1. That's surely not correct. Unreachable states are usually easy to see in graphical models, but can be hard to see in tabular models.

Unreachable states can be found by a simple algorithm. It can be applied to both graphical and tabular models.

1. The start state is reachable.
2. Consider every transition from a reachable state. Add that transition's next state to the set of reachable states. (If it's already in the set, ignore it.)
3. Stop when you've considered every transition. (Note that each new state added to the set adds a number of new transitions.)
4. After you've stopped, any states not in the set are unreachable.

Statecharts add a complication. Conditional transitions may produce bizarre effects. For example, if the transition from 1 to 2 has the condition [A] and the transitions from 2 to 5 and from 6 to 10 have the condition [not A], state 5 is unreachable (provided the value of A doesn't change). Because conditions can be arbitrarily complicated, there's no systematic way of discovering such problems, but they're probably rare.

Fig. 19-13

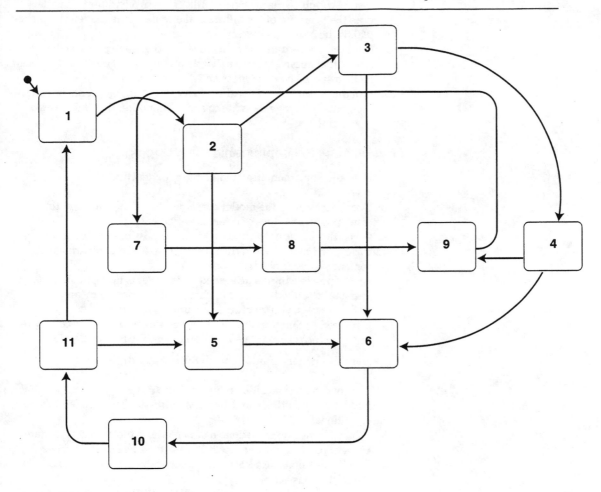

Dead states

Fig. 19-13 shows dead states, states that, once entered, cannot be left. (7, 8, and 9 are dead.) Unlike unreachable states, dead states sometimes make sense, but they're often a mistake. For example, those annoying graphical user interfaces that leave you trapped down deep in a menu hierarchy could be modelled by state machines with dead states.

Dead states can be found using the unreachable states algorithm. The only difference is that you consider every transition *to* a reachable state, instead of *from* it.

19.4.2 Inspect the Actions

The actions are names or brief descriptions. Somewhere, though, there is—or should be—a complete description. For each transition in the model, use the following checklist for the action.

1. Discover the action's preconditions. Is there a path through the model that can violate one of them? If so, and the precondition is assumed, you've discovered a fault. If the precondition is validated, does the handling of the failure make sense in the model? In particular, is the next state correct?
2. Consider all the data the action uses. Is there a path through the model that doesn't initialize that data or update it correctly? (This is really a special case of Question 1.)
3. Can the action affect the value of any state variable? That is, can it accidentally change the state to something other than the desired next state?

19.4.3 Check the Implementation Mapping

Does the implementation match the state machine?

1. Does each state in the model correspond to some clearly defined combination of values of internal variables?
2. Given those internal variables, are there possible combinations that correspond to no state in the model? Unusual combinations are sometimes overlooked.
3. Are all possible inputs described by the events in the model? If any of the undescribed inputs can change or be affected by any of the state variables, you've probably found a fault.
4. Is there code that implements each transition? Does this code produce the correct next state and implement the required action?

Does the implementation match the statechart?

1. Are conditional transitions implemented?
2. Has a transition that should be unconditional been implemented as conditional?
3. When a transition is made to a superstate, is the correct start state chosen? Or, if the superstate has history, is the last state chosen?
4. Do **all** transitions into a state implement the entry action and start the continuous action?
5. Do **all** transitions out of a state implement the exit action and stop the continuous action?

19.5 Testing State Machines and Statecharts

In most subsystems built from state models, the vast majority of the code implements the actions or is completely outside the scope of the model. The model helps organize the rest of the subsystem.

The same is true of testing. You'll get a few test requirements from the model and many more from other sources. The model requirements will provide an organizing structure. They do this by adding variety to tests you'd write anyway.

CHAP. 19 STATE MACHINES AND STATECHARTS

Because the model's test requirements duplicate straightforward checks already made in the inspection, they will not by themselves find many faults. They find most faults indirectly by improving other tests. They are more likely to find faults directly if the implementation is implicit, especially if it was written before the model. (There will be more faults to start with, and a higher percentage may slip past inspection.)

Use the test requirements even if there is no chance they will directly find faults. This would be the case if the framework was automatically generated from the model. The variety they add is useful, and it costs little.

19.5.1 Test Requirements

Model test requirements cause every possible transition to be exercised. Suppose you have this state machine:

	state1	state2	errorstate
eventA	errorstate / error	state1 / action1	errorstate / error
eventB	state2 / action2	errorstate / error	errorstate / error
eventC	state2 / action3	-	errorstate / error
resetevent	errorstate / error	errorstate / error	state1 / reset

You would have this test requirement checklist:

state machine transitions
    event A in state 1
    event A in state 2
    event A in errorstate
    event B in state 1
    event B in state 2
    event B in errorstate
    event C in state 1
    event C in errorstate
    resetevent in state 1
    resetevent in state 2
    resetevent in errorstate

Fig. 19–14
Test requirements
for a state machine

A few matters require explanation.

Duplicate transitions

Many of the transitions are duplicates. They should do exactly the same thing: perform the same action and lead to the same next state. But they might not. Each should be tested, though you might DEFER duplicates if you're short of time.

Error transitions

Several of the requirements are for transitions to an error state. Why aren't they marked as ERROR requirements? Don't they violate a precondition that says certain events should not occur in certain states?

The purpose of the ERROR notation is to prevent an error requirement from being combined with other requirements in situations that prevent those requirements from affecting the program. What requirements could an error transition mask?

1. It couldn't mask requirements derived from the transition action. Indeed, those requirements only have effect during the error transition. As a concrete example, suppose the action in an error transition formats and sends a message to a central logging facility. Requirements derived from the size of the message should certainly be combined with the requirement that causes the error transition.
2. It can't mask other transition requirements. Indeed, transitions out of the error state can only take effect after the error transition.

Since there is no chance of ineffectual requirements, an ERROR marking is not appropriate.

Which faults do these test requirements target?

These test requirements target the following faults, all of which can happen whether or not an explicit framework is used. Note that a targeted fault isn't necessarily revealed, as is discussed later.

1. The wrong transition might be selected. That could be caused by an incorrect `switch` statement (including a missing `break`) or by an incorrect initialization of the internal representation (an array in the case of a state machine, something more complex in the case of a statechart). If there is no explicit framework, this fault corresponds to a logic fault somewhere in the subsystem.
2. A transition might be wrong. The next state is incorrect, or the wrong action is taken.
3. A transition might be missing. The subsystem cannot handle a particular event happening in a particular state. This might be caused by leaving out a `case` in a switch statement. Such a fault is much more likely in implicit implementations.

Which faults don't they target?

There are other plausible faults not targeted by these requirements. This section explains why.

Action faults independent of the model

A transition's action might fail in a way independent of the model. For example, a particular transition might cause the subsystem to format and send a series of messages containing user input, but it happens that a particular input triggers an off-by-one fault. That fault should be found by test requirements derived from the action's specification and code.

Transitions that do not work together

Suppose the state machine is as shown in Fig. 19-15. The transition from state 4 to state 5 may succeed when state 4 was reached from state 3, but fail when it was reached from state 2. The action done in the 2-4 transition does something the 3-4 transition doesn't, and that something affects the 4-5 transition. The fault could be in the 4-5 transition if it fails to handle the results of the 2-3 transition. It could also be in the 2-3 transition, but the failure is only revealed during the 4-5 transition. Or it could be in both.

Fig. 19-15

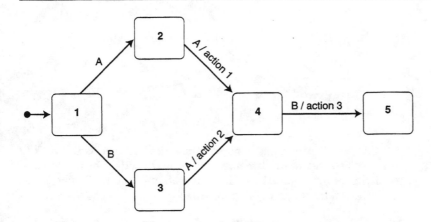

Subsystem testing does not produce test requirements that directly force particular combinations of transitions. Instead, as with other similar situations, indirect means are used:

1. Suppose there's a dependency between two transitions. If so, the test requirements for the data used in the second should force tests to pass through the first on the way to the second. The justification for this assertion is given in Part 5.
2. Failing that, complexity and variety may cause the needed combination. If you are particularly suspicious, you may add pairs or even larger combinations of transitions as explicit test requirements. Part 5 will help you determine which combinations are useful.

Faults in one transition that are only revealed during a later one are a test implementation issue, not a test requirement issue. (See Section 19.5.4 on page 333.)

Checklist organization

As discussed earlier in the book, a complete subsystem will have many checklists. There is one checklist for the overall specification (perhaps more than one, if that's more manageable) together with individual checklists for individual routines. Most usually, the state machine checklist is simply appended to the specification checklist. Requirements from the routines that implement actions could be used as refinements to the appropriate transition requirements, but it's rarely profitable to do so.

There is one exception. Consider the following state machine:

Fig. 19–16

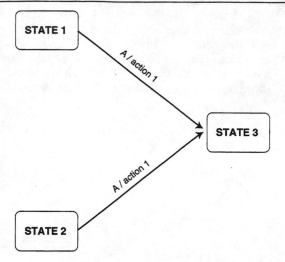

Although both transitions have identical actions, you may know that they're actually implemented by separate code. In that case, the requirements for `action1` should refine both transitions. (You might also think about removing redundant code.)

19.5.2 Test Requirements from Statecharts

As with state machines, test requirements exercise all transitions. In addition to writing a test requirement for each arrow, you need to treat some of the statechart features specially.

Transitions from superstates

Fig. 19–17

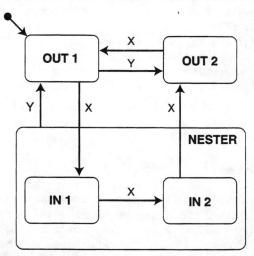

A transition from a superstate requires a test requirement for each nested substate. For example, the Y transition from the NESTER superstate should work in each of its two substates. That is, the following would be incorrect:

> X in OUT1
> Y in OUT1
> X in OUT2
> X in IN1
> X in IN2
> **Y in NESTER**

The correct checklist would specify the two substates:

> X in OUT1
> Y in OUT1
> X in OUT2
> X in IN1
> X in IN2
> Y in NESTER
> > **Y in IN1**
> > **Y in IN2**

That is, the notational simplicity of transitions from a superstate does not simplify testing.

Transitions to states with history

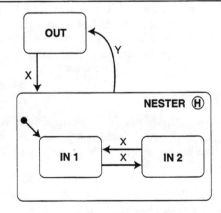

Fig. 19–18

A transition to a superstate with history is, in effect, several possible transitions to several possible substates. Each should have its own test requirement:

> X in OUT
> > leads to IN1
> > leads to IN2

Conditional transitions

A condition is a boolean expression attached to a transition. The test requirements for the boolean are used to refine the transition requirement:

Fig. 19–19

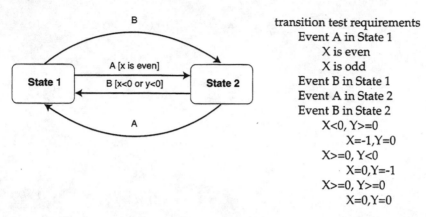

transition test requirements
Event A in State 1
    X is even
    X is odd
Event B in State 1
Event A in State 2
Event B in State 2
    X<0, Y>=0
      X=-1,Y=0
    X>=0, Y<0
      X=0,Y=-1
    X>=0, Y>=0
      X=0,Y=0

(I also used the catalog requirements for relational operators.)

State Actions

Fig. 19–20

SOME_STATE
entry: action
exit: other action
do: continuous action

State actions are handled just like transition actions. Test requirements don't come from the model, which is too terse. Instead, they come from other parts of the specification or from the code.

You will have to decide whether to duplicate the action test requirements for each transition that leads to the state or to list them independently and use them round robin in all the transitions. The former is appropriate for duplicated code; the latter when the state actions are all handled by the same code. The latter is more likely.

19.5.3 Test Specifications

There are two steps in making a test specification. First, you select a sequence of transitions, each of which satisfies a model test requirement. Then you flesh out that sequence with test requirements from other sources.

Sketch the Transition Sequence

In the absence of dead states, any state can be reached from any other state. A single transition sequence could satisfy every test requirement. For example, here's one that satisfies every one of Fig. 19–1''s requirements:

CHAP. 19 STATE MACHINES AND STATECHARTS

```
/* Initially in state 1 */
Input:    event B
Expect:   description of result of action2      /* Moves to state 2 */

Input:    event A
Expect:   description of result of action1      /* Moves to state 1 */

Input:    event C
Expect:   description of result of action3      /* Moves to state 2 */

Input:    event B
Expect:   error                                 /* Moves to error state */

Input:    event B
Expect    error                                 /* Moves to error state */

Input:    event A
Expect:   error                                 /* Moves to error state */

Input:    event C
Expect:   error                                 /* Moves to error state */

Input:    reset
Expect:   output of RESET command               /* Moves to state 1 */

Input:    event A
Expect:   error                                 /* Moves to error state */

Input:    reset
Expect:   output of RESET command               /* Moves to state 1 */

Input:    reset
Expect:   error                                 /* Moves to error state */

Input:    reset
Expect:   output of RESET command               /* Moves to state 1 */

Input:    event C
Expect:   description of result of action3      /* Moves to state 2 */

Input:    reset
Expect:   error                                 /* Moves to error state */

Input:    reset
Expect:   output of RESET command               /* Moves to state 1 */
```

The question is whether that's a good idea. Or would it be better to write many sequences, each of which exercises only a few transitions?

The general advice of this book is to make test specifications as complex as is tractable, stopping just before the point where the complexity overwhelms you. State machine test specifications are no exception. You may not bother with a single test specification that uses all transitions, but each specification should exercise many transitions. By doing this, you increase your chance of finding faults, including transitions that don't work together.

This advice contradicts [Beizer90], who recommends simple tests. This is good advice for system testing, which should be concerned, in part, with failures many users might see. It would be disastrous if the system handled complex tests, but not the simple series of events that 99 percent of the customers use. Subsystem testing has a different goal, removing the most likely faults before system testing so that system testing needn't duplicate work that can be done more efficiently earlier.

When choosing transition sequences, look for interesting ones: plausible sequences of events that might not have been tried before, ones that make you or the developer say, "That's interesting—I wonder if it works." The graphical representation can help. Selecting paths through that graph is more intuitive than selecting transitions from a table.

There's an extra expense when complex tests find bugs. When an early step in the sequence fails, you may have to write a new test to exercise the later steps—a definite expense. However, the savings of starting out with small tests would be dwarfed by the cost of missed faults.

Fleshing out

A transition sequence is not a complete test specification. It does not describe the exact inputs corresponding to each event (unless each input is a unique event). Use other test requirements to help select those. For example, if each event is a command, there will be test requirements from the command's syntax, its preconditions and postconditions, and so on. Each time a transition sequence uses that event, you have the opportunity to satisfy some of those requirements.

You can also use test requirements that add new inputs, not just flesh out events. Suppose a command's results are independent of the state and can be given in any state. That command should have been left out of the model—it would clutter it up to no good purpose. However, it will still have test requirements, and there's no reason not to use them in the same tests as the state machine requirements. This will—by chance—test whether the command is independent of the state. (It will probably not test whether the command is truly independent of every state. If you have reason to suspect it might not be, you should add explicit test requirements.)

Remember to review each test specification to find problems with the model. Do the expected results make sense from the user's perspective?

Rules for test form

Up to now, all subsystems in the book have used only one-step processing. They took inputs and produced results. Test specifications described any required setup of the test's environment, one set of inputs, and one set of expected outputs. State machines process in many steps, so test specifications must specify a sequence of exact inputs. They must also specify the corresponding sequence of exact expected results. It is not enough to specify only the final results: There must be a description of all visible results at every step along the way.

As before, maintenance (removing, reworking, or reordering tests) will be much simpler if tests do not depend on earlier tests to set up their environment. And more failures will be found if multiple tests are run in

each invocation of the subsystem. Both these rules are most easily satisfied by designing every test specification to begin in the starting state,
traverse other states, then end up back in the starting state.

Rules for test content

You want incorrect transitions to produce different results from correct ones. The basic problem is the usual one of propagation: An exercised
fault might not produce a visible failure. Here are three particular cases.

1. The wrong action executes, but it produces the same visible result as
   the correct one.
2. The wrong next state is selected, but the action is correct, so the state
   machine produces the correct visible result. The following transition (if any) would be from the wrong state, but might still appear
   correct if it happened to again produce the right visible result. Bad
   luck thus might lead to a wrong path with the correct visible behavior (and perhaps some untested transitions or states along the correct path).
3. The correct action executes, but an incorrect action also executes—
   but that incorrect action produces no visible result. (This dual execution could happen if a `break` is missing from a `switch`.)

Each of these problems can be caught by inspections, expecially in
explicit frameworks. Selecting inputs that distinguish the correct transition from any possible incorrect one is difficult. I recommend against it
for subsystem testing. Rely on inspections. When the subsystem reveals
so little that faults are likely to be masked, add test support code (see Section 19.5.4). Of course, keeping the desirability of unique output in mind
certainly can't hurt, and variety in the tests will make it harder for faults to
hide.

If you wish test specifications to be immune to visibility problems,
you should look to the literature on conformance testing of networking
protocols. [Fujiwara91] is a good place to start a literature search.

19.5.4 Test Implementation

Event-driven subsystems are usually organized cyclically. They
return often to a central dispatching routine. That dispatching routine is
an excellent place to put code that reveals internal variables, thereby
increasing the visibility of failures. A very simple example of such code is
one that prints the current state and the incoming event. The expected
output of such a subsystem then includes a trace of the transitions
through the state machine, which is useful for finding test implementation
mistakes as well as subsystem failures.

The central dispatching routine is probably a place where the subsystem is in a steady state. There, you can make strong statements about
consistency relationships that should hold between subsystem variables.
Add code that explicitly checks those statements.

Test support code will increase the chance that a faulty transition
fails immediately. That will make it less likely that a problem in one transition will be visible only when it's followed by a particular other transi-

tion. This reduces the need for testing pairs of transitions or, more generally, particular paths through the state machine graph.

19.5.5 Coverage

The goal of the test requirements is to exercise every transition. You need to be alerted when the implemented tests miss some. The transition traces mentioned in the previous section do nicely. Failing that, ordinary branch coverage often suffices when the explicit implementation is built from `switch` statements. The only weakness is that error transitions are often grouped together under the `default` case, in which case you can't tell which ones have not been taken. If an array of transition functions was used, coverage that measures which routines have been entered is helpful. (This coverage is common in tools that implement the other types described in Chapter 7.) When a function is used for several duplicate transitions, this method cannot tell which were not taken.

Even in an implicit implementation, there should still be branches corresponding to unique transitions. They simply are not as localized or as readily identifiable. In such a situation, keep the state machine in mind when examining coverage. Remember that a single unused transition may be a clue that your test design is weak. Do more than exercise that transition: Consider whether you also missed tests that would discover unimplemented transitions.

19.6
Multiple State
Machines

Communicating state machines are described in [Harel87] and [Rumbaugh91]. Both have useful large examples. This section begins by describing the simple case, independent state machines, then considers those that can affect each other. To understand this section, you must have read the section on statecharts, though most of what's in it can be applied to simple state machines.

19.6.1 Independent State Machines

A subsystem may contain more than one state machine. If the state machines do not communicate, there is little effect on testing. Fig. 19-21 shows an example of two independent state machines, using Harel's notation.

What does this picture represent? There are two outer-level states, but one of them is divided up into two "orthogonal" states by a dashed line. When DOUBLE_STATE is entered, *both* ORTHO1 and ORTHO2 begin execution in their respective start states. Some things to note:

1. DOUBLE_STATE is a label on the outside of the divided state, unlike other types of states which are labeled on the inside. This is purely to reduce the number of boxes; DOUBLE_STATE could be in a box itself.
2. The two states can respond in tandem to some events (COMMON), but other events may be specific to one of them. SPECIFIC applies only to ORTHO2—it has no effect on ORTHO1.
3. The states will simultaneously exit when the OUT event arrives.

CHAP. 19 STATE MACHINES AND STATECHARTS

4. Both will also exit when SPECIAL_OUT arrives while ORTHO1 is in state INNER1B. You can never leave only one of a set of orthogonal states.

Fig. 19-21

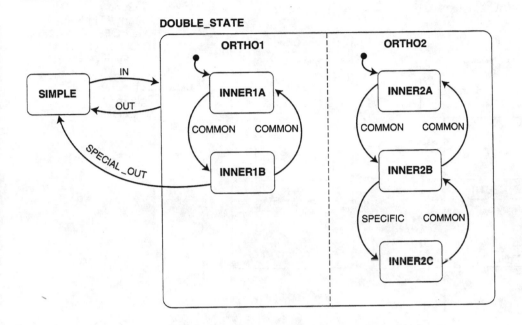

What does this model represent? Entry to DOUBLE_STATE could represent the start of two independent threads of execution (perhaps with a POSIX fork()). In an object-based system (see Chapter 21), the two orthogonal states might represent two objects which are created on entry to DOUBLE_STATE, then destroyed on exit. It's also quite possible that they simply model the processing of a single object with two independent groups of state variables. DOUBLE_STATE could be represented by a non-orthogonal six-state statechart, with one state for INNER1A-and-INNER2A, another for INNER1A-and-INNER2B, and so on. But if ORTHO1 describes the use of one global variable, and ORTHO2 describes the use of another, and the variables are used independently and by different code, a six-state state machine makes no sense and just adds complexity.

As before, each of the orthogonal state machines will have a test requirement for each of its transitions. Since the machines are independent, they can be tested independently. That is, the SPECIFIC transition from INNER2B must be tested, but it makes no difference whether ORTHO1 is in state INNER1A or INNER1B during that test. However, if there will be several tests that exercise that transition, there's no reason not to try both of those states. Keep that type of variety in mind as you create test specifications.

Sometimes, state machines are even more independent in that they don't even share events. Consider Fig. 19–22. Here, there are two independent state machines. They could be divided by a dashed line, but there's really no point to that. The first responds to signals from a heat-

Fig. 19–22

ing/cooling system, the second responds to a photosensitive toggle. The list of test requirements would be:

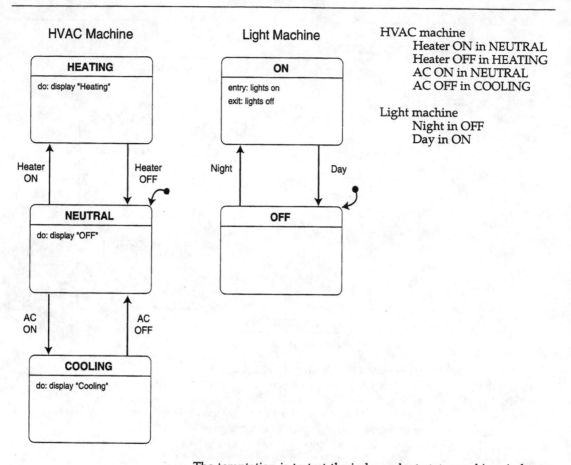

HVAC machine
    Heater ON in NEUTRAL
    Heater OFF in HEATING
    AC ON in NEUTRAL
    AC OFF in COOLING

Light machine
    Night in OFF
    Day in ON

The temptation is to test the independent state machines independently. One set of tests would take paths through the HVAC machine, another through the light machine. However, it would be better to test both machines simultaneously by interweaving events for both machines in the same test specifications. After all, the machines are only *supposed* to be independent. What if they're not? Independent test specifications will certainly not detect that, whereas interwoven ones might. However, since there's no explicit evidence of dependency, rely on chance and variety to detect it. That is, don't insist on tests that satisfy all of:

    heater on at night
    heater on in the day
    heater off at night
    heater off in the day
    AC on at night
    AC on in the day
    AC off at night
    AC off in the day

(Of course, if you have enough test requirements from other sources that you can satisfy all these, do so, provided the additional bookkeeping isn't too much trouble.)

19.6.2 Communicating State Machines

Things are more interesting when the state machines can influence each other. They can do this in two ways. A transition's action may cause an event, and a transition's guard condition may query the state of another state machine. Fig. 19-23 shows an example.

Fig. 19-23

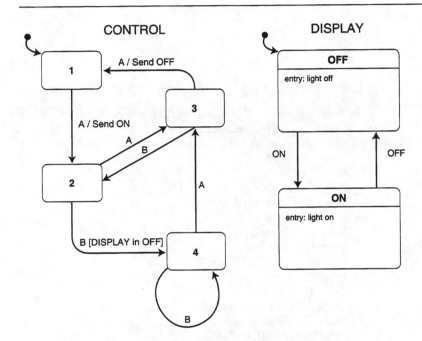

The CONTROL state machine performs various operations, and the DISPLAY state machine displays them. The CONTROL machine controls the DISPLAY machine, which gets no events from the outside world. When the A event arrives in state 1, the control machine sends ON to the DISPLAY machine.[1] That event forces the DISPLAY machine into the ON state.

The DISPLAY machine also affects the CONTROL machine. Event B in CONTROL's state 2 has an effect only if the DISPLAY machine is in the OFF state; otherwise, it is ignored.

Communicating state machines open up many new possibilities for specification problems. For example, neither of the two state machines seems to have an unreachable state. In particular, you can trace a path

---

1. In Harel's original statecharts, events are broadcast, so that many state machines may receive them "simultaneously." Such systems must be checked for time dependencies. That type of testing is outside the scope of this book. Events can also be targeted to particular state machines, which is far more likely in subsystems.

from CONTROL's state 1 to state 4 and back again. However, to get from 1 to 4, DISPLAY must be in OFF while CONTROL is in 2. That's impossible— the only time DISPLAY is in OFF is when CONTROL is in 1. (This raises the question of why there's a separate state machine, but this is only an example.) The machines collectively have unreachable states.

There are algorithms to discover specification problems in communicating state machines, most of them developed for networking protocols. They are outside the scope of this book. To learn more, see [Holzmann91].

If a conditional transition queries the state of another machine, it must be tested when the machine is both in and not in that state. The test requirements for Fig. 19–3 would include

> CONTROL machine
>> Event B in state 2
>>> DISPLAY in OFF state
>>> DISPLAY not in OFF state

When the subsystem contains more than one machine, there must be test requirements for each machine's transitions. Consider Fig. 19-24. If the machines were treated independently, the test requirements would be:

> COMMAND machine
>> Event ON in state C1
>> Event OFF in state C1
>> Event ON in state C2
>> Event OFF in state C2
>> Event ON in state C3
>> Event OFF in state C3

> RECORDER machine
>> Event ADVANCE in state R1
>> Event RETREAT in state R1
>> Event ADVANCE in state R2
>> Event RETREAT in state R2
>> Event ADVANCE in state R3
>> Event RETREAT in state R3

The requirements for the two machines are independent. For the first RECORDER requirement, it makes no difference if the ADVANCE comes from the C1-C2 transition or the C3-C1 transition. Insisting on independence is riskier when the machines communicate. Even simple communicating state machines are hard to get right, so a richer, more varied set of tests is justified. Further, the state machines are only partial models of the subsystem. There are likely to be nonstate variables used by both state machines, and more varied tests will detect more incorrect dependencies. Such dependencies are often caused when programmers don't realize a particular event can happen at a particular time. These are explicit reasons for a partial multiplication of test requirements, where every transition caused by another machine must come from each possible source:

Fig. 19-24

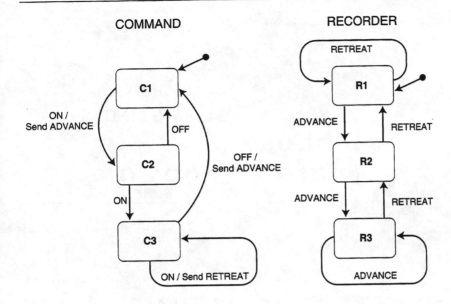

COMMAND machine
    Event ON in state C1   **-- redundant, can be removed**
    Event OFF in state C1
    Event ON in state C2
    Event OFF in state C2
    Event ON in state C3
    Event OFF in state C3   **-- redundant, can be removed**

RECORDER machine
    Event ADVANCE in state R1
-     **Caused by Event ON in state C1**
-     **Caused by Event OFF in state C3**
    Event RETREAT in state R1
    Event ADVANCE in state R2
-     **Caused by Event ON in state C1**
-     **Caused by Event OFF in state C3**
    Event RETREAT in state R2
    Event ADVANCE in state R3
-     **Caused by Event ON in state C1**
-     **Caused by Event OFF in state C3**
    Event RETREAT in state R3

(Note that RETREAT can only be sent in one transition, so there's no need to refine the RETREAT transitions of RECORDER.)

20

Testing Subsystems that Use Reusable Software

The producer of a reusable software library provides a part of your subsystem. The producer tests this reused part, but you must test the rest. This chapter addresses the question of how the producer should help you test (and what to do if you get no such help).

20.1 Test Requirements

As far as test design is concerned, it makes no difference that the library was written by someone else. You use reusable software as you use your own, you make the same type of mistakes, and you need to test for misuses in the same way:

1. When you call reusable functions, you may call them incorrectly or handle their results incorrectly. The integration test requirements of Chapter 3, Section 3.10, should be used.
2. If the reusable software provides variables, their test requirements should be satisfied for any routine that uses them (or perhaps should use them).

These integration test requirements should then be combined with test requirements from the part of the subsystem you wrote.

There is, however, one practical difference between calling a function you wrote and calling one used by thousands of other programs. The more that function is reused, the less sense it makes to have every reuser derive test requirements afresh. The library's producer should provide a catalog of reusable test requirements.

Fig. 20–1 illustrates this point. The subsystem uses two libraries, A and B, meaning that routines inside the subsystem call routines inside the libraries. To test the correctness of those calls, catalogs for the libraries would be useful. They would be used in addition to the standard catalog and all other sources of test requirements.

Fig. 20-1

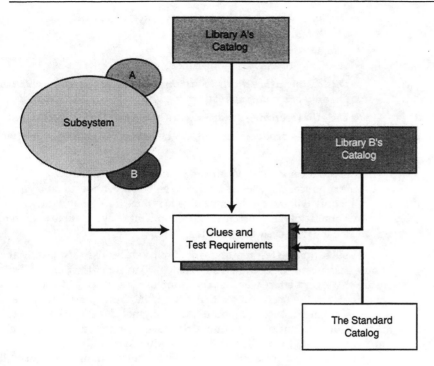

To emphasize: Except incidentally, these requirements do not test whether the library is correct. Instead, they check for incorrect uses of it. Such a catalog for the C library might contain entries like these:

```
char *bsearch ((char *) key, (char *) collection, number_elements,
               sizeof (*key), compar)
unsigned number_elements;
int (*compar)( );
```

➡ *bsearch is a binary search routine; it uses the same requirements as the searching operation in the standard catalog except that the INLINE requirement (match in first position) is not useful.*

- Match not found
- Match found (more than one element, exactly one match)
- More than one match in the collection
- Single match found in last position

➡ *This can catch a misuse where the index of the last element is passed in as number_elements.*

char *strrchr(char *string, int character)

➥*strrchr searches for the last occurrence of the character in the string.*

- Match not found
- More than one match in the collection

➥*This distinguishes a call to strrchr from a call to strchr, which is only one typographical error away.*

➥*The other searching conditions are not useful for this function.*

The library's producer should be the catalog's distributor for two reasons:

1. The producer is the most efficient distribution channel.
2. The producer can use the catalog to gain competitive advantage. Not only will the producer be able to reduce the cost and increase the quality of their customers' development, they'll be able to do the same for their customers' testing.

A subset of the test requirements the producer used for testing the library will make a good starting catalog. This subset would at least ensure that every effect was exercised, forcing the caller to handle each one. However, the users are the true experts in all the imaginative ways the library can be misused, because the original developers know too much about correct use. For example, the developer of strrchr probably did not anticipate the faults caused by writing strchr by accident, else the routine would have a different name. A conscientious producer will gather misuse information from customers and distribute it via a catalog, and they will make documentation or interface changes to reduce the chance of future misuse. At this writing, no vendor of reusable software provides test requirement catalogs.

20.2 Coverage

There's more to testing than designing tests—there's also measuring whether they do what they're supposed to do. Coverage tools fill that role. Consider this coverage report:

"lc.c", line 256: if was taken TRUE 0, FALSE 11 times.
"lc.c", line 397: operator < might be <=. (L==R)

The first line may remind you of an untested feature. The second line may be a symptom of forgetting to test Intervals. Both lines are clues of weaknesses in test design. They don't tell you precisely which test requirements you missed, especially if the requirements are for faults of omission.

For the special case of reusable test requirements, though, coverage can do better. This sort of report is possible:

"lc.c", line 218: strrchr(s,c): never two instances of c in s.
"lc.c", line 256: if was taken TRUE 0, FALSE 11 times.
"lc.c", line 397: operator < might be <=. (L==R)
"lc.c", line 403: bsearch never failed to find a match.

The last line might refer to this code:

```
elt_pointer = (elt_type *) bsearch ( (char *)key, (char *)collection,
                             size, sizeof(*key), elt_type_cmp);
elt_pointer->times_seen++;
```

The code is incorrect. There's no check for the null pointer that's returned if the `key` is not found in the `collection`. Writing a test to satisfy the coverage condition would find the fault. (So would simply looking at the code to see what test was needed.) In this case, the coverage condition is a test requirement targeted to a fault of omission, not just a clue. Of course, not all faults of omission are of this type, so the coverage condition should also be treated as a clue of other potential weaknesses in the tests.

Along with reusable test requirement catalogs, producers should provide modules to plug into coverage tools. Those modules would measure whether your test suites satisfied the integration requirements. To my knowledge, ViSTASIM® from Veritas Software is the only tool that supports this type of coverage. The most efficient use of such a tool is during creation of the initial test suite. It gives you integration requirements to combine with the requirements from all other sources.

21

Testing Object-Based Software

Object-based programming is object-oriented programming minus some features. When testing object-oriented software, much of the work is in testing the object-based part, so that testing deserves a chapter of its own. The next three chapters consider the extensions that make software object-oriented.

Subsystems that are not object-oriented often have object-based parts. This chapter will be useful when testing them.

This discussion first assumes you have time to test as thoroughly as subsystem testing allows. The last section describes what to do when time is short.

Figure 21-1 illustrates this chapter's fundamental idea. Object-based subsystems organize code and data into cohesive groups, commonly called *classes*. Each such grouping can have its own catalog of test requirements. The structure of that catalog mirrors the relationships in the class.

Fig. 21-1

Class Hash_Table	Hash_Table Catalog
Class String	String Catalog
Class Motor	Motor Catalog

Object-based software organizes subsystems around data structures. Each different type of data structure has an associated constellation of routines. Here is a typical C declaration of a hash table object together with an example of its use:

```
typedef struct
{
  token *elements;                  /* Pointer to an array of tokens. */
  int sz;                           /* Size of the array. */
} hash_table;

hash_table *new_hash_table(int size);
boolean insert_hash_table(hash_table *, token);
token retrieve_hash_table(hash_table *, char *);
boolean remove_hash_table(hash_table *, token);
int hash_table_size(hash_table *);

        hash_table *ht = new_hash_table(17);  /* Create a hash table, ht, with 17 entries. */
        token tok = new_token("dawn");        /* Create a token named "dawn". */
        token tok2;

        insert_hash_table(ht, tok);           /* Put the token in ht. */
        ...
         tok2 = retrieve_hash_table(ht, "dawn"); /* Retrieve a copy of the token. */
```

The routines define the interface to the hash table. Their declarations define the syntactic interface, and their preconditions and postconditions define the behavior. As long as the interface remains the same, the underlying data structure and algorithms can change without affecting external code.

Not all objects use a pure functional interface. For example, rather than calling `hash_table_size(table)`, hash table users could simply use `table->size`. That limits future changes to the hash table's implementation, so such "violations of encapsulation" are frowned upon. Of course, they still happen, so testing must take them into account.

The term "object-based" is due to [Cardelli85]. People can (and do) argue about the difference between objects and "abstract data types," first introduced by [Liskov74]. For subsystem testing, the distinction makes no difference.

21.1.1 Terminology

Some terminology is needed to make the discussion clear. Although understanding C++ is not a prerequisite for this chapter, I will use typical C++ terminology (and mention other common terms for people who use other languages).

❑ **class**

A class is the definition of an object. It describes both its interface and its internal structure. In C, the class is composed of a `struct` and related functions. It is not always clear which functions belong to the class, because there's nothing in the language that forces the programmer to identify them. In C++, the class is a language construct in its own right. In some languages, the class's interface and internal structure are described separately, but both are needed for testing.

❑ **data member**

The fields in the structure are called the data members of the class. In the hash table class, `elements` and `sz` are data members. Data members are sometimes called "instance variables."

❑ **member function**

The related function declarations are called member functions. `new_hash_table`, `insert_hash_table`, `retrieve_hash_table`, `remove_hash_table`, and `hash_table_size` are the member functions of the hash table class. Often, but not always, member functions are the only routines allowed access to a data member. For example, routines outside the class should not read `sz`; they should call `hash_table_size` instead. Member functions are sometimes called "methods."

❑ **object**

An executing subsystem may contain many instances of a particular class; for example, there may be many hash tables that share the same interface but are physically distinct (have different addresses in memory). "Testing the hash table" means creating one or more of those objects and exercising the associated member functions.

❑ **class invariants**

Each individual member function in a class has (or could have) preconditions and postconditions. The class as a whole can have an invariant. It tells what must always be true of an object of that class, no matter what member functions are called, what their arguments, and what order they're used in. Every member function can treat the invariant as an assumed precondition, and it must maintain the invariant no matter what else it does. For the hash table, an invariant is that it never contains two tokens with the same name. (Otherwise, which one would `retrieve_hash_table` retrieve?)

21.1.2 Other Approaches

This chapter discusses how to apply subsystem testing to this special style of programming. There are other approaches to test design, most based on variant styles of writing the class specification. See [Gannon81], [Hayes86], [Jalote89], [Doong91], and [Zweben92]. Many of the references in the next chapter are also relevant.

For object-based software, the smallest reasonable subsystem is the class. Member functions call each other, so testing them in isolation would require stubs. In most classes, the effort of writing the stubs would be perilously close to the effort of writing the real member functions, and it would obscure the interaction errors that you are (in large part) looking for.

Is the class also the largest reasonable subsystem? This section argues that it is not. Object-based software should, like other software, be tested in large subsystems augmented with judicious amounts of internal test support code. If you already believe that, you can skip to the next section.

This discussion will use two example faults.

Example 1: A hash table

Suppose the hash table satisfies its invariant (no two tokens with the same name) with this `insert_hash_table` postcondition:

> IF an entry with the same name exists
> THEN that entry is deleted before the new entry is added

That postcondition produces this test requirement:

> insert_hash_table called with matching entry in the hash table

But the code does not implement the specification. It doesn't delete the old entry, but only obscures it. That fault is not visible in the observable results of `insert_hash_table`. `retrieve_hash_table` will retrieve the new entry, not the old, so its results also do not reveal the bug. It will be revealed only if the new entry is deleted and the old entry retrieved (which should fail, but doesn't).

Example 2: A list

Consider a Container implemented as a doubly-linked list, one containing both forward and back links. The `insert` routine adds a new element `new` between the current element `elt1` and the following element `elt2`. The new element becomes the current element. The fault is one of missing code. `elt2`'s back link is not set to `new`; it remains pointing to `elt1`. The fault will only be revealed if that back link is traversed.[1]

21.2 Subsystem Size and Test Implementation

---

1. This example was inspired by [Zweben92] and subsequent discussion with Professor Zweben. It's a pretty common fault in doubly-linked lists.

A typical way to test classes is in isolation, via the class interface. The class is tested by calling a member function, checking its return value, and then calling other member functions to see if the object's state was appropriately changed. Data members not part of the official class interface are not accessed. (In C, nothing prevents the test code from doing so; languages with strong class interfaces, like C++, enforce them.)

The hash table fault would be found with a test like this:

```
/* Setup */
old_token.name = "dawn";
insert_hash_table(ht, old_token);

/* Insert the duplicate entry - previous should be erased. */
insert_hash_table(ht, new_token);

/* Check whether it was erased. */
remove_hash_table(ht, new_token);
retrieved_token = retrieve_hash_table(ht, "dawn");
            /* Tokens not in the table return a special value */
if (retrieved_token != nonexistent_token) FAIL;
```

The list fault would be found by this sequence of operations:

1. insert new while the current element is elt1.
EXPECT: new is the current element
2. move forward, then back
EXPECT: new is the current element (but it won't be)

However, one driver per class is expensive. Just as with other types of software, using a larger subsystem as the single driver for many classes is cheaper. Further, it provides a safety net: Complex tests for the subsystem will exercise individual classes in a variety of ways, possibly satisfying overlooked test requirements.

But object-based software makes larger subsystems harder. As the examples showed, finding a fault is not necessarily a simple matter of calling a member function, getting a wrong result, and seeing that result propagate. Because classes are designed to hide information, a carefully tailored sequence of member functions may be needed to coax the failure to the class interface. It can be hard to figure out which inputs to a distant subsystem interface will force that sequence.

The solution? Rather than coaxing failures to the class interface, put code inside the class to detect them as soon and as straightforwardly as possible. There are two types of such code. One type is added to a member function and checks one or more of its effects. The perhaps more effective kind is a new member function that checks the class invariant.

1. When `insert_hash_table` is called, its last action could be to call a new member function, `check_invariant_hash_table`, that loops through the hash table looking for duplicates. A test of insertion of an element that's already present would not need to call `remove_hash_table` and `retrieve_hash_table` after `insert_hash_table`.

2. When an element is inserted into the linked list, the structure could be checked to make sure that backward and forward links are consistent.

But wait: Is this really cheaper? Isn't adding internal testing code to each class effectively the same as writing an external driver for each class—or at least as expensive? Not really. The most important reason is that you should only write code for failures likely to be obscured. For example, consider the linked list example. Is that failure really hard to observe? It is when the tests are simple: ones that insert elements, check them, and then never reuse them. A proper test is complex with variety, so it will inevitably traverse many links in both directions. That's especially true of larger subsystem tests, which will use the list class heavily in the process of exercising the rest of the subsystem.

For efficiency's sake, only write internal code to reveal faults that you believe are unlikely to produce observable failures at the subsystem interface.

Internal checking code can still be expensive to write. A further way to reduce the cost is to make it only partially internal. The internal code displays (via `printf`s or some other mechanism) a complete description of the internal state in a form that's easy to compare to an expected state. The expected results of a subsystem test would include a sequence of displays of the state of the object. That is, the test specification would look like this:

SETUP:
   ...
TEST:
   ...
EXPECTED:
      Hash table internal state (first call): ...
      Hash table internal state (second call): ...
      Hash table internal state (third call): ...
      Hash table internal state (fourth call): ...
      Results from subsystem: ...

It's often easiest simply to have a single routine that displays the entire internal state. You can also cause each member function to display only the state relevant to it. That can simplify the comparison of actual to expected results.

Though usually cheaper, display code is less useful than internal checking code. Display code is only useful when running designed subsystem tests that specify expected results. Checking code contains its own expected results, so it can be used during all kinds of testing, including testing through normal use. Internal checking code is especially useful when objects are to be reused.

21.2.1 Two Special Cases

Groups of classes are often designed to work together. Groups may have their own collective invariant. For example, the three classes `object_to_be_displayed`, `visual_representation`, and

---

keyboard_controller might have the invariant that any object_to_be_displayed will have at most one visual_representation, and that it will have the same number of keyboard_controllers (zero or one). Groups of related classes should always be tested together. It makes no sense to test visual_representation in isolation since it is always used in conjunction with a keyboard_controller.

If a class is designed in isolation and is intended to be reused in many applications, it makes more sense to test it in isolation. Note, however, that classes are often not designed from scratch but plucked from existing subsystems, refined and polished, and put into a reuse library. In that case, you might want to use the original application as a test driver, thus testing both it and the class derived from it.

21.2.2 Another Approach

In [Doong91], Doong and Frankl describe a clever way to keep costs down, raise effectiveness, and test classes in isolation. They generate all possible sequences of member functions (up to a certain maximum length). Rather than creating expected results, they pair the sequences. Each member of a pair should put the object in the same state. If they don't, there's a fault. All that is required is a way of comparing two objects. The paper describes a tool that automates test generation.

Their approach is not appropriate for all classes, and it does not target all faults. However, it's possible that the faults it misses will largely be caught by testing the class as part of a larger subsystem (without adding internal test support code). The two approaches have not yet been tried together.

21.3
The Class
Requirements
Catalog

Suppose the hash table class is used in a routine, store_names, that formats and stores names and phone numbers. store_names must be tested to see if it uses the hash table correctly. The relevant test requirements could be found as in Part 1. Chapter 3, Section 3.10, tells how to find integration test requirements for hash table member functions called by store_names. Since the hash table is a variable that store_names uses, the Collection and Container requirements from the catalogs in the appendices also apply.

However, the hash table will surely be used in other routines. It may even be reused in other subsystems. It makes no sense to rederive these integration requirements every time new code uses a hash table. Instead, they should be listed once and for all in a *class requirements catalog* (often simply called "class catalog"). Testing any user of the class then involves less work: simply copying the class requirements from the class catalog to the routine's test requirement checklist.

When reuse is organized around classes, the class catalog is the reuse-specific catalog called for in the previous chapter. It's a bit more, as well. Since the class's own member functions use the class (call other member functions), the class requirements catalog is also used when testing them.

CHAP. 21 TESTING OBJECT-BASED SOFTWARE

This section discusses the class catalog in detail. The next describes its use. These sections are summarized in appendix F. To avoid confusion between the custom class catalogs and the catalogs in the appendices, the latter will be called the "standard catalogs".

21.3.1 Organization

Here is a template for the class requirements catalog, followed by a description of its parts.

Object use requirements
    from the class as a data type
    from the class invariant
    data member 1 requirements
    data member 2 requirements...
    from error guessing

State machine requirements (if relevant)
    the states of the state machine
    transition requirements

Member function requirements
    member function 1
        integration requirements (for testing calling code)
            one effect of the function
            another effect of the function...
    member function 2
        integration requirements...
    member function 3...

❐ **Object use requirements**

These requirements are those that are useful no matter which member functions are called. They apply even if no member functions are called. For example, a C structure with no member functions could still have Object Use Requirements derived from its fields.

❐ **State machine requirements**

If the class has a state machine or statechart model, the requirements from that model can be stored in this section. They're especially useful for adding variety to tests.

❐ **Member function integration requirements**

These are requirements useful for testing callers of class member functions. They are derived in the same way as those in Chapter 3, section 3.10.[1]

The following steps describe how to produce a class requirements catalog.

---

1. The structure is somewhat odd. Each member function has a single subsection because this same template will be expanded for object-oriented testing.

21.3.2 Step 1: Object Use Requirements

The Class as a Data Type

If the class, thought of as a data type, matches any standard catalog entries, write down appropriate requirements. For example, many classes describe Collections or Containers. A hash table is one of them.

The Class Invariant

The invariant is an assumed precondition. If it contains at least one OR, the OR rule (or the tables in appendix E) will produce several test requirements. Each of them may represent a situation the using code fails to handle. The invariant might also be phrased as a consistency relationship, in which case Chapter 18 applies. Even if the invariant is not in either of these forms, try to think of distinct ways in which it might be true, and list those ways as test requirements.

Data Member Requirements

Each data member may have requirements of its own. For example, you might choose to list Count requirements for the sz field of the hash table. "Count is zero" is probably illegal (if not, why not?).

When copying requirements, retain any IN or OUT annotations. Because the vast majority of class requirements are IN/OUT, you can treat that as the default, and not bother with a specific annotation.

Mark whether the data members are supposed to be used only by the member functions, or whether they are externally visible. When testing external code, the test requirements for invisible (private) data members are irrelevant. Effects they have on code outside the class should be captured by test requirements for externally visible member functions. (Be sure to check that this is so.) In C, these markings will also help you notice cases where external code accesses data members it shouldn't.

Error Guessing

Also write down any other test requirements you can think of that might reveal likely misuses of the class.

21.3.3 Step 2: State Machine Requirements

If the class can be (or has been) described as a state machine or statechart, write down the states as requirements. For example, a hash table has a natural statechart with three states: empty, partially full, and full. (Note that all of these are redundant with the Collection requirements.) If there is a single data member that contains the state, its requirements should be the same as the state requirements. Don't list the state requirements, but do make a note that names the data member. That way, whenever you would have used only the state requirements, you'll know to use that data member's requirements.

Separately list the transition requirements. Note that the state requirements are redundant with the transition requirements, but they're used for different purposes. (State requirements are used for testing member functions; transition requirements are used for testing under schedule pressure.)

21.3.4 Step 3: Member Function Integration Requirements

Precondition and Postcondition Effects

Find these requirements using the procedure described in Chapter 3, Section 3.10. Require each member function to execute each of its postconditions and violate each of its preconditions. In this step, you do not need to list the different ways each of these effects could happen. (There's no need to apply the AND or OR rules.) For `insert_hash_table`, the result of this step might look like this:

Member Function Use

   ...

     insert_hash_table
       element already present - error return[1]
       table is full - error return
       element is inserted

The Standard Catalogs and Error Guessing

Don't get stuck in the rut of listing only precondition and postcondition effects. If the member function matches (perhaps partially) a standard catalog entry, some requirements may be relevant to its callers. For example, suppose the function searches. The "no match found" catalog entry should be redundant with a precondition or postcondition. The "more than one match in the collection" probably is not but it's useful in cases where the caller might incorrectly ignore further matches. By adding it to the class catalog, it will be easier to notice. Also spend a few moments in error guessing. Are there ways of calling the member function that might provoke likely faults in the caller?

Do Effects Add More Data Member Requirements?

If the member function changes a data member, perhaps the change suggests a useful requirement. For example, if a member function sets an integer variable to a number in the range [5,15], that's a hint to treat the integer variable as an Interval.

Check against the State Machine Model

If there's a state machine model, the member function integration requirements probably force satisfaction of all the transition requirements. For example, `insert_hash_table` should have a precondition that the table is not full. To check it, a test would have to fill the table, thus exercising the Partially Full to Full transition. If the transition requirements aren't automatically satisfied, ask why not. The reason might be an omission in the specification or a mistake in the state machine model.

---

1. Note that the results of violated preconditions are not marked with ERROR. ERROR tags apply only to test requirement checklists, not catalogs. As discussed in Chapter 13, Section 13.1.3, the ERROR tag is appropriate only if it would prevent other requirements from having an effect. Without knowing what code is using `insert_hash_table`, it's impossible to know if that would happen.

21.3.5 Step 4: Collections of Objects

Often, classes are designed to be used together. Each class describes part of an ensemble of objects that forms a working whole. Each class will have its own catalog. There may also be invariants or consistency relationships that apply to the entire collection. Consider whether they add new requirements to each class's object use requirements.

21.4 Using the Class Requirements Catalog

An external routine that uses an object is tested almost like any other routine: Its test requirement checklist is created, filled with requirements from the specification and code, then used to produce test specifications. The only difference is that some of the requirements come from the used object's class requirements catalog.

❏ **member function integration requirements**

If a member function is called, copy its integration requirements into the checklist. You will often find that some of those requirements are impossible, in which case you shouldn't copy them.

❏ **object use requirements**

Copy at least some of the object use requirements. Certainly you should copy those from data members that are used in the external routine. Also think hard about whether any other public data members should perhaps have an effect. If you're suspicious, add their test requirements rather than relying on variety to produce a test that satisfies them by chance.

❏ **state machine states**

The state machine states represent meaningful combinations of data member values. List them as requirements, provided (1) they're not redundant with other requirements and (2) they either have an effect or plausibly should have an effect.

These sources of test requirements test the integration of the external routine with the object. Other sources of test requirements (the specification, common operations, and so on) test whether the rest of the routine works.

Member functions of the class itself are treated almost the same as external routines. The only difference is that member functions don't ignore test requirements of private data members.

As always, schedule pressure limits the amount of testing you can do. The guidelines of Chapter 15 apply to testing external routines that use objects. However, they do not apply well to testing classes themselves. Classes are usually tightly integrated, so there should be a shift of focus toward integration test requirements. The following is an ordered list of sources of test requirements. The most important ones come first. The particulars of individual classes may cause you to rank sources differently.

21.5 Schedule Pressure

☐ **State machine transition requirements**

These require you to exercise the most important member functions in ways that are meaningful from an external viewpoint. In many cases, of course, classes won't come with state machine models. For more complicated classes, the effort of building models is probably worthwhile. It's essentially a systematic inspection process that's good at finding faults.

☐ **The effects of each member function**

Forcing each member function to produce each of its possible effects will catch gross errors in its implementation. You might skip error effects if time is very short.

☐ **Object use requirements applied to each member function**

These requirements force each member function to be called in a variety of situations (with different values of data members and so forth). These requirements target faults of omissions where the programmer failed to anticipate some special case value of the object.

☐ **Integration requirements for called member functions**

When member functions are small, many faults are likely to be integration faults. Also, calling another member function tests both the caller and the called function. This category includes calls to member functions of another class if that class is being tested alongside this one.

☐ **Specification requirements**

This includes applying the AND rule and OR rule. It also includes requirements from operations and variables found in the specification.

☐ **Internal requirements**

These include requirements from inline operations, internal variables, and calls to routines that have already been tested.

Schedule pressure usually leads to testing many classes together as part of a single larger subsystem. Testing a class in isolation is not an option. You also may not be able to add test support code to the class. If so, a good tactic is to run the tests once under a debugger and manually check what the support code would have. Expected results visible at the subsystem interface should still be checked by an automated subsystem driver, not by hand.

22

Object-Oriented
Software 1:
Inheritance

Before reading this chapter, you should know object-oriented programming, and you should have a basic reading knowledge of C++. You must
also have read the previous chapter. The next chapter is devoted to a
detailed example of testing derived classes; you may find it helpful.

For simplicity, first assume you begin with a single class. That class
has a class requirements catalog, as described in the previous chapter. A
new class is created, derived from the old one. What happens?

1. The new class gets its own class requirements catalog, created by
   modifying the old class's. Some test requirements are inherited; others are added.
2. Member functions in the derived class get test requirement checklists. Not all member functions will need test requirements. Certainly any newly written code will. But some old, unchanged
   member functions will as well.
3. New test specifications are created. These must satisfy only the new
   test requirements, which you hope adequately capture all the ways
   in which the new class differs from the old. Some old test requirements might also be satisfied as a source of variety, but only if it can
   be done easily. Often, old tests can be applied to the new class.

After this flurry of activity, you have two classes. Each has a class
requirements catalog. When testing code that uses the new class, you use
only its class requirements catalog. Inheritance is no longer an issue. It
doesn't matter how the class was created: from scratch or through inheritance.

In short, the inheritance structure of object-oriented subsystems
leads to an inheritance structure in test design documents. Figure 22-1
shows the parallels.

Inheritance encourages change and reuse by structuring code into parts—data members and member functions—that can easily be replaced. Genericity (implemented in C++ by templates) has the same goal but uses a different replaceable part, namely, type names. This chapter also discusses testing generic classes.

An Example

Suppose you have a class `refrigerator`:

```
class refrigerator
{
public:
    void set_desired_temperature(int temp);
    int get_temperature();
    void calibrate();
private:
    int temperature;
};
```

`set_desired_temperature` allows the temperature to be between 5°C and 20°C centigrade. `calibrate` puts the actual refrigerator through various cooling cycles and uses sensor readings to calibrate the cooling unit.

A new, more capable model of the refrigerator is then created. It can cool to -5°C degrees centigrade. The `better_refrigerator` class is derived from `refrigerator`. `set_desired_temperature` is replaced with a version that accepts the lower `temperature`. `calibrate` is unchanged. Clearly,

`better_refrigerator::set_desired_temperature`

needs to be tested since it's new code. *Question*: does

`better_refrigerator::calibrate`

also need to be tested? Or can we assume it works, since the exact same code worked when invoked as `refrigerator::calibrate`?

Fig. 22–1

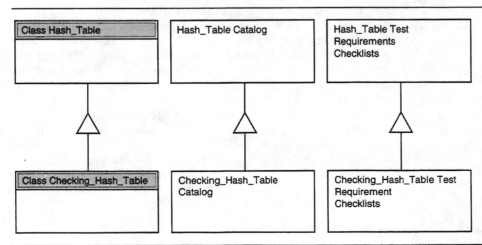

Unfortunately, no. Suppose that `calibrate` works, in part, by dividing sensor readings by `temperature`. What if `temperature` is zero? That's possible in a `better_refrigerator`, where it will cause a divide-by-zero failure that cannot happen in a `refrigerator`.

A Second Example
Suppose now that this code exists external to the class:

```
handle_refrigerator(refrigerator &ref)
{
        extern record Global_array[212];
        int index = ref.get_temperature();
        if (Global_array[index].count > 0) ...

          ...

}
```

This code uses the temperature as an index into an array. Though odd, that's at least legal for an object of class `refrigerator` because the temperature must be in the range [5,20]. However, `ref` is a C++ reference, and it may also refer to an object of the new derived class `better_refrigerator`. If so, the temperature may be in the range [-5,20], which allows an invalid array access.

Because you cannot tell what `ref` refers to until run time, it is said to be *dynamically bound*. The ways in which dynamic binding affects testing are the topic of the Chapter 24.

Disclaimer

Be suspicious of any testing advice that hasn't been extensively validated against real systems. The advice in these chapters hasn't been. Balance it against your own experience and advice from other sources. Let me know what you find out: The testing of object-oriented systems is still in its infancy, and we all have a lot to learn, especially about balancing cost and effectiveness.

Other Sources

The major issue of this chapter, reuse of testing information, was first described in [Perry90]. Most later discussions refer to this paper. See [Berard93] for a good recapitulation of the paper (which may be hard to find). The issue is central to [Harrold92b], [Hoffman93], and [Murphy92]. It is also touched on by many of the remaining papers. My approach is closest to [Harrold92b], but the particulars of subsystem testing (most notably, the strong distinction between test requirements and test specifications) cause major differences.

For experience reports, see [Fiedler89] and [Wilke93].

Other sources that describe object-oriented testing (usually also including object-based testing) are [Cox88], [Cox91], [Fiedler89], [Firesmith92], [Jacobson92], [Turner92], [Smith92], and [Siegel93].

[Binder94] is a good survey of the literature. Doug Shaker maintains a bibliography which periodically appears in the USENET newsgroup comp.object.

Terminology

This chapter mostly uses standard C++ terms, taken from [Ellis90]. A *member* is either a data member or member function. A *derived class* inherits from a *base class*. An immediate ancestor of a base class is called a *direct base*; otherwise, it's an *indirect base*. The *class lattice* shows the inheritance relationships of a set of classes.

When a derived class contains a member function that matches a function in the base class, the one in the derived class is called the *overriding member function*.[1] A *new member* is a data member or member function that is defined in a derived class and does not match any member in the base class. A member that is either new or overriding is called a *changed member*. If a derived class does not override a member, that member is available in the derived class, where it is called an *inherited member*.

As with the rest of the book, the real heart of this chapter is the careful creation of test requirement checklists. Consider these two classes:

22.1
Test Specification and Implementation

```
class A
{
public:
    virtual void member1();
    virtual void member2();
protected:
    Count count1;
    Count count2;
};

class B : public A
{
public:
    void member1();
    void member3();
protected:
    Count count3;
};
```

To test B you will create three test requirement checklists, one for each of member1, member2, and member3. Because member1 and member3 are new code, their checklists must be complete—they will contain all the requirements you'd expect after reading Part 1. Because member2 is unchanged code, its new checklist will contain only requirements that test interactions with member1 and member3. (Although member2 cannot call member3, it can interact with it if they share a data member.) In the happiest of worlds, member2 will be completely unaffected by any new behavior of the changed members. In that case, its new checklist will have no test requirements.

---

1. In C++, a match requires that the functions have the same name and argument list and that the function in the base class be declared virtual. Other languages define matches differently. Because this discussion is about inheritance, assume that all member functions are declared virtual.

Once the test requirements have been created, they can be satisfied in the usual way. Because the new checklists contain only requirements for new code and inherited code affected by the change, this might require much less work than testing B from scratch.

Because test requirements can never be perfect—you'll always miss something—tests should contain the usual amounts of complexity and variety. The test requirement checklists for class A are one good source of variety.

If A was tested in isolation, it is often easy to rerun A's tests against B. Rerunning existing tests on the new class is useful in two ways:

1. They may satisfy some of the new test requirements, saving you work writing test specifications.
2. They can be a cheap way to exercise class B more thoroughly, helping you stumble over faults you didn't think to write test requirements for.

To rerun tests, you must arrange to use the correct objects, and you must change the tests to correspond to the difference between the classes. With well-designed inheritance, this difference may be only additional expected results. In poorly designed inheritance, the difference may be so large that the tests would require too much rewriting.

When a base class was not tested in isolation, reusing its tests is harder. That strengthens the argument for small subsystems in object-oriented testing. However, small subsystems are not essential because reusing existing tests isn't. For example, in many cases A was created without any expectation that it would later be used for inheritance, so it was tested as part of a larger subsystem. B was created, not because of a grand scheme of reuse, but because someone working on another subsystem found that A didn't quite do what was required. Neither of the two benefits of rerunning A's tests would justify the expense of making them reusable. (They might not have justified it even had the reuse been anticipated.) B will still be adequately tested as long as its new test requirements are satisfied by tests with complexity and variety. Testing B as part of its subsystem is a good way to achieve that.

22.2 Types of Derivation

Object-oriented programming allows reuse of code and of specification. Testing must take both into account. Naming the different types of class derivation makes the discussion clearer. The types of changes considered here are more general than those recommended in writings on object-oriented design. See [Meyer88] for a good exposition. The differences are because the tasks are different: producing good designs versus testing what you've been given. Well-designed derivation makes testing much easier.

The example classes in this section will be used throughout the chapter.

CHAP. 22 OBJECT-ORIENTED SOFTWARE 1: INHERITANCE

Pure Addition

A derived class may add a member function or data member to the direct base class. Suppose this is the base class:

```
class simple
{
public:
    int simple_int;
    virtual void simple_function(int);
};
```

This derived class contains two pure additions:

```
class additions : public simple
{
public:
    int additions_int;
    virtual void additions_function(int);
};
```

Implementation-Only Change

Every member function has a specification (though perhaps not written down). The derived class may override a base class member function with one that ostensibly satisfies the same specification. The job of testing is to show that it doesn't. Here is an example of an implementation-only change:

```
class base
{
public:
    int data;
    virtual int f(int);
};

/* base::f(int i)
 * PRECONDITIONS:
 * 1.      Assumed: I is even.
 * 2.      Validated: I >= 0
 *            On failure:  return value is BADVAL
 * POSTCONDITIONS
 * 1.      DATA is set to twice the value of I.
 * 2.      The return value is the original value of DATA.
 */
int
base::f(int i)
{
    int retval = data;
    if (i < 0) return BADVAL;
    data = 2 * i;
    return retval;
}
```

```
class reimplemented_base : public base
{
public:
    virtual int f(int);
};

/* Same specification as base */
/* Note the two bugs. */
/* bad error check and wrong return value*/

int
reimplemented_base::f(int i)
{
    if (i <= 0) return BADVAL;
    data = i + i;              /* Different implementation. */
    return data;
}
```

Change in Defining Term

Recall that a defining term is the trigger for both preconditions and postconditions. It describes the domain of inputs to which the condition applies. This overriding member function makes several changes to defining terms:

```
/* derived::f(int i)
 * PRECONDITIONS:
 * Assumed precondition deleted.
 * 1.     Validated:  I > 0 && I <= MAXINT/2
 *            On failure:  return value is BADVAL
 * POSTCONDITIONS:
 * 1.     IF I > DATA
 *            THEN DATA is set to twice the value of I.
 * 2.     The return value is the original value of DATA.
 */
```

1. The effect "return value is BADVAL" originally applied to all inputs I<0. It now applies to a different domain: all inputs I<=0 (note that there's an extra input in this region) and all inputs I>MAXINT/2.
2. The assumed precondition has been dropped. Its domain has changed from half the integers to a region containing nothing. This represents an expansion of the domains of all the postconditions, which now apply to twice as many inputs.
3. The effect "DATA is set to twice the value of I" originally applied to all inputs that satisfied the precondition. It now applies to only those where I>DATA.

New Effect

A overriding member function may produce different effects. Here is a new version of f that illustrates some of these. Note that it overrides derived: :, not base: : f.

```
/* even_more_derived::f(int i)
* PRECONDITIONS:
* 1.      Validated: I > 0 && I <= MAXINT/2
*         On failure: return value is RANGEVAL.
* POSTCONDITIONS:
* 1.      IF I > DATA
*         THEN DATA is set to I + 2.
* 2.      The return value is the original value of DATA.
* 3.      An INCREASE message is sent to the global LOGGER object.
*/
```

1. Precondition 1 has a new effect: it returns RANGEVAL instead of BADVAL.
2. Postcondition 1 sets data to I+2 not 2*I. Note that it produces the same DATA value when I is 2. Even though that one particular input produces the same value for the two classes, the overall effect is nevertheless different.
3. There is a new effect that applies whenever the preconditions are satisfied: An INCREASE message is sent.

Be sure to consider the sudden lack of effect as a new effect. There was an instance in pnderived::f. While base::f always sets DATA to twice I, derived::f sometimes does not. There's a new "lack of process-ing" effect that a caller might not anticipate. It's important to keep such missing effects in mind, because they're easy to overlook and potentially important.

22.3 The Derived Class Requirements Catalog

Because this discussion is long, you may find it easier to keep track of where you are if you refer to the summary in Appendix F. Refer to the glossary if you forget the definition of a term.

Just like any other class, a derived class requires a class require-ments catalog. It is used when testing both external routines and the class itself. Inheritance creates the need for a new section of member function requirements, the *domain shift requirements*:

> Object use requirements
> State machine requirements
> Member function requirements
>   member function 1 (overriding)
>   integration requirements
>   **domain shift requirements**
>   member function 2 (inherited)
>   integration requirements
>   **domain shift requirements**
>   member function 3 (new)...

The integration requirements will contain all effects, including those new to the derived class. The domain shift requirements describe inputs that cause a different effect in the derived class than in the base class. That is, they capture changes in defining terms. Both new and shifted effects can cause failures in calling code.

22.3.1 Copying the Base Class Requirements Catalog

The first step in testing a derived class is to make a copy of the base class requirements catalog. This copy contains all the requirements that apply to the new class, leaving out only the requirements you know will have to be rethought.[1]

The Member Functions

For each inherited member function, copy the integration requirements but not the domain shift requirements. Give each changed (overriding or new) member function a blank entry (no requirements). You'll find it convenient to note whether a member function is overriding, new, or inherited.

For example, suppose again that you were given these two classes:

```
class A
{
public:
    virtual void member1();
    virtual void member2();
protected:
    Count count1;
    Count count2;
};
```

```
class B : public A
{
public:
    void member1();
    void member3();
protected:
    Count count3;
};
```

B's class catalog would be initialized as follows. `member1` would have a blank entry; its requirements would not be copied. `member2`'s integration requirements would be copied, but not any domain shift requirements. `member3` would have a blank entry since it's a new member function.

Data Member Requirements

Copy all the object use requirements to the derived catalog. Leave out data members that are invisible to member functions in the derived class.[2]

---

1. Another alternative would be to "inherit" test requirements. When using the catalog, though, you want all the information in one place. You don't want to search up inheritance hierarchies. This, however, does mean that a later modification to a base class can "ripple down" to all classes derived from it. That's not necessarily bad—it forces you to consider the change in the context of its effects on each derived class.

If the derived class contains new data members, create clues for them but don't add any test requirements yet. Tag the data members as new.

The previous example's class catalog would be updated as follows:

object use requirements
- **count1 requirements**   **// these are copied**
-     0   **IN/OUT**
-     1   **IN...**
- **count2 requirements**   **// these are copied**
-     0   **IN/OUT**
-     1   **IN...**
- **count 3 requirements (new)**

state machine requirements
member function requirements
    member1 (overriding) ...

The Other Object Use Requirements and State Machine Requirements

Even if the invariant or state machine model has changed, simply copy their requirements into the derived catalog. You'll continue to use variants of them later. Do the same for the other object use requirements.

22.3.2 Handling New Members

The derived class may contain new data members or member functions. These are easy to handle.

New Data Members

A new data member is treated the same as any other variable. You get test requirements from its type, such as Count, Interval, Collection, and so forth.

In the example of class B inheriting from class A, this step would produce the following change to the catalog:

object use requirements
    count1 requirements...
    count2 requirements...
    count3 requirements (new)
-     0   **IN/OUT**
-     1   **IN**
-     >1   **IN/OUT...**

state machine requirements
member function requirements
    member1 (overriding)...

---

2. In C++, base class data members can be invisible to a derived class if they were private, not protected. They may also be invisible in the derived class if it declares a new member with the same name—unless a scope operator is used, as with `base::x`. Overriding a variable name is bound to cause confusion about which one is called in inherited member functions, so have clues for both variables in the checklist (with appropriate scope names). That will force you to think about which one is meant and which one should be meant.

New Member Functions

Add a new member function's integration requirements in the usual way. (See Chapter 3, Section 3.10.)

If a new member function changes the possible values a data member could have, consider whether that change requires new test requirements. If so, add them to the object use requirements. Tag them with "NEW". In the example that opened the chapter, `better_refrigerator::set_desired_temperature` changes the `temperature` data member from an Interval [5,20] to an Interval [-5,20]. That adds a new test requirement, -5. (It could also add -6, but that's impossible to satisfy if `set_desired_temperature` rejects illegal values, is correct, and is the only way to set the temperature.) The old test requirement of `temperature=5` can be removed. I would tend to keep it as a DEFER requirement on the general principle that old special cases are often useful even for changed code, though that's unlikely in this instance.

Object Use Requirements
   temperature
     20
      5   **DEFER (from `refrigerator` class)**
•   -5   **NEW**

22.3.3 Handling Overriding Member Functions

An overriding member function produces test requirements in several ways.

Normal Integration Requirements

First create integration test requirements in the usual way. (If the overriding member function has the same specification as the one it overrides, the base class's integration requirements can be copied.) If an effect can sometimes occur and sometimes not occur, be sure to list both possibilities as integration requirements. When adding integration requirements, mark them as NEW if they are not redundant with requirements in the base class.

For `derived::f`, the two effects are

integration requirements
   DATA is set to twice the value of I
   DATA is left unchanged   **NEW**

New Requirements for Data Members

If the overriding member function changes the possible values a data member could have, handle it as with a new member function.

Changes in Defining Terms (Domain Shifts)

Next consider dropped preconditions, dropped postconditions, and changes in defining terms. These describe how an overriding member function produces the same effects as the base class's member function, but for different inputs. An effect may take place for a larger or smaller domain. In either case, the difference can be described by test require-

ments. These test requirements should be added as domain shift requirements. They will be used to test inherited member functions and (in Chapter 24) virtual function calls. Here are some examples:

1. `base::f` had an assumed precondition that `I` is even, which `derived::f` dropped. Effects now happen for odd numbers, when they couldn't before. "`I` is odd" can be added as a domain shift requirement.
2. `base::f` had a precondition that applied to `I>=0`. `derived::f` changed it to `I>0 && I<=MAXINT/2`. `I=0 OR I>MAXINT/2` describes the changed domain. Because they're widely separated regions (and because `I=0` is such a suspicious change), two requirements should be added to the inheritance section: `I=0` and `I>MAXINT/2`.
3. In `base::f`, Postcondition 1 applied everywhere, but it only applies when `I>DATA` in `derived::f`. However, this change created the new effect "`DATA` is left unchanged". Any test satisfying that requirement will also exercise the domain shift, so a domain shift requirement would be redundant. In general, the addition of a defining term to a postcondition that didn't have one always creates a new effect and its associated integration test requirement, so another test requirement isn't needed.

Here are the domain shift requirements for `derived::f`. The integration requirements are also shown.

Class Requirements Catalog for DERIVED

f requirements (overriding)
    integration requirements
        return value is BADVAL (violated precondition)
        DATA is set to twice the value of I
        DATA is left unchanged.   **NEW**
    domain shift requirements
-     **I is odd**
-     **I is 0**
-     **I>MAXINT/2**

➥*Note: The domain shift requirements don't have to be tagged with "NEW" since they are always new.*

22.3.4 Handling Inherited Member Functions

Suppose there's a function `base::call_f` implemented as

```
call_f(int i)
{
  int retval = f(i);
  if (retval == BADVAL)
    return retval;
  // other code.
}
```

`call_f` is not overridden in `derived`. Nevertheless, its specification changes. `base::f` did not return BADVAL for I=MAXINT, but `derived::f` does. `derived::call_f` "inherits" this behavior. Its specification changes, even though its code does not. Whereas before it had this partial specification:

```
/* base::call_f(int i)
 *
 * PRECONDITIONS:
 * 1. Validated:  I>=0
 *           On failure: return value is BADVAL
 */
```

now it has this one:

```
/* derived::call_f(int i)
 *
 * PRECONDITIONS:
 * 1. Validated:  I>0&&I<=MAXINT/2
 *    On failure: return value is BADVAL
 */
```

This specification change must be reflected in the `derived` class catalog. Since the change is to a defining term, it is captured by adding domain shift requirements to `call_f`'s catalog entry:

derived::call_f requirements (inherited)
  integration requirements (copied from base)
    return value is BADVAL (violated precondition)
    other inherited requirements
  domain shift requirements
- **I is 0**
- **I>MAXINT/2**

Had the change been a new effect, it would have been added to the integration requirements.

In short, an inherited member function can be affected through its calls to overriding member functions. The changes to their specifications may propagate to its specification. If so, its catalog must be updated—just as if it were overriding, not inherited. Of course, its callers may now be affected in turn. These callers may be inherited, overriding, or even new. You must propagate change throughout all callers. In a well-designed derived class, the propagation will quickly die out (will no longer have an affect on the caller's specification).

It's important to trace this propagation, as it's likely to lead you to faults. Suppose `call_f` is also inherited by `even_more_derived`. It now calls `even_more_derived::f`, not `derived::f`. As a result, it must expect a RANGEVAL return value where `derived::call_f` got an BADVAL. If you look at the `call_f` source code, you'll see that it apparently does not expect RANGEVAL. Most likely, it will incorrectly treat RANGEVAL like any other non-error return value.

Notes:

1. If you do discover a specification change, document it. You want programmers who use `derived::call_f` to understand its true behavior.
2. The effects of a change can propagate to any type of function. For example, a change to an overriding function's specification can affect another overriding member function that calls it. However, the most dangerous situation is when one of the two functions is unchanged. Examine all types of propagation if you think it worthwhile, but be sure to examine the two most important types. The first is when an unchanged (inherited) function calls a function whose specification or code has changed. The second is when any function calls a function whose code is unchanged but whose specification is different.
3. In the real world, you're working with specifications you've created from the code, under time pressure, so you'll miss things. What then? The answer is, as it has been in the past, variety, complexity, and testing larger bodies of code.

22.3.5 Updating the Remaining Object Use Requirements

The derived class may have a new invariant. If so, the invariant requirements may need to be updated, typically to add new ones. Be especially suspicious of invariant requirements that are now impossible. That might be a sign of a design mistake. Retain invariant requirements that are possible but wouldn't be gotten from the new invariant—they may still represent fault-prone special cases.

Do the same with other object use requirements—throw out impossible ones, retain "useless" ones, add new ones if needed, and be suspicious of changes that might suggest design mistakes.

Tag new requirements with "NEW".

22.3.6 Updating the State Machine Requirements

New data members may mean more states in the state machine model. New member functions may mean new events, and changed member functions may mean changed or new transitions. Update the State Machine Requirements section of the class requirements catalog. Tag new requirements with "NEW".

A new state machine model may also have fewer states or transitions than the old one. Remove the related requirements, but be suspicious.

22.3.7 Multiple Inheritance

Multiple inheritance causes no major changes in this process. When first creating the derived class's catalog, copy entries from each of the base classes. Thereafter, treat new and overriding members just as in single inheritance.[1]

---

1. Languages like CLOS allow overriding functions to be synthesized from more than one base class, rather than selected from among them. This synthesized function could be written as an overriding member function that calls the base member functions in a particular pattern. It should be tested the same way.

Any member function—new, overriding, or inherited—may gain test requirements and thus need new tests.

22.4.1 New Member Functions

A new member function is completely new code and should be tested in the same way as member functions in the previous chapter. (That is, use the techniques taught in Part 1. When the member function uses other members, look to the class catalog. Ignore domain shift requirements. They target inherited functions that the domain shift might "take by surprise," since the code might have been written with a different domain in mind.)

22.4.2 Overriding Member Functions

An overriding member function is treated like a new member function, but with two additional sources of test requirements. Get test requirements from the normal sources first.

The Function's Own Domain Shift Requirements

Consider this member function's own catalog entry, and ask if its domain shift requirements would be useful. They describe how this member function produces the same effects as the base class's, but for different inputs. The reasons behind the original defining terms might not have been well understood by the person overriding them.

For example, one of derived::f's domain shift requirements is "I is odd". That won't be in derived::f's checklist because it represents a dropped assumed precondition—there's nothing in the specification or (we assume) the code to focus attention on odd numbers. Yet odd numbers must have been ruled out in base::f for *some* reason, and it will be interesting to see if that reason still applies in derived::f. The other two domain shift requirements (I=0 and I>MAXINT/2) will be redundant with requirements gotten from normal handling of the specification.

The Overridden Function's Test Requirement Checklist

You now have a checklist for the overriding member function. The function it overrides also has a checklist. Compare the two. (That is, if you're testing derived::f, compare its checklist to base::f's.) If the "overridden checklist" has a requirement not redundant with any in the new checklist, ask if it's relevant. Suppose a base::f requirement tested handling of a special case. Is derived::f really immune to that special case? Or was it just overlooked?

22.4.3 Inherited Member Functions

An inherited member function has unchanged code. Since it has already been tested in the base class, retesting is used only to detect faults caused by interactions with changed members. Do not create test requirements from the normal sources (the specification, clichés in the code, and so on). Use only two sources.

NEW Requirements in Calls to Member Functions

When the inherited member function calls another member function, copy that function's new integration test requirements into the checklist. Also copy the domain shift requirements (which are by definition new). The new requirements capture all the ways in which the called member function in the derived class differs from its version in the base class. (At least you've done the best you can to ensure they do.)

Here is an example. `call_f` is a function that calls f. In `base`, it had this checklist:

base::call_f checklist

call to F
      return value is BADVAL (violated precondition)
      Normal return (DATA is twice I, etc.)

other requirements

The checklist in `derived` contains only new requirements for the call to `derived::f`:

derived::call_f checklist

call to F
      DATA is left unchanged
      I is 0
      I>MAXINT/2
      I is odd

Requirements like "normal return (DATA is twice I)" do not need to be retested in the derived class. The code has already been tested to see if it can handle such an effect. Retesting concentrates on seeing if it can handle new effects and old effects in new circumstances.

Other NEW Requirements

The other NEW requirements in other parts of the class catalog capture less direct interactions between changed and inherited code. Examine the rest of the class catalog and copy any relevant NEW requirements into the inherited member function's checklist. New data member requirements are most important.

22.5 Test Requirement Checklists for Changed External Routines

Some external code was probably changed to take advantage of the new derived class. The simplest change would have been to make the declaration of `my_var`, below, use `derived` instead of `base`.

```
external_call_f(int i)
{
    base my_var;

    // some code
    int retval = my_var.f(i);
    if (retval == BADVAL)
        return retval;
    // other code.
}
```

This changed version of `external_call_f` needs exactly the same new test requirements as the inherited member function `call_f`. That is, it needs to be exercised with test requirements that describe the different behaviors of `base::f` and `derived::f`.

A more complicated change would combine the use of a `derived` variable with other changes to `external_call_f`'s code. The test requirement checklist for that change would combine the NEW class catalog requirements with requirements targeting the changed code (as described in Chapter 15).

Dynamic binding allows new classes to affect external routines that haven't been changed at all. See Chapter 24.

22.6 Genericity (Templates)

Genericity allows classes to be parameterized by a type. For example, a Set generic class could describe a common interface and implementation for sets of integers, sets of strings, sets of output devices, and so on. For testing, the important question is whether a set of files will contain bugs that a set of integers does not. To see how a change of this type can cause problems consider this example, written in C++ notation:

```
template <class Type>
class Special
{
public:
    Type value;
    void bigsubtract() { value -= 1000000; }
};
```

Suppose that the `bigsubtract` specification says

Preconditions: None
Postconditions:
1. VALUE is set to value - 1000000.

This template class can be *instantiated* with any type that supports the -= operator. Here's an instantiation and use of the integer type:

```
Special<int> var;
var.value = 10;
var.bigsubtract();
cout << var.value << endl;
```

The output would be -999990. Instantiating the template with the unsigned integer type would require only this changed declaration:

```
Special<unsigned int> var;
```

However, executing the call to `bigsubtract` would produce (on my machine) 4293967306, which violates the specification.

Template bugs occur when the type used to instantiate the template causes it to behave differently than the programmer expected. One way to avoid the problem is to be clear about behavior—to write good specifications. That might have been enough to prevent the unsigned integer bug—when reading the specification, did you say, "Wait a minute—this won't work for unsigned integers?" However, when prevention isn't reliable enough, we test. An instantiation with unsigned integer causes `value` to be a data member in the Interval [0, maximum integer], which would lead to two test requirements: zero, and the maximum possible integer. Testing with zero would discover the fault (mostly likely when trying to decide on the expected result).

`bigsubtract` isn't right for integers, either, since it will give the wrong answer for the most negative integer. That value would be used in a test if you realized that `value` was a data member in the Interval [most negative integer, most positive integer]. Note that the test to find that problem is different than the test to find the unsigned integer problem.

Given that discussion, here is a procedure for testing a template class. It assumes that template classes are supposed to fulfill the same specification, no matter what type is used to instantiate them. The purpose of testing is to discover when that's not true. The same procedure can be adapted to test specifications that are type-dependent.

1. The template class catalog captures what is common to all instantiations. Individual instantiations will create instantiated class catalogs. They usually differ only in small ways from the template catalog.
2. Because the template class's member functions contain code, their test requirement checklists can be written. The requirements may not be complete, since some may still be created from the particular instantiating types. But they're usually nearly complete.
3. When the template class is instantiated, it can be tested. Requirements due to the instantiating type are added to the template requirement checklists and then turned into test specifications in the normal way.
4. Thereafter, a new instantiation of the template class would have to be tested with only requirements derived from the new instantiating type. In this way, testing of another instantiation is similar to the testing of a derived class.

Creating the Template Class Catalog

The template class catalog is created in the normal way. Some of the data members will be generic. For example, in the `Special<Type>` class, the object use section would look like this:

Special<Type> Class Catalog

Object Use Requirements
    value, a <Type>   INSTANTIATE

The INSTANTIATE tag is to make sure the line is reexamined when the template class is instantiated.

A `Set<Type>` class would probably have a generic data member like this:

Set<Type> Class Catalog

Object Use Requirements
         elements, a collection of <Types>   INSTANTIATE
           empty
           one element
           full

Notice that there are some test requirements already; they apply no matter what `Type` instantiates `Set<Type>`. Other requirements may come later.

A template class that provides an interface to objects that behave like files (are opened, read, written, and closed) might have a data member like this:

File_Wrapper<File> Class Catalog

Object Use Requirements
        true_file, an underlying File   INSTANTIATE

Creating Template Test Requirement Checklists

There is code for all the member functions, so their test requirement checklists can be created. They will be incomplete if the functions manipulate any generic variables. `Special<Type>::bigsubtract` can get requirements from its specification but none from the generic `value` it operates on. A member function in `Set<Type>` can use "empty", "one element", and "full" as test requirements, though that may not be the final list of `elements` requirements. `File_Wrapper<File>` probably has some code that looks like this:

```
template <class File>
void File_Wrapper<File>::manipulate()
{
  int fid = true_file.open();
  if (fid < 0) ...
    ...
}
```

In addition to data member requirements for `true_file`, there will also be integration requirements for the instantiating class's `open` member function. Quite likely, some of these integration requirements are common to all file opens, so they can be written down.

        true_file, the underlying file   INSTANTIATE

        true_file.open(),   INSTANTIATE
           open fails
           open succeeds

Others may be added later, when `true_file`'s class is known.

Instantiating the Template Class Catalog

When a template class is instantiated, the template class catalog can be instantiated along with it.

Wherever the generic type has been used in the template class catalog, zero or more requirements can be added to the clues marked INSTANTIATE. In the case of Special<unsigned int>, the instantiated Object Use requirements would be:

Special<Type> **Class Catalog**

instantiated with unsigned int,
an Interval [0, maximum possible integer]

object use requirements
    value, **an unsigned int**
-    0
-    **maximum possible integer**

Not all requirements will be appropriate. For example, the Set<Type> class may only manipulate pointers. Since it never dereferences the pointers, the requirements of the objects they point to are irrelevant. They shouldn't be put in the instantiated catalog. In that case, the Set<int> and Set<Output_device> class catalogs would have identical requirements.

Check whether the instantiating type causes a change in other object use requirements or the state machine requirements. That's very likely a bug. (The member function integration requirements are checked below.)

Instantiating the Template Test Requirement Checklists

Now that the instantiating type is known, the test requirement checklists can be completed. Update all the clues marked INSTANTIATE. In the case of File_Wrapper<File>::manipulate, the requirements for true_file can be copied from the instantiated class catalog, and the two existing requirements for true_file.open can be augmented by taking member function integration requirements from whatever class true_file is. (They might also be reduced. Perhaps open can never fail for the instantiating class, in which case the "open fails" requirement cannot be satisfied.)

When updating the test requirements checklist, check if satisfying a new requirement will cause the member function to violate its specification.

Testing the Instantiated Class

Testing the first instance of a template class is no different from testing any other class, except that you have to use an instantiating type. If possible, isolate the type-specific parts of the test, such as the initial creation of objects and the checking of expected results.

Testing a later instantiation requires testing only the new requirements from the instantiating type.

Since every instantiation should have the same specification, existing tests can often easily be converted to exercise the new class. Though not required, this may be worth doing. Reusing old tests can uncover oversights in your test design.

Testing External Code that Uses an Instantiated Class

Routines that use template members are tested in the usual way. Most often, the different instantiated class catalogs are identical as far as users are concerned: Member functions have unchanged specifications (and thus integration test requirements), and data members that depend on the instantiating type are invisible. If that's true, the template class catalog can be stored with the template class and used regardless of the instantiating type.

22.6.1 C++ Notes

C++ allows isolated template functions as well as template classes. One such function would be

```
template<class Type> void
sort(ordered_collection<Type> collection);
```

This function sorts ordered collections of a particular type. It would be used like this:

```
ordered_collection<int> int_collection;
// ...
sort(int_collection);
```

An isolated template function is tested like a template class member function. `sort` would have a template test requirement checklist containing requirements from its specification, its code, and the variables it uses. One of those variables is its argument. Part of `sort`'s template checklist would look like:

collection, an ordered collection of Type   INSTANTIATE
    zero elements
    one element
    full

These test requirements for `collection` would be gotten from the `ordered_collection<Type>` template class catalog. When `sort` was instantiated with a particular type, the instantiated `ordered_collection<Type>` catalog would be checked for more requirements to be used to instantiate `sort`'s template checklist. Most likely there wouldn't be any.

C++ also allows classes to be parameterized with constants. These are probably most often used for declaring sizes. A `Set` class might be declared and used as follows:

```
template <class Type, int size>
class Set
{
public:
    Type buffer[size];
};


main()
{
  Set<int,33> s;
}
```

For testing purposes, the `size` argument has little effect. It determines how big a full Set is.

23

An Example
of Testing
Derived Classes

This chapter contains an extended example of the procedures described in the previous chapter.

1. A class is created and tested. It's a special kind of class, called an *abstract class*, which exists only to serve as a base class. There are some testing implications.
2. A simple derived class is created. It's an example of the best kind of class: One that requires no retesting of inherited code.
3. Another simple class is derived. One of its overriding functions forces retesting of an inherited member that calls it.
4. The class is turned into a template class. The testing implications are shown.

Here's a hash table class:

abstract_hash_table class	Fig. 23-1

```
// This is a simple hash table class. Tokens are hashed on their
// names (which are strings).
// Invariant: No two entries in the hash table can have the same name.
// State Machine: none.

class abstract_hash_table
{
public:
    abstract_hash_table(unsigned int init_size);
    virtual bool insert(token &);
    // other member functions

protected:
    token *elements;                        // storage for elements.
    unsigned int sz;                        // size of hash table.
    virtual unsigned int hash(char * tag) = 0;     // where to look first.
    virtual unsigned int next_hash(char * tag, unsigned int current) = 0;
                                            // where to look next
    bool slot_in_use(unsigned int slot);
                            // tells when looking again is needed
    virtual unsigned int insertion_collision(token &tok,
                                unsigned int where);

};
```

For this example only one public member function will be defined. Here it is:

Fig. 23–2	**abstract_hash_table::insert**

```
// bool abstract_hash_table::insert(token &tok)
// Preconditions:
// 1. Assumed: TOK is not already in the hash table.
// 2. Validated: The hash table has room for a new element
//     On failure: FALSE is returned
//
// Postconditions:
// 1. TOK is inserted in the hash table. A later call to RETRIEVE with a string
//     equal to TOK.NAME will return a copy of TOK.
// 2. The return value is TRUE.
//
// Obligations:
// 1. TOK may be deleted after the call; a copy is stored in the hash table.

bool abstract_hash_table::insert (token &tok)
{
    unsigned int where = hash(tok.name);
    if (slot_in_use(where))
    {
        where = insertion_collision(tok, where);
        if (slot_in_use(where))
            return false;
    }
    elements[where] = tok;
    return true;
}
```

insert first uses hash to convert a token into a slot in the elements array. If that slot is in use, insertion_collision finds one that isn't. (If it can't, the hash table is full. insert tells its caller that by returning false.)

`insertion_collision` is separate from insert not because it's inherently a distinct operation, but to make the example more pertinent. Here is its definition:

| | abstract_hash_table::insert_collision | Fig. 23–3 |

```
// Preconditions:
// 1. Assumed: WHERE is in [0, SZ-1].
// 2. Assumed: WHERE contains a token.
//
// Postconditions:
// 1. IF the hash table is full
//      THEN the return value is an already-used slot (slot_in_use will be TRUE)
//      ELSE it's an empty slot.

unsigned int abstract_hash_table::insertion_collision(token &tok, unsigned int where)
{
    unsigned int starting_where = where;
    for (where = next_hash(tok.name, where);
        where != starting_where;
        where = next_hash(tok.name, where))
    {
        if (! slot_in_use(where))
        {
            return where;
        }
    }
    return starting_where;              // to indicate no empty slot was found.
}
```

`next_hash` tells where to look next. `next_hash` will return every possible index before it repeats the first one, so a repeat of the original where argument means the hash table is full.

The two functions `hash` and `next_hash` are so-called "pure virtual functions" (that's what the "= 0" in their class declaration means). (Fig. 23–1, p. 379) As such, they have no definitions. A class containing pure virtual functions is an *abstract class*. An abstract class exists only as a base for derived classes; it can never have objects itself. As we'll see, this has relatively little impact on testing.

When the functions are later defined, they must satisfy certain specifications, else `insert` and `insertion_collision` cannot work. These specifications are given below:

Fig.23–4	**hash and next_hash specifications**

unsigned int hash(char * tag)
Preconditions:
1.   Assumed: TAG is a null-terminated string.
Postconditions:
1.   A value in the range [0,SZ-1] is returned.
2.   The same string always yields the same return value.

unsigned int next_hash(char * tag, unsigned int current)

HASH is always called first. Then there are a series of calls to NEXT_HASH, each of which returns a different index in the hash table. When no more distinct indices are possible, HASH's original value is returned.

Preconditions:
1.   Assumed: TAG is the same string given to the last call to HASH.
2.   Assumed: CURRENT is the value of the last call to HASH or NEXT_HASH.
3.   Assumed: No more than SZ calls are made to NEXT_HASH.
Postconditions:
1.   A value in the range [0,SZ-1] is returned.
2.   SZ-1 calls with no intervening call to HASH will return SZ-1 distinct values.
3.   The SZ'th call returns the same value as HASH(TAG).

Note that some of these postconditions could be written in "IF..THEN" form such as "IF the call to NEXT_HASH is the SZ'th one, THEN the return value is the same as HASH(TAG)." I'm deliberately writing in this form because specifications often contain implicit defining terms; recognizing them is a part of testing.

23.1.1 Testing abstract_hash_table

Here is the class requirements catalog for `abstract_hash_table`. Only the member functions described above have entries.

Object Use Requirements
  Hash table as a collection of inserted elements
      empty
      one element
      more than one element
      full
  SZ field, a count (will be deleted; see Note 2.)
      1   IN
      >1
  elements, a pointer to the contents (a collection); (see Note 3.)

Member Function Requirements
  insert
      integration requirements
          returns false (no token added)
          returns true (token added)
      domain shift requirements

  insertion_collision
      integration requirements
          return value is an already-used slot
          return value is an empty slot
          return value is 0
          return value is SZ-1
      integration requirements

  hash
      integration requirements
          return value is 0
          return value is SZ-1
      domain shift requirements

  next_hash
      integration requirements
          return value is 0
          return value is SZ-1
          return value is the same as hash(tag) (This is the SZ'th call)
          return value is a new value (fewer than SZ calls since last call to hash.)
      domain shift requirements

Notes:

1. Because this catalog only includes the functions along one control
   flow path (starting at `insert`), there is a lot of apparent redundancy. For example, what is the point of having a requirement that
   `next_hash` return 0? Isn't that redundant with
   `insertion_collision`'s requirement? Whenever
   `insertion_collision` returned 0 it must have gotten it from

next_hash. Yes—in this catalog. But a complete catalog would contain other routines that call next_hash, and it wouldn't necessarily be redundant in those routines.

2. It's unlikely that anyone will ever use a single-element hash table, so that requirement can easily be dropped. (Of course, if anyone ever does, that case is one of the more likely to fail— simply because it's unexpected.)

3. The elements clue is a Collection, but has no Collection test requirements that aren't redundant with those of the hash table as a whole. It's also a pointer, so it might have a "null pointer" requirement. However, the class's constructor (not shown) always initializes elements, so that requirement would be impossible to satisfy.

Here is a set of test requirements for insert:

Fig. 23–6	**abstract_hash_table::insert checklist**
	Test requirement checklist for abstract_hash_table::insert

hash table as a collection of inserted elements (from class catalog)
    inserting into an empty table
    inserting into a one-element table
    inserting into a full table   ERROR
the hash table is an ordered collection (from standard catalogs)
    inserting into first slot (there's more than one) (see Note 4.)
    inserting into last slot (there's more than one)
call to insertion_collision (from class catalog) (see Note 3.)
    insertion_collision resolved (returns a slot not in use)
    returns 0   DEFER (see Note 5.)
    returns SZ-1   DEFER
call to hash (from class catalog)
    returns 0   DEFER
    returns SZ-1   DEFER

Notes:

1. Requirements from insert's validated precondition are redundant with the "inserting into a full table" object use requirement.

2. The class invariant naturally makes one think of trying to insert a token twice, but that violates an assumed precondition. (That is, the caller is responsible for maintaining the invariant.) (Fig. 23–2)

3. The class catalog requirement that insertion_collision return an already-used slot is redundant. That can only happen when the table is full. Therefore, it is omitted.

4. The requirements for inserting code into the first and last slots seem dubious. After all, how much can go wrong with

```
elements[where] = tok;
```

However, those slots have to be filled anyway, to produce a full hash table, so they don't cause any extra work.

5. The deferred requirements are different ways of causing insertion into the first and last slots. Given insert's code, there seems little value in requiring that the 0 come from both insert_collision and hash, but it doesn't hurt to cause both if it's easy.

All the undeferred test requirements could be satisfied in one test specification. However, it couldn't be implemented, since you can't create an object of an abstract class. Instead, abstract_hash_table will have to be tested via a "concrete" class that defines hash and next_hash. Where can such a class be found?

It's rare to find an abstract class in isolation. Either it was created by generalizing from some concrete class, or its design was validated by trying it out with a concrete class. Such classes are often good ones to use for testing. When I created abstract_hash_table, I tried it out using this derived class:

	test_hash_table class	Fig.23-7

```
class test_hash_table : public abstract_hash_table
{
public:
        test_hash_table(unsigned int init_size);

protected:
        unsigned int hash(char * tag) { return tag[0] % sz; }
        unsigned int next_hash(char *tag, unsigned int current) { return (current + 1) % sz;}
};
```

Though perfectly suitable for testing, this class doesn't make a very good hash table. hash tries to put all tokens starting with the same first letter into the same location. This tendency to cluster will be worsened by next_hash, which forces insertion_collision to search linearly for empty slots.

Here's a test specification. It contains several steps, each of which inserts into the hash table. The test requirements satisfied by each step are listed with the step. retrieve is used to check whether the insertion was done correctly. If this were real testing, those calls would also be chosen to satisfy some of retrieve's test requirements. That is, this single test specification would use insert to set up the hash table for retrieve testing and retrieve to check insert's expected results.

Notice the usual attempt to increase the variety of tests by using a variety of names and by doing retrievals in different orders.

Fig. 23–8	**abstract_hash_table::insert test**

	Setup: Create a hash table of size 3
	
	1. insert token1, with name "Dawn" and value 1
	    - inserting into an empty table
	    - hash returns SZ-1
	    - inserting into last slot
	EXPECT:
	    return value is true and a copy of the token is in slot 2.
	    retrieve("Dawn") returns a copy of token1.
	
	2. insert token2, with name "D" and value 0
	    - inserting into a one-element table
	    - insertion collision resolved
	    - insertion_collision returns 0
	    - inserting into first slot
	EXPECT:
	    return value is true and a copy of the token is in slot 0.
	    retrieve("D") returns a copy of token2.
	    retrieve("Dawn") returns a copy of token1.
	
	3. insert token3, with name "Erin" and value -1
	    - hash returns 0
	    - insertion_collision resolved
	EXPECT:
	    return value is true and a copy of the token is in slot 1.
	    retrieve("Erin") returns a copy of token3.
	    retrieve("Dawn") returns a copy of token1.
	    retrieve("D") returns a copy of token2.
	
	4. insert token_extra, with name "xebediah_Jones_the_3rd" and value 232
	    - inserting into a full table
	EXPECT:
	    return value is false, and the hash table is unchanged.
	    retrieve("Dawn") returns a copy of token1.
	    retrieve("xebediah_Jones_the_third") returns a copy of token_extra.
	    retrieve("Erin") returns a copy of token3.
	    retrieve("D") returns a copy of token2.

Tests of this hash table probably do not need internal support code. The only thing that can't be observed is where elements are placed, which is more a property of the hash functions in the derived class than of the base class we're testing. Errors in placement would likely be observable— either insert wouldn't return false when the hash table should have been full or `retrieve` would fail to find some tokens. Classes derived from this one might add more test support code.

23.2 Hash_table: A Derived Class

The following derived class is a more typical hash table. It uses all the characters in the token's name in a way that spreads entries more evenly throughout the hash table. The rehashing algorithm will further reduce clustering by giving each hash value a different "step size". For example, in a five-element hash table, a hash value of 0 will lead to probes at array indices 0, 1, 2, 3, and so on. The step size is 1. A hash value of 4 will lead to probes at 4, 2, 0, 3, and 1. The step size is 3.

hash_table class	Fig. 23–9

```
class hash_table : public abstract_hash_table
{
protected:
        unsigned int hash(char * tag);
        unsigned int next_hash(char *tag, unsigned int current);
private:
        unsigned int hashkey;        // communication between hash and next_hash.
};

unsigned int hash_table::hash(char * tag)
{
        hashkey = 0;
        for (; *tag != NULL_CHAR; tag++)
        {
            hashkey += (unsigned int) *tag;
            // Mix up the bits.
            hashkey = (hashkey << 5) + (hashkey >> 20);
        }
        return hashkey % sz;
}

unsigned int hash_table::next_hash(char *tag, unsigned int current)
{
        return (current + (sz - 2 - (hashkey % (sz - 2)))) % sz;
}
```

The specifications for `hash` and `next_hash` are unchanged except for the addition of one assumed precondition:

> Assumed: SZ is a prime number.[1]

---

1. `hash` does do something new, namely set `hashkey`. I am treating it as an internal detail, hidden from the outside world by the `private` label. It could be described in a new postcondition, but a reasonable external description would be vacuous: "hashkey can be set to any unsigned integer value, except that the same TAG always yields the same value."

As you might expect, the definitions of these two functions will have little effect on testing. The following sections will go through all the steps in meticulous detail. In real life, the process would be considerably abbreviated.

23.2.1 The Hash_table Catalog

Copying the Base Class Requirements Catalog

1. The inherited member functions (everything except hash and next_hash) have all their integration requirements copied (from Fig. 23–5, p. 383) into a new hash_table class catalog. Were there domain shift requirements, they'd be left behind. hash and next_hash have no requirements yet.
2. All the data member requirements are copied.
3. There's a new data member, hashkey. It's given a clue.
4. Other object use requirements would be copied, were there any.

Here is the result:

Fig. 23–10	**hash_table catalog**
	object use requirements
	Hash table as a collection of inserted elements...
	• **hashkey, an unsigned integer (NEW)**
	insert (inherited)
	integration requirements
	returns false (no token added)...
	domain shift requirements
	insertion_collision (inherited)
	integration requirements
	return value is an already-used slot...
	integration requirements
	hash (overriding)
	integration requirements
	domain shift requirements
	next_hash (overriding)
	integration requirements
	domain shift requirements

Handling New Data Members

hashkey is a new data member. It could be treated as an Interval from zero to the maximum positive integer.

hashkey, an unsigned integer (NEW)
    0
    largest possible integer

Integration requirements for new member functions
There are no new member functions.

Normal integration requirements for overriding functions
Because `hash` and `next_hash` don't change their specification, they have the same integration requirements as in the base class.

New requirements for data members due to overriding functions
`hash` and `next_hash` have no new effects on data members, so there are no new test requirements. They have an effect on hash-key, to set it to an unsigned integer value. Test requirements for such an output Interval have already been listed.

Changes in defining terms of overriding functions
The new assumed precondition is arguably a change to the range of inputs for which `hash` and `next_hash` have their effects. However, it doesn't lead to a domain shift requirement. The difference between the base class and the derived class could be described by this requirement:

> SZ is not prime.

But that would violate the assumed precondition, so is by definition impossible.

Handling inherited member functions
Inherited member function `insert` calls `hash`, and `insertion_collision` calls `next_hash`. However, those two overriding functions have unchanged specifications. There is therefore no change to `insert`'s or `insertion_collision`'s integration or domain shift requirements.

Updating the remaining object use requirements
There is no change to the invariant. Old requirements still apply to the new class.

Summary
The derived class requirements catalog looks almost like the base catalog (Fig. 23–5, p. 383). There's one new clue (`hashkey`) with two new test requirements. Because `hashkey` is a private variable, users of `hash_table` can see no functional difference between the derived and the base class. That was, after all, the whole point: A `hash_table` is an `abstract_hash_table`; all that's special about it are its performance characteristics.

23.2.2 Test Requirement Checklists
for Hash_table Member Functions

There are no new member functions, so all there is to worry about are the two overriding functions and possible new requirements for inherited functions.

Test Requirements for Overriding Member Functions

`hash` and `next_hash` can be treated in the normal way. The requirements for `hash` are easy to derive:

1. `hash` takes a string as an argument, so the standard catalog gives "the empty string" as a requirement.
2. The return value is in the Interval [0, SZ-1], so the boundary requirements apply. (They are already in the integration requirements.)
3. The specification (Fig. 23–4, p. 382) suggests a requirement that `hash` be called twice on the same string. The test would check that both calls yield the same return value. Such a requirement would catch a change that deleted the `hashkey = 0` initialization.

More requirements can be gotten using the `hash_table` class catalog. The catalog applies to member functions as much as to external routines. (The complete `hash_table` catalog isn't given, but it's the same as Fig. 23–5 with the `hashkey` requirements added).

1. The "hash table as a collection" requirements are irrelevant. They do not have an effect on `hash`, and it's hard to imagine any way in which they should.
2. `hashkey` is an output variable for `hash`. The purpose of OUT test requirements is, in part, to pick extreme values that the code will be unable to produce, or that will trigger faults along the way. A very large `hashkey` raises the possibility of arithmetic overflow. C++ implementations are allowed to trap overflow (though most do not). This implementation has an unstated assumed precondition: that overflow is not trapped. It would be useful to produce a regression test that would fail if it were. A 26-character `tag` will cause overflow for even the oddest sizes of bytes and integers.
3. The previous requirement was error guessing inspired by the `hashkey` requirements. What of those requirements themselves? Because the `hash` algorithm does not treat "`hashkey` is the maximum unsigned integer" specially, rather relying on hardware rounding to produce it, I won't bother with it. An output of 0 is redundant with the "empty string requirement".

Here are the `hash` requirements:

> tag, a string
> > the empty string
> > at least 26 characters
> return value, an Interval [0,SZ-1]
> > 0
> > SZ-1
> postconditions
> > hash is called at least twice on same tag

`hash` doesn't call any other member functions, so it gets no requirements from their catalog entries.

The `next_hash` requirements would be gotten the same way and would look like this:

> current, an Interval [0,SZ-1]
>> 0
>> SZ-1
>
> return value, an Interval [0,SZ-1]
>> 0
>> SZ-1
>
> postconditions
>> return value is the same as hash(tag) (This is the SZ'th call)
>> return value is a new value (fewer than SZ calls since last call to hash.)

(Because `next_hash` ignores its string argument, the String requirements are irrelevant. `next_hash` does not change `hashkey`, so the overflow requirement is also irrelevant. Values of `current` outside the Interval [0,SZ-1] are prohibited by assumed Precondition 2, Fig. 23–4, p. 382.)

Test Requirements for Inherited Member Functions

Test requirements are added to an inherited member function's checklist if members it uses have requirements tagged "NEW". There are no such requirements in the class catalog—I have found no way in which the new definitions of `hash` and `next_hash` can affect any other member functions. (`hashkey`'s requirements cannot, since it's private.) Of course, I trust my own infallibility as much as I do any programmer's, so I'll tailor my test implementation to increase the chance of exercising test requirements I missed. The first way to do that is to rerun old tests.

23.2.3 Hash_table Test Specification and Implemention

It is trivial to rerun the `abstract_hash_table` test (Fig. 23–8, p. 386). All that's required is that the hash table be created with `hash_table ht(3)` instead of `test_hash_table ht(3)`. These tests will exercise all the hash table functions, perhaps finding faults in the interaction of inherited and overriding functions.

A little bit of planning helped make test reuse simple. Making the hash table size 3 was no accident—I knew that many hashing algorithms require the size to be prime, so I knew a size 4 hash table would be less reusable. In general, when testing a base class, especially an abstract class, devote effort toward designing test specifications you think are likely to be reusable in any derived class. You'll sometimes be wrong, of course, but the work is usually well worth it. Testing an abstract class via a simple concrete class aids reusability.

Although easy to run, the reused tests may not satisfy the new `hash` and `next_hash` requirements. For example, consider the requirement that `hash` return 0. That was satisfied in the reused tests—but only for `test_hash_table::hash`, not necessarily for the overriding function `hash_table::hash`. New tests will be required for the new code.

Hashing functions are hard to test, since their whole purpose is to hide information and not allow easy prediction of outputs from inputs. For example, how should I pick an input that will cause hash to return

SZ-1? One way would be to hash a random selection of various names and use the first one that satisfied the requirement. I decided on a faster approach, implemented in this single test that satisfies all the requirements:

1. Insert seven tokens into a seven-slot hash table. These tokens are named "1@tya", "1@tyb", "1@tyc", ..., "1@tyg". If you think about the hash algorithm a moment, you'll see that such a sequence is likely—but not guaranteed—to hash to seven distinct values, including 0 and SZ-1. I confirmed that they do by using a debugger to set a breakpoint on insertion_collision. Since it was never called, the hash table was filled.[1]
2. The table is now full. Trying, and failing, to insert a 26-character name satisfies an additional requirement and should cause current and next_hash's return value to take on all possibilities (in particular, those called out in the test requirement checklist).
3. Another requirement is to try to insert an empty string. The insertion will fail, but not before hash returns.
4. The requirement that hash be called at least twice on the same tag is satisfied by calling retrieve after each insertion; in particular the first retrieve must call hash. If hash doesn't hash to the same value on each call, the retrieval will fail.

23.3 Checking_ hash_table: Another Derived Class

This is another example of testing a derived class. It's explained in less detail so that you can have a chance to work through the process yourself.

After some use of hash_table, people will get tired of a deficiency: It assumes you will never try to enter a duplicate. It should detect the error and return some error indication. This feature will be added in a derived class.

Unfortunately, insert returns a Boolean. It's either true, meaning the insertion succeeded, or false, meaning the insertion failed because the hash table was full. The only way to add a third value is to overload the meaning of false. It now means the insertion failed for one of two reasons. If the caller wants to find out the reason for the failure, it must call one of two member functions, full or duplicate.[2]

---

1. Note that the names don't have much variety. All the loop iterations perform the same computation, except the last. I could have chosen one-character tags, whose hash values are easy to compute and just as lacking in variety. This approach was almost as easy and forced me to think a little more about the code.
2. This class is intended to be a good example, not necessarily a good solution to the problem.

CHAP. 23 AN EXAMPLE OF TESTING DERIVED CLASSES

Here is the new class:

---

checking_hash_table class	Fig. 23-11

```
class checking_hash_table : public hash_table
{
public:
    bool full() { return last_error == FULL; }
    bool duplicate() { return last_error == DUPLICATE; }

protected:
    unsigned int insertion_collision(token &tok, unsigned int where);
    enum { FULL, DUPLICATE } last_error;
};
```

It turns out that insertion_collision is the best place to check for duplicates, so it is overridden. When it finds a duplicate, it records the find in last_error. It will also record discovery of a full hash table there.

Here are the specifications of the new members and the amended specification of insertion_collision:

---

checking_hash_table specifications	Fig. 23-12

bool checking_hash_table::full()
Precondition 1: Assumed: called only after INSERT returns FALSE
Postcondition 1: Returns TRUE if the reason INSERT failed was a full
                hash table, otherwise FALSE

bool checking_hash_table::duplicate()
Precondition 1: Assumed: called only after INSERT returns FALSE
Postcondition 1: Returns TRUE if the reason INSERT failed was a
                duplicate entry, otherwise FALSE

Preconditions for insertion_collision:
1. Assumed: WHERE is in [0, SZ-1].
2. Validated: The hash table is not full
    On failure: LAST_ERROR is set to FULL and the return value is
           an already-used slot.
3. Validated: The token's NAME is not already in the hash table
    On failure: LAST_ERROR is set to DUPLICATE and the return
           value is an already-used slot.

Postconditions:
1. The return value is an empty slot.

23.3.1 The Checking_hash_table Catalog

Copying the Base Class Requirements Catalog
The integration requirements are copied for the inherited member functions and are left behind for `insertion_collision`. All the domain shift requirements are left behind.

All Object Use requirements are copied. `last_error` becomes a clue.

Handling New Data Members
New data member `last_error` has two requirements:

      last_error
          FULL
          DUPLICATE

Integration Requirements for New Member Functions
The new functions get straightforward integration requirements from their postconditions:

      full
          integration requirements
              true
              false
          domain shift requirements

      duplicate
          integration requirements
              true
              false
          domain shift requirements

Normal Integration Requirements for Overriding Functions
`checking_hash_table::insertion_collision` gets requirements in the normal way, from an examination of its specification and code. Because both are similar to those of the overridden version, the test requirements are similar to those in Fig. 23–5, p. 383. It does add two requirements, marked below:

      insertion_collision
          integration requirements
              return value is an already-used slot
         •   **last_error is set to FULL**
         •   **last_error is set to DUPLICATE**   **NEW**
              return value is an empty slot
              return value is 0
              return value is SZ-1
          domain shift requirements

The first requirement is not marked NEW because it describes the old reason for that return value.

New Requirements for Data Members due to Overriding Functions

No data members can take on different values because of `insertion_collision`.

Changes in Defining Terms of Overriding Functions

`insertion_collision` can now fail to return an empty slot in situations where it once did, namely if it encounters a duplicate along the way.

> insertion_collision
> > integration requirements...
> > domain shift requirements
> - **discovers a duplicate**

This requirement is redundant with the new integration requirement, so it needn't be retained.

Handling Inherited Member Functions

`insert` (Fig. 23–2, p. 380) calls `insertion_collision`. Is it affected by the new integration and domain shift requirements? Because
```
 checking_hash_table::insertion_collision
```
returns an already-used slot where
```
hash_table::insertion_collision
```
wouldn't, `checking_hash_table::insert` must handle one where `hash_table::insert` did not. Indeed, that was the whole point of this derivation—but it's a point that I "forgot" to reflect in `insert`'s specification, which should be updated to change this precondition (Fig. 23–2, p. 380):

> 1. Assumed: TOK is not already in the hash table.

to this one

> 1. Validated: TOK is not already in the hash table
>   On failure: FALSE is returned, and later calls to DUPLICATE will return TRUE.

This is a contrived example of how a change in one function's specification, captured in its test requirements, can make you discover the need for specification changes in an inherited function. This discovery would lead to two integration requirements being added to `insert`'s catalog entry.

- **returns false, duplicate() will return true**   **NEW**
- **returns false, full() will return true**

Updating the Remaining Object Use Requirements

The invariant is the same, though the enforcement mechanism is different. There are no new test requirements.

23.3.2 Test Requirements Checklists for Checking_hash_table Member Functions

The two new functions get simple requirements from their specifications:

duplicate
      called when previous insertion failure was due to a duplicate
      called when previous insertion failure was due to a full hash table

full
      called when previous insertion failure was due to a duplicate
      called when previous insertion failure was due to a full hash table

As a body of new code, `insertion_collision` will be tested in the normal way. For example, the standard catalog would give these requirements:

searching for a duplicate
      found in first position (of several entries)
      found in last position (of several entries)

`insert` also needs to be tested. It calls a function, `insertion_collision`, that has changed behavior, which causes new and changed behavior for `insert`. That behavior should be tested. There should be a requirement like this:

call to insertion_collision
      attempt to insert a duplicate   ERROR

The other requirements for `abstract_hash_table::insert` given in Fig. 23–6, p. 384, need not be retested.

23.3.3 Implementing Checking_hash_table Tests

The `insertion_collision` checklist requires searches for duplicates along "collision chains" of tokens whose names all hash to the same value. Tests that satisfy those requirements would look like this:

1.   insert token1
Expect: ...
2.   insert token2 (different name than token1, but same hash value)
Expect: ...
3.   insert token3 (another different name than token1, but same hash value)
Expect: ...
4.   insert a token with same name as token 1
      - satisfies "found duplicate in **first** position"
Expect: insert returns 0, full() is false, duplicate() is true.
5.   insert a token with same name as token 3
      - satisfies "found duplicate in **last** position"
Expect: insert returns 0, full() is false, duplicate() is true.

This again raises the question of picking names that hash to particular values, this time pairs of names that hash to the same value. Because their hash values are easy to predict, I'll pick one-character names. (This will also satisfy a coverage condition that the earlier tests did not—that the hash loop be iterated exactly once.) In an 11-element hash table, three names that hash to the same value are "3", ">", and "I".

The abstract_hash_table and hash_table tests can be rerun on checking_hash_table by changing only the type of the hash table in the test setup. That's useful, since they exercise insertion_collision well.

23.4 Abstract_hash_table<Item, sz>: A Template Class

Hash tables are useful for more than just tokens. They should be able to insert any object with a name field. Such a generic hash table would be declared like this:

	a template class	Fig. 23–13

```
template <class Item, int sz>
class abstract_hash_table
{
public:
        abstract_hash_table();
        virtual bool insert(Item &);
        Item retrieve(char *name);

protected:
        Item *elements;
        virtual unsigned int hash(char * tag) = 0;
        virtual unsigned int next_hash(char * tag, unsigned int current) = 0;
        virtual unsigned int insertion_collision(Item &item, unsigned int where);
        bool slot_in_use(unsigned int slot);
};
```

Item is used wherever token was before. Notice that sz has been made a template argument. This makes sense, since the size was constant during the life of any particular hash table object. However, this design choice makes it awkward to later add a member function that changes the hash table size.

23.4 ABSTRACT_HASH_ TABLE<ITEM, SZ>: A TEMPLATE CLASS   397

Both `insert` and `insertion_collision` use the `Item::name` data member:

Fig. 23–14	**template functions**

```cpp
template <class Item, int sz>
bool abstract_hash_table<Item, sz>::insert (Item &item)
{
    unsigned int where = hash(item.name);
    if (slot_in_use(where))
    {
        where = insertion_collision(item, where);
        if (slot_in_use(where))
            return false;
    }
    elements[where] = item;
    return true;
}

template <class Item, int sz>
unsigned int abstract_hash_table<Item, sz>::insertion_collision(Item &item,
                                          unsigned int where)
{
    unsigned int starting_where = where;
    for (where = next_hash(item.name, where);
        where != starting_where;
        where = next_hash(item.name, where))
    {

        if (! slot_in_use(where))
        {
            return where;
        }
    }
    return starting_where;
}
```

Both functions have the same specification as before (Fig. 23–2, p. 380 and Fig. 23–3, p. 381), except for referring to "items" instead of "tokens").

23.4.1 Testing Abstract_hash_table<Item>

The template catalog looks the same as the original `abstract_hash_table` catalog (Fig. 23–5, p. 383). This is unsurprising in the case of the member functions, which have the same specification. What of the object use requirements, though?

abstract_hash_table<Item,sz> catalog	Fig. 23–15
object use requirements	
Hash table as a collection of inserted elements INSTANTIATE	
empty	
one element	
more than one element	
full	
sz, a count INSTANTIATE	
1 IN	
>1	
elements, a pointer to the contents (a collection) INSTANTIATE	

The hash table is a collection of objects of an undefined type, so it has all the normal collection requirements. sz is a template argument, not a field, but it has the same effect on the code in either case. (As with abstract_hash_table, I will decide not to bother testing the sz=1 case.) elements doesn't have a type yet, but it is still a pointer that cannot be null, and collection requirements for it would be redundant with those for the entire hash table.

The template test requirement checklist for insert will also be the same as abstract_hash_table's (Fig. 23–6, p. 384). The only potential difference is caused by statements like this one:

unsigned int where = hash(item.name);

item.name must be a character pointer (the compiler ensures this). It might not be a null-terminated string, which would violate hash's assumed precondition. It seems unlikely that the instantiating class will contain such a name field, but the requirement might be worth listing under hash's entry in the template class catalog:

    hash
        integration requirements
            return value is 0
            return value is SZ-1
            argument (item.name) is not a null-terminated string INSTANTIATE
                (should be impossible—violates assumed precondition)
        domain shift requirements

(It could equally well be added to the template test requirement checklist.)

Since all that the insert code does with the items it stores is use their name field, this template test requirement checklist will probably be useful for all instantiations. For the first instantiation, I would probably test using a template version of the test_hash_table class. For any later instantiation, I'd need to check two things:

1. elements will now be a collection of a new type of item. Should any test requirements from that type be added under the elements clue?
2. Is the name field a null-terminated string?

The answers would almost certainly be "no" and "yes", in which case no testing is required.

24

Object-Oriented
Software 2:
Dynamic Binding

Chapter 21 introduced a class hierarchy of base, derived, and even_more_derived. Consider this routine:

```
void
handle_an_object(base &my_var)
{
    int x = my_var.f(1001);
    /* More code */
}
```

my_var is not an object. It is a reference to a dynamically bound object, and the object it refers to may be a base, a derived, or any other class derived from base. myvar.f is not an ordinary function call, it is a *virtual function call*. You cannot know, until runtime, whether the call will actually execute base::f, derived::f, or even_more_derived::f.[1] The process of converting the *declared class* of my_var to the *object class* of the object to which myvar refers is called *resolving the reference*. A description of a virtual function call will often refer to both the name of the function and the declared class, as in "f is called through base".

Because the function actually invoked isn't known until runtime, handle_an_object must be tested against each possible class, not against just one. You must consider test requirements from all derived classes. This chapter is about how to do that efficiently.

---

1. Actually, you might. The use of a reference might be purely for efficiency with dynamic binding an unavoidable side effect. In that case, you might know that handle_an_object is always called with a base. This chapter is then not appropriate.

You do not want to worry about all the implications of dynamic binding every time you look at a virtual function call. You should do all the worrying once, write the results down in a *virtual call requirements catalog*, then use that catalog thereafter. That makes finding requirements for a virtual function call as easy as for statically bound calls to member functions:

1. For ordinary calls, you use the class of the object to find the class requirements catalog, find the name of the function in that catalog, and copy out the test requirements.
2. For virtual function calls, you use the name of the function to find the virtual call catalog, find the declared class, and copy out the test requirements.

Fig. 24–1 shows the relationship between the inheritance structure and the virtual call requirements catalog. The catalog is created by considering the differences between base classes and derived classes.

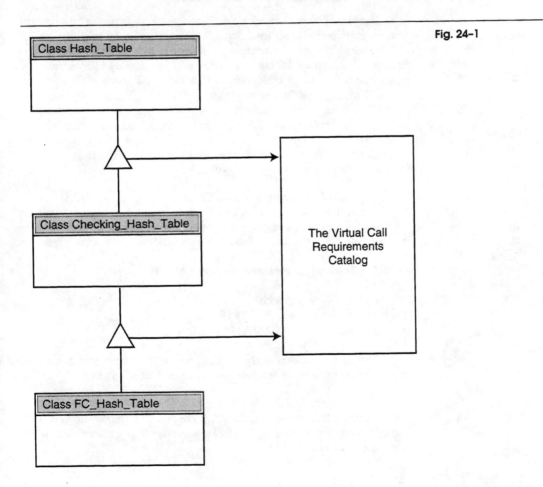

Fig. 24-1

The virtual call requirements catalog has this structure:

Virtual call catalog for member function BASE::F

> base is the declared class

> ⇒ *All requirements when F is called through BASE*

> derived is the declared class

> ⇒ *All requirements when F is called through DERIVED*

> even_more_derived is the declared class

> ⇒ *All requirements when F is called through*
> *EVEN_MORE_DERIVED*

24.1.1 Building the Virtual Call Catalog

For clarity, this discussion will first assume that you're building the entire virtual call catalog from scratch. Subsection 24.1.3 will discuss the (minor) implications of adding onto a virtual call catalog when a new derived class is created. This description will use the base, derived, and even_more_derived classes from Chapter 22. For your convenience, Fig. 24–2 repeats their specifications.

There is one virtual call catalog per member function. It begins with the class that first declares the member function. Each new derived class adds a new layer to the catalog, consisting of the integration test requirements for that function in that class. In addition, it may also modify the requirements for some previous layers.

Begin the Catalog from a Base Class
Begin with the base class. List the integration test requirements for the member function. These can be gotten directly from the class requirements catalog. For the base class, the requirements would be:

Virtual call catalog for member function BASE::F

> base is the declared class
> > return value is BADVAL
> > normal result (DATA is twice I, etc.)

The first requirement checks the precondition error effect. The second makes sure there's a test where the precondition is satisfied.

Add a Derived Class (Step 1)
When a derived class is added, there are four steps. The first is the same as adding a base class. The integration test requirements are copied into the virtual call catalog.

```
/*base::f(int i)
*PRECONDITIONS:
*1.    Assumed: I is even.
*2.    Validated: I >= 0
*      On failure: return value is BADVAL
*POSTCONDITIONS
*1.    DATA is set to twice the value of I.
*2.    The return value is the original value of DATA.


/*derived::f(int i)
*PRECONDITIONS:
*Assumed precondition deleted.
*1.    Validated: I > 0 && I <= MAXINT/2
*      On failure: return value is BADVAL
*POSTCONDITIONS:
*1.    IF I > DATA
*      THEN DATA is set to twice the value of I.
*2.    The return value is the original value of DATA.


/*even_more_derived::f(int i)
*PRECONDITIONS:
*1.    Validated: I > 0 && I <= MAXINT/2
*      On failure: return value is RANGEVAL.
*POSTCONDITIONS:
*1.    IF I > DATA
*      THEN DATA is set to I + 2.
*2.    The return value is the original value of DATA.
*3.    An INCREASE message is sent to the global LOGGER object.
*/
```

Fig. 24–2
The base, derived, and even_more_derived classes

Here is how the catalog would be extended for the `derived` class:

Virtual call catalog for member function BASE::F

    base is the declared class
        return value is BADVAL
        normal result (DATA is twice I, etc.)

    derived is the declared class
        return value is BADVAL
        DATA is set to twice the value of I
        DATA is left unchanged

`derived::f`'s postcondition 1 produces two integration requirements, one where DATA is changed and one where it isn't. The other postcondition (that the return value is the original value of DATA) doesn't need a separate test requirement—it would automatically be satisfied whenever either of the other postcondition requirements were.

The **even_more_derived** class would add the following:

> even_more_derived is the declared class
>> return value is RANGEVAL
>> DATA is set to I+2
>> DATA is left unchanged

The additional postcondition (that an INCREASE message is sent) has no new test requirement because its effect always happens whenever any postcondition effect does.

Updating Earlier Classes Because of New Effects (Step 2)

When a derived class's member function can have a new effect, a requirement to cause it should be added for its base classes (both direct and indirect). This checks for a common error: The programmer did not anticipate the specification change, so there's no code to handle the new effect.

Because of redundancy, not all new effects may be found in the class catalog. Generally, a requirement to cause an effect will not be listed if a requirement for another effect will automatically satisfy it. That's the case for the "return value is the original value of DATA" effect in base and derived, and the "An INCREASE message is sent to the global LOGGER object" effect in even_more_derived. Therefore, you must look to the specification for the effects.

Adding derived to the virtual call catalog would lead to this change to base:

Virtual call catalog for member function BASE::F

> base is the declared class
>> return value is BADVAL
> * **DATA is twice I (rewritten, used to be "normal result")**
> * **DATA is left unchanged (from derived)**
>
> derived is the declared class
>> return value is BADVAL
>> DATA is set to twice the value of I
>> DATA is left unchanged

The new effect (actually, the lack of an effect) is added. The parenthetical remark names the derived classes which can cause the effect. Notice that the "normal postcondition result" now only sometimes happens (it depends on I>DATA), so its requirement has been rewritten for clarity. F's return value is still always the previous value of DATA, no matter what, so there's no test requirement for that (it would be redundant with other test requirements).

Adding `even_more_derived` will lead to changes to both `base` and `derived`:

Virtual call catalog for member function BASE::F

> base is the declared class
> > return value is BADVAL
> - **return value is RANGEVAL (from even_more_derived)**
> > DATA is twice I
> > DATA is left unchanged (from derived, **even_more_derived**)
> - **DATA is set to I+2 (from even_more_derived)**
> - **An INCREASE message is sent to the global LOGGER object (from even_more_derived)**

> derived is the declared class
> > return value is BADVAL
> - **return value is RANGEVAL (from even_more_derived)**
> > DATA is set to twice the value of I
> > DATA is left unchanged
> - **DATA is set to I+2 (from even_more_derived)**
> - **An INCREASE message is sent to the global LOGGER object (from even_more_derived)**

> even_more_derived is the declared class
> > return value is RANGEVAL
> > DATA is set to I+2
> > DATA is left unchanged

The most noteworthy addition is the one about the INCREASE message. It is an effect that always happens when the object class is `even_more_derived`, but not when it's `base` or `derived`. A call of `f` through declared class `base` or `derived` may therefore sometimes produce that effect and sometimes not, so it should be listed under their entries.[1] Notice also that "DATA is left unchanged" can also happen when the class is `even_more_derived`, so the class has been added to that requirement's parenthetical list in `base`.

Updating Earlier Classes Because of Dropped Effects (Step 3)

A dropped effect is handled the same way as a new effect. In all base classes, the effect can either happen or not happen, so both possibilities should be added as requirements.

Updating Earlier Classes Because of Domain Shifts (Step 4)

A caller may be "surprised" not just by a new effect, but by a new domain of an old effect. For example, `base::f` and `derived::f` return BADVAL in different circumstances. A caller written with `base::f` in mind might avoid ever causing it to return BADVAL and hence might not contain any code to handle BADVAL. That caller will fail when it is used on an object of class `derived`.

---

1. The "send an INCREASE message" is actually redundant with the "DATA is set to I+2" requirement, which can only happen in `even_more_derived`. That's not unusual. As with other checklists, not noticing the redundancy does no real harm.

These requirements are gotten the same way as the domain shift requirements for overriding member functions. When the declared class is a direct base class of the true object class, the domain shift requirements can be copied. That would be the case when a `derived` object is called through a `base` reference or an `even_more_derived` through a `derived`. When the declared class is an indirect base class, the relevant requirements aren't in the class catalog. That would be the case when an `even_more_derived` object is called through a `base` reference.

Here are the effects of overriding `base::f` with `derived::f`.

base is the declared class
    return value is BADVAL
*   **I is 0 (from derived)**
*   **I>MAXINT/2 (from derived)**
    return value is RANGEVAL (from even_more_derived)
    DATA is twice I
    DATA is left unchanged (from derived, even_more_derived)
    DATA is set to I+2 (from even_more_derived)
    An INCREASE message is sent to the global LOGGER object (from even_more_derived)
* **I is odd (derived)**

The first two additions refine a requirement that applies to both `base` and `derived`. They describe the new values for which `derived::f` returns BADVAL.

The last requirement describes a new range of inputs where any of the effects could happen. (In `base`, that range was outlawed by an assumed precondition.) It could be used to refine all the effect requirements, so that you'd be forced to test a return value of BADVAL with I odd, a result where DATA was set to twice an odd I, and so on. By placing it where it is, normal test specification variety will combine it with most—but not necessarily all—of the effect requirements. Which placement is better depends on context—why did the original assumed precondition exist?[1]

The next step is to add test requirements for calls to `even_more_derived::f` through declared class `base`. They can't be gotten from the class requirements catalog. However, they are easily derived. The assumed precondition is dropped, as with `derived`. There's also been a change in the validated precondition:

    Validated: I >= 0
    On failure: return value is BADVAL

has become

    Validated: I > 0 && I <= MAXINT/2
    On failure: return value is RANGEVAL.

---

1. Actually, an odd I should be impossible for any call through declared class `base`, unless the caller has some way of determining the true object class. The member function executed might be `base::f`, which would violate the assumed precondition. This requirement could be tagged "better be impossible" and used as a question to ask of each caller.

The range where the postconditions apply has shrunk. They used to apply to I=0 and I>MAXINT/2, but those values now return RANGEVAL. The two requirements could be used to refine the "return value is RANGEVAL" requirement. That would lead to this catalog:

> base is the declared class
>   return value is BADVAL
>   I is 0 (derived)
>   I>MAXINT/2 (derived)
>   return value is RANGEVAL (from even_more_derived)
> - **I is 0 (even_more_derived)**
> - **I>MAXINT/2 (even_more_derived)**
>   DATA is twice I
>   DATA is left unchanged (from derived, even_more_derived)
>   DATA is set to I+2 (from even_more_derived)
>   An INCREASE message is sent to the global LOGGER object
>   (from even_more_derived)
>   I is odd (derived, **even_more_derived**)

That might be unnecessary, because the BADVAL requirements already test whether the caller can handle an unexpected error return for those inputs. (The only difference is the value of the error return.) Deferring the requirements might be reasonable.

Note that "I is odd" has been tagged with even_more_derived, because the dropped precondition applies to both classes.

The change to Postcondition 1 (adding the I>DATA defining term) produces no new test requirements. There is a change in the range of the "DATA is twice I" effect, but it is exactly redundant with the "DATA is left unchanged" effect requirement, which is already in the catalog.

One combination of true object class and declared class remains. A call of derived::f could resolve to even_more_derived::f. However, since derived::f and even_more_derived::f have the same defining terms, nothing needs to be added to derived's entry in the catalog.

24.1.2 What about Data Members?

You could also have a virtual call catalog for data members. ("Call" is a misnomer in this case—data members are used, not called.) A data member will have different test requirements depending on the class of its object. For example, better_refrigerator created a new range of allowable temperatures. temperature has these test requirements when its object is a refrigerator:

> temperature
>   5
>   20

When the class is a better_refrigerator, the requirements are:

> temperature
>   -5
>   20

Suppose there is a function like this:

```
handle_refrigerator(refrigerator &r)
{
    ...
}
```

All of the test requirements might be useful (`temperature=5` perhaps the least so). Therefore, it makes sense to build a virtual call catalog for publicly accessible data members.[1] It would look like this:

Virtual Call catalog for data member REFRIGERATOR::TEMPERATURE

refrigerator is the declared class
   -5
   5
   20

better_refrigerator is the declared class
   -5
   20

24.1.3 Building the Virtual Call Catalog during Change

In usual practice, the virtual call catalog won't be built all at once. Rather, as each new class is derived, the catalog will be updated, and the updates will be used to determine what retesting is needed.

Add the new class to the end of the catalog. Then add test requirements to its base classes. Mark each new test requirement with "NEW." As described below, these new requirements are used to retest unchanged code that might be affected by the new class. Once that retesting is complete the "NEW" tag can be removed.

24.2
Using the Virtual Call Requirements Catalog

Virtual calls are made by code outside the class. You look up test requirements in the catalog in two circumstances: when a derived class has been added, and when new external code is written.

24.2.1 When New External Code is Written

When new external code contains a virtual function call, find the catalog for that function and copy all the requirements for the declared class. Some requirements may come from derived classes that you know are not possible object classes for this particular call. In that case, those requirements will either be impossible (in the case of effects) or strictly irrelevant (in the case of domain shifts). You should document the impossible ones—because maintenance has a way of turning statements like "`handle_an_object` can never be called

---

1. A private or protected data member can only be used within class member functions. Its class is fixed, so there's no need for a virtual call catalog. The object use requirements suffice.

with an `even_more_derived`" into lies. For that reason, testing the (momentarily) irrelevant requirements may also be wise.

24.2.2 When a Derived Class Has Been Added

When a derived class is added, any virtual function call could suddenly produce unexpected results. After updating a particular member function's virtual call catalog, find all virtual calls of that function. For each, look up its declared class in the catalog. If there are new requirements, add them to the caller's test requirement checklist and write new tests, if possible.

Quite often, objects of the new class cannot be passed to the code making the virtual function call, so the new test requirements are impossible or irrelevant.

24.2.3 Maintenance

All this has frightening implications for maintenance. Whenever a new class overrides an existing member function, you have to think—perhaps think hard—about *every* virtual call to that member function. The temptation to skimp will be overwhelming. Even if you're dutiful, the chance of error is high.

This risk can be reduced by being careful about class design. The best kind of refinement is additive, so that the overriding member function completely fulfills the overridden member function's specification, but adds a new effect. Quite often, that new effect is irrelevant to the processing of almost all callers, so they don't need new testing. The callers that are affected are likely to be in code changed at the time the derived class was created. Those callers are easy to find (or, if missed, are likely to be involved in complex tests that exercise the ones you didn't miss).

Part 5

MULTIPLYING TEST REQUIREMENTS

U ntil now, each new test requirement was put into the checklist only once. Underlying that rule is the assumption that test requirements never interact or, if they do, that the standard combining rules will produce complex tests that detect interaction faults.

Suppose two test requirements are dependent and their interdependencies need to be tested explicitly. One approach would be to try more combinations of the requirements. So, if the checklist looked like this:

      clue 1

          requirement 1A

          requirement 1B

      clue 2

          requirement 2A

          requirement 2B

          requirement 2C

the standard combining rule could be abandoned in favor of trying all combinations. That would require six tests instead of the three required by the standard rule.

A better approach is to put the combinations into the checklist explicitly. One clue's requirements are multiplied and used to refine each of the other clue's requirements. Such a checklist would look like this:

> clue 1
>
> clue 2
>
> > requirement 2A
> >
> > > and requirement 1A
> > >
> > > and requirement 1B
> >
> > requirement 2B
> >
> > > and requirement 1A
> > >
> > > and requirement 1B
> >
> > requirement 2C
> >
> > > and requirement 1A
> > >
> > > and requirement 1B

This is better because the checklist remains the complete documentation of what you thought was worth testing. It also lends itself to an approach between complete independence and all possible combinations. It does have the disadvantage that the multiplied requirements are no longer visually linked to the clue that originated them, but that was never invariably true anyway.

Chapter 25, Simpler Test Requirement Multiplication, discusses the simpler ways to use multiplication. Chapter 26, Multiplying Operation Test Requirements, discusses more complex ways.

Simpler
Test Requirement
Multiplication

Chapter 13 discussed larger subsystems. It mentioned an oddity in basic subsystem testing: Effort is spent ensuring that every routine that uses a global is exercised with all of that global's test requirements. But that effort stops at the routine boundary. There's no attempt to deliver those requirements to every internal operation that uses the global. Further, requirements derived from other variables also only have to be satisfied at the routine boundary.

There are two reasons for the boundary. First, it simplifies the explanation of the basic technique. Second, the requirements from breaking the routine boundary have less value. It is best to apply the basic technique first, then—if there's time—add new requirements. Those new requirements, however, are not too difficult to discover, and the first section of this chapter tells you how.

The discussion in Chapter 3 said that the operators in complex expressions (those combining ANDs and ORs) should be treated independently, but mentioned that this was not a reliable assumption. The second section in this chapter explains what that assumption means, when it holds, and what to do with complex expressions.

Both these sections shed further light on the question of when to create definitions while summarizing a specification.

The last part of the chapter discusses the relationship between the topics of this chapter and a new type of coverage called data flow coverage. It also touches on some of the theory of testing.

sreadhex has two searching clues:

> Searching for a value for an odd DIGIT.
> Searching for a value for an even DIGIT.

25.1
Variable
Requirement
Reachability

The catalog entry for Searching was applied to each of them, and each got its own copy of the resulting requirements:

Searching for a value for an odd DIGIT.
    all of several elements are hexadecimal (none filtered)
    exactly one of several elements is not hexadecimal (one filtered)
    exactly one of several elements is hexadecimal (all but one filtered)
        only hexadecimal character is first of several
        only hexadecimal character is last of several
    none of several elements are hexadecimal (all filtered)

Searching for a value for an even DIGIT.
    all of several elements are hexadecimal (none filtered)
    exactly one of several elements is not hexadecimal (one filtered)
    exactly one of several elements is hexadecimal (all but one filtered)
        only hexadecimal character is first of several
        only hexadecimal character is last of several
    none of several elements are hexadecimal (all filtered)

This makes sense: Exercising the first search with all elements hexadecimal says nothing about what would happen when the other search is so exercised. (Well, since the loops are practically identical, testing one does increase your confidence in the other. Since this is a discussion of general issues, pretend the two searching loops are vastly different.)

This is not an example of multiplying test requirements, since independent test requirements were found for distinct operation clues. They just happen to look the same. However, not all test requirements that can exercise an operation are gotten from the operation clue. sreadhex had variable clues as well as operation clues. One of them had this entry in the checklist:

    S, a string
        empty
        a single element

But the only purpose of S is to be searched by the searching loops. Exercising the first searching loop with S empty says nothing about what would happen when the other search is so exercised. Yet, unlike the searching requirements, there's no guarantee that both loops will be exercised. It seems that the S requirements should be multiplied and added to each of the searching clues:

S, a string

Searching for a value for an odd DIGIT.
    all of several elements are hexadecimal (none filtered)
    exactly one of several elements is not hexadecimal (one filtered)
    exactly one of several elements is hexadecimal (all but one filtered)
        only hexadecimal character is first of several
        only hexadecimal character is last of several
    none of several elements are hexadecimal (all filtered)
- **S is empty**
- **S has a single element**

Searching for a value for an even DIGIT.
    all of several elements are hexadecimal (none filtered)
    exactly one of several elements is not hexadecimal (one filtered)
    exactly one of several elements is hexadecimal (all but one filtered)
        only hexadecimal character is first of several
        only hexadecimal character is last of several
    none of several elements are hexadecimal (all filtered)
- **S is empty**
- **S has a single element**

If you look at the sreadhex tests, you'll see that they happen to satisfy the second pair of requirements, but not the first. So the original set of tests would have been improved had I multiplied S's requirements to ensure they reached each place they're used. For the sreadhex code, the multiplication seems to add little value (mainly because the two loops are so similar). Suppose, though, that the first loop divided by the length of S. That will fail when S is empty, but the existing tests won't detect it. Tests written for the multiplied requirements would.

The sreadhex example illustrates the idea of multiplication for *variable requirement reachability*. More complicated multiplications are discussed in the next chapter.

There are a number of variations on this theme. They'll be illustrated by a series of routines that look like this:

```
function F(char *string, int A, int B, int C)
{
    if (A == B + C)
        /* operation 1 (uses string). */
    else
        /* operation 2 (also uses string). */
}
```

Each operation will have two test requirements. string will have a single requirement, that it be empty. For the above code, the multiplied checklist would look like:

operation 1:
    operation requirement 1A
    operation requirement 1B
    string is empty

operation 2:
    operation requirement 2A
    operation requirement 2B
    string is empty

There are two parts to the meaning of the indented "string is empty":

1. Operation 1 must be executed.
2. It must be executed with string empty.

The second of these is the original test requirement, and the first ensures reachability. A test must satisfy both parts of the compound requirement. In a checklist as written above, it's easy to miss the need for reachability, so I often write such multiplied requirements as

> operation 1:
>> operation requirement 1A
>> operation requirement 1B
>> **and** string is empty

Alternately, you could spell it out completely:

> operation 1:
>> operation requirement 1A
>> operation requirement 1B
>> **operation 1 executed with string empty**

Do whatever works for you—just make sure you avoid the mistake of passing in an empty string without realizing that a particular operation must be its destination.

Not all variables are arguments, but internal variables make no difference. Consider this code:

```
function F(int A, int B, int C)
{
    ...
    string = some_operation(A, B, C);
    ...
    if (A == B + C)
        /* operation 1 (uses string). */
    else
        /* operation 2 (also uses string). */
}
```

The string test requirements are again multiplied and used as refinements of both operations. The checklist looks the same. The test may be more difficult, since values of A, B, and C must be chosen to both produce a null string and to exercise a particular operation.

The previous examples both used IN variable requirements. But consider this code:

```
if (A == B + C)
    string = some_producer_operation();
else
    string = some_other_producer_operation();
/* Some more code */
```

Here, there will be an OUT requirement that `string` be null. Remember that OUT variable requirements have two purposes: to exercise the code that produces those variables, and to pass failure-provoking values along to the following code. The second purpose is satisfied no matter which operation is invoked: As far as later code is concerned, a null string is a null string, regardless of which operation produced it. But the first purpose requires multiplied test requirements. If `some_producer_operation` fails when producing a null string, you'll be unhappy if the single unmultiplied requirement was only used to exercise the other operation.

The multiplied test requirements are indented under the operation clues in the usual way:

> some_producer_operation:
>   some_producer_operation requirement A
>   some_producer_operation requirement B
>   and string is empty
>
> some_other_producer_operation:
>   some_other_producer_operation requirement A
>   some_other_producer_operation requirement B
>   and string is empty

Only the interpretation is different. In this case, the `string` is produced by the operation, not consumed by it.

As a final example, consider this code:

```
if (A == B)
    string = some_producer_operation();
else
    string = some_other_producer_operation();
...

if (A == B + C)
    /* Operation 1 (uses string). */
else
    /* Operation 2 (also uses string). */
```

The "null `string`" test requirement must be doubled for the producer operations. It must also be doubled for the consuming operations. Does that mean it's quadrupled? No. The working assumption of subsystem testing is that all relevant information about a variable is captured by its test requirements. Since they say nothing about where a variable is produced, that location is irrelevant to all consumers. A variable requirement by itself will not lead to testing combinations of operations. Other requirements may, of course. For example, a postcondition that combines specification elements may, in effect, read "IF the first producer operation is executed AND the second consumer operation is executed THEN...". The AND rule would lead to test requirements that force three of the four combinations.

The next chapter is concerned with rules about combinations of operations. For this chapter, the rule is simple: no explicit combinations. Therefore, the checklist would look like:

```
some_producer_operation:
    some_producer_operation requirement A
    some_producer_operation requirement B
    and result string is empty

some_other_producer_operation:
    some_other_producer_operation requirement A
    some_other_producer_operation requirement B
    and result string is empty

operation 1:
    operation requirement 1A
    operation requirement 1B
    and string is empty

operation 2:
    operation requirement 2A
    operation requirement 2B
    and string is empty
```

Two tests can satisfy all the requirements involving an empty string.

25.1.1 The Procedure—Working from the Specification and Code

There are two main steps when considering variable requirement reachability: identifying the clues to consider, then deciding whether any requirements should be multiplied.

Identifying Clues

Find all variable clues and all operation clues in the test requirement checklist. In addition, you may also want to consider operations not in the checklist. All the checklist operations come from function calls and clichéd operations. The code will do a lot more, and the variables will probably have an effect on the code not described in any checklist clue. This extra code can also be handled, but it needs to be done efficiently.

Identify blocks of code that perform abstract operations with some coherent purpose. You should be able to point to the code and say, "This code does X," where X is a relatively simple sentence. Often, the code produces a particular effect described in the specification. Most usually it will be at least several statements long—as large as a typical cliché (such as a searching loop), or larger. In fact, the operations you're looking for would *be* clichés, were they only used in many programs. Here are some examples:

1. "The code from line 34 to 43 checks the consistency of the two arguments."

2. "The code around line 53 selects an alternate route when the primary route times out."
3. "The code at line 565 finds and discards duplicate file names."

This definition is vague, but don't worry: These operations are easier to recognize than to define.

Notes:

1. Don't worry about overlapping operations. Treat them independently. They are likely to interact, but that's the topic of the next chapter.
2. The operations are often joined by "connective tissue," code that doesn't have a distinct purpose other than transmitting values from operation to operation. This code can be ignored—it will be exercised by test requirements for other purposes.
3. Typically, the operations are fairly compact. When an operation like validating inputs is spread out over the entire routine, that's a sign of trouble. That case is handled in the next chapter.

Add the new operations to the checklist as clues. In some cases, the clues may be redundant. For example, if an operation implements a postcondition's effect, there's no reason to add it separately.

The Variable Use Criterion

Now you have to decide which variable requirements affect the operations you identified. There's a simple (too simple) rule: If the variable is used in the operation, multiply the requirements. For IN variables, "used" means its value is referenced. For OUT variables, "used" means its value is set.

One problem is deciding when a variable is used in an operation. Checklist variables don't correspond exactly to code variables.

1. The code may use temporaries to contain parts or aspects of what the checklist refers to as a single variable. For example, in sreadhex the temporary val1 contains the original value of *ODD_DIGIT and limit is a temporary that fills the role of RLEN. In such cases, any use of a temporary counts as a use of the original.
2. Also, the checklist variable may be a convenience definition. The simple kind stands in for more than one actual variable. For example, a Collection variable may refer to a set of two pointers and a count. Any use of any of the variables can be considered a use of the Collection.
3. The more complicated convenience definition corresponds to no data at all, but to the results of processing. The variable is "used" in the operations that do that processing. In some cases, there may be no such processing. For example, NUM_HEX_CHARS in sreadhex can't be localized anywhere in the code. It's either used everywhere or nowhere, so multiplication is meaningless.

The Requirement Usefulness Criterion

The variable use criterion has a problem: It will result in too much multiplication. Variables will be used in places where the test requirements do not seem useful. That is, the test requirements don't exercise the operation in any way that seems likely to find faults. So only multiply if the requirement usefully affects the operation. "Requirement is useful" is a much fuzzier criterion than "variable is used", and you'll find yourself agonizing whether a requirement is useful or not. I have three recommendations:

1. Force yourself to decide after no more than a couple of minutes of thought. I suspect that spending more time rarely leads to better decisions.
2. It is probably easier to rank variable-operation pairs by usefulness than decide on absolute usefulness. Do that, and select a small (predetermined) number of the most useful.
3. Improve your judgement with feedback from faults you miss.

Another problem with the variable use criterion is that it ignores faults of omission. In addition to looking at all the operations where a variable is used, spend a little time looking at those where it's not used. Ask if perhaps it should be. For example, be suspicious if a variable is used in all but one of the cases of a switch.

Do not spend time tracing through the code to see if the variable in question could affect another variable, which could affect another variable, which could usefully affect the code in question. If the other variables are significant, they should have their own clues, and *their* requirements should be the ones that are multiplied.

Updating the Checklist

When you decide a variable clue's requirements apply to an operation, place a copy of the requirements under the operation, together with an annotation assuring that you'll read those requirements as meaning "operation executed and variable requirement satisfied".

If you think the variable might have a useful effect, but aren't sure, you can DEFER the requirements. A test requirement may be useful in only some of the operations it reaches. You may DEFER it in the others.

You can now erase the original variable requirements; they're redundant. Don't erase them if all the copies were deferred.

25.1.2 The Procedure—Working from the Specification Alone

The procedure is the same as using both the specification and code, except that you'll have fewer clues, and you can't examine the code to check either the variable use or requirement usefulness criteria. That's not fatal or even necessarily bad—you can often tell simply by reading the specification whether a variable has an effect on an operation. In fact, you may discover an effect that should exist, but that the programmer failed to implement. You're more likely to miss such faults of omission if you're looking at the code instead of the specification.

25.1.3 Implications for Testing Large Subsystems

Testing larger subsystems involves creating test requirement checklists from the subsystem interface and perhaps from individual routines. Variable requirement reachability applies only to routine checklists. When you build test specifications, you treat multiplied test requirements just like any other routine test requirements. That is, your test must exercise the routine while satisfying the test requirement. That provides reachability from the subsystem's interface to the routine interface to the operation affected by the requirement.

25.1.4 Example: Consistency Checking

Consistency checking (Chapter 18) offers another example of variable requirement reachability. Remember that the dependency statement

Statement 1: LEFT in range [0,1] requires RIGHT in the range [0-5]

is expected to be implemented with code like this:

```
switch(new_LEFT)
{
    case 0:                 /* Enforce dependency statement 1*/
    case 1:                 /* Enforce dependency statement 1*/
        if (RIGHT < 0 || RIGHT > 5) { error(); return; }
        break;
    ...
}
```

and will result in these test requirements:

```
consistency checking: LEFT and RIGHT
    statement 0 exercised
        LEFT is 0
        LEFT is 1
        RIGHT is -1          ERROR
        RIGHT is 0
        RIGHT is 5
        RIGHT is 6           ERROR
    ...
```

The code executed in case 0 or 1 is a distinct operation, that of "checking dependency statement 1". The RIGHT requirements from the Interval [0-5] certainly have an effect on that operation, so they are grouped with requirements that force it to be executed. In this case, there's no multiplication involved, since there's only one block of code to which the RIGHT requirements apply. However, the analysis is the same: What is needed to deliver a requirement to where it will do good?

25.1.5 Example: Working with the sreadhex Specification

In the original sreadhex specification, START was a definition, a convenience variable derived from *ODD_DIGIT. It had two IN test requirements:

*ODD_DIGIT == -1
*ODD_DIGIT != -1

Should it be multiplied? Here is an abbreviated section of the sreadhex code. *ODD_DIGIT becomes the initial value of val1. To avoid confusion between the initial value and later values, I'll continue to refer to *ODD_DIGIT when I mean val1's starting value. There are three operations: the outer loop, which selects which loop to run, and the two inner loops. *ODD_DIGIT might be used by all three.

```
49       byte val1 = (byte)*odd_digit;
61       if ( val1 <= 0xf ) goto d2;
62   d1: while ( (val1 = decoder[sgetc(s)]) > 0xf )
63          {  if ( val1 == hex_eofc ) { *odd_digit = -1; goto ended; }
64          }
65   d2: while ( (val2 = decoder[sgetc(s)]) > 0xf )
66          {  if ( val2 == hex_eofc ) { *odd_digit = val1; goto ended; }
67          }
68       *ptr++ = (val1 << 4) + val2;
69       if ( ptr < limit ) goto d1;
70       *nread = rlen;
71       return 0;
72   ended: *nread = ptr - str;
73       return 1;
```

1. The first inner loop (lines 62–64) immediately overwrites val1, so its processing cannot be affected by the initial value of *ODD_DIGIT. It does set the value of *ODD_DIGIT, but these test requirements are IN requirements, so the first inner loop does not satisfy the variable use criterion.

2. The second inner loop (lines 65–67) satisfies the variable use criterion, since the initial value of *ODD_DIGIT is used on line 66. It doesn't satisfy the requirement usefulness criterion. All the loop does is store the value and then exit. Processing is not affected—any value of *ODD_DIGIT will have exactly the same effect.

3. The outer loop (lines 61–69) is affected by *ODD_DIGIT, but only in how it begins—later iterations are unaffected. The two requirements for *ODD_DIGIT are already guaranteed to reach the beginning of the loop, so there's nothing to do.

Here's another way of looking at it. In the discussion of coverage in Chapter 7, these clues were considered:

    clue: *ODD_DIGIT
            a digit value
            -1

    clue: main loop iteration
            1 time
            more than once

I wondered if they should be multiplied to form

    main loop iteration
        1 time
                1 time, with a digit value for *ODD_DIGIT
                1 time, with a -1 value for *ODD_DIGIT
        more than once
                more than once, with a digit value for *ODD_DIGIT
                more than once, with a -1 value for *ODD_DIGIT

However, `*ODD_DIGIT` cannot affect later iterations of the outer loop. After the first time through, `val1` is overwritten and the value of `*ODD_DIGIT` is inaccessible. It can't possibly affect later iterations, so the multiplication is not justified.

25.1.6 Example: Building the sreadhex Specification

Chapter 12 had to decide between these two possibilities for part of the `sreadhex` specification:

    Possibility 1:
        START
            IF (*ODD_DIGIT == -1)
            THEN
                    START is 0
            ELSE
                    START is 1

        Postcondition 1:
                (An even number of digits that don't fill STR: use them all)
                IF (START+NUM_HEX_CHARS < RLEN*2) ...

    Possibility 2:
        Postcondition 1:
                IF (NUM_HEX_CHARS < RLEN*2 AND *ODD_DIGIT = -1)
                    OR
                (NUM_HEX_CHARS < RLEN*2-1 AND *ODD_DIGIT in [0,15])...

The two other postconditions follow the same pattern.

The latter will require some test requirements the former doesn't. In the first possibility, the `*ODD_DIGIT` test requirement is independent of which postcondition test requirement is selected. In the second, it's not since the AND rule will produce requirements like

NUM_HEX_CHARS < RLEN*2, *ODD_DIGIT=-1
NUM_HEX_CHARS < RLEN*2, *ODD_DIGIT in [0,15]

...

In effect, the latter possibility multiplies the first possibility's `*ODD_DIGIT` requirements by the requirements that trigger the postconditions. Is that needed, or does the simpler form suffice?

The three postcondition effects are caused by the three ways of reaching the `ended` label. The three ways are via `gotos` from the two inner loops and falling out of the outer loop. Those three operations have already been analyzed. `*ODD_DIGIT` doesn't need to be multiplied because of them, so the first specification possibility is sufficient.

25.2
Complex Boolean
Expressions

Chapter 3 said that, by default, the expression A AND (B OR C) should lead to these test requirements:

A true,	(B OR C) false
A false,	(B OR C) true
A true,	(B OR C) true

B true, C false
B false, C true
B false, C false

Why are the two operators treated independently? Variable requirement reachability justifies that independence if the code looks like this:

```
int t = b || c;
...
if (a && t)
{
    ...
}
```

T is a Boolean variable, with two test requirements (that it be true and false). It is irrelevant to the consumer of T (the `if`) how it is produced; all that matters is that the requirements are satisfied.

Such code is certainly not uncommon, especially in more complicated cases. Truly complex mixtures of `&&`'s and `||`'s are relatively rare. When they do occur, they should be tested more thoroughly because programmers find them hard to get right.

So the decision about how to test a boolean expression from the specification depends on the implementation:

1. If the specification expression contains a mixture of the two operators, but the code contains no expressions that mix them, treating the operators independently (as in Chapter 3) is sufficient. This case was the default assumption in that chapter because that was not the time to explain about reachability.

2. If the specification expression is directly implemented in the code, more reliable requirements must be used. The next section describes what "reliability" means and how those requirements are derived.

In practice, it's usually best to use the more reliable requirements in both cases. That saves you the trouble of determining if operators are really independent, isolates your tests from code changes, usually doesn't add many test requirements, and often doesn't add any tests (because the extra requirements can be used in tests required for other requirements).

Note: If the expression is exclusively composed of either AND or OR, the requirements from Chapter 3's AND rule and OR rule are exactly those that would be derived from the procedure in the next section.

25.2.1 Deriving a Catalog of Requirements

Given an implementation like

```
if (a && (b || c))
{
    ...
}
```

one could argue that each way `b||c` could be true should be exercised with each `&&` requirement that needs it to be true. That multiplication of requirements would look like this:

```
        A true, (B OR C) false
            A true, B false, C false
        A false, (B OR C) true
            A false, B true, C false
            A false, B false, C true
        A true, (B OR C) true
            A true, B true, C false
            A true, B false, C true
```

For `A and (B or (C and D))`, this *complete multiplication* would lead to this checklist:

	A true, (B or (C and D)) false
	A true, B false, (C and D) false
0	A true, B false, C false, D true
0	A true, B false, C true, D false
	A false, (B or (C and D)) true
	A false, B true, (C and D) false
0	A false, B true, C false, D true
0	A false, B true, C true, D false
	A false, B false, (C and D) true
0	A false, B false, C true, D true
	A true, (B or (C and D)) true
	A true, B true, (C and D) false
0	A true, B true, C false, D true
0	A true, B true, C true, D false
	A true, B false, (C and D) true
0	A true, B false, C true, D true

The eight numbered requirements are the final result of the multiplication. But not all are needed. The purpose of these requirements is narrow: to cause all plausible misimplementations (faults) of A and (B or (C and D)) to take the wrong branch of the if. For example, if the programmer implemented that specification as

```
if (B || (C && D))   /* forgot A */
{
    ...
}
```

the input (A false, B true, C true, D false) would cause the program to take the then branch instead of the correct else branch. That failure might not propagate to the output, but that's a separate issue (which applies to all tests and all test requirements). What requirements suffice depends on your definition of "plausible fault." Here is the one this book uses for boolean expressions:

❏ **negate a term**

"Term" means both individual operands like A and subexpressions like (C&&D).

❏ **drop a term**

❏ **change an operator**

&& is changed to || and vice-versa

❏ **drop parentheses**

This catches the common error of implementing (A and (B or C)) as (A && B || C).

❏ **rearrange an OR term and drop parentheses**

The programmer doesn't necessarily use the same ordering as the specification, so (A && C || B) is also a plausible fault for (A and (B or C)).

❏ **add parentheses to an OR 'term'**

Example: Implementing A and B or C as (A && (B || C)). These faults are less plausible than the others.

A reliable set of test requirements causes each plausible fault to take the wrong branch. Appendix E provides a Requirements for Complex Booleans Catalog. It contains all the 3-operand, 4-operand, and some of the N-operand expressions that mix AND and OR. If your program has a N-operand expression that isn't in that catalog, use a complete multiplication.

25.2.2 An Example

See "More about greport" in the next section.

This new way of handling boolean expressions seems straightforward: When a boolean expression uses either only AND or only OR, use the simple rules; otherwise, always use the Requirements for Complex Booleans Catalog. Why did Chapter 3 treat operators independently? The reason was to avoid confusion in Chapter 12, which explained how to summarize specifications. An important part of that process is creating convenience definitions. As far as that chapter was concerned, there was absolutely no difference between writing

> Postcondition 1:
>   IF (A1 AND A2) OR (B1 AND B2)
>   THEN ...

and writing

> Definition
>   IF A1 AND A2
>   THEN A allows the effect

> Definition
>   IF B1 AND B2
>   THEN B allows the effect

> Postcondition 2:
>   IF A allows the effect OR B allows the effect
>   THEN ...

The test requirements were identical. They are not identical when the Requirements for Complex Booleans Catalog is used. In Chapter 12, a convenience definition was justified solely by convenience; now, it is justified only if variable requirement reachability allows it. That is, you can create a definition only if code corresponding to the definition is physically separate from the code that uses the definition. For example, Chapter 12 created a POTENTIALLY VISIBLE definition that was used as follows. (The specification has been slightly simplified for this discussion.)

> Definition POTENTIALLY VISIBLE
>   IF   none of the visibility options are given
>   OR the line's file is named in a -vf option
>   OR the line's file is named in a -visible file option
>   OR the line's routine is named in a -vr option
>   OR the line's routine is named in a -visible-routine option
>   THEN the line is potentially visible

> Postcondition LINE SHOWN
>   IF (a line is potentially visible AND the line contains a zero)
>   THEN that line is shown in the output.

The definition is justified if the code looks like:

```
potentially_visible = ...

...

if (potentially_visible && line_contains_zero)
```

or

```
if (no_visibility_options
      || file_visible(filename)
      || routine_visible(routine))
{
    ...
    if (line_contains_zero)
    {
        show_line();
    }
}
```

It is not justified if the code looks like:

```
if (line_contains_zero && no_visibility_options || file_visible(filename) || routine_visible(routine))
{
    show_line();
}
```

(especially since the code is wrong). However, this latter code does support two smaller definitions:

Definition FILE VISIBLE
    IF   the line's file is named in a -vf option
       OR the line's file is named in a -visible file option
    THEN this file is potentially visible

Definition ROUTINE VISIBLE
    IF   the line's routine is named in a -vr option
       OR the line's routine is named in a -visible-routine option
    THEN the routine is potentially visible

These are justified because of the function calls used in the if. The code that handles the two separate options for file visibility is far removed from the code that checks whether a particular file is visible.

25.3.1 The Procedure

Here is the recommended procedure for creating and using boolean convenience definitions. You should, as always, adapt these general guidelines to your specific situation.

Creating Definitions with Code Available

You can create a convenience definition for an expression if it is physically separate from the expression that uses it. That includes all the cases above (intermediate variables, flow of control, and function calls).

Take extra care when the convenience definition corresponds to a macro. Consider this buggy code:

```
#define visible(file, routine)\
        no_visibility_options || file_visible(file) || routine_visible(routine)

    /* The && will group with the first term in visible(), because of precedence. */
    if (line_contains_zero && visible(file, routine))
    {
        show_line();
    }
```

If the macro's definition is not completely surrounded by parentheses, the chance of a fault (if not now, then during maintenance) is high. The code should be fixed. Unless it is, you can't use the convenience definition.

This type of fault is also listed in the Question Catalog for Code Inspections, but check specially for it while creating convenience definitions.

Creating Definitions, Code Not Yet Available

If you are working only with the specification but will later look at the code, create the definition and check it later. Creating the definition is justified because the assumption of independence is usually correct—what's convenient for you, the tester, is probably also convenient for the developer. Guessing wrong will cost you some extra work, but—on average—less work than avoiding definitions whenever there's any doubt about independence.

When you later examine the code and find you guessed wrong, substitute the definition's defining term into all expressions that use it, then create the requirements for those expressions, then make sure you have tests that satisfy those requirements. (Many of them will be satisfied by old tests.)

For example, if the specification read:
Definition
        IF A1 AND A2
        THEN A allows the effect

Postcondition 2:
        IF A allows the effect and the destination is available
        THEN ...

Postcondition 3:
        IF A allows the effect AND the user is privileged
        THEN

and it was discovered that the definition had no independent existence in the code, the substitution would be

Postcondition 2:
        IF A1 AND A2 AND the destination is available
        THEN ...

Postcondition 3:
        IF A1 AND A2 AND the user is privileged
        THEN

and the test requirements would be

Postcondition 2
    A1 true, A2 true, destination available
    A1 true, A2 true, destination not available
    A1 true, A2 false, destination available
    A1 false, A2 true, destination available

Postcondition 3
    A1 true, A2 true, user privileged
    A1 true, A2 true, user not privileged
    A1 true, A2 false, user privileged
    A1 false, A2 true, user privileged

You should work with the expressions in the specification rather than simply deriving test requirements from whatever the code uses. You want to test whether the code is wrong, not simply exercise it.[1]

Creating Definitions, Code Never Available

If you will never look at the code or don't want to look at it very carefully, guessing wrong has a higher cost. Decide, case by case, whether you want to assume independence. A bias toward creating definitions is still reasonable, but it should be less strong than in the previous scenarios.

Building Test Specifications

You can now treat definitions independently of the expressions that use them, as before.

A Note on Coverage

You'll find multicondition coverage useful. It will point out when you underexercised a boolean expression because you thought part of it was handled independently. It will not catch all such mistakes.

25.3.2 The greport Example

The greport code has the following rough structure:

```
main()
{
        process arguments, including visibility options
        while there are more lines in the input
                fetch a line
                evaluate the line's visibility
                if it contains one count field
                        call one_count_routine();
                else if it contains two counts
                        call two_count_routine();
                else if it contains four counts
```

---

1. In most cases the code's expression and the specification's expression will be identical. It may seem odd, then, to exercise that code with test requirements intended to discover if it's been misimplemented as a faulty version of itself. Of course it hasn't been. These requirements can, however, discover if the code (and the specification) is in fact incorrect and should be one of those faulty versions. ([Hamlet77] is an early example of this approach.) The faulty versions are all simpler than or as complex as the expression itself, and the expression is more likely to have missing code than extra code (that is, to be a fault of omission). These test requirements are not adequate to guarantee such faults will be revealed, but they may reveal them anyway if aided by variety and test complexity.

```
        call four_count_routine();
}
```

All count routines have roughly the same structure. The `two_count_routine` looks like this:

```
two_count_routine(line)
{
    if (!line->visible)
        return;

    if (line->first_count_on_line == 0 | | line->second_count_on_line == 0)
        show_line();
}
```

Irrelevant details have been suppressed for this example. Those details explain why `main` calls the `count` routines even when it could know the line is invisible.

The definition of POTENTIALLY_VISIBLE corresponds to the code in main labelled "evaluate the line's visibility". That code actually looks nothing like the definition of POTENTIALLY_VISIBLE, but it has the same effect. The use of an independent POTENTIALLY_VISIBLE definition is justified. The ways in which a line can be visible are irrelevant to `two_count_routine`; only the boolean fact of visibility matters.

Line visibility is tested in each of three routines. In each, it must be both true and false. The five ways in which POTENTIALLY_VISIBLE can be true can be spread throughout the three routines, making a total of five tests. The single way in which it can be false must be repeated for each of the three routines. This multiplication occurs because each routine takes a boolean input, so each routine's checklist requires that input to be both true and false.

25.3.3 More about greport

This same code provides another example of how the techniques in this chapter are used. Part of the specification for `greport` describes when the output line contains a trailing count in brackets. It happens under these conditions:

```
Postcondition APPENDED_NUMBER:
    IF (-all option given OR -n option given)
        AND the line does not normally show a count
        AND the line is to be shown in the output
    THEN the line shows an appended [number]
```

"Line normally does not show a count" could be defined as

```
IF a line is one of these types:
        operator line
    OR  operand line
    OR  call line
    OR  routine line
    OR  race line
THEN it does not show a count
```

This, however, is only an elaborate way of describing which values of a Case variable have a particular property. There's no reason to use boolean operators if another kind of description works just as well. The routine specifications reveal that the lines that do not normally show a count are precisely those handled by `one_count_routine`. A restatement of the postcondition could be

> Postcondition APPENDED_NUMBER:
> IF (-all option given OR -n option given)
>   AND **the line is handled by one_count_routine**
>   AND the line is to be shown in the output
> THEN the line shows an appended [number]

This is obviously of no use to a user, but it's just as good, or better, for testing. The postcondition contains both ANDs and ORs. Here's the matching entry from the Requirements from Complex Booleans Catalog:

(A || B) && C && D

A	B	C	D	Expression
1	0	1	1	true
0	1	1	1	true
0	0	1	1	false
0	1	0	1	false
1	0	1	0	false

The resulting checklist looks like:

Postcondition APPENDED_NUMBER
    -all given, -n not given, line handled by one_count_routine, line to be shown in output
    -all not given, -n given, line handled by one_count_routine, line to be shown in output
    -all not given, -n not given, line handled by one_count_routine, line to be shown in output
    -all not given, -n given, line not handled by one_count_routine, line to be shown in output
    -all given, -n not given, line handled by one_count_routine, line not to be shown in output

The first three of these are straightforward. Three tests have to be written. Each can handle a different type of input line; one could be an `operand` line, one an `operator` line, and one a `routine` line. That is, the three tests can satisfy three of the Case variable test requirements. Which three doesn't matter, since there's no evidence of interaction between the type of line and these test requirements. (This can be confirmed by looking at the code for `one_count_routine`.)

The fourth requirement contains the clause "line not handled by one_count_routine". If it's not handled by `one_count_routine`, which is it handled by? There are two other routines. In neither case is the count to be appended to the output. There are several ways to look at this. The default way is to pick one of the two routines and consider the requirement satisfied. There is no reason to multiply the requirement by testing both routines. This is not a case where variable requirement reachability applies (since these are not variable requirements).

One could even argue that *neither* of the routines should be tested with this requirement. The routines are not supposed to append a count. If they do, that's a fault. It is almost certain the fault manifests itself as additional code:

```
print_the_first_part_of_the_line(line);
if (N_option_given || ALL_option_given)
    append_a_count(line);
```

If the fault exists, and the test isn't run, coverage will tell of the omission. Examining the coverage results will lead to the fault's discovery. (Though there's some danger that the coverage will be interpreted wrongly, as a missed test rather than extra code.)

But not all faults will be revealed by coverage. One arguably plausible fault is this code:

```
print_the_line(line, N_option_given | ALL_option_given);
```

Here, `print_the_line` takes an argument that determines whether it adds an appended count. That argument should be 0 except in `one_count_routine`, but it's not. (Note the use of the bitwise-or operator, which evades multicondition coverage.) The risk of a missed fault might be enough to justify testing both routines.

A reasonable compromise would be to test the requirement on one of the routines. If there is a fault, there's a fair chance that it won't be unique to one of the routines. For example, perhaps all three routines implement the code as

```
print_the_line(line);
```

and `print_the_line` is the routine that checks `N_option_given` and `ALL_option_given`. If so, a single test will suffice. Exercising the requirement on the other routine could be marked DEFER and used if convenient.

The final requirement is

-all given, -n not given, line handled by one_count_routine, line not to be shown in output

This is the only one with "line not to be shown in output". You may recall from Chapter 12 that that clause was added to guard against a test that violated one of the rules for test content. It was used there to reinforce those rules, and to provide a more complex boolean expression for this chapter. It can be ignored (or used anyway, if convenient).

25.4 Data Flow Testing

Data flow testing is a type of testing related to variable requirement reachability. This section discusses a particular simplified type of data flow testing. There are other variants. The discussion also leaves out details important in actual use. For more information about data flow testing, see [Laski83], [Ntafos84], [Rapps85], [Frankl88], and [Beizer90].

Here is an example of a reachability problem.

```
F(int count, int use_how)
{
    switch(use_how)
    {
    case USE_ONE:
        use_count_one_way(1/count);      /* Fault */
        break;
    case USE_TWO:
        use_count_another_way(count);
        break;
    }
}
```

(`use_count_one_way` and `use_count_another_way` represent any arbitrary code that uses `count`, not necessarily a function call.) Data flow testing can be described by saying

1. `count` is given a value at the beginning of the function. Call this a *DEF*.
2. `count`'s value is used at two points in the function. Each of these points is a *USE*.
3. A path from a DEF to a USE is called a *DEF-USE pair*. In this example, a single test can satisfy only one of the two DEF-USE pairs.

Data flow testing requires that all DEF-USE pairs be exercised.

DEFS are not always input variables. Consider this program:

```
if (whitespace)
    some_var = W1();
else
    some_var = W2();

if (case)
    C1(some_var);
else
    C2(some_var);
```

(Again, the function calls represent arbitrary code. `C1` and `C2` use `some_var`, perhaps in addition to other variables.) Each of the two assignments to `some_var` is a separate DEF. Each of the uses is a USE. There are four paths—four DEF-USE pairs—between the DEFS and USES. Data flow testing requires that all four be exercised. In this way, it requires more than variable requirement reachability does.

25.4.1 How Data Flow Testing Fits In

Data flow testing requires both less and more than variable requirement reachability. They begin from the same premise—flow of information is important—but differ in what types of information they consider.

1. In data flow testing, what "flows" is the fact that a DEF was executed. In variable requirement reachability, test requirements are what flow.
2. Data flow testing uses the programming language definition of "variable". Subsystem testing has a more abstract but less precise definition.
3. Data flow testing uses the programming language definition of "DEF" and "USE". A USE is a reference to a variable's value; a DEF is an assignment of a new value to that variable. Variable requirement reachability looks at typically larger operations such as clichés. Like variables, these operations have a coherent purpose meaningful to humans but they cannot be described precisely enough for a compiler to find them.

The first of these differences is intended to make variable requirement reachability more powerful. In this code,

```
case USE_ONE:
      use_count_one_way(1/count);      /* Fault */
      break;
case USE_TWO:
      use_count_another_way(count);
      break;
}
```

what matters is that count=0 reach each set of complicated code, which is not the same as each DEF of count reaching each USE. What DEF set count to 0 is unimportant.

The assumption behind data flow testing is that if one body of code sets a variable used elsewhere, that body of code is assumed to do something unique that might provoke a failure in the using code. In essence, the existence of a DEF-USE pair is assumed to mean there's a test requirement that can be satisfied only by that DEF. The hope is that executing the DEF will satisfy the requirement, which will then provoke a failure on the way to the USE.

The assumption behind subsystem testing is that all the relevant test requirements can be discovered. That given, you don't have to rely on indirectly provoking unknown requirements.

Both assumptions are often wrong, of course. In both cases, the solution is the same: to write tests with complexity and variety in the hope of satisfying missed requirements by chance.

Variable requirement reachability has a higher base cost than data flow testing because typically more than one requirement must flow to an operation. The cost is partly reduced by not requiring requirements to flow from all producers. In the following example, each of the users of count must be exercised with count=0, but that zero count may come from any of the cases in the first `switch`:

```
switch(calc_how)
{
case CALC_ONE:
    count = calculation_method_one();
    break;
case CALC_TWO:
    count = calculation_method_two();
    break;
case CALC_THREE:
    count = calculation_method_three();
    break;
}
...
switch(use_how)
{
case USE_ONE:
    use_count_one_way(count);
    break;
case USE_TWO:
    use_count_another_way(count);
    break;
}
```

That would require two tests for the `count` requirement. Data flow testing would require each of the six DEF-USE pairs to be traversed for a total of six tests.

The other way in which variable requirement reachability's cost is reduced is by considering variables and operations at a coarser level of granularity (or, to make it sound better, at a higher level of abstraction). There are fewer potential sources of test requirements to think about, and fewer potential destinations. Tracing test requirements from all DEFS to all USES was called "complete variable reachability" in Chapter 13. Besides being more expensive than data flow testing, it would be an unnatural activity in the context of subsystem testing, which is based on an assumption that faults associated with such small operations are best found by targeting the larger, human-meaningful bodies of code that contain them.

Data Flow Testing as Coverage

The previous discussion made data flow testing sound unappealing compared to variable requirement reachability. However, it has an advantage that should not be underestimated: It can be measured. The hard part is identifying DEF-USE pairs. The general problem is difficult, but useful subsets can be handled with variants of familiar compiler technology. Once the DEF-USE pairs are identified, measuring how well they're covered is easy. Execution of the DEF is remembered. Execution of a USE then satisfies a DEF-USE pair. Several data flow coverage tools have been built ([Frankl88] [Harrold92] [Horgan91] [Ostrand91] [Weiss88]).

A tool to measure complete variable reachability would be much more difficult. It is not enough to remember the execution of a DEF. The tool must also check which test requirements are satisfied at that point.

That requires interpretation, such as determining that an "int" is used as a Count. It also requires measuring whether a test requirement is satisfied. "count=0" is easy, but what about "count=maximum"? A coverage tool for complete variable reachability is beyond the state of the art.

Variable requirement reachability is harder still, since it requires abstraction. Code variables have to be put into correspondence with variable clues, and groups of statements have to be recognized as cohesive enough to be treated as (effectively) a single USE or DEF.

As with the rest of testing, if we can't measure what we want, we measure an approximation. In the case of variable requirement reachability, data flow coverage is that approximation. Just as with other types of coverage, it would be inefficient and misleading to look at the coverage conditions before designing the original tests. Instead, the tests should be designed as described in the rest of this chapter. Then data flow coverage could be used to point to test design mistakes. Unfortunately, as of this writing there are no readily available coverage tools suitable for production use.

If you have read the optional last section of the Introduction, you'll remember that producing a failure from a fault requires three conditions:

25.5
Some Theory

❏ **reachability**

To provoke a failure, the program's inputs must cause the faulty statement to be executed.

❏ **necessity**

Next, the faulty statement must produce a different result than the correct statement.

❏ **propagation**

Finally, the incorrect internal state must propagate so that it becomes visible in the program's results.

Until this chapter, the concentration was on necessity: If a test requirement were delivered to a fault, it should satisfy the necessity condition. That delivery—the reachability condition—was left largely to chance (with limited exceptions like global variable reachability). The results of this chapter are test requirements that should satisfy both reachability and necessity. (Neither reachability nor necessity are guaranteed, of course. Necessity could only be guaranteed if the fault were known, and reachability requires its exact location. Neither of these are available. Subsystem testing works with plausible faults and approximate locations; this gains efficiency but loses any guarantees.) Propagation remains largely a matter of chance, though the rules for test content make it more likely, as does modifying the system to reveal more of its internal state.

Data flow coverage is, in a sense, the converse of basic subsystem testing. Rather than concentrating on necessity and hoping for reachability, it concentrates on reachability and hopes for necessity. In the general case, the reachability is from the input to a DEF and thence to a USE. In some cases, the input itself defines the variable's value (is itself a DEF), so the reachability is from the input to a USE.

Multiplying Operation
Test Requirements

The previous chapter showed how and when to multiply variable test requirements. The focus was restricted to those requirements because they're easy to handle. This chapter considers multiplying operation test requirements, which is harder to do.

In this chapter, "operation" will refer to clichés, function calls, and the groups of cohesive code described in the previous chapter. (That is, fairly compact code with an easily identifiable purpose.) The last part of the chapter considers operations that are not at all cohesive.

Why isn't multiplying variable requirements enough? Variable requirement reachability has three weaknesses:

1. *Omissions*

   It concentrates on whether variable requirements reach all operations that use the variables. But faults of omission may result in an operation not using a variable it should. Those faults should also be caught.

2. *Missing Requirements*

   You will inevitably miss test requirements. Basic subsystem testing (including variable requirement reachability) assumes those missing requirements will be satisfied by chance if you make tests complex and varied. But that's not a very satisfying solution. If there's any pattern to the missed requirements, perhaps it can be exploited to improve the chance they'll be satisfied. There is such a pattern: Such requirements are often due to subtle interactions between operations.

3. Coarse Granularity

Those interactions are undetected because of the coarse granularity of subsystem testing, which abstracts the code into function calls, clichés, and a few other larger operations. Here's an example, where two different operations that produce the "same" test requirements actually have important differences. A bug is found only when one of them produces the requirement that reaches a using operation.

```
unnoticed_variable = 1;
switch(calc_how)
{
case CALC_ONE:
    count = calculation_method_one();
    if (some_flag) unnoticed_variable = 0;
    break;
case CALC_TWO:
    count = calculation_method_two();
    break;
}
...

switch(use_how)
{
case USE_ONE:
    use_count_another_way(count/unnoticed_variable);  /* Fault */
    break;
case USE_TWO:
    use_count_one_way(count);
    break;
}
```

The fault will be found only if `calc_how` is `CALC_ONE`, the execution of the `CALC_ONE` case causes `unnoticed_variable` to be set to zero, and `use_how` is `USE_ONE`. This example is unlikely because `unnoticed_variable` is quite noticeable, and it's easy to see exactly what test is needed. But suppose

`unnoticed_variable`

is assigned in `calculation_method_one` and used in `use_count_another_way` (not passed in as part of an argument). In that case `unnoticed_variable` really would be easy to overlook. Or suppose there were so many variables that tracing all the requirements was too hard.

Finding a fault in an example is easy because you know it's there. In real testing, you have to find it more indirectly. The best you can do, given a particular test requirement checklist, is multiply test requirements. If you had a clue there was a hidden interaction between the code that calculates `count` and the code that uses it, you could exercise every producer test requirement with every consumer test requirement to try to discover the fault. That would lead to these test requirements:

```
USE_ONE operation
    and count 0
        and comes from CALC_ONE  (may find fault)
        and comes from CALC_TWO
    and count 1
        and comes from CALC_ONE  (may find fault)
        and comes from CALC_TWO
    and count >1
        and comes from CALC_ONE  (may find fault)
        and comes from CALC_TWO

USE_TWO operation
    and count 0
        and comes from CALC_ONE
        and comes from CALC_TWO
    and count 1
        and comes from CALC_ONE
        and comes from CALC_TWO
    and count >1
        and comes from CALC_ONE
        and comes from CALC_TWO
```

This is expensive: Twelve test specifications will be required, twice as many as with variable requirement reachability. None of them will guarantee the discovery of the fault because none of them guarantee some_flag will be true. There are three that might find the fault—given good variety in the test suite, this makes it likely that one of the three cases will give the right value to some_flag.

Since not every clue's requirements can affordably be multiplied with every other one's, you can at best select a small subset of possible pairs of clues. The only information available to make that selection is the amount of information that flows between operations. Two operations with greater information flow are more likely to have interaction faults. (The term "information flow" is used deliberately—as you'll see, it includes more than just the flow of even abstract variables.)

Note that the standard combining rule does take interactions into account. It requires that each test be complex and that test requirements be used round robin. That's so that each test requirement is combined with many others, as multiplication does. The difference is that the standard rule stops short of requiring extra test specifications just for unused combinations. It's a trade-off between the cost of more testing and the likelihood of that testing being worthwhile. Like any hard-and-fast rule, it will be wrong for some situations.

26.1
The Procedure

The procedure is like data flow testing: Make sure every producer of information supplies it to every possible consumer. Beyond that, make each of these information flows satisfy useful test requirements for both the producer and consumer.

26.1.1 Finding Interacting Clues

Scan the code looking for dependencies between operation clues you've already written down. You are trying to answer the two questions "Can the processing of *this* clue affect the processing of *that* clue? Should it, even if it doesn't?" A 'yes' answer is a hint that you should try some or all combinations of the test requirements for the two clues.

Here are several of the most common situations. They are presented in order of difficulty to discover in the code.

Code Overlap

If the text for two operations overlap, that's usually a clue about dependency. If the code's structure is

```
do a little bit of work for clue A
if (X)
        do some more work on clue A
        and some work on clue B
else
        do some more work on clue A
finish up clue B
finish up clue A
```

just the rough structure is a signal that the clues are more dependent than in code like

```
/* Handle A */
do a little bit of work for clue A
if (X)
        do some more work on clue A
else
        do some more work on clue A
finish up clue A

/* Handle B */
if (X)
        some work on clue B
finish up clue B
```

Information Overlap

Considering the interface between two overlapping operations can clarify their relationship. Consider this code:

```
for (i = 0; NULLCHAR != string[i]; i++)
{
  if (isspace(string[i]))
      whitecount++;
  else if (isupper(string[i]))
      upper++;
  else if (islower(string[i]))
      lower++;
}
```

The processing for the clues (counting white space and case) is textually close together, but shares little information (only a character in a string). The single loop could easily be split into independent loops. This code gives no reason not to treat the clues independently.

As another example, consider this code:

```
for (rover = list; rover != NULL; rover=rover->next)
{
    if (match(rover, sought))   /* searching operation */
    {
        count_characters(rover);   /* processing operation */
    }
}
```

There is little connection between the searching operation and the processing of the matching element. They have a narrow interface (`rover`) and the processing code depends very little on the actions of the searching code—it just accepts matching elements.

But now consider this code:

```
for (rover = list; rover != NULL; rover=rover->next)
{
    if (match(rover, sought))
    {
        /* Remove the element */
        rover->prev->next = rover->next;
        rover->next->prev = rover->prev;
        rover = rover->next;
    }
}
```

In this case, the searching operation and the processing operation share more information: both `rover` itself and its position in the list. Because they share information, generating test requirements especially concerned with their interdependence may be worthwhile. In particular, because they are both concerned with the element after `rover` (`rover->next`), perhaps all these cases might be worthwhile:

> an unmatching element is followed by a match
> an unmatching element is followed by an unmatching element
> a matching element is followed by a match
> a matching element is followed by an unmatching element

The third of these will in fact cause a failure. Because this operation is a cliché, that test requirement is found in the catalog. However, many interdependent operations are not found in the catalog, and you'll have to derive test requirements by noting how they interdepend. The larger the overlap, the greater the chance of faults.

Abstract Data Flow

Programmers make errors handling interactions partly because they get swamped by complexity. It's hard to get swamped by the complexity of a single Count variable passing from one operation to another. It's much easier to get swamped by the complexity of two Count variables, a Collection, and an Interval. In such a case, you might easily forget to consider the case where both Counts are zero, or you might omit checking yet another variable that's relevant.

Consequently, watch out for operations that share a great deal of data.

26.1.2 Doing the Multiplication

At this point you have pairs of clues you believe interact. Their entries in the checklist will look like this:

Operation 1:
    Requirement 1A
    Requirement 1B
    Requirement 1C
Operation 2:
    Requirement 2A
    Requirement 2B

They can be multiplied to produce

Operation 1:
    Requirement 1A
        and Requirement 2A
        and Requirement 2B
    Requirement 1B
        and Requirement 2A
        and Requirement 2B
    Requirement 1C
        and Requirement 2A
        and Requirement 2B
Operation 2:

In addition, you must ensure that both clues are reached. That may be implied by the checklist above, but you may also want to make it explicit:

Operation 1:
    Requirement 1A satisfied when operation 1 reached
        and Requirement 2A satisfied when operation 2 reached
        and Requirement 2B satisfied when operation 2 reached
    Requirement 1B satisfied when operation 1 reached
        and Requirement 2A satisfied when operation 2 reached
        and Requirement 2B satisfied when operation 2 reached
    Requirement 1C satisfied when operation 1 reached
        and Requirement 2A satisfied when operation 2 reached
        and Requirement 2B satisfied when operation 2 reached
Operation 2:

In addition, spend some time thinking about what the two elements have in common, and whether there are any test requirements implied by that. This is what was done in the previous example that combined a searching clue and an element deletion clue.

26.1.3 Coverage

Data flow coverage is the coverage best at finding oversights when multiplying operation requirements. Suppose you find an unexercised DEF-USE pair. If the DEF is in one operation and the USE in another, that might mean you missed the information flow between them. (It also might mean that you noticed it but decided multiplication wasn't justified.)

Data flow coverage will not discover two operations that overlap but don't share data. Therefore, it won't give you a clue to test situations that might reveal that the operations *should* share data.

Because I do not have a data flow coverage tool, I must rely on ordinary coverage. If some operation is underexercised, the chances are that its interactions with other operations are also underexercised. Careful thinking about the reasons behind missed coverage can reveal those missed interactions. I've found multicondition coverage surprisingly good at that.

26.1.4 An Example

How does operation multiplication apply to the `sreadhex` example? Here's the code containing the three major operations.

```
49        byte val1 = (byte)*odd_digit;
61        if ( val1 <= 0xf ) goto d2;
62   d1:  while ( (val1 = decoder[sgetc(s)]) > 0xf )
63             {  if ( val1 == hex_eofc ) { *odd_digit = -1; goto ended; }
64             }
65   d2:  while ( (val2 = decoder[sgetc(s)]) > 0xf )
66             {  if ( val2 == hex_eofc ) { *odd_digit = val1; goto ended; }
67             }
68        *ptr++ = (val1 << 4) + val2;
69        if ( ptr < limit ) goto d1;
70        *nread = rlen;
71        return 0;
72   ended: *nread = ptr - str;
73        return 1;
```

The two inner loops share very little data. All they have in common is that they both get characters from the same source. Individual characters are not shared, though. The only likely problem is that one of the loops will consume the wrong number of characters, leading to duplicated or omitted digits. Such a defect could be caught by multiplying any test requirements that cause a searching loop to find a character. (There's no reason to try all the requirements, and no reason to pick any one of them.) Such a multiplication might look like this:

> Searching for a value for an odd DIGIT.
> > an odd digit is found (any of several requirements satisfied)
> > > after a (different) even digit was found

> Searching for a value for an even DIGIT.
> > an even digit is found (any of several requirements satisfied)
> > > after a (different) odd digit was found

The requirement that the digit found by the other search be different than that found by this search is really an application of the rules for test content, but it doesn't hurt to make note of it in the test requirement. That's not the only application of those rules: Each search must actually be exercised, meaning there must be room in STR to place the results.

What practical effect do these requirements have? They *require* each loop to be executed after the other loop. Most of the other requirements could be satisfied by simple tests where one of the inner loops was executed, then `sreadhex` returned a value. Not all, though: There's already a requirement that will force both new requirements to be satisfied:

> hexadecimal character, in range ['0' .. '9', 'A'.. 'F', 'a' .. 'f']
>   All of 1-8, B-E, b-e

So there's no need to look at the tests to see if the new requirements were satisfied by chance. (I knew they had been anyway, just from remembering the tests. In real testing, I wouldn't have bothered writing the new requirements. I would have noticed the shared information, thought briefly about possible faults, and realized immediately that existing tests would catch them. In fact, in real testing, I would have probably seen that there was little information flow between the two loops and not bothered thinking about their interactions at all.)

The outer loop overlaps the inner loops, which is evidence of interaction, namely that the outer loop determines whether the inner loops are called, and in what order. That interaction has already been tested well. Abstract data flow to the outer loop also doesn't lead to multiplied test requirements. Although the inner loops produce variables consumed by the outer loop, little data crosses the interface, and it is used in a very simple way: `val1` and `val2` contain values which the outer loop places in `STR`. The values of the variables do not affect the processing, so interaction faults that might be caught by multiplication seem unlikely.

26.2 Diffuse Operations

Typically, operations are mostly compact. They may contain other operations (as `sreadhex`'s outer loop does), or they may overlap other operations, but you could easily circle a body of code and say, for example, "This is the code that checks whether input is correct." In other cases, you couldn't. You'd have to circle several bits of code and say, "Part of input checking is done here, but another part is done here, and the third argument is checked when needed, which is only in this code over here."

An operation spread out over an entire routine is a sign of trouble. The programmer has tailored the operation to many special cases. Some of the cases are likely to have been handled incorrectly, or over-generalized, or simply omitted. Something approaching complete multiplication of the operation's requirements is justified. For example, if some error checking is done only when a variable A has a certain value, you should strongly consider multiplying all of the error checking requirements by all of A's requirements.

Part 6

APPENDICES

his part of the book contains two types of reference material:

1. Catalogs that contain information used in the process. You will always use these.
2. Checklists that summarize parts of the process. After you become experienced, you'll rarely refer to any other part of the book.

Test Requirement Catalog
(Student Version)

This version of the Test Requirement Catalog has been pruned down so that people just learning subsystem testing will find it easier and quicker to use. More examples and explanations have also been added.

Some entries are marked "specification only." By this, I mean that the test requirements should be included only when they match an element in an external description of the program. For example, comparison operators used in the code shouldn't have test requirements written for them specially—they'll be well tested via other test requirements (or failing that, by coverage).

A.1   BOOLEAN   SIMPLE
                                                                DATA TYPES

- 1 (true)   IN, OUT

- 0 (false)   IN, OUT

- Some true value not 1   IN

A.2   CASES

V1 might be any of (C1, C2, ... Cn).

Specification only.

- V1 = each possible case.   IN, OUT

- V1 = some impossible case.   IN

> (If possible, choose boundaries like C1-1 when the cases are integers.)

Example:

A search routine can take four arguments: 0 (search forward from the start), 1 (search backward from the end), 2 (search forward from the current position), or 3 (search backward from the current position). Each of these should be tested. When choosing an illegal case, 4 would be a good choice.

The test requirements would be the same if the arguments were symbolic constants instead of explicit numbers.

A.3   NUMBERS

Comparison Operators

Specification only

epsilon is 1 for integers.

$<, >=$
- $V1 = V2 - epsilon$
- $V1 = V2$

$>, <=$
- $V1 = V2$
- $V1 = V2 + epsilon$

$==, !=$
- $V1 == V2$
- $V1 != V2$

If floating point numbers
- $V1 = V2 + epsilon$
- $V1 = V2 - epsilon$

Examples:

If the specification talks about $X < 2$, where X is an integer, the two test requirements would be

X = 1
X = 2

If X were a floating point number, the following requirements would be better:

X = 1.9999999999
X = 2

If the specification talks about X<Y, where both are integers, the two test requirements would be

X = Y - 1
X = Y

A.4 COUNTS

number of iterations, number of data items, etc.

Note that Counts are related to Intervals (A.5).

Specification only.

• -1	IN
• 0	IN/OUT
• 1	IN
• > 1	IN/OUT
• maximum possible value	IN/OUT
• one larger than maximum possible value	IN

If a program deals some number of cards from a standard deck, the IN test requirements would be

-1 ERROR

0

1

52

53 ERROR

If the program is a vision program that counts the number of cards a human deals, the OUT test requirements would be

0

52

The values -1 and 53 are impossible. The value 1 generally does not cause failures when it's a pure output value.

Use the "> 1" requirement when the maximum is unknown or difficult to test. (In the latter case, try to test the maximum once and then use some large numbers in other tests when you need variety.)

A.5 INTERVALS

Intervals describe values selected from a range including its endpoints [A,B], or from a range that doesn't (A,B).

Epsilon is 1 for intervals of integers.

Note: On computers, there's no such thing as an interval to infinity. Treat them as closed intervals ending in the largest or smallest possible numbers, or at least very large numbers.

[A, B] (Both A and B are in the interval)

- V1 = A - epsilon   IN
- V1 = A   IN, OUT
- V1 = B   IN, OUT
- V1 = B + epsilon   IN

[A, B) (A is in the interval; B is not.)

- V1 = A - epsilon   IN
- V1 = A   IN, OUT
- V1 = B - epsilon   IN, OUT
- V1 = B   IN

(A, B] (A is not in the interval; B is.)

- V1 = A   IN
- V1 = A + epsilon   IN, OUT
- V1 = B   IN, OUT
- V1 = B + epsilon   IN

(A, B) (Neither A nor B are in the interval.)

- V1 = A   IN
- V1 = A + epsilon   IN, OUT
- V1 = B - epsilon   IN, OUT
- V1 = B   IN

Counts have the same requirements as intervals of [0, maximum], except that "1" is added as a requirement (because subsystems use Counts slightly differently than intervals, so there are extra faults that requirement catches).

Pairs of Intervals

If there is more than one interval-valued variable, consider adding these requirements:

- Let both V1 and V2 have the smallest possible values.
- Let both V1 and V2 have the largest possible values.

It doesn't matter if the variables describe the same interval or not. Restrict the pairs you list to variables likely to interact.

Example:

> page size, interval [0,66]
>
> number of pages, interval [0, 1000]

If the amount of memory allocated is page size *x* number of pages, the two requirements would apply.

If the card dealing program used in the Counts example took two arguments, the number of cards and the number of players, two new requirements would be

> Zero players get zero cards each.
>
> More than one player gets 52 cards each (programs should flag this as an error)

In this case, it would also be reasonable to consider "total number of cards dealt" as an interval from [0,52].

A.6 GENERAL COLLECTIONS

Spotting collections requires creativity. Here are some examples:

> lines in a file (if the file is processed line-by-line)
>
> slides in a presentation
>
> slides to be printed (a subcollection)
>
> paragraphs on a page
>
> highlighted paragraphs on a page (a sub-collection)
>
> elements in an array
>
> a linked list
>
> the argument list to a function (from the point of view of the compiler)

• empty	IN/OUT
• a single element	IN/OUT
• more than one element	IN/OUT
• full	IN/OUT
• duplicate elements	IN/OUT
(may be an error case, or impossible)	

Note: More than one of the following categories can apply to a single collection.

General Operations on Elements of Ordered Collections

Whenever you're doing something to particular elements of an ordered collection (one with a first and last element), use the following requirements:

- Doing it to the first element   **INLINE**

 (There should be more than one)

- Doing it to the last element   **INLINE**

 (There should be more than one)

Examples:

 printing a single page of a document

 deleting an element of a linked list

In most languages and programs, collections have an ordering whether you know it or not. This ordering is often hidden from the specification. You may need to defer knowing which is the first element until you can look at the code.

Selecting One or More Elements from a Collection

The selected elements are a subset of the original collection. See the next entry. Selecting even a single element makes a subset.

Making Subsets of a Collection

You should also generate test requirements from both the starting and ending collection (even if the ending collection is never actually present as a distinct variable in the code, but created by ignoring elements of the original collection).

In all cases, the starting collection should have more than one element.

- Filtering out no elements (subset is same as original)
- Filtering out one element
- Filtering out all but one element
- Filtering out all elements (subset is empty)

A.7 STREAMS (SEQUENTIALLY PROCESSED COLLECTIONS)

These are Collections that are processed by taking each element in turn and doing something with it.

Examples:

> processing each line in a file sequentially
>
> accepting commands from a terminal
>
> processing incoming packets on a network connection
>
> adding up elements of an array

In the test requirements, streams are abbreviated as letters in parentheses, like (a b c). When letters are repeated, it means that two elements are the same. As an example, in (a b a) the first element and third elements are the same and the second is different. What "the same" means depends on the type of stream and is discussed below.

You can expect to see loops when you have streams. Most of the stream test requirements are derived from faults in those loops. For each test requirement, at least two sample streams are given.

When using streams, remember that streams are Collections, so you should also look for Collection test requirements (A.6). Remember that several of the subcategories below may apply to any particular stream.

Streams that May Contain Repeated Elements

> These are streams in which repeated identical elements are expected to affect the processing. For example, if the elements are machines to send updates to, repeated elements might be ignored—and that condition should be tested. On the other hand, if the elements of the stream are just integers to be added up, repeated elements don't make a difference and aren't worth testing.
>
> Often, several of these requirements can be satisfied in one test specification.

- No duplicates   IN/OUT

  Examples: (a b c) (c a b d)

- All duplicates   IN/OUT

  Examples: (a a) (b b b)

- An element is duplicated more than once   IN/OUT

  Examples: (b b b) (a b a c a d)

- More than one element is duplicated   IN/OUT

  Examples: (a a b b) (a b b a b c d c)

- An element is duplicated immediately   IN/OUT

  Examples: (a a) (b a a c)

- An element is not duplicated immediately   IN/OUT

  Examples: (a b a)

Streams with Two Kinds of Values

The previous category was for streams with a wide variety of elements, some of which may be repeated. The streams in this category have only a narrow variety of elements, namely two. That could mean there are actually only two possible values, such as 1 or 0. It could also refer to the interpretation of the elements. For example, in a stream of machine names, the two values might be whether the machine was available or not available. There are really a wide variety of elements (the machine names), but only two meaningful values (available or not).

- Two or more elements, each with the first value   IN/OUT

  Examples: (0 0) (0 0 0)

- Two or more elements, each with the second value   IN/OUT

  Examples: (1 1) (1 1 1)

- Two or more elements, each appears   IN/OUT

  Examples: (1 0) (0 1) (1 0 1) (0 1 0 1)

- null pointer   IN/OUT
- pointer to a true object   IN/OUT
- if several arguments are pointers of the   IN
  same type, Have them all point to the
  same object.

The last requirement targets faults where the routine uses the argument when it should have made a copy. Consider

```
func(object *p, object *other_p)
{
    p->field = true;

    ...

    if (other_p->field)

    ...

}
```

when called with

```
func(&object, &object);
```

The effect is probably not what was intended, since the same object's `field` is first set and then tested.

This section concerns itself with data types made up of structures linked together with pointers. Simple linked lists don't have anything special about them—they're treated just like any other Collection or Stream, so you won't find anything about them here.

DATA TYPES USING POINTERS

Specifications usually don't contain any references to pointers, but you can use these test requirements if you discover any sort of tree or circular structure in the specification.

A.9   TREES

Trees are Collections (A.6). There are also two Counts (A.4) involved. The first is the number of immediate children of a node. Does any node have zero children, one child, more than one child, and so on? The second is the depth of the tree. In particular, you want a maximally deep tree (or at least one with depth > 1).

A.10 LINKED STRUCTURES

- The structure is circular INLINE

The structure is circular if you can start at some node and follow some chain of pointers that brings you back to the starting node.

STRINGS AND TEXT

Notice that strings are Collections (A.6) of characters, that they're often treated as Streams (A.7) of characters, and that programs use Pointers (A.8) to manipulate them. So lots of other catalog entries apply—here are some that are particular to strings and text.

A.11 STRINGS

- The empty string. IN, OUT

Comparing Strings

- V1 and V2 same length, differing in last element. INLINE

  Example: "abc" and "abd"
- V1 has same elements as V2, but one element shorter. INLINE

  Example: "ab" "abc"
- V2 has same elements as V1, but one element shorter. INLINE

  Example: "abc" "ab"

FILES

A.12 FILES

Checking Whether a File Exists

- file exists
- file does not exist

Opening a File for Reading

- file does not exist
- file is readable
- file exists, but not readable

A.13 EQUALITY COMPARISON

SIMPLE
OPERATIONS

This applies to many data types, not just numbers. Some data types are indexed separately because they have several false cases, or more refined false cases. See, for example, Numbers (A.3) and Strings (A.11).

Specification only.
- Equal
- Not equal

A.14 OTHER COMPARISON OPERATORS

Some data types have a < or <= relationship defined for them, even though they're not Numbers.

Specification only.

<, >=
- V1 < V2
- V1 = V2

>, <=
- V1 = V2
- V1 > V2

In the inequality cases, make the two variables "close together" whenever the ordering allows it.

For example, in string comparisons "fooc" is both less than "food" and also nearly equal to it.

A.15 GENERAL SEARCHING REQUIREMENTS

SEARCHING

- Match not found

    Example: searching for "a" in ["b", "c", "d"]

- Match found (more than one element, exactly one match)

    Example: searching for "c" in ["b", "c", "d"]

- More than one match in the collection

    Example: searching for "c" in ["b", "c", "d", "c"]

- Single match found in first position (it's not the only element)

    INLINE

    Example: searching for "b" in ["b", "c", "d"]

- Single match found in last position (it's not the only element)

    Example: searching for "d" in ["b", "c", "d"]

If the search is backward, the "last" element is actually the first in the collection.

A.16 USING THE POSITION OF THE MATCHING ELEMENT

In general, programs don't care where the element is found. In this case, the program uses the position.

- Single match found in first position
  (it's not the only element)

- Single match found in last position
  (it's not the only element)

Continued Searching

Here, searching can be resumed from the last element found.

- Further match immediately adjacent to last match

  Example: searching for "c" in ["b", "c", "c", "d"]

This is a good requirement to apply to searching text. For example, if searching for $-delimited keywords, one test specification might be $key1$$key2$. Because there are no characters between the end of one keyword and the beginning of the next, an off-by-one error can cause the second keyword to be missed.

OPERATIONS ON PAIRS OF COLLECTIONS

A.17 GENERAL OPERATIONS

- V1 and V2 empty   IN
- V1 has 1 element, V2 none   IN
- V2 has 1 element, V1 none   IN
- Both V1 and V2 have more than one element   IN

A.18 OPERATIONS ON EQUAL-SIZED COLLECTIONS

The collections are supposed to have the same number of elements.

- V1 has N (>= 1) elements, V2 N+1   IN
- V2 has N (>= 1) elements, V1 N+1   IN

A.19 ORDERED COLLECTIONS WITH MATCHES

Here, two collections are processed in order. Elements from one collection may match elements in the other. (The program may expect that all will match, or none, or some—these test requirements are useful regardless of the expectation; all that changes is whether they are error cases or not.)

APP. A TEST REQUIREMENT CATALOG (STUDENT VERSION)

In the test requirements below, variants of the word "match" indicate elements that are identical in the two collections; variants of "mismatch" indicate elements are not identical to their corresponding element in the other collection. You can freely make longer collections that satisfy several of the test requirements at once.

- V1 = (match another-match) V2 = (match another-match)   IN
- V1 = (match MISMATCH) V2 = (match mismatch)   IN
- V1 = (MISMATCH match) V2 = (mismatch match)   IN
- V1 = (MISMATCH ANOTHER-MISMATCH)   IN
  V2 = (mismatch another-mismatch)

Here is a pair of collections of integers that satisfies each of the test requirements:

(1 2 3 4 5 6 7 8)

(1 2 3 A B 6 C D)

The following requirements always apply to collections with at least two elements.

- First elements match   IN, INLINE
- First elements mismatch   IN, INLINE
- Last elements match   IN, INLINE
- Last elements mismatch   IN, INLINE

In the case where the collections are of different length, the "last element" is the last element of the shorter collection. Here is an example of last elements mismatching:

("foo" "bar" "baz" "quux")

("foo" "bar" "bazz")

B

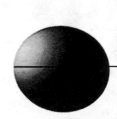

Test Requirement Catalog
(Standard Version)

The italicized text in this appendix is there for the benefit of new users. It's italicized as a signal that the experienced reader can safely ignore it.

Some entries are marked "specification only". By this, I mean that the test requirements should be included only when they match an element in an external description of the program. For example, comparison operators used in the code shouldn't have test requirements specially written for them—they'll be well tested via other test requirements (or, failing that, by coverage requirements).

SIMPLE DATA TYPES

B.1 BOOLEAN

- 1 (true)   IN, OUT
- 0 (false)   IN, OUT
- Some true value not 1   IN

B.2 CASES

V1 might be any of (C1, C2, ... Cn).
Specification only.

- V1 = each possible case.   IN, OUT
- V1 = some impossible case.   IN
  (If possible, choose boundaries like C1-1
  when the cases are integers.)

B.3 NUMBERS

Comparison Operators

Specification only

epsilon is 1 for integers.

<, >=

- V1 = V2 - epsilon
- V1 = V2

>, <=

- V1 = V2
- V1 = V2 + epsilon

==, !=

- V1 == V2
- V1 != V2

If floating point numbers

- V1 = V2 + epsilon
- V1 = V2 - epsilon

Numbers Used in Arithmetic Operations

The code under test does arithmetic more complicated than simple addition or subtraction.

- V1 = 0
- V1 = epsilon
- V1 = -epsilon
- V1 = largest possible
- V1 = smallest possible

B.4 INDICES

An index into an array
Specification only.

Indices into One Dimensional Arrays

• 0 (the smallest possible index)	IN/OUT
• -1 (one less than smallest)	IN
• largest possible index	IN/OUT
• one larger than the largest possible index	IN

Indices into N-Dimensional Arrays

• all values the smallest possible	IN/OUT
• all values the largest possible	IN/OUT
• First index less than smallest possible	IN
• Second index less than smallest possible	IN
(and so on)	
• First index larger than the largest possible	IN
(and so on)	

B.5 COUNTS

The number of iterations, number of data items, etc. Note that Counts are related to Intervals (B.6).

Specification only.

• -1	IN
• 0	IN/OUT
• 1	IN
• > 1	IN/OUT
• maximum possible value	IN/OUT
• one larger than maximum possible value	IN

B.6   INTERVALS

Intervals describe values selected from a range including its endpoints [A,B], or from a range that doesn't (A,B). Epsilon is 1 for intervals of integers.

Note: On computers, there's no such thing as an interval to infinity. Treat them as closed intervals ending in the largest or smallest possible numbers, or at least very large numbers.

[A, B]
- V1 = A - epsilon   IN
- V1 = A   IN, OUT
- V1 = B   IN, OUT
- V1 = B + epsilon   IN

[A, B)
- V1 = A - epsilon   IN
- V1 = A   IN, OUT
- V1 = B - epsilon   IN, OUT
- V1 = B   IN

(A, B]
- V1 = A   IN
- V1 = A + epsilon   IN, OUT
- V1 = B   IN, OUT
- V1 = B + epsilon   IN

(A, B)
- V1 = A   IN
- V1 = A + epsilon   IN, OUT
- V1 = B - epsilon   IN, OUT
- V1 = B   IN

Pairs of Intervals

If there is more than one interval-valued variable, consider adding these requirements:

- Let both V1 and V2 have the smallest possible values.
- Let both V1 and V2 have the largest possible values.

It doesn't matter if the variables describe the same interval or not. Restrict the pairs you list to variables likely to interact. Example:

page size, interval [0,66]

number of pages, interval [0, 1000]

If the amount of memory allocated is page size x number of pages, the two requirements would apply.

B.7   PERCENTAGES

- Treat percentages as an Interval [0,100].
- If the percentage is being calculated from some count, make sure that count is 0   IN

COLLECTIONS

B.8   CONTAINERS

Containers are objects that can contain variable amounts of data. For example, a buffer of characters, a C-style string, etc. Containers are a kind of Collection (B.9).

Appending to a Container's Contents

This includes the case where several elements are being added at once. Some requirements are not applicable when adding elements one at a time.

- Container initially empty.
- Container initially not empty.
- Adding just as many elements as will fit.
- Full container, attempt to add one element.
- Partially full container, add one too many elements.
    - *Example*: Adding "cdef" to an array of six characters that contains "ab"
- Add just enough to leave room for exactly one element   INLINE
  (can catch unchecked "small, harmless" additions)
    - *Example*: Adding "cd" to an array of six characters that contains "ab"
- Add zero new elements.

Overwriting a Container's Contents

This includes the case where several elements are being added at once. Some requirements are not applicable when adding elements one at a time.

- New contents have 1 more element than will fit.
- New contents just fit.
- New contents leave room for exactly one element   INLINE
  (can catch unchecked "small harmless" additions)
    - *Example*: putting "abcd" in an array of six characters
- 0 elements added (is container correctly emptied?)
- Some elements added, but fewer than in original   INLINE
  container (are old contents correctly cleared?)
    - *Example*: Putting "xy" in an array containing "abc"

B.9 GENERAL COLLECTIONS

Spotting collections requires creativity. For example, the formal parameters to a C macro definition are a collection—and an old bug in the GNU C preprocessor could be found using these rules.

Note also that you might apply individual element requirements to all the elements at once. For example, if an array is used in arithmetic, you would want all elements 0 in one test.

• empty	IN/OUT
• a single element	IN/OUT
• more than one element	IN/OUT
• full	IN/OUT
• duplicate elements	IN/OUT

  (may be an error case, or impossible)

General Operations on Elements
of Ordered Collections

Whenever you're doing something to particular elements of an ordered collection (one with a first and last element), use the following requirements:

• Doing it to the first element	INLINE
(There should be more than one)	
• Doing it to the last element	INLINE
(There should be more than one)	

In most languages and programs, collections have an ordering whether you know it or not. This ordering is often hidden from the specification. You may need to DEFER knowing which is the first element until you can look at the code.

Making Subsets of a Collection

You should also generate test requirements from both the starting and ending collection (even if the ending collection is never actually present as a distinct variable in the code, but created by ignoring elements of the original collection).

In all cases, the starting collection should have more than one element.

- Filtering out no elements (subset is same as original)
- Filtering out one element
- Filtering out all but one element
- Filtering out all elements (subset is empty)

Deleting Elements from a Collection

Subsetting is general in that it includes making copies of some of the original elements, skipping some of the original elements during processing, or actually changing the original collection. This category adds some requirements in the case where the original collection is changed.

- The collection has one element   INLINE
- The collection has no elements (nothing to delete)

B.10 ARRAYS

- If elements are numerical, have each element be an   IN illegal index.
  Example: Initialize "int array[5]" with
  -1000000, -1000000, -1000000, +1000000, +343224,
  (Large values are more likely to cause obvious failures.)

Comparing Arrays

- V1 and V2 same length, differing in last element.   INLINE
  Example: [5 6 4] [5 6 5]
- V1 has same elements as V2, but one element shorter.   INLINE
  Example: [5 6] [5 6 5]
- V2 has same elements as V1, but one element shorter.   INLINE
  Example: [5 6 4] [5 6]

B.11 STREAMS (SEQUENTIALLY PROCESSED COLLECTIONS)

These are collections that are processed by taking each element in turn and doing something with it: Input from a file or a terminal or a network connection, for example. You can expect to see loops when you have streams. Most of the stream test requirements are derived from faults in those loops.

Notation: Streams are usually written as letters in parentheses, like (a b c). Identical letters mean that the elements are the same. In (a b a), the first and third elements are the same.

When using streams, remember that streams are Collections (B.9), so you should also look for test requirements there. Remember also that several of the subcategories below may apply to any particular stream.

Streams that May Contain Repeated Elements

These are streams in which repeated identical elements are expected to affect the processing. For example, if the elements are machines to send updates to, repeated elements might be ignored—and that condition should be tested. On the other hand, if the elements of the stream are just integers to be added up, repeated elements don't make a difference and aren't worth testing.

Often, several of these requirements can be satisfied in one test specification.

• No duplicates	IN/OUT
Examples: (a b c) (c a b d)	
• All duplicates	IN/OUT
Examples: (a a) (b b b)	
• An element is duplicated more than once	IN/OUT
Examples: (b b b) (a b a c a d)	
• More than one element is duplicated	IN/OUT
Examples: (a a b b) (a b b a b c d c)	
• An element is duplicated immediately	IN/OUT
Examples: (a a) (b a a c)	
• An element is not duplicated immediately	IN/OUT
Examples: (a b a)	

Streams with Two Kinds of Values

This refers to either the actual elements (such as a stream of 1's and 0's) or the interpretation of the elements. For example, in a stream of machine names, the two values might be whether the machine was available or not available.

- Two or more elements, each with the first value   IN/OUT

  Examples: (0 0) (0 0 0)
- Two or more elements, each with the second value   IN/OUT

  Examples: (1 1) (1 1 1)
- Two or more elements, first kind appears after the second   IN/OUT

  Examples: (1 0) (1 0 1) (0 1 0 1)
- Two or more elements, second kind appears after the first   IN/OUT

  Examples: (0 1) (1 0 1) (0 1 0 1)

Streams with Error Handling

These streams may contain elements that trigger error handling. For example, the program may cease processing if a file-name is unreadable.

- A stream containing only an error   IN

  Example: (error)
- One or more correct items, an error, one or more   IN

  correct items.

  Example: (correct, error, correct)

In the second example, the first correct item gives you a chance to see whether error handling undoes the effects of the first item (if that's what error handling is supposed to do). The second correct item gives you a chance to see whether error handling truly does stop further processing (if that's what it's supposed to do).

Error-Handling Streams with Recovery

More tests should be written if the program is supposed to recover from the error and continue processing.

- A stream with two errors in a row, then a correct item   IN

  Example: (error, error, correct) (correct, error, error, correct)

Streams with a Fixed Number of Elements

The number of elements may be predetermined, or it may be calculated from one of the early elements

- A stream that ends one element prematurely.   IN

This test is especially good for I/O streams, which often don't check for end-of-file and end up treating it like valid input.

Streams with an In-Band End-of-Stream Marker

An example of such a stream is the input to a program that calculates an average of numbers typed in, stopping when the number 999999999 is the input.

- (>1 element, proper end marker)   IN
  Examples: (5 999999999) (2 3 999999999)
- No end marker   IN

  (This may be impossible for the program to detect.)
- An element after the end marker   IN
  Examples: (5 999999999 3) (2 3 999999999 4)
- An element that almost matches the end-marker, but is longer   IN
  Examples: (5 9999999990 3 999999999)

Ordered Streams

"Ordered" here refers to the values of the elements. We'll assume the stream should be increasing.

No Plateaus Allowed

- Steadily increasing   IN, OUT
  Example: (a, b, d, f) (a, b, c, d)
- Increasing with plateaus (error case)   IN
  Example: (a, b, b, d)

Make sure that in at least one case, the increase is by the smallest possible unit. (For example, in a stream of integers (..., 2, 3, ...), and in a stream of characters, (..., c, d,...).

Plateaus Allowed

- Increasing, with plateau   IN, OUT

    Example: (a, b, d, f)

- Decreasing (error case)   IN

    Example: (a, b, a, d)

In the decreasing case, make the decrease by the smallest possible unit.

Streams with Complex Elements

Suppose the stream is composed of C-language records, or perhaps it's a stream of 10-element arrays, or a stream of lists.

- Consider the sequences of components as streams themselves.

    Example: Given

      (elt1, elt2, elt3)

    apply stream entries in the catalog to

      (elt1->first_field, elt2->first_field, elt3->first_field)

    and

      (elt1->second_field, elt2->second_field, elt3->second_field)

POINTERS   B.12   POINTERS

- null pointer   IN/OUT
- pointer to a true object   IN/OUT
- if several arguments are pointers of the same type,   IN
  have them all point to the same object.
  (This targets faults where the routine uses the
  argument when it should have made a copy.)
      Example: func(&object, &object)

Pointer Equality Testing

A common error is confusion about whether equality means equality of pointers or equality of what's pointed to.

• Two pointer arguments are equal	IN
• Pointers are not equal, but objects pointed to have identical contents	IN
• Neither pointers nor objects are equal	IN

This section concerns itself with data types made up of structures linked together with pointers. Simple linked lists don't have anything special about them—they're usually treated just like any other Collection or Stream, so you won't find anything about them here.

DATA TYPES USING POINTERS

B.13 TREES

Trees are Collections (B.9). There are also two Counts (B.5) involved. The first is the number of immediate children of a node. Does any node have zero children, one child, more than one child, and so on? The second is the depth of the tree. In particular, you want a maximally deep tree (or at least one with depth > 1).

Trees: Calculating their Depth

The "first subtree" is whichever branch of the tree the traversal routine processes first.

• The first subtree is not the deepest (because the code may only descend one branch)	INLINE
• The depth is not equal to the number of immediate children of the root	INLINE

B.14 LINKED STRUCTURES

• The structure is circular	INLINE

The structure is circular if you can start at some node and follow some chain of pointers that brings you back to the starting node.

B.15   STRUCTURES SHARING PARTS

- Suppose that two objects might share a pointer to a third   common object. Construct a test specification in which

  1. The two objects do share the third object.
  2. Some operation on the third object is done via the first object.
  3. Some operation on the third object is done via the second object.
  4. The sequence is repeated.

STRINGS AND TEXT

This part is concerned with text processing, both of small strings and larger groups of strings (text). Notice that strings are collections (B.9) of characters, that they're often treated as streams (B.11) of characters, and that programs use pointers (B.12) to manipulate them. So many other catalog entries apply—here are some that are particular to strings and text.

B.16   STRINGS

- The empty string.   IN, OUT

Comparing Strings

These are the same rules as for arrays, repeated here for convenience.

- V1 and V2 same length, differing in last element.   INLINE
    Example: "abc" and "abd"
- V1 has same elements as V2, but one element shorter.   INLINE
    Example: "ab" "abc"
- V2 has same elements as V1, but one element shorter.   INLINE
    Example: "abc" "ab"

Case-Independent Comparisons

- Make sure all combinations
  of 'A' and 'a' are compared,   INLINE
  also all combinations of 'z' and 'Z'
    Example: "AAaazzZZ" "AaAazZzZ"

    • Unprintable characters   IN

Printing Text with Breaks

These could be page breaks, breaks across lines for formatted text, and so on.

    • Maximum amount that will fit on one page/line.   IN
    • One more than maximum amount for one page.   IN
    • Maximum amount that will fit on N pages. (N>1)   IN
    • One more than maximum amount for N pages. (N>1)   IN

Printing Text / Filled Output

Filling is when a sequence of items are to be laid out in groups of fixed size. (Such as the way text formatters lay out text to right-justify it.) In some cases, an item occupies more than one unit of output. For example, a "line" may be more than one physical line long when displayed. Or a character may be printed in octal form (\055), and occupy more than one character space. We are concerned only with such oversize items.

    • Oversize item straddles boundary, is almost past it.

        Example: For character, only \ showing)

    • Oversize item straddles boundary, is almost before it.

        Example: For character \055, \05 showing, final 5 hidden)

    • Oversize item ends just before the boundary.

In some cases, there may be more than one type of item that straddles the boundary. If it is likely that different code handles each type, write a separate test requirement for each type.

B.18   READING TEXT

The rules for Parsing (p. 482) can usually be applied to reading text.

Remember that what's read is probably put into a Container, so use the Container rules (B.8).

Text with Quoting or Other Special Characters

Certain text causes some portion of following text to be handled specially. Call these "quotes."

An unpaired quote quotes a single item. It doesn't require a close-of-quote marker. The backslash (\) is a common single-quote marker, as is the "//" comment in C++.

A paired quote a group of items. It requires a close-of-quote marker. C comment markers are paired quotes.

In the example, \ is used as an unpaired quote and "" is used for paired quotes.

For these tests, the text surrounding quotes should always be visible text (not white space), so that you can easily see whether extra characters were incorrectly used up. Similarly, the quoted text should not be white space.

Unpaired Quotes

- Quote mark as first character in text   IN
  Example: \xyz
- Quote mark as last character in text   IN
  Example: abc\

Paired Quotes

- Entire text quoted   IN
  Example: "text"
- Partial text quoted   IN
  Example: text"more text"text
- No closing quotes   IN
  Example: "text
- Opening quote as last character in text   IN
  Example: text"

Combinations

- Single-quoted double-quote mark.   IN
  Example: xxx\"xxx
- Double quote enclosing single quote   IN
  Example: xxx"\"xxx

(Note: Precedence may vary, so the double quote may quote the single quote or the single quote may quote the closing double quote)

Conversions

This refers to conversions between a text representation of an object and its internal representation in the program. See also the requirements for Parsing (p. 482). Remember that what's read is probably put into a Container (B.8).

Conversions to Numbers

Consider the range of possible numbers as an Interval, leading to these test requirements:

• As large as will fit	IN
• Barely too large	IN
• As negative as will fit	IN
• Barely more negative than will fit	IN

Consider also other clues from Numbers (B.3), such as "numbers used in arithmetic operations."

B.19 FILES

See also the POSIX-specific catalog (Appendix C) for UNIX or POSIX programs.

Checking Whether a File Exists

- file exists
- file does not exist

Opening a File for Reading

- file does not exist
- file is readable
- file exists, but not readable

Opening a File for Writing

- file does not exist but can be created
- file does not exist, can't be created
- file exists, but not writable
- file exists and is writable

B.20 EQUALITY COMPARISON

This applies to many data types, not just numbers. Some data types are indexed separately because they have several false cases, or more refined false cases. See, for example, Numbers (B.3), Strings (B.16), and Arrays (B.10).

Specification only.

- Equal
- Not equal

B.21 OTHER COMPARISON OPERATORS

Some data types have a < or <= relationship defined for them, even though they're not Numbers.

Specification only.

<, >=
- V1 < V2
- V1 = V2

>, <=
- V1 = V2
- V1 > V2

In the inequality cases, make the two variables "close together" whenever the ordering allows it.

For example, in string comparisons "fooc" is both less than "food" and also nearly equal to it.

B.22 GENERAL SEARCHING REQUIREMENTS

- Match not found
  If possible, a matching element should be placed just past the bounds of the search. If the boundaries are handled incorrectly, this increases the chance of an observable failure.
- Match found (more than one element, exactly one match)
- More than one match in the collection
- Single match found in first position   **INLINE**
  (it's not the only element)
- Single match found in last position
  (it's not the only element)

  If the search is backward, the "last" element is actually the first in the Collection.

B.23 USING THE POSITION OF THE MATCHING ELEMENT

In general, programs don't care where the element is found. In this case, the program uses the position. The requirements are the same as above, but the INLINE tag is removed.

- Single match found in first position
  (it's not the only element)

- Single match found in last position
  (it's not the only element)

B.24 SEARCHING BASED ON KEY FIELDS

Here, the elements in the Collection are structures. Matching depends not on the whole structure, but on whether some key fields match.

Multiple Keys

- For each key field, use an element where it is the only one that doesn't match   INLINE

  Example:
  The program is searching for an element with key1=1, key2=2, and key3=3. Here are three test requirements:

key1=1,	key2=2,	key3≠3
key1=1,	key2≠2,	key3=3
key1≠1,	key2=2,	key3=3

B.25 Continued Searching

Here, searching can be resumed from the last element found.

- Further match immediately adjacent to last match

This is a good requirement to apply to searching text. For example, if searching for $-delimited keywords, one test specification might be $key1$$key2$.

B.26 Delimited Searching

In this case, the search stops before the end of the Collection. For example, only the first 15 elements of a 30-element array are to be scanned, or a text string has special significance only in the header of a mail message.

- No match before the boundary, match just past boundary
- No match before the boundary, a match well past the boundary
  (This requirement applies only to searching free-form text.)

OPERATIONS ON PAIRS OF COLLECTIONS

B.27 GENERAL OPERATIONS

- V1 and V2 empty — IN
- V1 has 1 element, V2 none — IN
- V2 has 1 element, V1 none — IN
- Both V1 and V2 have more than one element — IN

B.28 OPERATIONS ON EQUAL-SIZED COLLECTIONS

The collections are supposed to have the same number of elements.

- V1 has N (>= 1) elements, V2 N+1 — IN
- V2 has N (>= 1) elements, V1 N+1 — IN

B.29 ORDERED COLLECTIONS WITH MATCHES

Here, two collections are processed in order. Elements from one collection may match elements in the other. (The program may expect that all will match, or none, or some—these test requirements are useful regardless of the expectation; all that changes is whether they are error cases or not.)

In the test requirements below, variants of the word "match" indicate elements that are identical in the two collections; variants of "mismatch" indicate elements are not identical to their corresponding element in the other collection. You can freely make longer collections that satisfy several of the test requirements at once.

- V1 = (match another-match) V2 = (match another-match) — IN
- V1 = (match MISMATCH) V2 = (match mismatch) — IN
- V1 = (MISMATCH match) V2 = (mismatch match) — IN
- V1 = (MISMATCH ANOTHER-MISMATCH) V2 = (mismatch another-mismatch) — IN

The following requirements always apply to collections with at least two elements. In the case where the collections are of different lengths, the "last element" is the last element of the shorter collection.

- First elements match — IN, INLINE
- First elements mismatch — IN, INLINE
- Last elements match — IN, INLINE
- Last elements mismatch — IN, INLINE

Any equality test requirements that apply to the elements (e.g., Comparing Strings, B.16) should be used. It is a good idea to refine both the "first elements" and "last elements" test requirements.

B.30 ORDERED COLLECTIONS WITH SORTED ELEMENTS

This is like the above, but more refined for the case where the collections are sorted.

In the test requirements, elements are represented by numbers. Equal numbers represent matching elements. Smaller numbers correspond to smaller elements.

A single test case will usually satisfy several of these test requirements at once. For example, the two Collections (1 3 1 2) and (2 4 1 2) satisfy the first two requirements.

• V1 = (1 3) V2 = (2 4)	IN
• V1 = (1 2) V2 = (1 2)	IN
• V1 = (1 2) V2 = (3 4)	IN
• V1 = (3 4) V2 = (1 2)	IN
• V1 = (1 2) V2 = (2 3)	IN
• V1 = (2 3) V2 = (1 2)	IN
• V1 = (1 3) V2 = (1 2 3)	IN
• V1 = (1 2 3) V2 = (1 3)	IN

In addition, use these requirements.

• V1's first element is smaller than V2's first element	IN, INLINE
• V1's first element equals V2's first element	IN, INLINE
• V1's first element is larger than V2's first element	IN, INLINE
• V1's last element is smaller than V2's last element	IN, INLINE
• V1's last element equals V2's last element	IN, INLINE
• V1's last element is larger than V2's last element	IN, INLINE

B.31 RELATIONAL DATABASE NATURAL JOIN

- V1 joins with a single instance of V2
- V1 joins with no instances of V2 (joins with nothing)
- V1 joins with N instances of V2 (N>1)
- N instances of V1 join with a single instance of V2 (N>1)
- An instance of V2 joins with nothing
- N instances of V1 join with two instances of V2 (N>1)

Here, we have grammar-structured input. The focus is not just on determining whether the grammar has been implemented correctly (in these days of parser generators, that's more likely), but also on using the grammar to discover faults in later handling of the input.

Use INLINE requirements only if a parser generator wasn't used.

Note: Parsing usually involves the filling of Containers (B.8).

B.32 HANDLING WHITE SPACE

These requirements assume that spaces, tabs, and newlines are white space. They are easy to adjust to other circumstances.

• 1 space	INLINE
• 1 tab	INLINE
• space and tab	INLINE
• tab newline space (all white space characters used)	
• newline newline	INLINE
• no white space (where lexically possible)	INLINE
• white space as first character in file	INLINE
• white space as last character in a complete statement	INLINE

(The one undeferred requirement tests whether the lexical analyzer has been given the correct list of white space characters.)

B.33 COMMENTS

• comment present	
(Comments should always comment text that would generate easily observable errors if not commented.)	
• no comment	
• comment starts on first character in file	INLINE
• unterminated comment	INLINE

B.34 BOUNDARY CASES

• empty input	
• end of file in "middle" of statement	INLINE

(Most likely the end-of-file case will lead to multiple requirements. Each tests a different place where a "bad" end-of-file
could happen. Beware of spending too much time testing this
type of error handling. You may find yourself without time for
more important testing.

B.35 SYNTAX

Syntax descriptions are written in a notation adapted from
[Beizer90]. The requirements are explained in more detail in
Chapter 16.

Syntax statements are enclosed in double quotes when used as part of running text.
Optional elements are surrounded by square braces: .
   [optional]
Alternatives are separated by vertical bars:
   "option1 | option2" means choose option1 or option2.
   "[option1 | option2]" means choose either option1, option2, or neither.
Ellipses mean iteration:
   "element..." means one or more iterations
   "[element]..." means zero or more iterations
Braces are used for grouping:
   "{ element1 | element2 } element3" means either element1 followed by element3
      or element2 followed by element3.

Syntactic statements can be named and referred to by other statements.
The names and references are written in bold font:
   tree: left + right

   tree - tree

Such references have little effect on testing.

The following requirements apply both to entire statements and
substatements. For example,

   { A B } | { C D }...

contains two sequences, an alternative, and an iteration.

Sequences

These are statements where there are a fixed number of items, each of which must be present. "A B" is a sequence. "A B [C D]" contains two sequences, "A B" and "C D".

- Last item missing   INLINE
- Extra item   INLINE
- Nearby items

  (Try one for each item in the sequence.)

Alternatives and Optional Items

Examples:

"A | B", "[A]" (choose A or nothing), "[A | B]"

- Each of the legal alternatives
- None of the alternatives
- An illegal (but nearby) alternative.   INLINE

Simple Repetition

Example: A...

- The minimum number of repetitions
- One less than the minimum number of repetitions
- 1 repetition
- > 1 repetition
- The maximum number of repetitions (if known)
- One too many repetitions
- Incorrect but nearby item as last   INLINE

  Example: "09:" given syntax "numeral..."

Repetition and Alternatives

Example: "[a | b | c]..."

- Each element is omitted in at least one test
  This would lead to requirements like "a not used",
  "b not used", etc.
- Everything used, in reverse order from that given
  in the description. (*Example*: "cba")

Recursive References

Statements that indirectly contain themselves.

- A recursive use that repeats the original statement.

  Examples:

  For C's **if** statement:
      if **test** if **test statement**
  For C's **switch** statement:
      switch **test** { switch **test statement** }

- At least one recursive use in which the original
  statement is not repeated.

  Example:

  while **test** if **test statement**

      or

  while **test** do **test statement**
  There would be no requirement to have both.

POSIX-Specific Test Requirement Catalog (Sample)

This is an example of a catalog specific to a particular application area, in this case UNIX and POSIX programs. It is by no means a complete catalog.

PATHNAMES, FILES, and OPEN FILE DESCRIPTORS

C.1 PATHNAMES

- Beginning with -   IN
  Example: "-file"
  (Sometimes useful in command-line arguments.)

- Containing component ".."   IN, INLINE
  Example: "../../dir/X"

- Null string   IN
  Example: ""
  (Surprisingly, this is equivalent to ".".)

- Absolute   IN, OUT
  Example: "/tmp/X"

- Relative   IN, OUT
  Examples: "../tmp/X", "tmp/X", "X"

Decomposing Pathnames

There are many opportunities for errors when decomposing pathnames into their component parts and putting them back together again (for example, to add a new directory component or to expand wildcards).

- <text>/
- <text>/<text>
- <text>/<text>/<text>
- <text>//<text>

Also consider the directory and file components as Containers of variable-sized contents.

C.2   FILES

Opening a File for Reading

- file exists, but not readable

  (Note: If a setuid program, make it not readable by effective UID but readable by real [or vice-versa, if appropriate for the application])

Opening a File for Writing

- file exists, but not writable.

  (Note: If a setuid program, make it not writable by effective UID but writable by real [or vice-versa, if appropriate for the application])

C.3   OPEN FILES

Note: These apply to **each** read or write system call, and there may be many in the subsystem. You may need to defer these requirements if you can't look at the code.

Reading Open Files

- Read succeeds
- End of file.
- Failure with no data.
- No data, no failure.
- Partial data (with failure)
- Partial data (without failure)

"Partial data" means that the buffer is partly filled with data, but either EOF or some error is signaled. Does the program handle the data? When data is lines, consider especially a file with no trailing new line.

Writing Open Files

- Write succeeds
- Write fails

COMMAND LINES

This describes the conventions for POSIX commands:

1. *Options come after a command name.*
2. *Options may have arguments.*
3. *Options are ended by " - - " or by the first argument without a leading dash.*
4. *After the options, there may be from MINARGS to MAXARGS more arguments*

C.4 Options

For multicharacter option names, consider the Comparing Strings requirements and the Syntax requirements. (Some of these requirements are redundant with the Syntax requirements; they're repeated here to make sure they're not missed.)

- All options present

  (It's mildly useful to provide them in the opposite order from the one the documentation uses.)

- No options present
- Repeated option

  (If the option takes an argument, it should take a different value the second time.)

- Option with missing argument as last option

    Example: "tar -f"

  (You often get a null-dereference core dump in this case.)

- Missing option argument followed by option

    Example: "tar -f -e"

  (This usually exposes not coding errors, but non-robustness in the specification: POSIX programs don't generally do a lot of sanity checking of arguments.)

- Partial option

    Example: "cat -"

- Unknown option

C.5 Arguments

Treat as an Interval [MINARGS, MAXARGS].

• MINARGS-1 arguments	IN
• MINARGS arguments	IN
• MAXARGS arguments	IN
• MAXARGS+1 arguments	IN

Question Catalog for Code Inspections

For each function (or other chunk of code), scan this catalog, first checking whether the question applies anywhere, next whether the answer is yes. A yes answer means a probable fault. The questions are predominantly for faults that dynamic testing is poor at discovering. Other faults are better found via testing.

This catalog is to be kept short. A catalog with too many entries will not be used.

DECLARATIONS

D.1 LITERAL CONSTANTS

- If these are parameterized with #ifdefs, are any of the different values incorrect? For example:

```
#ifdef PDP10
#define BYTESIZE 7        /* Should be 6 */
#else
#define BYTESIZE 8
#endif
```

Such errors often slip past because all values are not tested (much less all combinations of values).

D.2 CHANGES TO EXISTING CODE

- If a new field is added to a declaration, have any initializing definitions not been changed? Consider

```
struct foo
{
  int i;
  int j;
  int m;
};
struct foo myfoo = { 1, 2, 3}
```

If the structure is changed to

```
struct foo
{
  int i;
  int k;
  int j;
  int m;
};
```

the insertion of k into the middle of the structure means that myfoo's j will no longer be initialized to 2, but to 3.

- If a new field is added to a declaration, has any initializing code not been changed?

This is really the same as the previous case, but worth noting specially. If, in the example above, instances of the structure are normally initialized with

```
s.i = 1; s.j = 2; s.m = 3;
```

all such initializations must be updated when k is added.

DATA ITEMS

D.3 STRINGS

- Can this string ever not be null-terminated?

D.4 BUFFERS

- Are there always size checks when copying into the buffer?

- Is this buffer ever too small to hold its contents?

  For example, one program had no size checks when reading data into a 12-character buffer because the *correct* data would always fit. But when the file it read was accidentally overwritten with incorrect data, the program crashed mysteriously.

D.5 BITFIELDS

- Are there possible ordering problems (portability)?

INITIALIZATION

D.6 LOCAL VARIABLES

- Are local variables initialized before being used? (Compilers and related tools do *not* catch all cases of this -- only most of them.)

MACROS

- If a macro's formal parameter is evaluated twice, is the macro ever expanded with an actual parameter that has side effects?

  For example, what happens in this code?

  ```
  #define max(a,b) ((a)<(b)?(b):(a))
  max(i++, j)
  ```

- If a macro is not completely surrounded by parentheses, is it ever invoked in a way that will cause unexpected results?

  ```
  #define max(a,b) (a)<(b)?(b):(a)    /* Should be ((a)<(b)?(b):(a)) */
  result = max(i, j)+3;
  ```

- If a macro's arguments are not surrounded by parentheses when used in its definition, will this ever cause unexpected results?

    ```
    #define check(A)  (A && global)    /* Should be ((A) && global) */
    result = check(i | | j)
    ```

- Is the argument to `sizeof` an incorrect type?

    A common error is using `sizeof(p)` instead of `sizeof(*p)`.

- Is too little (or too much) space allocated?

- Malloc and similar functions allocate uninitialized storage. Does the code assume it's been initialized to zero?

- When dynamically allocated structures or arrays are initialized, are any of the fields not set?

- Is allocated data never freed?

- If a function is called that returns static storage, is that function ever called again before the caller is finished using the first value?

    ```
    char *
    give_storage(int data1, int data2)
    {
     static char retval[SIZE];   /* Place return value in here. */
     /* Initialize contents of retval. */
     return retval;
    }


     ...

    storage1 = give_storage(upper1, upper2);
    storage2 = give_storage(lower1, lower2);   /* storage1 has just been overwritten. */
    ```

REALLOCATING DATA

- When allocating more space with `realloc`, is the additional space assumed to be initialized to zero?

- When allocating more space with `realloc`, are there pointers to the old copy of the data?

FREEING DATA

- Are you freeing already freed storage?

- Does the freed storage still have pointers to it, pointers that could still be dereferenced? (Some versions of `free` overwrite some parts of the freed data; most do not.)

- Are you freeing storage that is not supposed to be freed? (Perhaps it was allocated with a routine that says "do not free returned value" in a code header.)

- Is it possible for the pointer being freed to be null?

    (Note: POSIX-compliant implementations of `free` accept null pointers. Not all implementations conform.)

FILES

- Can a temporary file not be unique?

    (This is a common design bug.)

OPEN FILES

- Is a file pointer reused without closing the file?

    fid = open(...); fid = open(...);

- Is a file not closed in case of an error return?

    For example, a file is opened, processing continues, some error occurs, and the function returns without closing the file.

- Is a file never closed for any other reason?

- Are parentheses used incorrectly?

  The following error is very common, of course:

  > if (a = function() == 0)

  used instead of the correct

  > if ((a = function()) == 0)

  but there are more subtle cases:

  > if (function(X,Y, (expression != test)))

  used instead of the correct

  > if (function(X,Y, expression) != test)

  or

  > malloc(strlen(name+1))

  used instead of the correct

  > malloc(strlen(name)+1)

- Sometimes two or more variables must all be updated together. For example, one may cache values calculated from another. If one variable changes, are all synchronized variables updated?

- Is division by zero possible?

- Are exact equality tests used on floating point numbers?

- Are null pointers always cast to the correct type when passed as a function argument?

  > execl(name, arg0, arg1, ..., argn, 0)

  used instead of the correct

  > execl(name, arg0, arg1, ..., argn, (char *)0)

- Is an unsigned integer used when a signed one should be (or vice versa)?

POINTERS

- When dereferenced, can a pointer ever be null?

- Suppose this routine copies a pointer value. Should it instead have copied what that pointer points to?

  For example, suppose Routine1 takes a pointer as an argument and stores it in a global for later use by Routine2. Then consider what happens in this situation:

  ```
  routine1(&some_data);
  some_data.count++;
  routine2();   /* Will use updated value of some_data.count */
  ```

ASSIGNMENT

- Do the units of the expression and variable match?

  For example, you might be calculating a number of bytes when the number of words was meant—if the result is used for allocation, you'd be using too much memory.

FUNCTION CALLS

- Is this function correct? Should it be a different function with a similar name? (E.g., strchr instead of strrchr?)

- Could this function violate the assumed preconditions of a called function?

MISCELLANEOUS

- Has unintended debug code been left in?

- Does the program have a specific exit value or does it just "fall off the end?"

Requirements for Complex Booleans Catalog

This catalog applies to operators that combine ANDs and ORs. As a reminder, here's how to derive test requirements for homogenous expressions:

>   A1 AND A2 AND ... AND An:
>   all terms true
>   N cases, each of which has exactly one term false
>
>   A1 OR A2 OR ... OR An:
>   all terms false
>   N cases, each of which has exactly one term true

Two Operators

In these tables, && is used for AND and || is used for OR. That makes it easier to find the expression you're looking for. The value 1 is used for "true" and 0 is used for "false". That makes the tables easier to read.

(A && B) || C			
A	B	C	Whole Expression
1	1	0	true
0	1	1	true
1	0	0	false
0	1	0	false

A && (B || C)			
A	B	C	Whole Expression
1	1	0	true
0	0	1	false
1	0	0	false
1	0	1	true
0	1	0	false

A || (B && C)			
A	B	C	Whole Expression
1	1	0	true
0	1	1	true
0	0	1	false
0	1	0	false

(A || B) && C			
A	B	C	Whole Expression
0	1	1	true
0	0	1	false
1	0	0	false
1	0	1	true
0	1	0	false

Several cases have more than one set of equally good test requirements. One of them has been arbitrarily chosen. In a few of these cases, the general rules given in Section E.3 can be used to derive the other sets.

Some of these tables could be derived from each other. However, it's less error-prone to spell everything out than force you to do the derivation.

E.1 One AND

				(A && B) || C || D
A	B	C	D	Whole Expression
1	0	0	0	false
0	1	0	0	false
1	1	0	0	true
1	0	1	0	true
0	1	0	1	true

				((A || B) && C) || D
A	B	C	D	Whole Expression
1	0	1	0	true
0	0	1	0	false
0	1	0	0	false
0	1	1	0	true
1	0	0	0	false
0	0	1	1	true

				A && (B || C || D)
A	B	C	D	Whole Expression
1	0	0	0	false
1	1	0	0	true
1	0	1	0	true
1	0	0	1	true
0	0	1	1	false

				A || (B && (C || D))
A	B	C	D	Whole Expression
0	1	0	1	true
0	1	0	0	false
0	0	1	0	false
0	1	1	0	true
0	0	0	1	false
1	1	0	0	true

				A || (B && C) || D
A	B	C	D	Whole Expression
1	1	0	0	true
0	1	1	0	true
0	0	1	1	true
0	0	1	0	false
0	1	0	0	false

				A || B || (C && D)
A	B	C	D	Whole Expression
0	0	0	1	false
0	0	1	0	false
0	0	1	1	true
0	1	1	0	true
1	0	0	1	true

				(A || B) && (C || D)
A	B	C	D	Whole Expression
0	1	1	0	true
1	0	0	0	false
0	0	1	0	false
1	0	0	1	true
0	1	0	0	false
0	0	0	1	false

				(A || B || C) && D
A	B	C	D	Whole Expression
0	0	0	1	false
0	0	1	1	true
0	1	0	1	true
1	0	0	1	true
1	1	0	0	false

E.2 Two ANDs

(A && B && C) || D				
A	B	C	D	Whole Expression
1	1	1	0	true
1	1	0	0	false
0	0	1	1	true
0	1	1	0	false
1	0	1	0	false

((A && B) || C) && D				
A	B	C	D	Whole Expression
0	1	0	1	false
1	1	0	1	true
1	0	1	1	true
1	0	0	1	false
0	1	1	1	true
1	1	0	0	false
0	1	1	0	false

A && B && (C || D)				
A	B	C	D	Whole Expression
1	1	0	1	true
1	1	1	0	true
1	1	0	0	false
1	0	1	0	false
0	1	0	1	false

A && (B || (C && D))				
A	B	C	D	Whole Expression
1	0	1	0	false
1	0	1	1	true
1	1	0	1	true
1	0	0	1	false
1	1	1	0	true
0	0	1	1	false
0	1	1	0	false

A && (B || C) && D				
A	B	C	D	Whole Expression
0	0	1	1	false
1	0	0	1	false
1	1	0	0	false
1	0	1	1	true
1	1	0	1	true
0	1	0	1	false

(A || B) && C && D				
A	B	C	D	Whole Expression
1	0	1	1	true
0	1	1	1	true
0	0	1	1	false
0	1	0	1	false
1	0	1	0	false

(A && B) || (C && D)				
A	B	C	D	Whole Expression
1	0	0	1	false
0	1	1	1	true
1	1	0	1	true
0	1	1	0	false
1	0	1	1	true
1	1	1	0	true

A || (B && C && D)				
A	B	C	D	Whole Expression
0	1	1	1	true
0	0	1	1	false
0	1	0	1	false
0	1	1	0	false
1	1	0	0	true

E.3   Four or More Operators

Only some of the possible expressions are provided. If you have a different sort of expression, you can multiply the test requirements completely (see Chapter 25 for an example) or treat the ANDs and ORs independently (as in Chapter 3). Which you choose depends on whether you believe the terms are treated independently in the code (Chapter 25). Also keep in mind that complex expressions are just as hard for specification writers to get right as they are for programmers. Complete multiplication is worthwhile if it uncovers specification bugs.

(A1 && ... && An-1 && An) ‖ B
B ‖ (A1 && ... && An-1 && An)

There are three rules:

1. B is 0 and all the A's are 1.
2. Try every combination where exactly one A is 0. B remains 0.
3. B is 1 and two or more of the A's are 0. (It doesn't matter which ones.)

Here's an example:

(A1 && A2 && A3 && A4) ‖ B					
A1	A2	A3	A4	B	Whole Expression
1	1	1	1	0	true
1	1	1	0	0	false
1	1	0	1	0	false
1	0	1	1	0	false
0	1	1	1	0	false
0	0	0	1	1	true

(A1 && ... && Am) && (B1 ‖ ... ‖ Bn)
(B1 ‖ ... ‖ Bn) && (A1 && ... && Am)

There are three rules:

☐ **AND expression true, all ways OR expression true**

Write N test requirements. Each should have all the A's 1, all but one of the B's 0, and one B 1. A different B should be 1 in each requirement.

☐ **AND expression true, OR expression false**

Write one test requirement with all the A's 1 and all the B's 0.

☐ **all ways AND expression false, all ways OR expression true**

Write $\max(M,N)$ test requirements. In each, exactly one of A's should be 0 and exactly one of the B's should be 1. Each of the A's should be 0 in at least one test. Each of the B's should be 1 in at least one test. The choice of which A is 0 is independent of the choice of which B is 1.

Here's an example:

(A1 && A2 && A3 && A4) && (B1 ‖ B2 ‖ B3)							
A1	A2	A3	A4	B1	B2	B3	Whole Expression
1	1	1	1	1	0	0	true
1	1	1	1	0	1	0	true
1	1	1	1	0	0	1	true
1	1	1	1	0	0	0	false
0	1	1	1	1	0	0	false
1	0	1	1	0	1	0	false
1	1	0	1	0	0	1	false
1	1	1	0	0	1	0	false

(A1 ‖ ... ‖ An-1 ‖ An) && B
B && (A1 ‖ ... ‖ An-1 ‖ An)

There are three rules:

1. B is 1 and all the A's are 0.
2. Try every combination where exactly one A is 1. B remains 1.
3. B is 0 and two or more of the A's are 1. (It doesn't matter which ones.)

Here's an example:

(A1 || A2 || A3 || A4) && B					
A1	A2	A3	A4	B	Whole Expression
0	0	0	0	1	false
1	0	0	0	1	true
0	1	0	0	1	true
0	0	1	0	1	true
0	0	0	1	1	true
0	1	0	1	0	false

(A1 ‖ ... ‖ Am) ‖ (B1 && ... && Bn)
(B1 && ... && Bn) ‖ (A1 ‖ ... ‖ Am)

There are three rules

☐ **OR expression false, all ways AND expression false**

Write N test requirements. Each should have all the A's 0, all but one of the B's 1, and one B 0. A different B should be 0 in each requirement.

☐ **OR expression false, AND expression true**

Write one test requirement with all the A's 0 and all the B's 1.

☐ **all ways OR expression true, all ways AND expression false**

Write max(M, N) test requirements. In each, exactly one of A's should be 1 and exactly one of the B's should be 0. Each of the A's should be 1 in at least one test. Each of the B's should be 0 in at least one test. The choice of which A is 1 is independent of the choice of which B is 0.

Here's an example:

(A1 || A2 || A3) || (B1 && B2 && B3 && B4 && B5)								
A1	A2	A3	B1	B2	B3	B4	B5	Whole Expression
0	0	0	0	1	1	1	1	false
0	0	0	1	0	1	1	1	false
0	0	0	1	1	0	1	1	false
0	0	0	1	1	1	0	1	false
0	0	0	1	1	1	1	0	false
0	0	0	1	1	1	1	1	true
1	0	0	0	1	1	1	1	true
0	1	0	1	0	1	1	1	true
0	0	1	1	1	0	1	1	true
0	1	0	1	1	1	0	1	true
1	0	0	1	1	1	1	0	true

Checklists
for Test Writing

Use these checklists as reminders when testing. They'll save you the trouble of paging through the book.

Testing New Subsystems or Major Changes

This checklist describes typical testing of new subsystems or major changes to old subsystems. Expect to tailor it somewhat to your particular situation.

This checklist can be used when you have only the specification, only the code, or both. Some of the steps will differ in each case. The differences are noted.

F.1 Testing before development: Use test design to help subsystem design

1. During the development of the subsystem's external interface, find test requirements (as described below).
2. Use the test requirements in design and specification reviews.
3. Build test specifications from at least some of them. A test specification is a scenario, an example of one use of a subsystem. Discussing scenarios is a good way to find flaws in the subsystem's specification.

F.2 Find operation and variable clues in the specification you were given

See Chapter 3, section 3.1.

If you weren't given a specification, skip this step.

You will build at least one test requirement checklist from the subsystem's external specification. (For large subsystems, you may want several checklists, perhaps one per functional area. This will help you keep track of what you've done and what remains.)

1. The text of the specification provides two types of clues: variables and clichéd operations. List them in the test requirement checklist.

2. Pay special attention to result variables and globals— they're easy to miss.

F.3 Create an abbreviated specification (chapter 12)

Other clues are gotten by following this procedure. It can be applied to the specification you were given, the code, or both.

1. List the effects the specification describes. These can be error effects (precondition failure effects), normal effects (postcondition actions), or intermediate or convenience effects (definitions, which often corresponding to variables mentioned or implied by the specification).

   • List the effects separately from the test requirement checklist.

   • Be sure to note which effects are error effects.

   • Avoid effects with redundant information. Effects are redundant if they would give rise to the same requirements that you'd get from one of the test requirement catalogs. Watch out particularly for simple effects of the syntax. The effects of syntax errors are almost always redundant.

2. Write defining terms for each effect. Defining terms are boolean causes connected with AND and OR.

   • When writing defining terms, create definitions when they're convenient.

3. Copy effect names (not defining terms) into the test requirement checklist. They are clues.

4. Check your work.
   • Were any effects missed?
   • Does each effect's defining term include all its causes?
   • Are all of the causes used in at least one effect?

5. Check for specification bugs.
   • Is there any input to which no effect applies?

• Is there any input to which two apply? Which actually happens?

F.4 Use the code to find more operation and variable clues

See Chapter 3, section 3.2.

(If the code is not available now, you'll later come back to this step, find new clues, then repeat everything that follows for the new clues.)

1. Each routine should have its own test requirement check-list.
2. List variables that contribute new information. Don't forget globals.
3. List clichéd operations that weren't in the specification.
4. Least each function call separately.
5. This is a good time to inspect the code with the Question Catalog. If a routine has assumed preconditions, also ask the question, "Can any caller violate these preconditions?" (Chapter 6)

F.5 Add test requirements obtained from defining terms

See Chapter 3, section 3.4.

(Defining terms are what cause precondition, postcondition, and definition effects.)

1. Apply the AND and OR rules

> A AND B:
> > A true, B true
> > A true, B false
> > A false, B true

> A1 AND A2 AND ... AND An:
> > all terms true
> > N cases, each of which has exactly one term
> > false
> A OR B:
> > A false, B false
> > A true, B false
> > A false, B true

A1 OR A2 OR ... OR An:

all terms false

N cases, each of which has exactly one term true

2. If the defining term contains both AND and OR operators, use the Requirements for Complex Booleans catalog.

3. Be sure to mark ERROR requirements.

F.6 Add test requirements gotten from a test requirements catalog

See Chapter 3, Section 3.6.

Catalogs are indexed by clichéd variables and operations. Three catalogs are provided with this book; you can also build your own.

Scan the catalog sequentially, asking these two questions:

1. Does this catalog entry match a clue I listed?

2. Does this catalog entry match a clue I didn't notice but should have?

Remember that definitions may be variable clues (as well as having effects).

These rules help decide whether to list a catalog test requirement:

1. List IN requirements for input or intermediate variables.

2. List OUT requirements for output or intermediate variables.

3. List INLINE requirements when the operation is known to be implemented inline. Do not list them if the operation is implemented as a function call. If the implementation is not known because the code isn't available yet, mark the requirement DEFERRED.

4. Specification-only catalog entries don't apply to clues found only in the code.

5. Don't list a test requirement if it's redundant with one already listed.

6. If a test requirement refines one already listed, write the new one down indented under the old one.

7. Don't list test requirements that violate assumed preconditions.

8. When a test requirement violates a validated precondition, make sure to note that it's an ERROR requirement.

9. If the test requirement can't be satisfied, don't list it.

F.7   Add integration test requirements

See Chapter 3, section 3.10.

1. Get test requirements from the called subroutine's specification. The caller should be forced to handle each effect and also the case where that effect does not occur.

2. Some of these test requirements might produce indistinguishable effects. (Two requirements might produce effects that look the same to any caller, or only to this caller.) If you're sure that the effects are—and, more importantly, should be— indistinguishable, you need only use one of the requirements.

3. If the called function provides data to the caller, find the type of the data in the catalog and use IN requirements.

F.8   Use other sources of test requirements

1. If operation requirements were earlier DEFERRED (because the code was not available), decide whether they should now be used (Chapter 3, section 3.13).

2. Use intuition and experience in error guessing (Chapter 3, section 3.12).

   • If some clues have no test requirements, can you think of any?
   • Can you think of more or better test requirements for clues that have requirements?
   • Can you think of any missed clues?

F.9   Multiply test requirements, if needed

These steps (especially the second) are optional.

1. Check variable requirement reachability (Chapter 25).

   • Identify all operation and variable clues. (Variable clues will include convenience definitions. Operations include subroutine calls.)
   • For each variable, determine whether it could usefully exercise each operation.
   • If so, make sure that it will. The usual way is to indent a copy of the variable requirements under the operation clue. (Often, a variable requirement will automatically exercise the relevant operations, which is why this step is optional.)

2. Check whether operation requirements should be multiplied (Chapter 26).

- Find interacting operation clues. Overlapping code or much information flow between operations are signs of interaction.
- Refine each of one operation's requirements with each of the other operation's requirements. In many cases, you won't want to try all combinations, only a selected few suspicious ones.

F.10 Using groups of requirements (Chapter 13)

Select a manageable set of test requirements.

1. Each internal routine has its own test requirement checklist. Use all the requirements from a group of related routines.

2. Add a subset of the external requirements. Choose them with an eye toward forcing variety.

3. Build test specifications as described in the next section.

4. Don't write special test specifications for "straggler" requirements; merge them into the next set of requirements.

5. It is often best to implement a set of test specifications before moving on to the next set of requirements. This catches systemic testing errors early. You can also check coverage, but only to find gross mistakes.

6. Repeat with the next set of requirements. Continue until all of them have been used at least once.

F.11 Using individual test requirements (Chapter 4)

1. Error test specifications satisfy only one (ERROR) test requirement.

2. Normal test specifications satisfy as many as is reasonable.

3. If you must choose among several test requirements, pick the one that's been satisfied least.

4. Test specifications (including error tests) should have as much variety as is tractable.

5. Use DEFERRED test requirements when convenient.

6. Tag each test requirement with a list of the test specifications that satisfy it.

F.12 Check test specifications (Chapter 4, sections 4.5 and 4.6)

Rules for test form

1. Test inputs are specified exactly.

2. All test inputs are described.

3. Test specifications do not mention internal variables.
4. Expected results are given as exactly as possible.
5. All results are described.
6. Independent tests are best.
7. Multiple tests per invocation are best.

Rules for test content

1. Background modifications must be visible.

   Before running a test, initialize the background to known values. After the test, check that the background is unchanged.

2. Foreground modifications must be visible.

   For example, if the subsystem is to set a variable to 5, make sure it starts with some other value.

3. Alternate effects should cause visible differences.

   Will your test detect a bug where the wrong postcondition is applied?

4. Test requirements must be exercised.

   Consider changing the test's input so that a test requirement is no longer satisfied. If this can be done in a way that doesn't change the test's expected results, there's no evidence that the test requirement has any effect at all. An example is a test requirement that specifies the value of a list element that isn't used. An alternate way of asking whether a test requirement is exercised is to ask if it affects the subsystem's processing.

5. Make inputs distinct.

   If a function takes two variables and the test requirements don't call for them to have the same value, make sure they have different values.

The above are specific ways of answering these general questions:

❖ Will the test requirement be delivered to the appropriate code?

❖ Will any failures propagate to the output?

❖ Will the failures be readily visible?

F.13 Implement tests (Chapter 5)

1. Find, tailor, or build the test driver.
2. Find, tailor, or build the suite driver.
3. Implement your tests.

F.14 Measure coverage (Chapter 7)

1. Measure branch, multicondition, loop, and relational operator coverage.

2. Use coverage information to provide new clues.

3. Avoid the trap of writing tests only to satisfy coverage. Instead, generate new test requirements and new test specifications from coverage clues.

4. Keep complexity and variety in mind.

F.15 Clean up (Chapter 8)

Make sure what you did will make sense to you (or someone else) months from now.

1. Can the test requirements can be understood by someone else? (They tend to be rather terse and cryptic.)

2. Each test requirement has a list of test specifications that satisfy it. Is the list accurate? Are the test names given there adequate to find the implemented test?

3. Have the test specifications been saved? They're usually easier to understand than their implementations.

This checklist applies to testing small changes. If the change is large, test the entire changed routine in the normal way. You may need to follow this checklist for all callers of the changed routine.

Testing Bug Fixes or Other Changes (Chapter 14)

F.16 Definitions

❏ **changed code**

Consider the scope of the change to be the block enclosing the actual changed text. Two enclosing blocks is sometimes better. An enclosing cliché can make an especially good unit of change.

❏ **changed variables**

The changed code contains variables used or set exactly as they were before the change. It also contains variables used or set differently. The latter are the changed variables.

❏ **demonstration requirement**

This is the test requirement that demonstrated the fault before the change. It causes the pre-change code to be executed in a way that produces incorrect results. The changed code will (presumably) produce correct results.

❏ **changed results**

These are what's different when the demonstration requirement exercises the changed code. They could include setting changed variables to different values. They could also include changing the execution path of the program.

F.17 Basic test requirements

1. List all variables in the changed code as clues. (Note: *All* variables, not just the changed variables.)

2. List variables related to the changed variables as clues. Perhaps these related variables, which are not mentioned in the changed code, also need to be handled differently. Typical related variables are different fields in the same structure, variables with similar purpose, and variables that are used together with the changed variables in other parts of the subsystem.

3. Consider the routine and subsystem specification. List any preconditions or postconditions that would cause the changed code to be executed (whether or not these are related to the demonstration requirement).

4. List operation clichés. Include operation clichés contained within the changed code and also any that contain it.

5. List function calls in the changed code.

6. Generate test requirements from these clues in the usual way. Case analysis of variables is particularly important.

7. Generate test requirements from the demonstration requirement. The demonstration requirement is a boolean expression, like a postcondition trigger. Treat it the same way. (This ensures that you have tests that do not demonstrate the bug, but rather exercise "nearby" parts of the code and subsystem input.)

F.18 Using the test requirements in an existing test suite

1. Eliminate requirements already tested.

2. Consider merging new test requirements into old tests.

3. Combine the rest as usual.

   By default, each test should satisfy the demonstration requirement. That is, you prefer tests that would have demonstrated the need for change. This is not always possible, since some of the test requirements are chosen to exercise nearby situations.

   Variety is especially important for these tests. Because you won't be working with as many test requirements, you have to be careful to force variety.

F.19 Using the Test Requirements Without a Test Suite

1. Write as many tests as you can.
2. Review requirements you can't afford to test.

   It is often helpful to write the test specifications, not implement them, and then walk through them ("hand execute" them).

F.20 Harder Test Requirements

Both of these kinds are harder to find, and harder to test. Once found, it may make more sense to use them in a review than to write the tests.

Propagation requirements

1. Find code that uses the changed result and might be affected by the change. This code is called a "user." List it as a clue. The corresponding test requirement is whatever it takes to transmit the changed result to the user.
2. Could the change require new users of the changed result? List them as clues.
3. When designing tests, it's best if the changed result changes the user's processing (instead of being handled just as before).
4. Consider also IN variable requirements, if they can apply to the changed result.

Similarity requirements

1. Find code like the changed code. Such code might have similar effects, use the same or similar variables, use the same operations or functions, and so on.
2. The corresponding test requirement is whatever it takes to exercise that similar code in the same situation that caused the original failure (the demonstration requirement or something like it).

F.21 Coverage

As always, you should measure whether you get the coverage you intend.

Because propagation and similar requirements require the execution of code potentially far from the original change, they're very susceptible to tests that don't test what they were supposed to test. Be sure to measure whether the intended code was actually reached.

See Chapter 18. A consistency relationship is of the form

Statement 1:   left-hand-side-1 requires right-hand-side-1
Statement 2:   left-hand-side-2 requires right-hand-side-2
...
default: requires default-right-hand-side (or may always be an error)

Each routine (or user command) that can change one of the variables involved in the consistency relationship should have the following as part of its test requirement checklist:

Consistency checking (a clue)
  Statement 1 exercised
    a requirement from any left-hand-side that exercises statement 1
      different from misclassification as default   EITHER
      different from most likely misclassification   EITHER
    another requirement from any left-hand-side that exercises statement 1
      different from misclassification as default   EITHER
      different from most likely misclassification   EITHER

    ...
    right-hand-side-1 requirement A
    right-hand-side-1 requirement B   ERROR

    ...
  Statement 2 exercised
    a requirement from any left-hand-side that exercises statement 2
      different from misclassification as default   EITHER
      different from most likely misclassification   EITHER
    another requirement from any left-hand-side that exercises statement 2
      different from misclassification as default   EITHER
      different from most likely misclassification   EITHER

    ...
    right-hand-side-2 requirement A
    right-hand-side-2 requirement B   ERROR

    ...
  ...
  Default exercised
    a requirement from any left-hand-side that exercises the default
      different from most likely misclassification   EITHER
    another requirement from any left-hand-side that exercises the default
      different from most likely misclassification   EITHER
    default-right-hand-side requirement A
    default-right-hand-side requirement B   ERROR

To more thoroughly exercise the rest of the subsystem, refine the requirements that exercise statements with the requirement in bold below:

> a requirement from any left-hand-side that exercises statement 2
>> different from misclassification as default   EITHER
>>
>> different from most likely misclassification   EITHER
>>
>> **consistency satisfied**

Consider also putting right-hand side requirements under every "statement N exercised" test requirement they can satisfy (be consistent with), not just the one they came from.

When consistency checking is done by a library routine, that routine uses the above checklist. Each of its callers has a single consistency checking requirement:

> routine 1
>> **variable changed to inconsistent value**   ERROR
>>
>> *other test requirements from whatever else the caller does*

> routine 2
>> **another variable changed to inconsistent value**   ERROR
>>
>> *other test requirements from whatever else the caller does*

If more than one variable can change at once, a few more requirements should be added. Assume there are two variables, V1 and V2. (See Chapter 18 for the more general case.) Add the requirements in bold as refinements of each "statement N exercised" requirement.

> Statement 1 exercised
>> **only V1 changed, to inconsistent value**   ERROR
>>
>> **only V2 changed, to inconsistent value**   ERROR
>>
>> **both changed, unchanged V1 would have different result**   EITHER
>>
>> **both changed, unchanged V2 would have different result**   EITHER
>>
>> a requirement from any left-hand-side that exercises statement 1
>>> different from misclassification as default   EITHER
>>>
>>> different from most likely misclassification   EITHER

F.23 Building a Class Catalog

See Chapter 21.

The class catalog gives requirements for users of the class. In what follows, it is distinguished from the catalogs in Appendices A, B, and C by calling them the "standard catalogs."

> Object Use Requirements
> > from the class as a data type
> > from the class invariant
> > data member 1 requirements
> > data member 2 requirements...
> > from error guessing
>
> State Machine Requirements (if relevant)
> > the states of the state machine
> > transition requirements
>
> Member Function Requirements
> > member function 1
> > > integration requirements (for testing calling code)
> > > > one effect of the function
> > > > another effect of the function...
> > member function 2
> > > integration requirements...
> > member function 3...

F.24 Fill in the object use requirements

1. If the class, thought of as a data type, matches any standard catalog entries, copy the requirements.
2. The invariant is an assumed precondition. If the OR rule, consistency relationship rules, or error guessing discovers distinct ways in which it might be true, list those as test requirements.
3. Treat each data member as a distinct variable and find matching entries in the standard catalogs. Mark whether the data members should be visible to routines outside the class.
4. Guess errors: How might the class be misused? List ways of distinguishing correct from incorrect uses as test requirements.

F.25 Fill in the state machine or statechart requirements

If the class has been modeled with a state machine or statechart, do the following:

1. List the states as requirements.
2. List the state transitions as requirements.

F.26 List member function use requirements

1. These are the integration requirements found as in Chapter 3, section 3.10. If an effect might not happen, be sure to list that as a separate requirement.
2. If the member function, treated as an operation, matches any standard catalog entries, consider copying the test requirements. Copy only those that are likely to provoke a misuse in the caller (never INLINE requirements).
3. Guess errors: how might a caller misuse the member function? List the ways as test requirements.
4. If a member function changes a data member, consider whether the change adds a new test requirement for that data member. If so, list it under the data member's clue in the object use requirements section.
5. Check the member functions against the state machine model (if any). It is suspicious if the member function requirements do not force satisfaction of all the transition requirements.

F.27 Consider collections of objects

Often, classes are designed to be used together. There may be invariants that apply to the whole collection. If they produce new requirements, add them to each class's object use requirements.

F.28 Using a Class Catalog

See Chapter 21.

If a routine uses an object, that object's class catalog can provide some test requirements. It doesn't matter if the routine is a member function of that class, a member function of a different class, or a routine not part of any class.

1. If the routine calls a member function of the class, use the member function integration requirements.
2. Use any of the object use requirements that apply.
3. Use the state machine state requirements. They ensure the routine will use the object in each of its externally meaningful states.

F.29 Building A Derived Class Catalog

See Chapter 22.

Copy the base class requirements catalogs

1. Copy integration requirements for member functions. Do not copy domain shift requirements.
2. Overriding and new member functions get no requirements.
3. Copy all object use requirements from the base catalogs.
4. Copy state machine or statechart requirements from the base catalogs.

Add requirements for new members

1. Treat a new data member just like any other variable. Get test requirements from its type.
2. Get a new member function's integration requirements in the usual way.
3. If a new member function changes the possible values a data member could have, consider whether the data member clue should get new requirements. If so, add them, tagged with NEW.

Add requirements for overriding member functions

1. Create integration requirements in the normal way. Mark the requirements as NEW if they are not redundant with requirements in a base class.
2. If the overriding member function changes the possible values a data member could have, consider whether the data member clue should get new requirements. If so, add them, tagged with NEW.
3. If the overriding member function produces the same effects as the overridden function for different inputs, describe the change with domain shift requirements.

Check for new requirements for inherited member functions

1. If an inherited function calls a function with new integration requirements, consider whether they cause changes to the caller's behavior. If so, describe the changes as new requirements. Tag them as NEW.
2. Do the same for domain shift requirements.
3. Propagate the new requirements to any callers of the inherited function. If there's any effect, continue propagating it until it dies out.

Update remaining object use requirements

1. If the derived class has a new invariant, update invariant requirements. Tag them with NEW.
2. Do the same with other Object Use Requirements.

Update state machine requirements

1. If the new state machine has more states or transitions than the old one, update the requirements. Tag them with NEW.
2. If the new state machine has fewer, remove the old requirements—but be suspicious.

F.30   Using a derived class catalog

See Chapter 22. You use a derived class catalog when building test requirement checklists.

New member functions

A new member function in a derived class is tested the same way as any new object-based code.

Overriding member functions

1. First find test requirements in the normal way.
2. Consider whether the function's own domain shift requirements would be useful.
3. Consider the usefulness of any unsatisfied requirements from the *overridden* function.

Inherited member functions

Do not add test requirements derived from the unchanged code. Use only these two sources:

1. When the inherited member function calls another member function, use that function's NEW integration requirements. Use all domain shift requirements.
2. Copy all the relevant NEW Object Use and State Machine requirements.

Changed external routines

If external code is changed to use a new class, test it as if it were an inherited member function.

F.31   Building and Using a Virtual Call Catalog

See Chapter 24.

The catalog for a member function F, first declared in class BASE, would have this structure:

Virtual call catalog for member function BASE::F

base is the declared class
All requirements when F is called through BASE

derived is the declared class
All requirements when F is called through DERIVED

even_more_derived is the declared class
All requirements when F is called through
EVEN_MORE_DERIVED

F.32   Building the Catalog

The catalog begins with the class that first declares F. That first layer contains all of F's integration requirements from BASE's class catalog.

Each new derived class adds a new layer. The layer contains all the integration requirements for F in the derived class's class requirements catalog. The new derived class may also add requirements to previous layers:

1. When a derived class's member function can have a new effect, a requirement to cause that effect should be added for its base classes (both direct and indirect).

2. The same may also be done when a derived class removes an effect.

3. If an effect in the derived class has a different defining term than the same effect in a base class, a domain shift requirement should be added to the base class's layer. If the base class is a direct base, those requirements can be copied from the derived class's class catalog. If it's an indirect base, they must be deduced.

In all cases, annotate the requirement with the class it came from. That will make it easier to decide how to satisfy it.

There can also be a virtual "call" catalog for data members. Like the member function catalog, it begins with the base class that

first declares the data member. Each derived class that inherits the member may have new test requirements for it. If so, those requirements should be added to previous layers, tagged with the originating class.

F.33   Using the Catalog

When new external code contains a virtual function call, find the catalog for that function. Add all requirements from the declared class to the caller's test requirement checklist.

When a derived class is added, any virtual function call could suddenly produce unexpected results. If there are new and relevant requirements in the updated virtual call catalog, add them to each caller's test requirement checklist.

Bibliography

Victor R. Basili and David M. Weiss. "Evaluation of a Software Requirements Document By Analysis of Change Data". *Proceedings of the 5th International Conference on Software Engineering*, pp. 314-323, IEEE Press, 1981. **(Basili81)**

V. Basili and R.W. Selby. "Comparing the Effectiveness of Software Testing Strategies". *IEEE Transactions on Software Engineering*, vol. SE-13, No. 12, pp. 1278-1296, December, 1987. **(Basili87)**

Boris Beizer. *Software Testing Techniques*, 2/e. New York: Van Nostrand Reinhold, 1990. **(Beizer90)**

Boris Beizer. *Software System Testing and Quality Assurance*. New York: Van Nostrand Reinhold, 1984. **(Beizer84)**

E. Berard. *Essays on Object-oriented Software Engineering, Volume 1*. Englewood Cliffs: Prentice-Hall, 1993. **(Berard93)**

R. Binder. "Testing Object-Oriented Programs: a Survey". Robert Binder Systems Consulting, 3 First National Plaza, Suite 1400, Chicago, IL 60602, 1994. **(Binder94)**

Grady Booch. *Object-Oriented Analysis and Design*. Redwood City: Benjamin/Cummings, 1994. **(Booch94)**

L. Cardelli and P. Wegner. "On Understanding Types, Data Abstraction, and Polymorphism". *ACM Computing Surveys*, vol. 17, No. 4, December, 1985. **(Cardelli85)**

T.S. Chow. "Testing software design modeled by finite-state machines". *IEEE Transactions on Software Engineering*, vol. SE-4, No. 3, pp. 178-187, May, 1978. **(Chow78)**

(Cox88)   B. Cox. "The Need for Specification and Testing Languages". *Journal of Object-oriented Programming*, June/July, 1988.

(Cox91)   B. Cox and A. Novobilski. *Object-Oriented Programming: An Evolutionary Approach*. Reading, Mass: Addison-Wesley, 1991.

(DeMillo78)   R.A. Demillo, R.J. Lipton, and F.G. Sayward. "Hints on test data selection: help for the practicing programmer". *Computer*. vol. 11, no. 4, pp. 34-41, April, 1978.

(Dennett91)   Daniel C. Dennett. *Consciousness Explained*. Boston: Little, Brown, 1991.

(Doong91)   R. Doong and P. Frankl. "Case Studies on Testing Object-Oriented Programs". *Proceedings of the ACM SIGSOFT Symposium on Testing, Analysis, and Verification*, October, 1991.

(Ellis90)   M. Ellis and B. Stroustrup. *The Annotated C++ Reference Manual*. Reading, Mass: Addison-Wesley, 1990.

(Fiedler89)   S. Fiedler. "Object-oriented Unit Testing". *Hewlett-Packard Journal*, vol. 40, No. 2, April 1989.

(Foster80)   K.A. Foster. "Error-Sensitive Test Cases Analysis". *IEEE Transactions on Software Engineering*, vol. SE-6, No. 3, pp. 258-264, May, 1980.

(Frankl88)   P.G. Frankl and E.J. Weyuker. "An Applicable Family of Data Flow Testing Criteria". *IEEE Transactions on Software Engineering*, vol. SE-6, No. 10, pp. 1483-1499, October 1988.

(Freedman90)   Daniel Freedman and Gerald M. Weinberg. *Handbook of Walkthroughs, Inspections, and Technical Reviews*. Little, Brown, 1990.

(Fujiwara91)   S. Fujiwara, G. v. Bochmann, F. Khendek, M. Amalou, and A. Ghedamsi. "Test Selection Based on Finite State Models". *Transactions on Software Engineering*, vol. SE-17, No. 6, pp. 591-603, June, 1991.

(Gannon81)   J. Gannon, P. McMullin, and R. Hamlet "Data-abstraction implementation, specification, and testing". *ACM Transactions on Programming Languages and Systems*, vol. 3, No. 3, pp. 211-223, July, 1981.

(Ghiselin55)   Brewster Ghiselin, ed. *The Creative Process*. Mentor Books, 1955.

(Glass81)   Robert L. Glass. "Persistent Software Errors". *Transactions on Software Engineering*, vol. SE-7, No. 2, pp. 162-168, March, 1981.

(Hamlet77)   R.G. Hamlet. "Testing Programs with the aid of a compiler". *IEEE Transactions on Software Engineering*, vol. SE-3, No. 4, pp. 279-289, 1977.

(Hamlet92)   Dick Hamlet. "Are We Testing for True Reliability". *IEEE Software*, July 1992.

(Hayes86)   I. Hayes. "Specification Directed Module Testing". *IEEE Transactions on Software Engineering*, vol. SE-12, No. 1, January, 1986.

(Harel87)   D. Harel. "Statecharts: A Visual Formalism for Complex Systems". *Science of Computer Programming*, vol. 8, 1987.

D. Harel. "On Visual Formalisms". *Communications of the ACM*, Vol. 31, No. 5, pp. 514-531, May, 1988. **(Harel88)**

M.J. Harrold and P. Kolte. "Combat: A compiler based data flow testing system". *Pacific Northwest Software Quality Conference*, October 1992. **(Harrold92)**

M.J. Harrold, J. McGregor, and K. Fitzpatrick. "Incremental Testing of Object-Oriented Class Structures". *Proceedings of the 14th International Conference on Software Engineering*, IEEE Computer Society Press, May, 1992. **(Harrold92b)**

D. Hoffman and P. Strooper. "Graph-based Class Testing". *The Australian Software Engineering Conference*, Christ Church, New Zealand, 1993. **(Hoffman93)**

Mark A. Holthouse and Mark J. Hatch. "Experience with Automated Testing Analysis". *Computer*, Vol. 12, No. 8, pp. 33-36, August, 1979. **(Holthouse79)**

Gerard J. Holzmann. *Design and Validation of Computer Protocols*. Prentice-Hall, 1991. **(Holzmann91)**

J.R. Horgan and S. London. "Data Flow Coverage and the C Language". *Proceedings of the ACM SIGSOFT Symposium on Testing, Analysis, and Verification*, October, 1991. **(Horgan91)**

W. E. Howden. "An Evaluation of the Effectiveness of Symbolic Testing". *Software - Practice and Experience*, vol. 8, no. 4, pp. 381-398, July-August, 1978. **(Howden78)**

W. E. Howden. "Functional Program Testing". *IEEE Transactions on Software Engineering*, vol. SE-6, No. 2, pp. 162-169, March, 1980. **(Howden80)**

W. E. Howden. "Weak Mutation Testing and Completeness of Test Sets". *IEEE Transactions on Software Engineering*, vol. SE-8, No. 4, pp. 371-379, July, 1982. **(Howden82)**

IEEE Standard Glossary of Software Engineering Terminology. ANSI/IEEE Std 729-1983. **(IEEE83)**

I. Jacobson, M. Christerson, P. Jonsson, and G. Overgaard. *Object-Oriented Software Engineering*. Reading, Mass: Addison-Wesley, 1992. **(Jacobson92)**

P. Jalote. "Testing the Completeness of Specifications". *IEEE Transactions on Software Engineering*, vol. SE-15, no. 5, May, 1989. **(Jalote89)**

W.L. Johnson, S. Draper, and E. Soloway. "An effective bug classification scheme must take the programmer into account". *Proceedings of the Workshop on High-Level Debugging*, Palo Alto, CA, 1983. **(Johnson83)**

W.L Johnson, E. Soloway, B. Cutler, and S.W. Draper. *Bug Catalogue: I.* Yale University Technical Report, October, 1983. **(Johnson83b)**

(Knight86) John C. Knight and Nancy G. Leveson. "An Experimental Evaluation of the Assumption of Independence in Multiversion Programming". *IEEE Transactions on Software Engineering*, Vol. SE-12, No. 1, January, 1986.

(Laski83) J. Laski and B. Korel. "A Data Flow Oriented Program Testing Strategy". *IEEE Transactions on Software Engineering*, vol. SE-9, No. 3, pp. 347-354, May, 1983.

(Liskov74) B. Liskov and S. Zilles. "Programming with Abstract Data Types". *ACM SIGPLAN Symposium on Very High Level Languages*, 1974. Published in SIGPLAN Notices, volume 9, number 4, 1974.

(Marick91) Brian Marick. "The Weak Mutation Hypothesis", *Proceedings of the ACM SIGSOFT Symposium on Testing, Analysis, and Verification*, October, 1991.

(Marick91b) Brian Marick, "Experience with the Cost of Test Suite Coverage Measures", *Pacific Northwest Software Quality Conference*, October, 1991.

(Marick92) Brian Marick. "Generic Coverage Tool (GCT) User's Guide". Testing Foundations, 1992.

(Meyer88) B. Meyer. *Object-oriented Software Construction*. Englewood Cliffs: Prentice-Hall, 1988.

(Morell89) Larry J. Morell. *Unit Testing and Analysis*. SEI Curriculum Module SEI-CM-9-1.1, Software Engineering Institute, Pittsburgh, Pennsylvania, 1989.

(Morell83) Larry Morell. *A Theory of Error-Based Testing*. Ph.D. dissertation, University of Maryland, 1983.

(Morell90) L.J. Morell. "A Theory of Fault-Based Testing". *IEEE Transactions on Software Engineering*, Vol. SE-16, No. 8, August 1990, pp. 844-857.

(Morell91) L. Morell and J. Voas. "Inadequacies of Data State Space Sampling as a Measure of Trustworthiness". *ACM SIGSOFT Software Engineering Notes*, April 1991.

(Murphy92) Gail C. Murphy and Pok Wong. "Toward a Testing Methodology for Object-Oriented Systems". *OOPSLA 92* (Poster only). October, 1992.

(Myers78) Glenford J. Myers. "A Controlled Experiment in Program Testing and Code Walkthroughs/Inspections". *Communications of the ACM*, Vol. 21, No. 9, pp. 760-768, September, 1978.

(Myers79) Glenford J. Myers. *The Art of Software Testing*. New York: John Wiley and Sons, 1979.

(Ntafos84) Simeon Ntafos. "On Required Element Testing". *Transactions on Software Engineering*, vol. SE-10, No. 6, pp. 795-803, November, 1984.

(Offutt88) A.J. Offutt. *Automatic Test Data Generation*. Ph.D. dissertation, Department of Information and Computer Science, Georgia Institute of Technology, 1988.

A.J. Offutt and S.D. Lee. "How Strong is Weak Mutation?", *Proceedings of the ACM SIGSOFT Symposium on Testing, Analysis, and Verification*, October, 1991. **(Offutt91)**

W. Opdyke and R. Johnson. "Creating Abstract Superclasses By Refactoring". *Proceedings of CSC '93: 1993 ACM Computer Science Conference*, Indianapolis, Indiana, February 1993. **(Opdyke93)**

W. Opdyke. *Refactoring Object-Oriented Frameworks.* Ph.D. thesis, University of Illinois at Urbana-Champaign, 1992. Available as Technical Report No. UIUCDCS-R-92-1759. Postscript: /pub/papers/ opdyke-thesis.ps on st.cs.uiuc.edu. **(Opdyke92)**

T.J. Ostrand and E.J. Weyuker. "Error-Based Program Testing". *Proceedings of the 1979 Conference on Information Sciences and Systems*, Baltimore, MD, March 1979. **(Ostrand79)**

Thomas J. Ostrand and Elaine J. Weyuker. "Data Flow-Based Test Adequacy Analysis for Languages with Pointers". *Proceedings of the ACM SIGSOFT Symposium on Testing, Analysis, and Verification*, October, 1991. **(Ostrand91)**

G. D. Papagiannakopoulos. *On Generating Test Cases from the Syntax of a Specification.* M.S. thesis, University of Illinois, 1990. **(Papagiannakopoulos90)**

David L. Parnas and David M. Weiss. "Active Design Reviews: Principles and Practices". *Proceedings of the 8th International Conference on Software Engineering*, pp. 132-136, IEEE Press, 1985. **(Parnas85)**

Dewayne E. Perry. "The Inscape Environment". *Proceedings of the 11th International Conference on Software Engineering*, pp. 2-12, IEEE Press, 1989. **(Perry89)**

Dewayne E. Perry. "Adequate Testing and Object-Oriented Programming". *Journal of Object-Oriented Programming*, vol. 2, no. 5, Jan/Feb, 1990. **(Perry90)**

Andy Podgurski. "The Role of Statistical Reliability Assessment". 24th Symposium on the Interface: Statistics and Computing, College Station, Texas, March 1992. **(Podgurski92)**

Sandra Rapps and Elaine J. Weyuker. "Selecting Software Test Data Using Data Flow Information". *Transactions on Software Engineering*, vol. SE-11, No. 4, pp. 367-375, April, 1985. **(Rapps85)**

J. Rumbaugh, M. Blaha, W. Premerlani, F. Eddy, W. Lorensen. *Object Oriented Modeling and Design.* Englewood Cliffs: Prentice-Hall, 1991. **(Rumbaugh91)**

S. Siegel. "Strategies for Testing Object-oriented Software". *Software Quality World*, vol 5, no 1, 1993. **(Siegel93)**

M. Smith and D. Robson. "A Framework for Testing Object-oriented Programs". *Journal of Object-oriented Programming*, June, 1992. **(Smith92)**

(Spohrer85) J.C. Spohrer, E. Pope, M. Lipman, W. Scak, S. Freiman, D. Littman, L. Johnson, E. Soloway. *Bug Catalogue: II, III, IV*. Yale University Technical Report YALEU/CSD/RR#386, May 1985.

(SQE85) Software Quality Engineering. *Systematic Testing* (course notes), Jacksonville, FL, 1985.

(Turner92) C. Turner and D. Robson. "The Testing of Object-Oriented Programs". Technical Report TR-13/92, University of Durham, 1992.

(Voas91a) Jeffrey Voas, Larry Morell, and Keith Miller. "Predicting Where Faults Can Hide from Testing". *IEEE Software*, March 1991.

(Voas91b) Jeffrey Voas. "Factors That Affect Software Testability". *Pacific Northwest Software Quality Conference*, October, 1991.

(Weiss85) David M. Weiss and Victor R. Basili. "Evaluating Software development by Analysis of Changes: Some Data from the Software Engineering Laboratory". *IEEE Transactions on Software Engineering*, vol. SE-11, No. 2, pp. 3-11, February, 1985.

(Weiss88) Stewart Weiss. "A Report on the Development of MacASSET, a Macintosh Software Testing Environment," Technical Report CS-TR-88-04, Hunter College, 1988.

(Wilke93) G. Wilke. *Object-Oriented Software Engineering: The Professional Developer's Guide*. Reading, Mass: Addison-Wesley, 1993.

(Zweben92) S. Zweben and W. Heym. "Systematic Testing of Data Abstractions Based on Software Specifications". *Journal of Software Testing, Verification, and Reliability*, vol. 1, No. 4, pp. 39-55, 1992.

Glossary

In an N-way AND expression, N+1 test requirements: N where a single term is false and all the rest are true, and one where all terms are true. **AND Rule**

In object-oriented programming, a class that cannot have objects. Its only purpose is to serve as a base class in inheritance. **Abstract Class**

Those variables that would be ignored by a correct test execution (but might not be by an incorrect one). See also Far Background and Immediate Background **Background**

A class used in object-oriented programming. Derived classes inherit data members or member functions from a base class. **Base Class**

A test requirement that describes extreme values. If a subsystem takes inputs in the range [0 .. 12], 0 and 12 are boundaries. They're more likely to find bugs than interior values because programmers often make off-by-one errors. **Boundary Condition**

Part of a specification. A boolean component of an effect's defining term. The defining term describes the conditions under which an effect occurs. Causes are combined with Combining Operators to form the defining term. **Cause**

Any IF-THEN-ELSE statement in a specification. **Cause-Effect Statement**

In object-oriented programming, a member that is either new or overriding. **Changed Member**

See Test Requirement Checklist. **Checklist**

Class	In object-based or object-oriented programming, the definition of an object's interface and internal structure.
Class Lattice	The class lattice shows the inheritance structure of a group of classes. It allows you to determine which classes are direct and indirect base classes for other classes. In single inheritance, the class lattice is a tree; a full lattice is needed only for multiple inheritance.
Cliché	Any operation or type that's not predefined in the programming language, but is often used by programmers.
Clue	Some essential part of a specification or subsystem, such as a precondition, postcondition, variable, or operation. The first thing placed in a test requirement checklist, it leads to test requirements.
Combining Operator	AND or OR: these combine boolean values to make larger boolean expressions.
Combining Rules	See Standard Combining Rules.
Complete Multiplication	Multiplying every test requirement with every other one. Testing all combinations of all test requirements.
Complete Variable Reachability	This rule is satisfied when all test requirements for a variable reach all locations where that variable is used. Compare to Variable Requirement Reachability, the Global Reachability Rule, and Data Flow Testing.
Consistency Relationship	A relationship between the values of two or more variables. The specification defines the relationship; the subsystem must enforce it. See also Dependency Statement.
Coverage	A coverage metric is a measure of how thoroughly a test or test suite has exercised a subsystem. Different metrics measure different aspects of program execution. Coverage is an approximate measure of the quality of testing.
Coverage Condition	Information about a way the test suite has underexercised the subsystem. Coverage conditions are used as clues.
Data Flow Testing	A type of testing where the test requirements are that all DEF-USE pairs be exercised. Compare to Complete Variable Reachability.
Data Member	In object-based or object-oriented programming, the variables used in a class's implementation. Data members may or may not be visible to external code.
Declared Class	A reference or pointer names its declared class. The actual class of the object referred to may be any class derived from the declared class.
DEF	A location in the code where a variable is assigned a value. In compiler jargon, an lvalue.

A pair consisting of a DEF and a USE and, implicitly, paths between them. Data flow testing requires that all DEF-USE pairs be exercised. — **DEF-USE pair**

The definition of what combination of causes results in an effect. — **Defining Term**

When testing a bug fix, a requirement describing inputs that caused the original failure. After the change, testing this requirement should produce different results. See also User Reachability Requirement and User Demonstration Requirement. — **Demonstration Requirement**

A statement describing part of a consistency relationship. It describes allowable values of one variable when another has a particular value. — **Dependency Statement**

A derived class is one that inherits data members or member functions from a base class. — **Derived Class**

In object-oriented programming, a direct base is an immediate ancestor of a derived class. — **Direct Base**

When an overriding member function changes the defining term of an overridden function's cause-effect statement, the effect now applies to a different domain of inputs. A domain shift requirement captures the difference. — **Domain Shift Requirement**

A driver provides inputs to a subsystem under test. It may also collect the outputs and judge their correctness. — **Driver**

Names in a program's text are bound to program entities. If the entity cannot be located at compile time, it is dynamically bound. In the context of this book, dynamic binding refers mainly to functions called through a pointer or reference. Which code is executed can't be known at compile time. — **Dynamic Binding**

The action performed by a satisfied postcondition, violated precondition, or definition. Generally, either the THEN or ELSE clause of any IF-THEN-ELSE statement in a specification. — **Effect**

According to [IEEE83], an error is a mistake made by a person, resulting in one or more faults, which are embodied in the program's text. The execution of the faulty code will lead to zero or more failures. — **Errors, Faults, and Failures**

The distinct classes of inputs to which a state machine responds. — **Events**

See Errors, Faults, and Failures. — **Failure**

Those variables that the subsystem should never change. — **Far Background**

A measure of the percent of coverage conditions satisfied, leaving out ones that are impossible or too difficult to satisfy. — **Feasible Coverage**

See Errors, Faults, and Failures. — **Fault**

Fault of Omission	A fault which is corrected by the addition of text. For example, `if (p>setup == COMPLETE)` may contain the fault of failing to check whether p is a null pointer; It can be corrected by adding the omitted text: `if (p && p->setup == COMPLETE)`.
Foreground	Those variables whose values the subsystem is supposed to change in a particular test execution.
History File	The saved result of a run of a test suite. Used to see what's changed between two runs.
Global Reachability Rule	Basic subsystem testing mandates that test requirements for a global variable reach all routines that use that variable. Compare to Complete Variable Reachability and Variable Requirement Reachability.
Gold Program	An implementation of a specification that is assumed to be correct. If this assumption is true, it can be used to judge another implementation's correctness.
Ideal Fault Conditions	In the theory of testing, the Reachability, Necessity, and Propagation Conditions.
Implicit Implementation	A state machine has an implicit implementation when the model does not translate directly into an implementation framework.
Indirect Base	In object-oriented programming, an indirect base is an ancestor—but not an immediate ancestor—of a derived class. If Collection is derived from Object and Set is derived from Collection, Object is an indirect base of Set.
Inheritance	Inheritance supports programming through difference. It allows you to say, "this object is just like that one, except for X."
Inherited Member	In object-oriented programming, an inherited member is one defined in a base class and not overridden in a derived class.
Immediate Background	Variables a subsystem might modify in another test, but should not modify in the current test.
Inline Operation	See Operation.
Input	A general term meaning whatever data a subsystem operates on. Input may be actual file input, values passed in as function arguments, global values set up before a subsystem is invoked, and so on.
Instantiation	In this book, a specific term referring to the replacement of a generic type by a specific type. Instantiation is used in genericity (templates).
Instrument	To modify a subsystem so that it measures coverage while executing.
Integration Test Requirement	A test requirement derived from one routine's use of another (by calling it as a subroutine).

Testing to find faults involving one subsystem's use of another. In this technique, another part of ordinary test design. In other techniques, a separate stage.

Integration Testing

In object-based subsystems the invariant describes what must always be true of the object. Routines that change the object can use the invariant as an assumed precondition, and their effect must preserve it.

Invariant

A file containing the actual output when a test runs. Compared to the reference file.

Log file

A failure is masked when some operation fails, but the resulting incorrect internal state is corrected or obscured before it makes it to the output, where it can be seen by the tester.

Masking

A member is either a data member or a member function.

Member

In object-based or object-oriented programming, the routines used to implement a class. Member functions may or may not be visible to external code.

Member Function

Multiplying test requirements is done by making copies of one set of test requirements and placing them as refinements of others. This is typically done when two clues interact.

Multiplying Test Requirements

In the theory of testing, the requirement that a fault be exercised with values that cause the program to have the wrong internal state. See Reachability Condition and Propagation Condition.

Necessity Condition

A new member is freshly defined in a derived class. It does not match any member in any base class.

New Member

An object is a distinct instance of a class.

Object

Object-based subsystems are organized as collections of objects, which are essentially structures and collections of associated routines. Each type of object is (ideally) defined solely by its functional interface (the routines).

Object-Based Programming

The class to which an object belongs. Distinguished from the declared class of a reference or pointer to the object, which may be a base class of the object class.

Object Class

Object-oriented programming adds inheritance to object-based programming.

Object-Oriented Programming

Requirements from a class's data members, its invariant, and the class as a data type. These requirements are those useful whenever an object of that class is used as a variable; they are not dependent on which member functions are called (if any).

Object Use Requirements

An obligation says what a subsystem's caller must do at some point after the call. It may also say what must never be done after the call.

Obligation

Omission	See Fault of Omission.
Operations	An operation is any function call, use of a predefined operator, or pattern of computation.

Examples:

```
sqrt(x)          /* The square root operation. */
a = sqrt(x)      /* The assignment operation, as well. */
a < b            /* An inequality operation. */

/* An instance of the search operation: */
index = 0;
while (index < LENGTH)
{
        if (array[index] == target)
            break;
        index = index + 1;

}
```

The last operation is called an inline operation by analogy to inline functions in programming languages. The sqrt examples used an existing operation definition. The search example both defined a search operation and also used it. The distinction is important because you'd expect to have to test an inline search differently—more thoroughly—than a call to an already-tested search routine. With a few exceptions (the relational operators), the language's predefined operators are ignored in subsystem testing.

OR Rule	In a N-way OR expression, N+1 test requirements: N where a single term is true and all the rest are false, and one where all terms are false.
Oracle	A program that can judge the correctness of another program.
Output	Anything that is the result of a subsystem's execution. Output may be true file output, the return value from a routine, a change to a global variable, and so on.
Overriding Member Function	An overriding member function is one which is defined in both a class and one of its base classes.
Postconditions	Given inputs that satisfy the preconditions, the postconditions describe the subsystem's output.
Preconditions	The preconditions describe what must be true of valid inputs to a subsystem and what the results of invalid inputs will be.
Propagation Condition	In the theory of testing, the requirement that an internally incorrect state become visible in the program's results. See Reachability Condition and Necessity Condition.
Propagation Fault	A fault caused by a change to the system which violates some assumption relied upon by distant code.

In subsystem testing, the requirement that a test requirement exercise a particular operation. The term is derived from Reachability Condition, a term from the theory of testing.	Reachability
In the theory of testing, the requirement that the location of a fault be exercised.	Reachability Condition
A redundant test requirement describes the same (or larger) set of inputs as a test requirement already in the Checklist.	Redundant
A file that describes the correct results of a test specification. Compared to the log file.	Reference file
One test requirement refines another if it describes a smaller set of inputs that is more likely to discover a bug than the original.	Refining
A test suite. The term originally was specific to tests for changes. The regression test suite was rerun to discover whether any of those changes "came undone" in later releases. There's no particular reason to separate those tests from other tests, though.	Regression test suite
A reference or pointer names a declared class. The object referred to has an object class, which must be a class derived from the declared class. Resolving the reference converts the declared class to the object class.	Resolving a Reference
A precondition is satisfied when the input is valid (as far as it's concerned). A test requirement is satisfied by a test if it is true of that test's input.	Satisfied
The collection of faults all resulting from the same error. Bug fixes often fix only one of the collection.	Similarity Fault
A description of the interface to a subsystem. It describes what the system is supposed to do without much description of the mechanism. You cannot tell whether a system is correct without reference to a specification. The term is general: A user's manual can provide a specification of the system. Often important parts of the specification aren't written down, which makes things difficult.	Specification
The way in which test requirements are combined to form test specifications. Each test requirement is used at least once, each test specification satisfies as many test requirements as is reasonable, and test requirements are used equally if you have no reason to favor one of them.	Standard Combining Rules
The memory a state machine uses to determine how to respond to incoming events.	State
The response of a state machine to a particular event in a particular state.	State Transition

Stub	When a subsystem is tested in isolation from a subroutine it uses, the tester must write simpler version of that subroutine. This simpler version, which does only what is required for the test specifications, is called a stub.
Substate	In a statechart, a state that is nested within a superstate. The substate is part of a state machine that is completely contained in the superstate.
Subsystem	A part of the system small enough to test individually, but large enough that testing doesn't require too much writing of stubs and drivers. The word is used throughout the book, even when referring to individual functions, to emphasize that subsystem testing can be applied at any scale.
Suite Driver	A program that runs all the tests in a test suite. It will typically allow you to compare this run with a previous run.
Superstate	In a statechart, a state that contains a state machine nested within it.
System Testing	Testing the entire integrated system to see whether it does what the user wants, as well as whether it fulfills its specification.
Test Coverage	See Coverage.
Test Requirement	A test requirement is a note to yourself that says,"Make sure you write a test specification where X is true." It is expressed as a description of a set of inputs to a subsystem.
Test Requirement Checklist	A test requirement checklist begins with clues, which are essential parts of the specification and/or subsystem. The test design process derives test requirements from these clues. Thereafter, the completed checklist is used to design test specifications.
Test Specification	A test specification is a particular set of inputs to be used in testing a subsystem. A test specification satisfies one or more test requirements. For example, the two test requirements A<B and A<0 are satisfied by a single test specification where A=-1 and B=0. A test specification also includes a precise description of the expected result of executing the subsystem on those values.
Test Driver	A driver. A test driver always judges the success or failure of the subsystem under test.
Test Suite	A collection of tests.
Type	A generic term encompassing, but not limited to, a type in a programming language. The type describes what a variable is and is used for. "L is a length, I is a scratch integer, and P is list of matching words."
Unit Testing	Commonly, testing individual functions or subroutines in isolation. In most cases, requires stubs and drivers.

A location in the code where a variable's value is used. In compiler jargon, an rvalue.

USE

The user here is code that might be affected by a change to other code. The requirement is that the effect of the change exercise the user code in a way likely to provoke different results. See also Demonstration Requirement and User Reachability Requirement.

User Demonstration Requirement

The user here is code that might be affected by a change to other code. The requirement is that the effect of the change reach the user code. See also Demonstration Requirement and User Demonstration Requirement.

User Reachability Requirement

A generic term used to describe any container-of-data used by a subsystem. A variable may be a global variable, an argument passed to a subroutine, a file and its contents, and so on.

Variable

This rule is satisfied when all test requirements for a variable reach all operations where that variable's value is used. Operation here is restricted to the sort that might be written in the test requirement checklist. Compare to Complete Variable Reachability and the Global Reachability Rule.

Variable Requirement Reachability

A precondition is violated when incorrect input is given.

Violated

A catalog used to find integration requirements for calls to a member function through a reference or pointer. The catalog is indexed by the declared class.

Virtual Call Requirements Catalog

A call to a member function through a reference or pointer to an object, rather than through the object itself. Since the object's class is unknown (is dynamically bound), the function that will be executed by a virtual function call is not known until run time.

Virtual Function Call

Index

combining operators, test requirements from
  AND, 20, 45–46
  AND and OR, 46–47
  OR, 20–21, 42–45
  ERROR markers in, 42, 85
  as IF–THEN–ELSE statements, 180
  validated, simple, 20, 41–42
  violated vs. satisfied, 20–21
  See also MAX; Sreadhex
Program code. *See* Subsystem code; MAX; Sreadhex
Programmers as testers, 210–11
Propagation
  achieving, 14–15
  criterion for test content, 109
  propagation faults. *See* Faults

Q

Question Catalog for Code Inspection
  allocating data, 493
  assignment, 496
  casting, 495
  changes to existing code, 491
  computation, 495
  conditionals, 495
  data items
    bitfields, 492
    buffers, 492
    strings, 492
  declarations: literal constants, 490
  files, 494
  freeing data, 494
  function and use, 141, 143
  function calls, 496
  initialization: local variables, 492
  inspecting sreadhex code, 143–44
  macros, 492–93
  and MAX code, 265–67
  miscellaneous, 496
  open files, 494
  pointers, 496
  reallocating data, 494
  sizing data, 493

R

Reachability
  global, 201–2
  as ideal fault condition, 13, 14
  in maintenance testing, 222–23
  and theory of subsystem testing, 13, 14, 437
  variable requirement reachability. *See under*
      Test requirement multiplication
  See also Data flow testing

Redundancy
  in sreadhex test 2, 116–17
  in test requirements, general, 50
Reference files, 133–34, 139. *See also* Drivers
Refinements
  and added test requirements, 84
  advantages of, 51
  and deferred requirements, 92
  in sreadhex, 50
  tagging, 94–95
Regression test suite, 132
Repetition
  and alternatives, 237–38, 240
  notation for, 232
  simple, test requirements for, 236–37
Requirements for Complex Booleans Catalog
  introduction to, 497
  four or more operations, 501–3
  mixed AND/OR expressions, 46–47
  three operations
    one AND, 499
    two ANDs, 500
  two operations, 498
Resource exhaustion, 164–65. *See also* Test design
Reusable software
  coverage of, 342–43
  producer's responsibility for, 340, 342, 343
  test requirements for, 340–42
  VISTA coverage tool, 343

S

Safety nets, 84, 140
Scaffolding code, 136
Scale of testing. *See* Subsystem testing
Sequences, syntax testing, 235
Size, subsystem. *See* Subsystem testing
SOUGHT statements, 92
Special cases, 3
Sreadhex
  introduction
    motivation, 24–25
    program code, 28–29, 39, 144, 194
    reasons for selecting, 18
    specification, 25–27
  definitions in
    hexadecimal characters, 26
    postcondition test requirements, 55–56
  drivers for
    directory and file structure, 136–37
    drivers and stubs, 137
    run-suite test results, 138–39